Praise for Gary Eldred

"Donald Trump and I have created Trump University to offer the highest quality, success-driven education available. Our one goal is to help professionals build their careers, businesses, and wealth. That's why we selected Gary Eldred to help us develop our first courses in real estate investing. His books stand out for their knowledge-packed content and success-driven advice."

—*Michael W. Sexton, CEO Trump University*

"Gary has established himself as a wise and insightful real estate author. His teachings educate and inspire."

—*Mark Victor Hansen, Coauthor,* Chicken Soup for the Soul

"I just finished reading your book, *Investing in Real Estate*. This is the best real estate investment book that I have read so far. Thanks for sharing your knowledge about real estate investment."

—*Gwan Kang*

"I really enjoyed your book, *Investing in Real Estate*. I believe it's one of the most well-written books on real estate investing currently on the market."

—*Josh Lowry Bellevue, WA President of Lowry Properties*

"I just purchased about $140 worth of books on real estate and yours is the first one I finished reading because of the high reviews it got. I certainly wasn't let down. Your book has shed light on so many things that I didn't even consider. Your writing style is excellent. Thanks again."

—*Rick Reumann*

"I am currently enjoying and learning a lot from your book, *Investing in Real Estate*. Indeed it's a powerful book."

—*Douglas M. Mutavi*

"Thanks so much for your valuable book. I read it cover to cover. I'm a tough audience, but you've made a fan here. Your writing is coherent, simple, and clean. You are generous to offer the benefits of your years of experience to those starting out in this venture."

—*Lara Ewing*

INVESTING

in

REAL ESTATE

Seventh Edition

GARY W. ELDRED, PHD

WILEY

John Wiley & Sons, Inc.

Published by John Wiley & Sons, Inc., Hoboken, New Jersey.
Published simultaneously in Canada.

For general information on our other products and services or for technical support, please contact our Customer Care Department within the United States at (800) 762-2974, outside the United States at (317) 572-3993 or fax (317) 572-4002.

Wiley publishes in a variety of print and electronic formats and by print-on-demand. Some material included with standard print versions of this book may not be included in e-books or in print-on-demand. If this book refers to media such as a CD or DVD that is not included in the version you purchased, you may download this material at http://booksupport.wiley.com. For more information about Wiley products, visit www.wiley.com.

Library of Congress Cataloging-in-Publication Data:

Eldred, Gary W.
    Investing in real estate / Gary W. Eldred. — 7th edition.
        pages cm
        ISBN 978-1-118-17297-1 (pbk.); ISBN 978-1-118-22696-4 (ebk);
ISBN 978-1-118-24002-1 (ebk); ISBN 978-1-118-26460-7 (ebk)
        1. Real estate investment—United States.   I. Title.
    HD255.M374   2012
    332.63'24—dc23

                                                    2011046343

Printed in the United States of America
10 9 8 7 6 5

CONTENTS

2   OPM: BORROW SMART, RAISE CASH, BUILD EQUITY   21

6   PROFIT WITH FORECLOSURES

ACKNOWLEDGMENTS

Many people have contributed directly and indirectly to this 7th edition of *Investing in Real Estate*. Because of their efforts, this popular classic text on property investing will continue to provide beginning and experienced investors the timely, no-nonsense, practical know-how that has kept this book a bestseller for the past 25 years.

Accordingly, I thank Donald Trump and Michael Sexton for inviting me to work with them to help create some of the best real estate educational products and services available (especially Trump University books—all published by John Wiley & Sons). Working with the Trump team has provided me new perspectives on property investing.

I also express my appreciation to Dr. Malcolm Richards, dean of the School of Business and Management at the American University of Sharjah (AUS). In recognizing the critical need for real estate education in the Middle East—and the hypergrowth Sharjah/Dubai metroplex—Dean Richards designed a rewarding position for me from which I have added substantively to my knowledge and analytical abilities as they apply to international property markets. Under Dean Richards, the School of Business and Management of AUS has established itself as the premier school for business education in the Middle East—and I am pleased to have been able to participate in its development. Also, I thank Dennis Olsen, chair of the Department of Finance at AUS, for the counsel, insights, and collegial support that he has offered to facilitate my work and working environment at AUS.

My valued assistants at AUS, Mohsen Mofid, Faiza Farooq, Omer Shabbir, and Sadaf Ahmad Fasihnia, too, deserve recognition for their cheerful and competent assistance in my writing and teaching. (Alas, all have now graduated and I miss them greatly.)

My best-selling real estate titles—including *Investing in Real Estate*—have been translated into foreign languages such as Russian, Indonesian, Vietnamese, and Chinese. Thanks go to the skillful translators of these volumes and to my Asian property advisor Sit Ming (Laura) Lee.

Last, but far from least, I thank my supervising editor Shannon Vargo, senior production editor Deborah Schindlar, and the entire staff at John Wiley & Sons with whom I always enjoy working. This edition of *Investing in Real Estate* marks the 24th book manuscript that I have written for this 200-year-old company that represents the finest of publishing traditions. I look forward to completing many more.

—Gary W. Eldred

Prologue

INVEST IN PROPERTY NOW

Invest in property now. Or forever live with your regrets.

Listen to the wealth-building wisdom of Warren Buffett: *"Invest when fear, doubt, and uncertainty grip the mind of the crowd; sell when wild hopes and speculative fever burn away reason."*

The emotional herding of the crowd allows you and me to buy cheap and sell dear. Think through that wise advice offered by the Sage of Omaha. What type of markets offer the best opportunities for future profits? What type of market alleviates risk? To answer these questions, contrast those boom market conditions of yesteryear with the potential-filled market we experience today:

1. *Boom:* Builders brought to market more than 2 million housing units a year.

   Today: Housing starts have fallen to fewer than 400,000 per year (the lowest level of building since World War II).

2. *Boom:* Buyers crowded into open houses and model homes to beg sellers or builders to accept their above-asking-price bids. Sellers set prices. No matter how high, buyers willingly paid on the ill-founded assumption that any price would look cheap compared to 12 months later.

   Today: A majority of potential investors and home buyers remain cautious, uncertain, and fearful. Open houses remain sparsely attended. To attract mere lookers, builders are slashing prices and doling out buyer concessions and incentives.

3. *Boom:* Interest rates averaged plus or minus 6 percent.

   Today: Interest rates of 4.0 to 5.0 percent prevail (at least for now).

4. *Boom:* Inflation seemed under control as far into the future as the mind might imagine. Allan Greenspan, chairman of the Federal Reserve Board, was dubbed "The Maestro" for his then believed-to-be masterful handling of the money supply and interest rates.

   Today: Trillions of dollars of deficits, government borrowings, and quantitative easing seem likely to push inflation (and interest rates) to much higher levels within the coming decade.

5. *Boom:* Properties sell at prices 30 to 100 percent *above* their replacement (construction) costs.

   Today: You can buy properties at 20 to 70 percent *below* their cost to rebuild new.

6. *Boom:* Millions of buyers overborrow to purchase properties they cannot afford. Liars' loans proliferate. Appraisers deliver any market value figure that buyers, loan reps, and sellers want.

   Today: Tight credit and high unemployment lead many people to double up (or even triple up) on their housing. Boomerang kids and even three-generation households have increased to the highest levels since World War II. Loan reps and appraisers must comply with strict new regulations that inhibit collusion.

7. *Boom:* Most sellers can easily demand top dollar.

   Today: Financial distress and millions of short sales, foreclosures, and bank REOs (real estate owned) create a ready supply of desperately motivated sellers (and lenders). Buyers—not sellers—set prices.

8. *Boom:* Property prices are propelled far above the amounts that rental income will justify.

   Today: Market prices have fallen to the point where rental income yields from properties substantially exceed the income yields available from bonds and stocks (that is, interest and dividends). Investors can reasonably expect to achieve positive cash flows—either immediately or within a few years. Capitalization rates have increased. Gross rent multipliers have decreased. Rents are heading up, vacancies down.

9. *Boom:* Hundreds of thousands of new investors stretched financially and overpaid for rental properties that they did not know how to manage.

   Today: Many of those same starry-eyed investors have sadly awoken to the reality that safe investing requires reserves of cash and credit, knowledge, thought, an effective operating system, and a tenant-pleasing strategy.

10. *Boom:* Nearly all soothsaying economists forecast blue sky prosperity without serious recession.

Today: Talk shows and financial news spew out a steady stream of gloom and doom.

[For historical perspective, recall other previous times of economic hardship such as the early to mid-1970s, the early 1980s, and even as far back as 1937—when the hoped-for Depression recovery suffered a discouraging setback (the stock market again fell more than 30 percent. Or say Texas in the late 1980s and early 1990s when the RTC (Resolution Trust Corporation) was selling masses of foreclosures and nearly all of the banks and savings and loans within the state became insolvent. Or revisit the severe recession and real estate collapse that occurred in California during the early 1990s (La Jolla houses at less than $300,000; Los Angeles condominiums at less than $100,000).

Were those so-called bad times actually *good times* to invest in property? No doubt about it. Investors who bought during any of those doom-and-gloom eras earned extraordinary returns for their insight and foresight. Now's your sure opportunity to buy a winning ticket. You can match their gains. History does repeat itself. You do not need a "back to the future" time machine to return you to those past golden years.

Today when I travel and tell people that I live part of the year at my home in Florida, they predictably respond, "Florida! The real estate market there is really bad, isn't it?"

I reply, "Bad? What do you mean, *bad?* You are mistaken. The Florida market today represents one of the best property markets that I have ever seen—anywhere, at any previous time. I am an investor. Relative to income and cash flows, property prices look good. Relative to risk-adjusted potential for capital gain, property prices look great."]

TODAY'S ODDS POINT DIRECTLY TOWARD PRESENT AND FUTURE GAINS

In these seemingly bleak days of the real estate cycle, fear looms. Cash balances in banks build up. Most would-be investors and savers crowd onto a flight to quality. They accept certificates of deposit (CDs) and money market accounts that pay negligibly low-single-digit interest rates. These fearful and uncertain folks think, "Who cares about return *on* capital? I want to feel confident that I am protecting a return *of* my capital."

In his perpetually popular book, *The Intelligent Investor,* Ben Graham (Warren Buffett's graduate school professor at New York's Columbia

University) created the parable of Mr. Market. Mr. Market represents the crowd mentality whose moods swing like a pendulum from irrational exuberance to bewildered fear and confusion. Which market mood provides the best investment opportunities and possibilities? Which mood of Mr. Market lures investors into taking the highest degree of actual risk? Which mood of Mr. Market presents the least amount of actual risk?

Booms Enlarge Actual Risk

During the irrationally exuberant boom times, investors *perceive* little risk, but real risks loom larger and larger as prices climb higher and higher, rental income yields fall, and unsustainable amounts of mortgage debt pile up—even though rent collections remain too low to cover operating expenses and debt service.

During the boom in Las Vegas, so-called investors (actually speculators) believed that flipping properties for magnificent gains would never end. Few perceived that their property risks actually laid down poorer odds than the slots at Caesar's Palace. And who but a fool (or Panglossian optimist) would borrow money to play the slots?

Yet, Las Vegas property buyers loaded up with dangerously high loan-to-value (LTV) ratios of 90, 95, and 100 percent (or more). They naïvely assumed that the future would continue to pay off those same jackpots that they had won in the recent past. Those thousands of Californians stampeding to Vegas thought they had discovered another Sutter's Mill.

They did not see the fool's gold. They did not comprehend why the growing gap between mortgage payments and rent levels could not persist. On typically purchased Las Vegas properties, loan payments (principal, interest, taxes, and insurance [PITI]) often approached $2,000 a month. Potential rents for these same properties would reach no more than $1,200 a month.

When such a huge alligator is chewing off your leg, you are in a world of danger (and a world of hurt). As I have often written, high debt, low rental income yields, and exaggerated hopes for outsized continuing increases in price (for stocks, gold, or properties) always trigger a reversal of fortune. (See especially my *Value Investing in Real Estate*, John Wiley & Sons, 2002.)

True, the hot speculative fever in Las Vegas (as well as Miami, Dubai, coastal Spain, Ajman, Dublin, Phoenix, and so on) does stand out as beyond-the-norm mania. Most other cities did not experience such heightened frenzy among both builders and buyers. Nevertheless, irrational exuberance fueled the manic moods and mind-sets of property buyers and borrowers throughout much of the United States and other countries (though, during the boom of late, not Dallas, Berlin, or Tokyo—each of these cities had suffered its own irrationally exuberant property market 15 to 20 years back, and sat out this most recent party).

With most right-brain dominant speculative buyers now knocked out of the game, today *investing* in real estate once again offers outstanding profit potential with vanquished risk.

Market Downturns Vanquish Market Risk

During the past five years, property prices throughout the United States (and various other countries) have fallen by 15 to 70 percent from their previous peak levels. Relative to current rent levels and replacement (construction) costs, today's property prices offer the most favorable buying opportunities since World War II. With property prices sitting well below construction costs (for the most part), builders cannot profitably bring new product to market. Today's investors are protected from new competition. Builders will not even ramp up to half speed until the market prices of housing increase enough to generate a decent profit margin.

To make investing even better, mortgage interest rates have fallen to less than 5 percent (though these low rates are always subject to increase). I am taking advantage of today's property and mortgage market. During the past several months, I have purchased multiple properties (in good to excellent condition) at discounts of 50 to 65 percent off their earlier peak sales prices.

Of course, you may wonder: Is now really the time to buy? Might prices go lower? Could we encounter a double-dip recession? Will the pipeline of foreclosures flood the market with an increased number of distress sales? Even the good opportunities of today might be surpassed with even better bargains in the near future.

Possibly, yes. But, do not forget interest rates. Over a property holding period, the extra costs of higher interest rates could dwarf any savings that you might score in price. Nevertheless, if you do choose to delay, do so intelligently.

Monitor the market (foreclosures, existing home sales, interest rates, unemployment and employment figures, new construction starts, and so on). Detect turning points in the data as well as investor and buyer confidence. Intelligent monitoring and opportunistic waiting differ from inattentive procrastination. Moreover, property investing offers multiple ways to earn a good return, among which "market bottom, lowest price" represents only one—and not necessarily the most important—reason to invest.

Multiple Sources of Return

Journalists and their media molls (especially economists, Wall Street mavens, and mutual fund analysts), love to play the game of short-term forecasting. They do it with stocks, gold, commodities, interest rates, and, for the past 10 years, properties. Are prices climbing? Buy. Are prices falling? Get out of the game and watch from the sidelines. As they persistently obsess over short-term price movements, the media distort and confuse the idea of *investing* in real estate.

Contrary to media hype, most experienced and successful real estate *investors* do not emphasize short-term price forecasts. Instead, we typically look to an investing horizon of 3 to 10 years (or longer). We realize that property provides multiple sources of return. The smart money investors weigh, evaluate, and understand that to earn great returns, they need to achieve only several (maybe only one) sources of reward.

Here are many (but certainly not all) of the profit possibilities that property offers:

- ◆ Earn price gains from appreciation (a possibility that becomes nearly certain when you buy in down markets at below-replacement-cost prices.
- ◆ Earn price gains from inflation (especially when you invest while inflation rates remain subdued and obtain low interest rate financing).
- ◆ Generate unleveraged cash flows.
- ◆ Use leverage (financing) to magnify returns from price gains.
- ◆ Use leverage (financing) to magnify returns from cash flows.
- ◆ Grow equity through amortization (that is, use rent collections to pay down your loan balance).
- ◆ Refinance to increase cash flows (reduce your loan payments).
- ◆ Refinance to generate cash (lump sum cash-out).
- ◆ Buy at a below-market price.
- ◆ Sell at an above-market price.
- ◆ Create value through smarter management.
- ◆ Create value through savvy market strategy.
- ◆ Create value by improving the location of your property.
- ◆ Subdivide your bundle of property rights.
- ◆ Subdivide the physical property.
- ◆ Create plottage (assemblage) value.
- ◆ Convert the use of the property to one that generates more revenues (for example, residential to offices, retail to office—adapt a property use to changing markets).
- ◆ Convert type of tenure (for example, rental to ownership, as in rental apartments to condominiums or, as is now the case with so many fractured condo conversion projects in default, condos to rental).

♦ Shelter cash flows from taxes.
♦ Shelter (or defer) capital gains from taxes.
♦ Create and sell development or redevelopment rights.
♦ Diversify away from stocks and bonds.

I explain each of these possible sources of return in Chapter 1 and then illustrate and elaborate to varying degrees in the chapters that follow. With this extensive range of possibilities in view, you can always find profitable ways to invest in real estate.

Unlike investing (or speculating) in stocks, bonds, gold, or commodities, you can generate returns from properties through active participation (research, reasoning, knowledge, and entrepreneurial talents). When you buy stocks, you can only pray that the market price goes up, because that's your one single possibility to receive a reasonable return.[1] (Dividend yields on stocks now average around 2 percent—though many pay nothing, and a relative few pay 3 to 4 percent per year.)

Look for Solid Value–Not Necessarily a Market Bottom

Today's markets offer multiple low-risk, high-profit possibilities. Over a time horizon of three to seven years—if you follow the principles laid out in this book—you will earn high returns. I encourage you to invest now. No one can perfectly forecast price movements during the next year or two. But today, you can find and negotiate solid investments in any market.

Two frequent mistakes block people from profiting with property: (1) they wait too long to enter and then cannot exit an irrationally exuberant market, and (2) they wait too long to take advantage of the possibilities that are theirs for the taking (that is, they perpetually procrastinate and then regret).

DEVELOP YOUR INVESTMENT PLAN

As you read through the following chapters, you will discover how to create, develop, and exploit at least 22 sources of financial returns. To buy, improve, and hold income properties—*especially* when you invest in difficult economic times and finance with smart leverage—does offer the

---

[1]With some properties, I have earned a yearly return on equity of 25 percent or more—without a single dollar of price gain. If not price gain, how? Cash flow, amortization, and tax shelter (albeit tax shelter was larger then than it is today).

surest, safest, and, yes, even the quickest way to build your net worth. But even long-term investors like me will venture along other avenues when opportunities arise.

In addition to the buy, improve, and hold houses and apartment buildings approach, other profit-generating techniques include discounted paper, commercial properties, condominium conversions, fix and flip, adaptive reuse, tax liens, mobile home parks, self-storage centers, lease options, and triple net leases. (I discuss and explain each of these techniques in later chapters.)

To secure your future—a future free from financial worries, with a life that you can live as you would like to live—property, especially property in today's distressed markets, provides a near-certain route to personal freedom and prosperity. All that remains is for you to develop and execute your own investment plan now.

INVESTING

in

REAL ESTATE

Seventh Edition

1

ACHIEVE A PROSPEROUS FUTURE: 22 WAYS YOU CAN EARN PROFITS WITH PROPERTY

For at least the past 20 to 25 years, financial planners, mutual fund sales reps, Wall Street promoters, and various cheerleading professors of finance (most loudly, Jeremy Siegel of the Wharton School) have championed the mantra, "Stocks for the long run"; "Stocks for retirement." These advocates of equities assert that over the long run, stocks outperform all other types of investments. "If your retirement still sits at least 10 years into the future," they advise, "place 100 percent of your nest egg in stocks." (Admittedly, the 2011 bull market in bonds converted a few of the stock market enthusiasts to a more balanced view—but the majority seem undaunted.)

In his widely read (and praised) book, *Winning the Loser's Game*, Charles Ellis encourages investors to place all of their money in stock index funds rather than property because (according to Ellis),

> Owning residential real estate is not a great investment. Over the past 20 years, home prices have risen less than the consumer price index and have returned less than Treasury bills. . . . Own a home as a place to live, not as an investment.

Leave aside for a moment how Ellis arrived at his long-term house price figures—no data that I have seen (even if we factor in the recent downturn) report that long-term housing prices, relative to incomes or consumer prices, have become cheaper. However, Ellis errs most egregiously in another way. He does not understand how investors should measure the total potential returns that property offers.[1]

Neither Ellis, stock market enthusiasts, financial planners, nor you should evaluate property returns (past or future) simply on the basis of historical or expected price growth.

Frequently, even advocates of real estate investing often err in a similar way. I often read property investing advice such as, "Always buy from a motivated seller"; "Never buy unless you can buy at least 20 percent below market value"; "Always buy in an area poised for growth (or experiencing rapid growth)." Unfortunately, this stock market mentality that focuses upon price growth has infected the way too many people think about property.

22 SOURCES OF PROFIT FROM INVESTMENT PROPERTY

No question about it. I love price gains and will elaborate on this point as my next topic. Nevertheless, as you evaluate properties as investments, expand your perspective. Apply each one of the potential returns listed in the prologue and explained with examples in this chapter. You can achieve stock market–beating returns from property—at much lower levels of risk—in many different ways. When you fail to evaluate the *full* potential of a property, you not only bypass properties that could yield great profits (albeit in ways you may never thought of), you also slight the full range of profit possibilities that lie within the properties that you do buy.

Will the Property Experience Price Gains from Appreciation?

Passive price gains (as contrasted to gains from actively creating value) can arise from two unique sources: (1) appreciation and (2) inflation. Yet, in everyday conversation, most people do not differentiate between price gains that result from appreciation and those that result from inflation. Appreciation occurs when demand for a specific type of property, location, or both, grows faster than the supply of competing (substitute) properties, whereas inflation *tends* to push property prices up—even if demand and supply remain in

---

[1] His two-decade time horizon also fails as a representative period because it includes the late 1970s and the 1980s—Treasuries paid record-high interest rates during those years. Today, Treasury bills pay close to zero.

balance (although in cities such as Detroit or Buffalo, demand may slide so much that property prices lag the Consumer Price Index by a wide margin).

Homes in Central London, San Francisco's Pacific Heights, and Brooklyn's Williamsburg have experienced extraordinarily high rates of demand growth during the past 15 to 20 years. And since 1990, houses within a mile of the University of Florida campus have more than doubled (and in some cases tripled) in market price—primarily because UF students and faculty alike now prefer "walk or bike to campus" locations.

Areas Differ in Their Rate of Appreciation. Although properties located in Pacific Heights and Williamsburg have jumped in price at rates much greater than the rise in the Consumer Price Index (CPI), some neighborhoods in Detroit have suffered price declines of 60 to 90 percent. Appreciation does not occur uniformly or randomly. You can forecast appreciation potential using the right place, right time, right price methodology discussed in Chapter 15.

Likewise, you need not get caught in the severe, long-term downdrafts in prices that plague cities and neighborhoods that lose their economic base of jobs. Just as various socioeconomic factors point to right time, right place, right price, similar indicators can signal wrong place, wrong time, and wrong price.

Today's property markets seem to offer a best-of-both-worlds opportunity: You can earn good returns from cash flow—and good returns from appreciation when the economy and property supply and demand balances return to normal. In the past, in markets strong in longer-term appreciation potential (for example, coastal California or as with urban Vancouver now), investors had to sacrifice cash flow as a trade-off for expected price gain. Fortunately, that trade-off no longer exists to the degree that it used to.

You Do Not Need Appreciation. Should you invest in properties that are located in areas poised for above-average appreciation? Not necessarily. Some investors own rental properties in deteriorating areas—yet still have built up multimillion-dollar net worths. My first properties did not gain much from price increases (appreciation or inflation)—but they consistently cash-flowed like a slot machine payoff. With one of my early apartment buildings, a $10,000 down payment grew into $100,000 of equity over 10 years—just through mortgage amortization.

When you choose a quick turn, fix, and sell strategy, appreciation isn't needed. You achieve gains in equity that are unrelated to market temperature. Appreciation isn't necessarily required, either, when you buy at a price 15 to 30 percent *below market value.* Savvy buying can reward you with five years of appreciation-like price gains—instantly upon purchase. Throw out the popular (but erroneous) belief that you can't make good money with property unless its market price appreciates. Appreciation represents one highly rewarding goal to achieve, but by no means is it the only goal that counts.

Will You Gain Price Increases from Inflation?

In his book, *Irrational Exuberance*, the oft-quoted Yale economist, Robert Shiller, concludes (as does Charles Ellis, cited earlier) that houses perform poorly as investments. According to Shiller's reckoning, since 1948, the *real* (inflation-adjusted) price growth in housing has averaged around 1—at best 2—percent a year.

"Even if this $16,000 house [bought in 1948] sold in 2004," says the eminent professor, "at a price of $360,000, it still does not imply great returns on this investment . . . a *real* (that is, inflation-adjusted) annual rate of increase of a little under 2 percent a year." (Note that Shiller also omits rental income from his supposed investment results.)

Shiller Thinks Like an Economist, Not an Investor. Every investor wants to protect his wealth from the corrosive power of unexpected inflation. Even if we accept Shiller's inflation-adjusted rate of price growth—and I believe it reasonable (on average—though savvy investors need not accept average), yet certainly not beyond critique—even Shiller's data show that property prices have kept investors ahead of inflation in every decade throughout the past 75 years.

[Side Note: Not true for stocks (or bonds). Consider the most inflationary period in U.S. history: 1966–1982. In 1966, the median price of a house equaled $25,000; the Dow Jones Index (DJIA) hit 1,000. During the subsequent 18 years, the CPI climbed steadily from 100 to 300. In 1982, the median price of a house had risen to $72,000; the 1982 DJIA closed the year at 780—below its *nominal* level of 18 years earlier.]

Inflation Risk: Property Has Protected Better than Stocks. No one knows what the future holds. Will the CPI once again start climbing at a steeper pace? At the runaway rate at which the U.S. government prints money and floats new debt, the odds weight the scale in that direction. During periods of accelerating inflation, most people would rejoice at staying even. In fact, the popularity of Treasury inflation-protected securities (TIPS) reveals that goal (and worry).

Imagine that in the early to mid-1960s you were a true-blue stocks for retirement kind of investor—and you were then age 45. In 1982, as you approach age 65, your inflation-adjusted net worth sits at maybe 30 percent of the amount you had hoped and planned to accumulate. What do you do? Stay on the job another 10 years? Sell the homestead and downsize? Borrow money from a wealthy friend who invested in property?

Property Investors Do Not Buy Indexes and Averages. Economists calculate in the nether land of aggregates and averages. Investors buy specific properties according to their personal investment objectives. An economist's average does not capture the actual price gains (inflation plus appreciation) that real investors can earn—when they set price gain as their prime financial objective. Investors apply some variant of right time, right place, right price methodologies (see p. 315). If you want to outperform the *average* price increases of real estate—even though the long-term averages themselves look good—you can. And today's housing markets (especially) offer the right time to greatly outperform with long-term price growth (appreciation plus inflation).

Earn Good Returns from Cash Flows

Unlike the overwhelming majority of stocks, income properties typically yield (unleveraged) cash flows of 5 to 12 percent per year.[2] If you own a $1,000,000 property free and clear of financing, you can pocket $50,000 to $120,000 a year (mostly tax sheltered; see the following discussion). If you own a $1,000,000 portfolio of stocks, you might pocket cash flows (dividend payments) of $15,000 to $30,000 a year (fully taxable—although at the time this chapter was written, the income tax rate on dividends was just 15 percent, many in Congress would like to increase this rate).

Historically, the largest source of return for unleveraged properties has come from cash flow. Remember, too, rent increases add to the profit potential of cash flows. To grow a passive, inflation-protected stream of income, own income properties.

Economists and financial planners greatly embarrass themselves when they slight or ignore this critical source of return. Before Charles Ellis, Robert Shiller, and others of their ilk again take up their pens to write on real estate returns, they might set aside their misguided claims of expertise and first learn the actual practice of investing in real estate. If they did, they would also learn that nearly all property investors magnify their returns (cash flows and equity buildup) with leverage.

Magnify Your Equity Gains with Leverage

Misguided economists, financial analysts, and various media-anointed experts claim that property provides investors real (inflation-adjusted) returns of 1 to 2 percent a year. In doing so, these advisors omit the

---

[2]Yields in the United Kingdom, Asia, and most of Europe often fall somewhat below those available throughout the United States (which is one reason why U.S. property is attracting record amounts of international capital).

return-boosting power of OPM (other people's money—typically, bank or seller financing).

Low Rates of Price Gain Create Big (Inflation-Adjusted) Returns. Assume you acquire a $100,000 property. You borrow $80,000 and place $20,000 as down payment. During the following five years, we experience inflation similar to the late 1970s. The CPI advances by 50 percent. Your property's price, though, lagged the CPI. It increased by only 25 percent. Your real (inflation-adjusted) wealth fell, right? That's what Shiller, the economist, would conclude. But no, your real wealth increased.

You now own a property worth $125,000, but your equity wealth— your original $20,000 cash equity in the property—has increased more than 100 percent—to $45,000 (not including repayment of principal, that is, amortization). You more than doubled your money. To have stayed even with the CPI, your equity needed to grow from $20,000 to only $30,000 (a 50 percent increase to match the gain of the CPI).

Acorns into Oak Trees. Real estate investing builds equity because it grows acorns (relatively small down payments) into free and clear properties worth many multiples of the *original* amounts of invested cash. Let's go back to Shiller's house purchase example.

The homebuyer paid a price of $16,000 in 1948. Did that homebuyer pay cash? Not likely. Ten to 20 percent down then set the norm—say, 20 percent or $3,200 (.2 × $16,000). At Shiller's hypothetical 2004 value of $360,000, the homebuyer multiplied his original investment more than 100 times over. Even if the 2004 property value comes in at $180,000—the homeowner enjoyed a nearly 60-fold increase of his $3,200 down payment. (Of course, in 1948 some homebuyers could have used a nothing-down VA loan or a 3 percent down FHA mortgage. Their gains from OPM would have paid back much greater multiples of their original investment.)

What about stock gains during that period of 1948 to 2004? In 1948, the Dow Jones Industrial Average (DJIA) hovered around 200 (by the way, it was then still about 40 percent below its 1929 peak of 360). In 2004, the DJIA stood at about 8,000—a 40-fold gain. Not bad, but still less than the equity gains from property ownership (and much, much less when we bring cash flows and tax shelter into the return comparison). [Note: When I wrote this chapter in late 2011, the DJIA still sat at around 11,500, whereas property prices (in all but the most distressed areas) are still way up from 1999, which is the year that the DJIA first hit 11,500.]

Magnify Returns from Cash Flows with Leverage

Traditionally, investors not only magnify their equity gains from leverage (mortgage financing), they also magnify their rates of return from cash flows. You pay $1,000,000 cash for an apartment building that yields a net income (after all operating expenses) of 7.5 percent (no financing). Quite good when compared to CD interest rates of 1 to 2 percent, dividend yields from stocks of 2 percent, corporate bond interest of 4 to 5 percent, or 10-year Treasuries at 2 to 2.5 percent interest. Yet it gets better. If you finance $800,000 of that $1,000,000 purchase price at, say, 30 years, 5.75 percent interest, you invest just $200,000 in cash. Your net income equals $75,000 (.075 × 1,000,000) and your annual mortgage payments (debt service) will total around $56,000. You pocket $19,000 ($75,000 less $56,000). You've boosted your cash flow return (called *cash on cash*) from 7.5 percent to 9.5 percent ($19,000 divided by $200,000). You can achieve positive leverage with cash flows whenever your cap rate exceeds your mortgage loan constant (see Chapter 2).

Build Wealth through Mortgage Payoff

Assume for a moment that from your $1,000,000 apartment building, you pocket no cash flows. You pay every dollar of net operating income (and future rent increases) to reduce your mortgage balance of $800,000. After 20 years, you have paid off (fully amortized) your loan and own your property free and clear (a workable strategy). This apartment building experienced no gain in price. At the end of 20 years, its value equals your original purchase of $1,000,000.

No price gains from inflation, no price gains from appreciation, and no money pocketed from cash flows. Quite pessimistic, right? Yet, just from amortization over a 20-year period, you grew your equity from $200,000 to $1,000,000—a five-fold gain and annual compound growth rate of more than 8 percent. In today's low-rate world, an 8 percent return sounds pretty appealing. After 20 years, you pocket 100 percent of your net operating income—quite likely enough to live on comfortably.

Your tenants just bought you a $1,000,000 property. That's why I tell my college students, "Rent or buy?" asks the wrong question. Everyone buys—the real question is one of ownership. If you rent, you pay your landlord's mortgage. Your landlord reaps the rewards of ownership—while tenants pay the costs. Seems to me a good deal for property investors.

Over Time, Returns from Rents Go Up

Most property owners raise their rents. Maybe not this year. Maybe not next year. But over a period of five years or more, increasing rents yield increasing cash flows. If you've selected a right time, right place, right price property, demand will push rents up as more people want to live in the neighborhood where your property is located. Or perhaps, as government floods the economy with paper money, inflationary pressures force rents up. Either way, you gain. In fact, you can gain even if your rent increases fail to match the inflationary jumps in your expenses.

Return to our apartment building example. Gross rent collections equal $125,000; net operating income equals $75,000; mortgage payments equal $56,000; your cash flow equals $19,000.

Gross rents	$125,000
Vacancy and expenses	50,000
Net operating income	75,000
Annual mortgage payments	56,000
Cash flow	19,000

First, assume your rents and expenses each increase by 8 percent. Here are the revised amounts:

Gross rents	$135,000
Vacancy and expenses	54,000
Net operating income	81,000
Annual mortgage payments	56,000
Cash flow	25,000

An 8 percent increase in rents and expenses boosts your cash flow by 31 percent:

$$25,000 \div 19,000 = 13.1$$

If expenses had increased by 12 percent and rents stepped up mildly by just 6 percent per annum (p.a.), you would still increase your cash flow:

Gross rents	$132,500
Vacancy and expenses	56,000
Net operating income	76,500
Annual mortgage payments	56,000
Cash flow	20,500

$$20,500 \div 19,000 = 1.08$$

Caution: Engage your brainpower. Run multiple outcomes with these figures and other numbers presented throughout this chapter (and following chapters). No one guarantees the results that you want or expect.

Through market and entrepreneurial analysis, you estimate, negotiate, execute, and create the potential returns for the properties you buy. (Nevertheless, these examples do illustrate the time-tested principles and advantages of property investing.)

Envision each return possibility that property investing offers. Then as you evaluate markets, properties, and the outlook for your geographic areas of interest, figure the probabilities. Which of the listed (p. xxvi) sources of return look most promising? Which sources of return seem remote?

What risks could throw ice water against your expectations? What if interest rates increase? What if a local employer lays off hundreds (or thousands) of employees? What if tight local government budgets drive up property taxes? What if vacancies increase or rent collections fall, or both? Even though you can build your net worth with property with more safety and certainty than any other asset, such wealth does not accumulate automatically—or without some turbulence along the way. Anticipate potential storms: safety belts and life jackets are mandatory.

In a majority of cases, today's foreclosures have resulted because many unwise borrowers projected that blue skies and smooth flying would last forever. It never does. As Chapter 2 discusses, the property mentors, gurus, loan reps, banks, and authors who widely promoted "No cash, no credit, no problem" actually promoted their own immediate profits at the expense of their naïve and trusting customers.

Refinance to Lift Your Cash Flows

Increase your rents (or decrease your property's operating expenses, or both) and you increase your property's cash flows. But you also gain additional cash flow when you refinance your loan at a lower interest rate or for a longer term than the years remaining on your current loan. When might a refinance pay off with a lower interest rate?

First, if market rates fall—perhaps not likely from today's low levels. Yet, that's what most experts said when mortgage interest rates fell back to 6 percent during the early 2000s. So, who knows? Moreover, at some future time, we might again see mortgage interest rates of 7 to 10 percent. Under those market conditions, a refinance of a property purchase as those higher rates come back down becomes ever more attractive and cash generating.

Second, not everyone qualifies for the lowest interest rates available. Credit counts. Many credit-challenged investors accept higher interest rates at the time of purchase, then refinance as they build more equity in their property; establish a higher credit score; or the credit-damaging, adverse events (bankruptcy, foreclosure, late payments, judgments, and so on) are dropped from the credit bureaus' reporting files.

Third, LTV (loan-to-value) ratios influence interest rates. To maximize leverage, finance with a higher-interest-rate, higher-LTV loan. Then, as you build more equity in the property (inflation, appreciation, creating value, amortization, and so on), refinance your loan's existing balance. With more equity (which means a lower LTV), the lender may grant you a lower interest rate.

In addition to reducing payment amounts by refinancing into a lower interest rate, you can increase your cash flow (decrease mortgage payments) by refinancing into a longer term. Say your loan shows a current balance of $435,000 with 14 years remaining. Extend the term of your new loan to 30 years and your payments drop by 20 to 35 percent. (The exact amount of reduction depends on the terms and amount originally borrowed.)

Some investors want quick loan payoffs. Others want to maximize cash flow and cash-on-cash return. It's your call. But the point is that refinancing can place extra cash income into your pocket—if that's what you prefer. (We go through some payment examples in Chapter 2. For now, we explore possibilities that you can use to boost your returns.)

(*Additional Possibility for Profit:* Chapter 2 introduces a technique called a *wraparound mortgage*. Using this technique, you obtain the benefit of a lower-than-market interest rate by combining purchase money financing from the seller with an existing loan on the property. Wraparounds provide buyers a reduced interest rate and, at the same time, create another source of return for sellers; cf. p. 40–41.)

Refinance to Pocket Cash

Buy a property today and within 12 to 15 years (possibly sooner—depending on the speed of market recovery and your skill in selecting or improving the property), you can sell it for 50 to 100 percent more than the price you paid. You earn a large capital gain. But what if you do not want to sell? Can you still place some of that large equity that you have built up into your pocket? Absolutely. Arrange a cash-out refinance.

Here's how this possible source of return works. Say after 10 years your $1 million property has grown in price to $1.5 million. You've paid down your loan balance to $650,000. Your equity has increased from $200,000 to $850,000 ($1.5 million less the $650,000 that you owe to the mortgage lender). You obtain a new 80 percent LTV mortgage of $1.2 million. You pocket $550,000 tax-free! (Cash from a sale may be taxed as a capital gain, but cash into your pocket from a refinance remains free from the IRS.)

You can spend that extra cash (albeit a poor choice) or, much smarter, reinvest it. Buy another income property. You now pay higher amounts on your first property's mortgage each month and your cash flows from that property will decrease. But with the additional cash flows from your second property, your total cash flows will go up. How's that for having your cake and eating it, too?

Buy at a Below-Market Price

When the economists and financial planners (mis)calculate the returns that property investors can earn, they fail to note that savvy buyers can acquire properties for less than their *current* market value. Opportunity (grass-is-greener) sellers, don't-wanter sellers, ill-informed sellers, incompetent sellers, unknowledgeable sellers, and—most importantly in today's markets—banks and financially distressed sellers will all sell at below-market prices. Today's markets not only offer properties at much-reduced market values, savvy buyers can find or negotiate purchases at even steeper discounts.

And unlike during normal times, the financially stressed and distressed today include not only individual property owners but also mortgage lenders. Banks, Fannie Mae, and Freddie Mac (and other lenders) now hold an inventory of perhaps 2 million foreclosures (real estate–owned—REOs) that they must sell as quickly as they can line up buyers to take these properties off their books. Builders of new homes and non-distressed would-be sellers blame bank REOs for driving down property prices for all sellers.

How do you find and buy these properties for less than they are worth? See Chapters 5, 6, and 7.

Sell at an Above-Market-Value Price

Sometimes you can *buy* a property for *less than* its market value. Sometimes you can *sell* a property that you own for *more than* its present market value. How do you achieve this gain? Surprisingly, such a feat is neither rare nor difficult: Sell to a buyer who lacks knowledge about a property; or perhaps a buyer who is not well-informed about the local market; someone who's incompetent, or pressed by time. Offer seller financing, a wraparound mortgage, or a lease option. Apply your skills of promotion and negotiation (see Chapter 13). Match the unique features and benefits of the property to the unique needs of the buyer. Sell the property with a below-market-interest-rate assumable (or subject-to) loan.

Occasionally, buyers pay more than market value because they don't know (or do not care) what they're doing. Sometimes they pay more to obtain a much-desired feature or terms of purchase or financing. Whatever their reason, exploit this possibility and you've created another source of return.

Create Property Value through Smarter Management

Manage your properties *and* your tenants more intelligently. You increase a property's net operating income (NOI) and, correspondingly, its market value—without the need to (necessarily) raise rents; you reduce tenant turnover; you increase prospect conversions (that is, converting lookers to tenants); you spend more effectively for maintenance, promotion, and capital replacements. You enjoy peaceful, pleasant, and productive relations with your tenants.

Fortunately for you (and me), most (yes, most!) owners of small investor-size (as opposed to institutional-size) rental properties manage their investments poorly. Their shoddy or uncaring management creates opportunities for us. After you buy the ill-managed property, you execute a more promising and competitive management strategy. (I improve the management—and hence value—of every property that I purchase. Indeed, I especially seek out undermanaged and poorly managed properties. This opportunity leads to one of the surest means to create value and build your equity.)

How can you achieve maestro-like performance? Rely on Chapter 11 to develop your profit-maximizing management *and* market strategy.

Create Value with a Savvy Market Strategy

Although investors tend to ill manage their properties, they show even less skill as savvy marketers. Go to the property websites loopnet.com, and craigslist.org. Click through a sample of listings. Look at the listing promotional information provided. Look at the property photographs. Does the seller or agent tell a persuasive story about the property? A message that rings true? Does the sales message position that property against the tens of thousands of competing properties that also beg for attention? Do the photographs of properties reveal a well-cared-for property—a property that invites tenants to call it home?

I will provide you the answers. No! No! No! The implication? More opportunities for you to gain competitive advantage. When you combine the management know-how and marketing strategy lessons of Chapters 11 and 13, you earn higher cash flows; you provide a better home for your tenants; and when the time to sell arises, your property will command a higher price.

Create Value: Improve the Location

True or false? "You can change anything about a property except its location." A false and silly cliché. As Chapter 8 shows, you can improve a location, and doing so offers one of your most powerful sources of return.

Think for a moment. What does the concept of location include? What makes the location where you live desirable (or undesirable)? Accessibility and convenience, appearance, quiet, good public transportation, cleanliness, the character and lifestyles of people who live in the neighborhood, school quality, parks, shopping, nightlife . . . the list could go on and on. What's the best way to improve any or all of these attributes? Community action. Examples of improvement are available from throughout the United States and throughout the world (South Beach, SOMA, SOHO, Williamsburg, Lakeview, Hyde Park, to name just a few).

Convert from Unit Rentals to Unit Ownership

Buy wholesale, sell retail. A grocer buys a 48-can box of tomato soup and then sells each can individually along with a retail mark-up. Property investors execute a similar wholesale-to-retail strategy.

Buy a 48-unit apartment building. After completing legal approvals and documentation, sell each apartment individually. In principle, you can apply a similar condo-conversion strategy to office buildings, neighborhood shopping centers, self-storage warehouse units, mobile home parks, hotels, marinas, boat storage facilities, private aircraft hangars, and other types of rental real estate in which potential users might prefer to own versus rent. In each case, you pay less per unit (or per square foot) for an entire building than individual retail buyers are willing to pay for the smaller quantities of space that will meet their needs.

Opportunities for conversion profits run in cycles. As property markets change, potential profit margins swing from "make an easy million" to "call the bankruptcy lawyer" and back again to profit possibilities.[3] Orlando, Florida, during the boom years, seemed like the perfect condo conversion market to make that easy million. Today, the bankruptcy and foreclosure lawyers are working overtime. But the cycle will turn. To profit with this possibility, monitor your property markets for both conversion timing and product potential (see Chapter 9).

---

[3]In such distressed market conditions, you might profit from reverse conversions. Buy a fractured condo and operate it as a rental property.

Convert from Lower-Value Use to Higher-Value Use

Assume that because of undersupply in your city, single-family homes (SFRs) rent for, say, $2 per square foot (psf); offices rent for $1 psf (due to an excess supply). Five years from now, the market has reversed. Single-family space rents have fallen to $1.50 psf (due to excessive new housing construction), and because of a strong economy and high rate of job growth, office space rents have increased to $3 psf. What might you do (if zoning permits)? Convert your single-family house into offices.

To succeed with conversions of *use*, renovate (at least to some degree) the old, lower-value space to fit the market needs of the tenants for the higher-value use. When relative prices or rent levels grow progressively wider, conversion from lower-priced use to the higher-priced use can generate a lucrative source of returns. In the Wall Street area of Manhattan, various buildings with vacant office space found new life (and profitability) as million-dollar condominiums.

Subdivide Your Bundle of Property Rights

When you own a freehold estate in property, you own *divisible* property rights. Divisible means that you can sell or lease each of these rights to different persons. In some instances, the sum of the parts greatly exceeds the value of the whole. Such divisible rights may include (but are not limited to):

♦ Air
♦ Mineral
♦ Oil and gas
♦ Coal
♦ Access
♦ Subsurface
♦ Development
♦ Water
♦ Leasehold
♦ Grazing
♦ Timber
♦ Solar/sunlight
♦ Easement
♦ Life estate

When Donald Trump built his United Nations World Tower, a few lucky nearby property owners pocketed several million dollars. Why? Because Trump paid these owners to transfer a portion of their air rights to him. After purchasing their air rights, the City of New York permitted Trump to build 80 stories instead of 40 stories, the maximum height zoning then allowed. These owners could sell additional air space to Trump because their buildings had not maxed out their height allotment under the then-current zoning law.

After selling to Trump, these owners lost the right to rebuild their sites to the maximum height otherwise permitted [e.g., the owner of a 30-story building may have been able to build a new 40-story building on that site (or perhaps add 10 stories to the existing building). The owner instead sold those air rights to 10 additional stories to Trump. Unless the zoning law changes, 30 stories represents the most that can now be constructed on that site.]

When you are in Hong Kong, notice that high-rise apartments tower directly above some of the Mass Transit Railway (MTR) stations. Developers paid the Hong Kong government for the right to lease that airspace—even though the government retained ownership and use rights of the land beneath the apartment buildings.

Does a neighboring landowner need access to the beach through your property? Sell (or lease) him an easement. Do you own property near a stadium or popular event location? Grant short-term parking rights. Do you own a rental condominium or house with parking or storage spaces? Lease these spaces separately from the residence. Does your city recognize the right to sunlight? If so, sell this right to your neighbor when he wants to build an upper-floor addition onto his house that will place your backyard in the shade most of the day.

Timber, oil, gas, minerals, life estates—these and many other rights may offer profit possibilities. Match up advanced knowledge of local property law with the particulars of a given property. Stir in your fertile imagination. You can come up with some good ideas for parceling out your property's divisible package of rights.

Subdivide the Physical Property (or Space within a Property)

Condominium conversions represent one form of subdividing. But subdividing usually refers to selling or leasing land or buildings in smaller parcels, most commonly, a developer who buys, say, 500 acres, and then sells half-acre lots to homebuilders. Alternatively, consider a permanently closed Kmart store. A thriving big-box retailer might pay $10 per square foot to lease the entire now-vacant building. But subdividing (partitioning) the interior space might bring in higher rents.

A property entrepreneur could master lease the old Kmart property and partition the interior space into a variety of uses such as child care, offices, or smaller retail merchants. Each small tenant pays a higher price per square foot rental rate than would the Best Buy or Lowe's that might otherwise lease the entire building. If the new space users require lower parking ratios than the old Kmart, the entrepreneur might subdivide some of the parking lot area for additional retail or restaurant uses (outparcels).

Thoughtful entrepreneurs steeped in market knowledge and possibility thinking persistently search for properties to subdivide or partition. The sum of the parts may exceed the value of the whole.

Create Plottage (or Assemblage) Value

You create plottage or assemblage value when you combine smaller parcels into a larger parcel of land or space. Say you discover a perfect site to build a new neighborhood shopping center. Zoning and planners require a minimum of four acres for such a development. The site equals four acres but it is owned by eight different persons in one-half-acre lots. Individually, the lots are worth $10,000 apiece—or $80,000 in total.

However, as a four-acre shopping site, the land would sell for $250,000. You now see how to earn a good profit. Persuade each of the current owners to sell you her lot at its current market value (or even at a price that sits somewhat above market value). One of the most famous and profitable assemblages (Disney World) involved the Walt Disney Company. Over a period of 10 years, Disney secretly put together the smaller tracts of hundreds of landowners to accumulate a total of 25 square miles of Central Florida land at agricultural-valued prices. Once Disney had completed this assemblage, the value of the aggregated raw land probably exceeded their per acre purchase costs by a factor of 10 (or more).

Obtain Development or Redevelopment Rights

Return to the four-acre neighborhood shopping center example. You succeed. You acquire all eight lots at a total price of $130,000 (several of those owners did not want to sell—so you raised your offer). Can you start building the center? No. You must first secure a long list of government permits and approvals. So, the current site value of $250,000 applies only to the assembled parcel—devoid of permitting.

With development and construction permits approved, the land might command a price of $500,000. You could sell now for $250,000 and take your profit. Or you could stay in the action. Spend $50,000 (more or less) for lawyers, soil tests, public hearings, environmental clearance, traffic studies, and whatever else the city requires. This permit process might (with luck—and no unanticipated delays) continue for 12 to 24 months. Then, if all goes as planned, you sell for $500,000 and earn $320,000 ($500,000 less [$130,000 + $50,000]).

In real estate, government approvals add to the value of any property that is suitable for development, redevelopment, renovation, conversion— or even destruction.[4] Obtain those permits and the value of the subject property goes up.

Tax Shelter Your Property Income and Capital Gains

To build wealth, protect your income and capital gains from the grasp of government. Fortunately (under current tax law), investing in real estate provides you more opportunity to avoid paying taxes than any other asset class.

Depreciation (noncash) deductions might shelter all (or nearly all) of your positive cash flow. A Section 1231 exchange shelters your capital gain as you pyramid into larger investment properties. The $250,000/$500,000 capital gain exclusion provides you tax-free gains from the sale of your personal residence(s). A cash-out refinance (that your tenants will repay for you) deposits tax-free cash into your bank account. And if you buy a first-time home, you may qualify for a mortgage (tax) credit certificate.

Some naïve investors might remark, "I can build my stock market wealth tax free through my 401(k), 403(b), and IRA plans. That tax break beats real estate."

Unfortunately, those retirement programs do not provide tax advantages that are as favorable as most people think, because when you begin to draw on that cash during retirement, the government will tax every penny as ordinary income. Even though (if you invested successfully) much (perhaps most) of your withdrawals will have accumulated through capital gains, the IRS does not permit you to claim those withdrawals as a capital gain and therefore pay the much lower capital gain tax rates.

Another costly disadvantage: if you withdraw money from your retirement plan before you attain age 59½ (as nearly 50 percent of Americans do), the IRS will take 35 to 50 percent of those amounts (taxes plus penalties). If you die before you withdraw your benefits, the IRS still reaches in and pulls out its share from your estate.

To minimize loss of income and wealth to the IRS, buy investment real estate. But do not misinterpret my point. I own a 403(b) account that is exclusively invested in stocks and bonds. Diversity of assets has merit (see the following discussion). My property investments, however, generate more effective tax-avoidance possibilities (as will yours). (See Chapter 14 for a discussion of property taxes and income tax laws. In addition, many

---

[4]Yes, government even requires permits to tear down buildings. In Sarasota, Florida, the Ritz Carlton fought a four-year battle to obtain permission to tear down a historic house located on part of the site where the Ritz planned to build. In compromise, the Ritz eventually paid to move the house to another site.

investors today are switching to a self-directed IRA—within which you are permitted to hold investment real estate and many types of alternative assets other than stocks and bonds.)

Diversify Away from Financial Assets

Although some investors prefer stocks, those investors would prove themselves wise to diversify part of their portfolio into property. (And similarly, property enthusiasts are smart to own at least some stocks and bonds.)

During longer periods of expected and unexpected inflation, property prices have kept pace with (or exceeded) the rate of growth in the CPI. Even better, leverage transforms small price gains into double-digit rates of increase in your equity wealth. With smart financing, you can earn above-inflation returns with below-inflation gains in price.

Historically, property values have experienced less volatility than stock prices. The recent depression, surfeit of foreclosures, and price downturns for many properties seem less serious when compared to the precipitous periodic drops in stock prices. Even in the hard-times property markets, prices have only fallen back to their 2004–2005 levels. When I wrote this chapter, major stock indices (S&P 500, DJIA, NASDAQ) were sitting below their levels of the year 2000.

And do not forget income. During our continuing financial crisis, rent levels increased and vacancies decreased in most cities. In contrast, stock dividends fell significantly—especially the dividends paid by banks (which until the crisis accounted for 35 to 40 percent of all dividends paid by S&P 500 companies). If you want your investments to fund your retirement *income,* own investment properties.

Today, most financial planners encourage asset diversification. Historical as well as recent experience supports that view. The mantra "stocks, stocks, and more stocks for retirement" does not meet the test of experience. Add property to your investments—if not for its superior returns, then to reduce portfolio risks. As long as my tenants pay their rents, short-term paper gains or losses in property prices mean little to me.

IS PROPERTY YOUR BEST INVESTMENT CHOICE?

I referred to Jeremy Siegel (*Stocks for the Long Run*) as chief cheerleader for stocks. But some people think that I serve as head cheerleader for investing in real estate.

In one sense, they are right. The record shows that more average people have built sizable amounts of wealth through property than any other type of savings or investment. Despite the huge growth in IRAs and 401(k)s— and despite the downturn in home prices—home equity still provides the largest portion of household net worth.

However, I do not say, "Property will beat stocks or bonds any time, any place, at any price." As early as 2005, I told my investor audiences that I would not buy property in the then-current hot spots such as Las Vegas, Miami, Barcelona, Dublin, or Dubai. Hot money and speculative frenzy drove those markets—not reasoned fundamental evaluation of risks and rewards. I advocate *investing* (not speculating) in property. Be wary of any market or asset class that has attracted large amounts of hot money. When that speculative asset (whatever it might be at the time) begins to lose its glow, hot money leaves even faster than it arrived. [In Dubai, hot money built its momentum over a period of 4 years. That flow virtually disappeared within a period of three months after October 2008 (the market peak).]

When people ask me, as they often do, "Which asset provides the best returns—stocks or real estate?" I answer, "It all depends." (In fact, since 2007, in a general sense, quality corporate and government bonds have provided higher total returns than either stocks or property.)

Yes, it all depends. In 1989, I would rather have invested in the S&P 500 index fund than Tokyo real estate. In 1993, I would have preferred the DJIA to property in Berlin. In 1997, I would rather have bought Apple Computer stock than a Hong Kong condominium located on the Peak. (In fact, if you can identify the next Apple Computer–like company, please e-mail and let me know. I will gladly buy its stock—and even sell properties to do so.)

To choose assets wisely, rely on investment and market analysis. Investors do not always make more money with property than they do with stocks or bonds. I have never said otherwise. But that begs the question, "Which investment offers the best possibilities and probabilities today?"

Given today's real estate bargains relative to where property prices will likely stand 5 to 10 years from now; given the fact that you can build large increases in property wealth (equity) without big gains in price; given the relative income yields of property versus stocks (or bonds); given the tax advantages of property relative to all other investments; given the multiple sources of returns that property offers; and last—but far from least—given the entrepreneurial talents that you can apply to property to increase its price and cash flows; then, yes, in today's market, I am willing to lead the cheers for smart investing in real estate.

2

OPM: BORROW SMART, RAISE CASH, BUILD EQUITY

Build your net worth more quickly: use OPM (other people's money). Nearly all property investors rely on mortgage loans and/or seller financing—and in many instances, equity partners. To profit with property, you need not draw primarily on your own cash. Other people stand ready to provide all of the cash you need. But OPM presents risk as well as reward.

Used intelligently, financial leverage (OPM) magnifies your gains. OPM can increase your cash-on-cash return, magnify your equity buildup (acorns into oak trees), and help you acquire properties that you otherwise could not acquire—if you had to rely exclusively on your own cash balances. Used foolishly, leverage not only increases your chance of loss, it increases the amount of loss you suffer. Smart financing of your investments leads to financial independence and a feeling of security. Dumb financing leads to sleepless nights, drained bank accounts, forced property sales, and loss of reputation.

Today, excessive debt has dashed the hopes of many investors and homebuyers. To help understand why, look back to the faulty advice that (until recently) enticed millions of naïve and ill-prepared Americans to borrow dumb. As Ben Graham says, "The first rule of wealth building: Do not lose money." How not to use OPM stands even more important to investing than how to use OPM.

THE BIRTH OF "NOTHING DOWN"

In the early days of the get-rich-quick real estate gurus, property prices were shooting up 15 to 20 percent a year. Similar to 2001–2006, back then nearly every would-be investor wanted to grab a piece of the property action. Likewise, many renters longed to become homeowners. Yet a majority of these hopeful buyers lacked cash, credit, or both. They possessed the will, but they lacked the means.

Enter Robert Allen, Carlton Sheets, Tyler Hicks, Al Lowry, Mark Haroldson, Russ Whitney, and other advocates of "nothing down." To sell their books, tapes, CDs, DVDs, mentoring programs, and seminars, these pundits promised the ill-prepared a solution to their dilemma. "No cash, no credit, no problem." Just learn the tricks and techniques of creative finance (easy money) and you, too, can become a real estate millionaire.[1] Not surprisingly, the property boom of late enlivened those guru promises of easy wealth. Scores of books, CDs, seminars, and boot camps promoted all types of get-rich schemes that told wannabe investors that they can win big in real estate through lease options, short sales, foreclosures, flipping, and a sundry collection of other so-called no-cash, no-credit techniques.

In his book *Multiple Streams of Income: How to Generate a Lifetime of Unlimited Wealth* (John Wiley & Sons, 2004), Robert Allen recounts his famous boast to the skeptical *Los Angeles Times*: "Send me to any city," Allen told the newspaper. "Take away my wallet. Give me $100 for living expenses. And in 72 hours, I'll buy an excellent piece of property using none of my own money" (p. 140).

In response to this boast, the *Los Angeles Times* hooked Allen up with a reporter, and off they went. "With this reporter by my side," Allen writes, "I bought seven properties worth $722,715. And I still had $20 left over." The *Times* ate crow and headlined a follow-up article, "Buying Homes without Cash: Boastful Investor Accepts Challenge—and Wins." "Yes, these techniques do work," Allen writes.

No question, Robert Allen and others who have preached a similar gospel are right. You can buy with little or nothing down (even in today's much tighter credit market), but that begs the real question. The real question is whether you *should* buy with little or no cash or credit.

---

[1]The term *creative finance* eludes precise definition. In general, it refers to the use of multiple sources of credit (e.g., sellers, real estate agents, contractors, partners) and out-of-the-norm financing techniques such as mortgage assumptions, subject-to purchases, land contracts, lease options, second or third mortgages, credit card cash advances, master leases, and so forth. In some circumstances, investors can use creative financing to buy real estate even though they lack cash or good credit. Each of these topics is discussed in this chapter.

SHOULD YOU INVEST WITH LITTLE OR NO CASH OR CREDIT?

If investing in real estate with little or no cash or credit were a sure route to wealth, this country would be awash in real estate millionaires. Indeed, more than 10 million people have bought various nothing-down books, tapes, videos, courses, and seminars. With this hoopla elevating the promises of easy money, you might think that real estate wealth awaited anyone who bought property.

So where's the catch? Why, among the many have signed up with the gurus, can so few boast of success? Why have millions of easy money buyers perished?

What's Wrong with "No Cash, No Credit, No Problem"?

Many smart, savvy, experienced, and successful investors and homebuyers do use various forms of creative finance. I encourage the (smart) use of creative finance. Easy money enabled me to buy and finance my first 8 or 10 investment properties.

Notwithstanding this fact, I have seen many naïve, foolish, and sometimes dishonest borrowers crash and burn because many promoters of creative finance (including a slew of sleazy loan reps and mortgage brokers) oversold advantages and underplayed potential perils. And unfortunately, in today's world of tight lending and millions of people with wrecked credit, the charlatans have found a flowing stream of new prospects for their scams and deceptions (now including false promises of credit repair, stop foreclosure, and loan workout). Before you imbibe such intoxicating elixir as "no cash, no credit, no problem"—or other too-good-to-be-true offers, answer and address the following questions and issues:

Do You Live below Your Means? In their continuing bestseller *The Millionaire Next Door* (Longstreet, 1997), Thomas Stanley and William Danko reveal that self-made millionaires typically live well below their means. More often than not, they avoid prestige spending. They do not drive new Jaguars or BMWs, dress for success in Armani suits, spend lavishly with their platinum American Express cards, or wear $200 (let alone $2,000) wristwatches. Serious wealth builders display no foolish affectations of conspicuous consumption.

In contrast to the serious wealth builder, many of the dreamers who were attracted to the easy money schemes of the real estate gurus never learned to spend (or invest) wisely. They looked to real estate as a means to detour around their money and credit problems—a quick and painless way to live the envied lifestyles of television's rich and famous.

In fact, promoters of "no cash, no credit" shamelessly encouraged this lavish image. They typically displayed themselves in fabulous settings. Mark Haroldson's photo on the cover of his book (*How to Wake Up the Financial Genius Inside of You*) shows him lounging on the hood of a Rolls Royce. Irene and Mike Milan (*How to Buy and Manage Rental Properties*) instead chose a high-end Mercedes sedan for their photo backdrop. And, of course, nearly everyone has seen the TV infomercials that feature Carlton Sheets sitting next to his swimming pool while enjoying a beautiful Florida bayfront estate.

Look at yourself. Is your goal to sensibly pursue the inner security and confidence of a millionaire next door? Do you presently live well below your means? Do you save a large percentage of your earnings? *Or* do you frequently fail to discipline your fiscal frivolities? Do you try to show the world you've "made it"? Do you believe creative finance techniques can vanquish your need to add real muscle to your financial fitness?

If a borrow-and-spend profile describes you, realign your spending and saving habits to match your wealth-building priorities. The "no cash, no credit" gurus and commission-hungry loan reps have lured too many people into believing that, as one such author exclaims, "Nothing down can make you rich." Wrong! Little or nothing down can help you begin to invest in real estate, but only fiscal discipline can pave your path to a comfortably secure high net worth. Before you seek out easy-terms property financing, another credit card, or higher credit card limits, critique and adjust (revolutionize, if necessary) your habits of spending, borrowing, and saving.

Price versus Terms

In response to today's tighter credit market, increasing numbers of sellers offer OWC (owner will carry) financing. So, I present this advice: (1) take advantage of owner finance and (2) beware of owner finance. OWC offers both a bright side . . . and a dark side. Here's the dark side.

Some "no cash, no credit, no problem" gurus encourage want-to-be property investors to talk sellers into an owner-finance arrangement with this (now well-known) gambit: "You set the price, let me set the terms." In this way, the seller receives a price that exceeds his property's market value (along with great bragging rights). In exchange, the hopeful (yet often unprepared) buyer asks for terms that may include seller financing, little or nothing down, a below-market interest rate, lease option, or other seller concessions.

In their eagerness to jump into a seller's price–my terms deal, novice investors often fail to adequately inspect the property for problems. They also end up owing more than their properties are worth. When expenses arise that a buyer can't afford to pay for—or otherwise remedy—he also confronts the between-a-rock-and-a-hard-place difficulty of owning a property that can't be sold for a price high enough to pay off the mortgage balance. The seller repossesses the property, retains payments made to date, and seeks out another lamb. I know of sellers who have sold the same property multiple times—and multiple times their buyers have defaulted and lost all monies paid (to the benefit of the seller).

Sometimes, too, naïve or all-too-trusting OWC sellers get taken by an unscrupulous or irresponsible buyer. A dishonest buyer can pocket rent monies, avoid paying all but the most necessary property operating expenses; refuse to make loan payments to the seller; and then when the seller attempts to repossess or foreclose, the buyer uses sham defenses to delay legal process.

A good idea (OWC) can be twisted and perverted to harm one or sometimes both parties to the transaction.

The lesson: use owner finance (or any finance for that matter) only when you work the numbers and manage the dangers that lurk behind the easily obtained OPM. All too often, easy credit dulls the senses. Indeed, the new car industry thrives only when new car buyers can obtain easy credit. And how many of those now desperate subprime mortgage borrowers sought to investigate the perils lurking within the loan documents they so eagerly signed. (We discuss an OWC example of "You name the price, I'll set the terms" later in this chapter.)

Credibility versus Creativity

Many would-be investors use creative financing not just to buy with little or nothing down but also to work around credit problems (no credit record, slow pay, write-offs, bankruptcy, foreclosure, self-employment, and so on). Yet, regardless of the quality of your credit history (good or bad), before you attempt the use of OPM, establish your credibility.

Sometimes credibility and creativity clash. In contrast to the boom years, many of today's dealmakers have learned from the hard knocks of experience. If you suggest a finance technique that seems strange, risky, or otherwise off-the-wall, the other would-be participants in the transaction (broker, seller, mortgage lender) may doubt that you really know what you're doing. Or they may conclude that you fall too short on experience, cash, or know-how.

Before you negotiate an OPM arrangement (either debt or equity), sound out the views and possible responses of other potential players in the deal. If you leap too far from the reasonable, others may dismiss you as a pseudo big shot. They look at you as tall hat but no cattle. Establish credibility first. Otherwise, you'll lose good properties and potentially valuable relationships.

Perseverance versus Productivity

Nearly all no cash–no credit gurus admit (at least in their fine print) that the majority of sellers, brokers, and mortgage lenders will reject most of their financing techniques. "How often does a transaction like this happen?" Robert Allen (*Multiple Streams of Income*, p. 142) asks rhetorically after explaining one of his zero-down techniques. "Very rarely. One in a hundred. It takes luck, chutzpah, and quick feet."

So, will the search for easy money lead to success? For many people, that answer has been no. When these previously eager investors have met repeated rejection, they gave up. They came to see real estate investing as a waste of time. Or they did arrange a financing plan. But it proved unrealistic and unworkable. The buyer lost the property—or lost money with the property.

These would-be investors missed the success they would have achieved—had they first prepared themselves financially. OPM—either creative or conventional—should serve as a means to your goals. Think: What risks does this financing lay at my feet? Have I itemized the identifiable sources of potential concern? Am I assuming that all unknowns will land in my favor? Have I written off potential adverse (now referred to as black swan) events as "too improbable to worry about"?

Leverage: Pros and Cons

Many of today's troubled borrowers took on bad loans because they assumed (or were told) that attractive refinance possibilities could rescue them if they could not manage the agreed payments. Bad assumption, bad advice. Never let anyone tempt you into believing any deal represents a sure thing—that any adverse future contingency can be easily overcome. Rents can fall. Vacancies can increase. Adjustable rates can adjust up. Teaser rates end. Loan underwriting can tighten. In the short run, you may not be able to sell your property at a price high enough to pay off your loans. Investing for the long run means surviving through those potentially adverse short runs.

Used Smart, Leverage Magnifies Returns. With risks in view, we now place more emphasis on the advantages of OPM (leverage). The term *leverage* means that you use a relatively small amount of your own cash to acquire or control a property. To illustrate: you buy a $100,000 rental property that produces a net operating income (NOI) of $10,000 a year.[2] If you finance this unit with $10,000 down and borrow $90,000 (a loan-to-value ratio of 90 percent), you highly leverage your purchase.

You own and control a property. Yet you put up only 10 percent of the purchase price, whereas if you paid $100,000 cash for the property, you would not have leveraged your purchase (no OPM). (When Lehman Brothers went bust, it had leveraged up its equity capital 44:1.)

Here's how leverage can magnify your returns. The following four examples calculate rates of gain in equity from price increases based on various amounts of down payments: $100,000 (an all-cash purchase), $50,000, $25,000, and $10,000.

Example 1: $100,000 all-cash purchase

$$\text{ROI (return on investment)} = \text{Income (NOI)/Cash investment}$$
$$= \$10,000/\$100,000$$
$$= 10\%$$

In this example, you pocket the full $10,000 of net operating income (gross rental income less vacancy and operating expenses such as insurance, repairs, maintenance, and property taxes). If you instead finance part of your purchase price, you will make mortgage payments on the amount you borrow. If we assume you find financing at 8 percent for 30 years, you will have to pay your lender $7.34 a month for each $1,000 you borrow. Now, using various percentages of leverage, the following examples show the gains that leverage offers:

Example 2: $50,000 down payment; $50,000 financed. Yearly mortgage payments equal $4,404 (50 × $7.34 × 12). Net income after mortgage payments (which is called *cash throw-off*) equals $5,596 ($10,000 NOI less $4,404).

$$\text{ROI} = \$5,596/\$50,000 = 11.1\%$$

Example 3: $25,000 down payment; $75,000 financed. Yearly mortgage payments equal $6,607 (75 × $7.34 × 12). Net income after mortgage payments (cash throw-off) equals $3,394 ($10,000 NOI less $6,606).

$$\text{ROI} = \$3,394/\$25,000 = 13.6\%$$

---

[2]Obviously, in high-priced areas of the country, $100,000 won't buy a studio apartment. But to illustrate, it's an easy figure to work with.

Example 4: $10,000 down payment; $90,000 financed. Yearly mortgage payments equal $7,927 (90 × $7.34 × 12). Net income after mortgage payments (cash throw-off) equals $2,073 ($10,000 NOI less $7,927).

$$ROI = \$2{,}073/\$10{,}000 = 20.7\%$$

With the figures in these examples, the highly leveraged (90 percent loan-to-value ratio) purchase yields a cash-on-cash return that's double the rate of a cash purchase. In principle, the more you borrow, the less cash you invest in a property, the greater you magnify your returns. The actual rate of return you'll earn on your properties depends on the rents, expenses, interest rates, and purchase prices that apply to your investment properties. Work through those actual numbers at the time you buy to see how much you can gain (or lose) from leverage. (Lehman Brothers used high leverage to bet the ranch—and lost the bet.)

Here's another way that leverage magnifies your returns and builds wealth faster than a cash purchase.

Over the years (if well selected), your investment properties will increase in price. If the price of that $100,000 property we've just discussed increases at an average annual rate of 3 percent, you earn another $3,000 a year. If its price increases at an annual rate of 5 percent, you'll gain $5,000 more a year. And at a 7 percent annual rate of appreciation, your gains will hit $7,000 a year.

Add together annual net rental income and annual price gains and you'll earn these total returns:

$$Total\ ROI = Income + Appreciation/Cash\ investment$$

Example 1: $100,000 all-cash purchase and (a) 3 percent, (b) 5 percent, and (c) 7 percent rates of appreciation:

(a) Total ROI = $10,000 + $3,000/$100,000 = 13%
(b) Total ROI = $10,000 + $5,000/$100,000 = 15%
(c) Total ROI = $10,000 + $7,000/$100,000 = 17%

Example 2: $50,000 down payment and (a) 3 percent, (b) 5 percent, and (c) 7 percent rates of appreciation:

(a) Total ROI = $5,596 + $3,000/$50,000 = 17.2%
(b) Total ROI = $5,596 + $5,000/$50,000 = 21.2%
(c) Total ROI = $5,596 + $7,000/$50,000 = 25.2%

Example 3: $25,000 down payment and (a) 3 percent, (b) 5 percent, and (c) 7 percent rates of appreciation:

(a) Total ROI = $3,394 + $3,000/$25,000 = 25.6%
(b) Total ROI = $3,394 + $5,000/$25,000 = 33.6%
(c) Total ROI = $3,394 + $7,000/$25,000 = 41.6%

Example 4: $10,000 down payment and (a) 3 percent, (b) 5 percent, and (c) 7 percent rates of appreciation.

(a) Total ROI = $2,073 + $3,000/$10,000 = 50.7%
(b) Total ROI = $2,073 + $5,000/$10,000 = 70.7%
(c) Total ROI = $2,073 + $7,000/$10,000 = 90.7%

When you total returns from annual net rental income and price increases, highly leveraged properties may produce almost unbelievably high annual rates of return—even without unrealistically high average annual rates of price increases. That's why some investors in small rental properties have (over decades) built a net worth for themselves that runs into the millions of dollars. When you own rental properties, long-term rent and price increases grow acorns (relatively low down payments) into oak trees (property equity worth hundreds of thousands [or millions] of dollars).

As the years pass and you pay down your mortgage balances, a property portfolio of just 6 or 8 houses or perhaps 12 to 24 apartment units (more or less) can build enough wealth to guarantee a secure future. (Note, too, how potential investment property rates of return might easily exceed the widely believed [yet overstated] 10 percent average annual gains that the stock market has supposedly produced "over the long run.")

Manage Your Risks

The advocates of get-rich-quick real estate schemes often fail to warn their followers that highly leveraged real estate magnifies risks as well as returns. Many naïve (as well as underfunded) real estate buyers have lost their shirts. These dreamers optimistically expected the market values of their properties to realize steady price gains of 10 to 20 percent a year— year after year just as steadily as the pages of their calendars are turned. They lost touch with reality. In fact, many investors barely cared what purchase prices they agreed to, what rent levels they collected, or how they financed their properties. They just knew that they could sell their properties within a few years for twice the amount they had paid.

One such investor bought a $300,000 fourplex with a down payment of $30,000. After paying property operating expenses and mortgage payments, the investor faced an alligator (negative cash flow) that chewed up $1,000 a month. But the investor figured that $1,000 a month was peanuts. He believed the future selling price of his property would go up 15 percent a year. Based on his expected rate of gain, here's how this investor calculated the annual returns that he (unrealistically) hoped to receive:

ROI = Income + Appreciation/Cash investment
    = $12,000 (12 × $1,000) + $45,000 (.15 × $300,000)/$30,000
    = $33,000/ $30,000
    = 110%

As it turned out, this investor, like so many others, could not continue to feed his alligator $1,000 a month. He fell behind with his mortgage payments. As the market slowed, he was unable to sell (or refinance) the property. The lender foreclosed. The investor lost the property, his down payment of $30,000, the $24,000 of monthly negative cash shortfalls that he had covered prior to default, and his once-high credit score.

Here are four lessons you can take away from this investor's regrettable (yet all too common and perfectly avoidable) losses:

1. *Never expect the value of real estate, stocks, gold, antique automobiles, old masters, or any other type of investment to increase by 10, 15, or 20 percent year after year.* When you need high rates of price gain to make your investment look attractive, you set yourself up for a big loss. The longer a bull market runs, the more likely it will exhaust itself (and perhaps suffer a near fatal heart attack).

2. *Beware of negative cash flows.* If the income you earn from an asset does not support the price you pay, you magnify your risk and chance of loss. You are speculating more than investing. That's okay if that's what you want to do. Just recognize that speculators (whether they realize it or not) play in a high-risk game that produces far more losers than winners.

   As negative cash flows increase, the probability of severe price correction looms large. Indeed, in his 1937 classic, *The Theory of Investment Value* (Harvard University Press), John Burr Williams wrote,

Every thoughtful investor knows that he should not confuse the real worth of an investment with its market price. No buyer considers all investments equally attractive. On the contrary, the wise investor seeks "the best at the price". . . . Even then, he may not buy at all, for fear that everything is priced too high and nothing will give him his money's worth.

If he does buy, he buys as an investor. He holds for income; if as a speculator for [quick] profit at sale. But over the long run, speculators must sell to investors [unless you believe that somehow speculative price increases can forever outrun people's incomes and GDP] . . . therefore sooner or later, the ultimate values of all investments derive from a reasonable estimate of future income.

3. *Beware of financial overreach.* High leverage (a high loan-to-value ratio) usually requires large mortgage payments relative to the amount of net income that a property brings in. Even if at first you don't suffer negative cash flows, vacancies, higher-than-expected expenses, or large rent concessions intended to attract good tenants can push you temporarily into the swamps where alligators feed.

   Over a period of, say, 10 to 20 years, owning real estate will grow your net worth many times over. But to enjoy that long-term future, you will likely pass through several cyclical downturns. Without cash (or credit) reserves to defend against alligator attacks, you may be pulled into the swamps and eaten alive before you find the safety and comfort of high ground.

4. *Even when the property financing looks good, avoid overpaying for a property.* Overly optimistic investors buy overpriced properties with little-or no-down-payment deals. In the earlier fourplex example, the investor agreed to pay $300,000 for the fourplex not because the property's net income, that is, investment value, justified a price of $300,000. Rather, he paid $300,000 because he was excited about his easy-credit, low, 10 percent down payment financing. Compared with the $600,000 sales price that he expected to reap after just four or five years of ownership, his $300,000 purchase price looked cheap.

Again, I emphasize: I do not advise against low down payments (high leverage) per se. But when you do finance with high LTVs (loan to value), anticipate possible setbacks. To manage the risks of high-leverage OPM, adopt these six safeguards:

1. *Buy bargain-priced properties.* You build a financial cushion into your deals when you pay less than market value or pay less than a property is worth—which is not quite the same thing. Discover how in Chapters 4 through 7.

2. *Buy properties that you can profitably improve.* To build your net worth more quickly and reduce the risk of leverage, add value to your properties through creativity, sweat equity, remodeling, and renovation (see Chapter 8).

3. *Buy properties with below-market rents that you can raise to market levels within a relatively short time (6 to 12 months).* Increase your rental income and as a percentage of net operating income (NOI), your mortgage payments will become easier to pay. You will enjoy a larger margin of safety.

4. *Buy properties with low-interest-rate financing such as mortgage assumptions, adjustable-rate mortgages, interest-rate buydowns, or seller financing.* Low interest rates help you manage high debt. High interest rates make debt less affordable—especially beware of low interest rates that may disappear within just a few years (or less).

5. *Buy right time, right price, right place properties.* "All real estate is local" is an oft-cited cliché that contains a kernel of truth. Various neighborhoods and cities offer unique differences with respect to price, location, and market timing. To reduce risk and increase rewards, proactively study and select from such opportunities (see Chapter 8).

6. *When high leverage presents an anxious level of risk, increase your down payment to lower your loan-to-value ratio and lower your monthly mortgage payments.* If your available cash does not permit a higher down payment, bring in a money partner. Don't act penny-wise and pound-foolish. Share gains with someone else rather than chance wrestling with a fierce alligator.

What Are Your Risk-Return Objectives?

Little- or nothing-down finance can increase your returns. Smart borrowing, when linked with smart investing, will grow acorns into oak trees. But the higher your LTVs (other things equal), the more you must prepare for a downturn in the rental market, unexpected property operating expenses, or a potential setback in your personal wherewithal. When you highly leverage your properties, a slight fall in rents may push you into negative cash flows. A decline in your property's value can pull you underwater. Steer clear of sunshine-every-day optimism. Work through the investment numbers under several adverse scenarios. Decide what profits are worth pursuing and what risks you prefer to avoid.

If you can't find properties in your favored area(s) that generate the numbers you would like to see, look elsewhere. Shift your discovery efforts from cities (or neighborhoods) that lack what you want to areas that offer more potential for the sources of returns that you find attractive (and doable). In fact, some international investors now believe that Detroit properties are attractive for their high incomes and low prices. They expect strong returns from cash yield, amortization, and price growth as the local economy gradually revitalizes and rebuilds.

MAXIMIZE LEVERAGE WITH OWNER-OCCUPANCY FINANCING

You now know the pros and cons of high leverage OPM (little or nothing down). Use it; do not abuse it. Among the best high-LTV choices for beginning investors: owner-occupied property financing.

The easiest-qualifying and often the lowest-cost way to borrow most (or even all) of the money you need to buy a property remains owner-occupied mortgage financing. Even with tight credit standards, high-LTV owner-occupied loan programs are readily available on single-family homes, condominiums, townhouses, and two- to four-unit apartment buildings. Owner occupancy allows LTVs as high as 90, 95, 97, or even 100 percent.

If you do not arrange for owner-occupied financing (that is, you choose not to live in the property), most lenders (banks, mortgage bankers, savings institutions) limit their mortgage loans on investment properties to 70 percent to 80 percent LTV ratio.[3] Owner-occupied loans provide great advantage (as to LTV) relative to loans to finance purely rental properties. (However, some higher 85 to 95 percent investor loans are available, such as VA REOs—see Chapter 7.)

As another benefit, owner-occupants pay lower interest rates than investors. If lenders charge 4.0 to 5.0 percent for good-credit (say, FICO 720 or higher), owner-occupied loans, the interest rate for investor properties will probably range between 4.75 and 5.25 percent. As a beginning real estate investor, weigh the possibilities of owner-occupied mortgage loans. [Note: The spread between owner occupant interest rates and those rates available to investors does not remain constant. As lenders perceive greater loan risk, the spread widens. When blue sky forecasts prevail, interest rate (and LTV) spreads narrow. When len ders feel optimistic, the costs and terms for investor loans nearly match those available to owner occupants.]

---

[3]From the late 1990s to 2006, some lenders offered investor loans with total LTVs as high as 100 percent. When the property boom receded, such liberal lenders either went broke because of excessive borrower defaults or tightened their qualifying to match or exceed more conservative (safer) underwriting standards.

Owner-Occupied Buying Strategies

To begin investing in rental properties with little or nothing down, select a high-LTV owner-occupant loan program that appeals to you.[4] Buy a one- to four-unit property. Live in it for one year, then rent it out, and repeat the process. After you obtain owner-occupied financing, that loan can remain on the property even after you move out. Because the second, third, and even fourth homes you buy and occupy will still qualify for high-LTV financing (low or nothing down), you can—within a period of five or six years—accumulate as many as 8 to 16 rental units in addition to your own residence—all without large down payments.

You can work this homeowner gambit two, three, maybe four times. But you cannot pursue it indefinitely. At some point, lenders may shut you off from owner-occupied financing because they will object to your game plan. Also, some lenders will not count all of your rent collections as part of your qualifying ratios. In such cases, you will need to earn a large enough salary to continue your ability to qualify for new high-LTV mortgages. Nevertheless, serial owner-occupancy acquisitions can surely help you acquire (at least) your first two or three investment properties.

Current Homeowners, Too, Can Use This Method

Even if you own your own home, weigh the advantages of owner-occupied financing to acquire your next several investment properties. Here's how: Locate a property (condo, house, two- to four-unit apartment building) that you can buy and move in to. Find a good tenant for your current house or condo. Complete the financing on your new property and move in to it. If you like your current home, at the end of one year, rent out your most recently acquired property and move back into your former residence. Alternatively, find another "home" to buy and again finance this property with a new owner-occupied, high-leverage (LTV), low-rate mortgage.

Why One Year?

To qualify for owner-occupied financing, you are required to assure the lender that you intend to live in the house for at least one year. Intend, however, does not mean guarantee. You can (for good reason or no reason) change your mind. Beware: Do not lie about your intent to

---

[4]Many of these programs are described with applications in my book *The 106 Mortgage Secrets that Borrowers Must Learn—But Lenders Don't Tell,* 2nd ed. (John Wiley & Sons, 2008).

occupy a property. Lying to obtain a loan violates state and federal laws. Governments do prosecute for this offense.

During the past property boom, borrowers lied and loan reps winked. Many borrowers and loan reps brazenly failed to comply with the intent-to-occupy rule. In fact, a loan rep at Wachovia (a bank that subsequently went bust) suggested that I finance a new investment property that I was buying (out of state) as if it were a second home. I declined.

To succeed in real estate over the short and long term, establish, maintain, and nurture your credibility with lenders—and everyone else with whom you want to enter transactions or build a relationship of trust. To slip through loopholes, make false promises, sidestep agreements, or engage in other sleights will destroy your reputation for integrity. Unless you encounter an unexpected turn of events, honor a lender's one-year occupancy requirement.

Where Can You Find High-LTV Owner-Occupied Mortgages?

Everywhere! Even in today's tighter credit market, walk your fingers through the Yellow Pages to "mortgages." Then call banks, savings institutions, mortgage bankers, mortgage brokers, and credit unions. Mortgage lenders advertise in local daily newspapers and on the Internet. Check with your state, county, or city departments of housing finance. Many homebuilders and Realtors know of various types of low- or nothing-down home finance programs. Explore the websites hud.gov, va.gov, homesteps .com (Freddie Mac), and fanniemae.com.

WHAT ARE THE LOAN LIMITS?

The specific maximum amount you can borrow under these high-LTV programs varies by type of loan and area of the country. However, the loan limits are high enough to finance properties in good neighborhoods. For example, Freddie Mac and Fannie Mae programs nationwide will lend up to the following amounts (usually adjusted upward each year):

Number of Units	Contiguous States, District of Columbia, and Puerto Rico	Higher-Priced Areas
1	$417,000	$625,000
2	$533,850	$800,775
3	$645,300	$967,950
4	$801,950	$1,202,925

FHA varies its loan limits by county. Here are several examples:

Low-Cost Areas (FHA/HUD)

Type of Residence	Loan Limits
One-unit	$271,050
Two-unit	347,000
Three-unit	419,425
Four-unit	521,250

High-Cost Areas (FHA/HUD)

Type of Residence	Loan Limits
One-unit	$729,750
Two-unit	934,200
Three-unit	1,129,350
Four-unit	1,403,400

For VA loans, eligible veterans may originate—and veterans and non-veterans alike may assume—up to the following amounts:[5]

Lowest-Price Areas	Highest-Price Areas
$417,000	$625,000

Unlike Fannie, Freddie, and the FHA, the VA applies the same loan limit for one- to four-unit properties. The VA, however, has boosted its loan limit and, like the FHA, varies each specific limit according to the prevailing local price levels. One- to four-unit properties that are priced higher than these stated limits seldom bring in rents high enough to cover expenses and mortgage payments. When you select rentals that pay for themselves—even with a small down payment—the limits set by FHA and VA will not unduly limit your choice of properties. (FHA and VA adjust their loan limits periodically.)

---

[5]When a veteran makes a down payment, these loan amounts may be higher. Also, higher limits may apply in selected high-cost areas. The VA periodically increases its limits.

HIGH LEVERAGE FOR INVESTOR-OWNER FINANCING

Say that you've maxed out your high-LTV (low down payment) owner-occupancy financing possibilities. Or maybe you're happy in your present home. No way will you (or your spouse) move (even temporarily) to another property. Without owner-occupied, what other ways help you avoid placing 20 to 30 percent of the purchase price in cash from your own savings? What high leverage (low down payment) OPM (other people's money) techniques can you use to buy and finance your investment properties?

High Leverage versus Low (or No) Down Payment

Note this paradox: High leverage does not necessarily imply a low down payment. High leverage means that you've acquired a property using little cash (say, 10 to 20 percent of the purchase price, or sometimes less) from your own funds.

You find a property priced at $400,000, and your lender agrees to provide a first mortgage in the amount of $280,000. Because you can't (or don't want to) draw $120,000 from your savings to make this large down payment, you can find another way to raise all (or part) of the cash required. When successful, you will have achieved a highly leveraged transaction. You control a $400,000 property with relatively little money pulled from your own pocket.

You can gain the benefits (and risks) of high leverage in two ways: (1) originate (or assume) a high-LTV first mortgage, or (2) originate (or assume) a lower-LTV mortgage. Then to reduce (or eliminate) out-of-pocket cash, use other sources (loans, equity partners) to fill in some (or all) of the difference between the amount of the first mortgage and the purchase price of the property.

Creative Finance Revisited

Creative finance encourages you to think through multiple financing alternatives. The term gained popularity when property prices shot up and millions of hopeful buyers felt shut out of the fast and seemingly easy money because they lacked sufficient cash, credit, or both to enter the game. "The central theme of my course," wrote Ed Beckley in *No Down Payment Formula,* "is to teach you how to acquire as much property as you can without using any of your own money. . . . Starting from scratch requires that you become extremely resourceful. You need to substitute ideas for cash" (p. 69).

How might investors use creative thinking and resourcefulness to substitute for cash?

Look for a More Liberal Lender. Under today's tighter underwriting standards, most banks and savings institutions loan only 70 to 80 percent of an (non-owner-occupied) income property's appraised value. However, some specialty lenders will make 90 percent (or higher) LTV loans. When credit markets ease, lender competition will most likely (once again) edge up investor LTVs.

Also, some wealthy private investors provide high-LTV mortgages. Find these private investors through newspaper classified ads and websites: Advertise in the "Capital Wanted" section, or telephone those who list themselves in the "Capital Available" section. Also call mortgage brokers who may have contacts with as many as 20 to 100 sources of property financing. Through their lengthy list of lenders, mortgage brokers may find you a high LTV.

Beware: Read the fine print of the loan agreement. Many of these nontraditional (subprime, hard money) mortgages include costly up-front fees, high interest, and steep prepayment penalties. Foolish optimism plus subprime (or unconventional) loan equals foreclosure.

Second Mortgages

Before the credit crisis, some investment property lenders permitted what are called 70–20–10 loans, or other variations such as 75–15–10, or maybe even 80–15–5. The first figure refers to the LTV of a first mortgage; the second figure refers to the percentage of the purchase price represented by a second mortgage (often owner financing); and the third figure refers to out-of-pocket cash contributed by the buyer (or equity partners). A 70–20–10 deal for the purchase of a $100,000 property would require the following amounts:

First mortgage	$70,000
Second mortgage	$20,000
Buyer's cash	$10,000

The property seller makes the best source for second mortgage loans. Referred to as *seller seconds* or *seller carrybacks*, these loans require less red tape, paperwork, and closing costs. You can sometimes persuade a seller to accept an interest rate that's lower than what a commercial lender would charge. At a time when first mortgage rates were at 11 percent, and second mortgage rates were at 16 percent, one of my sellers carried back a

$75,000 interest-only mortgage loan at a rate of 8 percent.[6] (Sellers are more likely to offer below-market interest rates when market interest rates climb upward—unlike today's low market rates.) My deal looked like this:

Purchase price	$319,500
First mortgage at 11%	$180,000
Seller second at 8%	$75,000
Cash from buyer	$64,500

If the sellers won't cooperate, look to private investors, mortgage brokers, banks, and savings institutions. Before you do turn to loan-sharking commercial second mortgage lenders, think of friends or family members who might like to earn a relatively safe return of 6 to 8 percent (more or less) on their money. Compared to certificates of deposit and passbook savings that in most times pay interest between 2 and 5 percent, a 6 to 8 percent rate of interest could look pretty good (and especially good with today's CD rates of 2 percent or less).

Borrow against Other Assets

If you're a homeowner with good credit, arrange a home equity loan (that is, second mortgage) on your home. Through an equity line of credit you might raise cash for a down payment—but prepare for adverse changes in the market or your own finances. Home equity loans are often written with variable interest rates. Low interest today, but potentially higher rates tomorrow. Alternatively, consider a high-LTV, cash-out refinance of your home with a newly originated first mortgage.

What other assets can you borrow against? Retirement accounts, cars, jewelry, artwork, coin collection, life insurance, or vacation home? List everything you own. You may surprise yourself at what you discover. On the other hand, if you fail to discover other assets, reprioritize your spending and saving (see further on).

Convert Assets to Cash (Downsizing)

Rather than borrow against your assets, downsize. Friends of mine sold their 6,000-square-foot Chicago North Shore residence for $1,050,000. With those proceeds they bought a vacation home, a smaller primary residence,

---

[6]In this case, the seller second served primarily to reduce my overall cost of borrowing thanks to its low interest rate.

and an in-town condominium. In the United Kingdom, they call this popular practice *mouse-holing*.

Could you live comfortably in a smaller or less expensive home?
Are you wasting money on unproductive luxury cars, jewelry, watches,
or clothing? Are you one of the many Americans who live the high life—
for now—but fail to build enough net worth to support the twin goals of
financial security and financial independence?

In their study of the affluent, Thomas Stanley and William Danko
(*The Millionaire Next Door*) interviewed a sample of high-income professionals whom the authors named UAWs (under-accumulators of wealth).
They also chose a sample of PAWs (prodigious accumulators of wealth)—
who worked in less prestigious jobs and earned less income. Because of
wise budgeting and investing, the net worth of PAW households far surpassed the net worth of those higher-income, yet profligate spenders.
Downsizing now rewards with high payback later. (In keeping with the
theme of frugal living and smart investing, Stanley titled his latest book
Stop Living Rich.)

Wraparound Mortgage

A wraparound mortgage helps buyers obtain a high LTV while it provides
a seller with a good yield. Investors use wraparounds to gain some benefit
from a below-current-market-rate loan that exists against a property—and
yet also obtain a relatively high LTV.

To accomplish these twin goals, the investor wraps the existing
below-market loan with a new wraparound loan at a higher interest rate.
The seller continues to pay the existing low interest rate loan while the
buyer pays the seller on the new wraparound loan. The seller profits on the
spread in interest rates. The wraparound works best during periods when
interest rates shoot up. Figure 2.1 provides an example.

In Figure 2.1, the seller creates and carries a new loan of $210,000 at
9.0 percent. Payments on the seller's existing first mortgage total $1,077
per month. Payments on the new wraparound loan are $1,691 per month.
Therefore, the seller earns a $614 per month spread. As a return on the
$60,000 equity the seller has left in the deal, he earns a return of 12.28
percent $(12 \times 614 \div 60,000 = 12.28)$. The buyer-investor gains because the
interest rate charged him by the seller falls below the then-prevailing market interest rate on newly originated loans.

If, as a buyer, you wrap a so-called nonassumable mortgage, the
seller's mortgage lender may choose to exercise its due-on-sale clause. If
that happens, the sellers (or you) would have to pay off the seller's mortgage and arrange new financing. However, during the past 25 years—and
especially during periods of high foreclosures, lenders rarely throw their

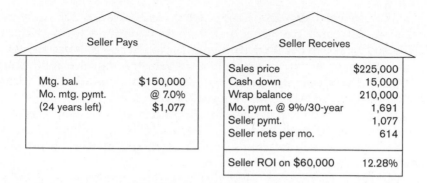

Seller Pays			Seller Receives	
Mtg. bal.	$150,000		Sales price	$225,000
Mo. mtg. pymt.	@ 7.0%		Cash down	15,000
(24 years left)	$1,077		Wrap balance	210,000
			Mo. pymt. @ 9%/30-year	1,691
			Seller pymt.	1,077
			Seller nets per mo.	614
			Seller ROI on $60,000	12.28%

Figure 2.1 Wraparound Loan Example

performing loans into default by demanding full payment because a seller breached a technical requirement of the loan agreement.

Use Credit Cards

Although inviting disaster, some investors take advantage of every credit card offer they receive in the mail. Then when they require quick cash to close a deal, they raise $10,000, $25,000, or even $50,000 from cash advances. Investors sometimes even pay cash for a property with the entire sum raised from credit cards.

It makes no sense to use credit card cash advances for long-term financing. Yet, on occasion, plastic might serve as a quick and convenient source to cover short-term needs. You might find a steal of a deal that you can buy (and renovate?), then immediately flip (resell) the property at a profit. Or maybe you need quick money to place great property under contract.

For my taste, credit card cash costs too much and exposes the borrower to excessive risk. But it remains a possibility if you realistically calculate that the potential rewards decisively trump the risks—and you see multiple unlocked exit doors.

Personal Loans

In the days before credit card cash advances (which are now the most popular type of personal loan), personal loans were called signature loans. As you build your net worth, lenders will grant you signature loans—at much lower fees and interest rates than credit card cash advances—in amounts of $10,000, $25,000, $50,000, or even $250,000, if your credit record and net worth can support repayment. Use the money from these signature loans for down payments or renovation funds.

Although mortgage lenders do not favor borrowers who use personal loans for down payments, investors routinely find ways to do so. OWC (owner will carry) sellers who finance property sales probably won't inquire (and maybe won't care) about the source of your down payment. If you're short on cash, compare the risks and benefits of using a cash advance or signature loan to raise money for your down payment.

But again, count the risk factors. Ill-conceived borrowing can push you into those ugly toss-and-turn, sleepless nights, if not financial ruin. Make sure repayment does not depend on some speculative (uncertain or unpredictable) contingency.

Land Contracts

A land contract—sometimes referred to as a contract for deed, contract of sale, or agreement of sale—permits buyers to pay sellers for their property in installments. The term *land contract* became popular because this type of financing was often used to buy acreage (especially farmland).

Under a land contract, a buyer agrees to purchase a property and pay principal and interest to the seller. Property title remains in the seller's name until conditions of the contract are fulfilled. The buyer takes possession of the property. If a buyer defaults on the agreement, the seller can typically repossess (not foreclose on) the property. Sellers favor repossessions because they're typically quicker, easier, and less costly than foreclosure. It's even common for buyers who default on land contracts to voluntarily return the collateral property to the seller. In this way, the buyer avoids the negative mark on his credit record that would otherwise result from a seller's suit for recovery of the property.

Verify State Law

Consumer protection laws in some states now entangle the property repossession process with more cumbersome requirements. As a buyer, you might welcome such protection. Yet, if entanglement endangers the simplicity of the agreement, sellers may choose to avoid offering OWC.

Contract for deeds may become useful when wrapping low interest rate financing (see the previous discussion of wraparounds). Caution: These contracts include pitfalls for buyers and sellers. Because evolving state law governs land contract sales, consult a competent, local real estate attorney before entering into this form of financing (either as buyer or seller.).

Often, properties financed with land contracts are nonconforming properties such as storefronts with living quarters in the rear or above, farmhouses with acreage, older properties in need of repair, or a large house that has been split up into multiple apartment units. My first investment was a five-unit property—a large, old house split into four one-bedroom apartments and a one-bedroom, one-bath carriage house that sat on the rear of the lot.

I paid $10,000 down, and the seller (an elderly widow) financed the $90,000 balance at 5 percent interest. She said that interest rate matched what she could receive from a bank and she didn't think it ethical to charge me a higher rate. That experience occurred decades ago. But, amazingly, a 5 percent interest rate might again look attractive to sellers today—as it far exceeds the bank CD rates now available.

In the present tight-credit market, a contract for deed serves the same purposes they always have (nonconforming properties or subpar cash or credit buyers). During the credit and property boom, land contracts diminished in use because mortgage lenders opened their vaults for almost anyone who applied for a loan. With lenders now tight-fisted, contract for deeds are making a comeback. And they are not limited to buyers who lack cash or credit. Even some creditworthy buyers might accept land contract financing to avoid the piled-higher-and-deeper paperwork required by banks.

In addition to land contracts, two types of easy credit, low-down-payment, seller-assisted financing have become widespread: lease-purchase and lease-option agreements (see Chapter 9). To some degree, many sellers prefer these rent-to-own alternatives because (if written properly), they eliminate the need for court action to recover a property—except perhaps the rental eviction process—if a defaulting lease-option buyer refuses to voluntarily vacate. Nevertheless, land contracts remain available to play a role in your property acquisition strategy (and later perhaps, in your disposition of properties).

Properly written, land contracts are low cost and relatively easy to complete; they offer flexibility in price, terms, and interest rate; and they can provide sellers quick remedies for borrower default while they protect buyers against unfair forfeiture and future title problems. If you find (or create) a good deal using a land contract, don't pass it up without thoughtful review (and, certainly, informed legal advice).

Sweat Equity (Create Value through Renovations)

You might buy some properties with 100 percent financing if you can enhance their value through improvements and renovations. Say you find a property that should sell (in tip-top condition) for around $250,000. Yet, because of its sorry state of repair, as well as an eager seller, you can buy the property at a price of $170,000 with short-term, no-money-down owner financing (maybe a lease option or lease purchase). You then contribute labor (sweat) and $17,500 in materials that you pay for with credit cards.

After you complete your work and bring the property up to its $250,000 market value, you arrange a 75 percent LTV mortgage with a lender. With your loan proceeds of $187,500 (.75 × $250,000), you pay off the seller and your credit card account. Voilà—you have not only achieved 100 percent financing for your acquisition price and rehab but also created $67,500 of instant equity.

More OPM Techniques

In addition to the high leverage techniques discussed, you might choose from the following OPM possibilities:

♦ *Bring in partners.* If you can't (or don't want to) draw on your own cash or borrowing power, find a good deal and then explain to potential money partners (friends, family, contractors, wealthy investors) how they will benefit if they join you in the transaction.

♦ *Agree to swap services or products.* Would the seller accept some service or expertise that you can provide? Take stock of your skills (law, medicine, dentistry, writing, advertising, carpentry, accounting, landscaping, architecture, and so on). How about products? Say you own a radio station or newspaper. Trade off advertising time or space for a down payment. Anything you can produce, deliver, or sell wholesale (at cost) might work.

♦ *Borrow (or reduce) the real estate commission.* Most brokers and sales agents hate this technique. Still, sometimes buyers and sellers do ask the agents involved in a transaction to defer payment until some later date. A few agents like to leave their commissions invested in a property. In doing so, they avoid (or defer) paying income taxes on their commission. At the same time, they earn interest or receive a piece of the action (equity in the property and future profits from a sale).

♦ *Simultaneously sell (or lease) part of the property.* Does the property include an extra lot, mobile home, or perhaps timber, oil, gas, air, or mineral rights that you could sell? Yes . . . then sell, lease, or license these rights simultaneously with your acquisition. These proceeds will help you fund your transaction.

♦ *Prepaid rents and tenant security deposits.* Buy an investment property and you are entitled to the existing tenants' security deposits and prepaid rents. Say you close on June 2. The seller (of a fourplex) is holding $4,000 in tenant security deposits and $3,800 in rent money that applies to the remaining days in June. Together, the deposits and prepaid rents amount to $7,800. In most transactions, these monies reduce your cash-to-close.

♦ *Create paper.* You've asked the seller to accept owner financing with 10 percent down. She balks. She believes the deal places her at risk. Alleviate her fears and bolster her security. Offer her a lien against your car or a second (or third) mortgage on another property you own. Write into the loan agreement that when principal payments and property appreciation (added together) lift your equity to 20 percent (LTV of 80 percent), the seller will remove the security lien she holds against your other pledged asset(s).

♦ *Lease/purchase options.* Because of their popularity, a more extensive discussion in Chapter 9 surveys the pros and cons of lease or purchase options.

Are High-Leverage Creative-Finance Purchases Readily Available?

I have used some type of creative finance (as either buyer or seller) in more than one-half of the property transactions in which I've been involved. To make creative finance work, however, know what you are doing. Envision ways the deal might turn against you. Calm your eagerness to make the deal. Concede, but also request quid pro quo.

Become Wary: Low-down, easy-money transactions tempt new investors into buying troubled properties or paying excessive prices. Honor commitments—but commit slowly and thoughtfully. Are you convinced that you will always want to fulfill this commitment? What contingencies might change your mind?

Fewer Sellers, Fewer Properties

Because creative finance bypasses conventional norms, your property purchase choices become fewer. Though nearly every seller will accept cash, a much smaller number will provide financing with little or nothing down. Nevertheless, such transactions not only occur, they sometimes occur unexpectedly. Sellers who first claim they're not interested will soften their attitude once you persuasively explain what's in it for them and then tender your signed offer.

Lower-Quality Overpriced Lemons

Beware of property owners who want to entice you into buying overpriced lemons. These sellers have read the nothing-down books. They know that advertising come-ons like "owner financing," "nothing down," "no qualifying," "make offer," and "EZ terms" will bring dozens of calls from the latest "graduates" of the Ima Guru School of Creative Finance and Credit Repair.

Standing ready to fleece these sheep, savvy sellers surreptitiously lead eager buyers into ill-advised purchase contracts. Maintenance and repair problems, disappearing tenants, phantom leases, illegal units, neighborhood crime, short-term balloon mortgages, troublesome neighbors, and undisclosed liens represent just a few of the setbacks naïve buyers have run in to. [For many other types of potential problems, see my book *The 106 Common Mistakes Homebuyers Make (and How to Avoid Them)*, 4th ed. (John Wiley & Sons, 2008.)] In other words, don't let the siren call of easy finance crash your boat onto the rocks before you've barely left port.

BUILD CONFIDENCE WITH LENDERS, INVESTORS, SELLERS, AND SALES AGENTS

How can you effectively raise debt or equity capital, or both (OPM) to convince potential lenders and partners that they can place their confidence in you? How do you instill their confidence? Prepare and present yourself to satisfactorily meet the 7 Cs (criteria of credibility) for raising money and attracting profitable opportunities.[7]

Here's what I mean: Evaluate this "call for help" posting from "Ralph" that I recently saw on a real estate website:

> Hi! I'm a new investor. . . . I want to concentrate on rehabbing and flip.
>
> As my credit score is 580, and my wife is back in school (no savings, and so on) . . . I'm having trouble finding 100 percent funding for that first deal. I've found several houses which I think would work well for fix and flip, but they slipped away before I could find the funding. . . . I keep hearing about building a small cash reserve by bird-dogging for others, but if I can come up with a 100 percent hard money loan here in the Denver area, and the numbers work for a high interest rate, back end points, and so on . . . I would prefer to jump right in.

Would you provide a mortgage loan to this newbie? Would you invest equity money in one of his deals? If you were a real estate agent,

---

[7]For a more extensive discussion of financing properties, see my book *The 106 Mortgage Secrets that All Homebuyers Must Learn—but Lenders Don't Tell*, 2nd ed. (John Wiley & Sons, 2008).

would Ralph make it onto your list of favored clients (that list of investors you alert first when a too-good-to-last new listing comes onto the market)?

Not likely, right? Nothing in this would-be investor's résumé instills confidence that he could carry out his fix and flip successfully. Look at Ralph's personal facts: low credit score, no experience or track record, no savings, and an almost desperate plea for money—he's even willing to accept whatever loan terms a hard money lender might require. And although he does not specifically admit it here, I suspect that all of Ralph's current income goes out to pay bills and living expenses—as fast as (or maybe faster than) it comes in.

With such risk factors piled up against him, he still wants to "jump right in." Ralph evidently sees no need to prepare. He seems to believe that real estate will remedy his precarious financial condition—if he could just find someone who will lend him the money he wants. Ralph represents a superb example of the "no cash, no credit, no experience" mindset. Ralph fails to understand the lesson that I conveyed at the beginning of this chapter. Rarely can property help anyone solve one's "no cash, poor credit" money troubles.

In fact, I would bet that if a hard money lender (or any lender, for that matter) did provide enough money for Ralph to acquire a fixer-upper, he soon would find himself in a sorrier fiscal condition than his current situation poses. As every experienced renovator has learned, most fix-and-sell projects take more time and more money than the original budget estimates. Cost overruns, contractor delays, unforeseen problems that show up after you have begun the work, mistakes in sequencing the work, and a slower-than-hoped-for resale can plague even the wisest of the fix and flippers.

If you think that my comments here are meant to discourage "jumping into real estate," you are right. I want you (and Ralph) to succeed in real estate . . . not merely invest per se. Before you jump in, use the 7 Cs of credibility to prepare your resume. Strengthen each of the 7 Cs. Capital and opportunities will seek you out.

The 7 Cs refer to the loan underwriting standards that lenders apply when they evaluate potential borrowers. But you also need to establish credibility with equity investors, property sellers, and real estate agents. No one in real estate wants to waste time with the unprepared and unqualified. For each of the following Cs, rate yourself. Then list and execute the steps that you will take to strengthen each one.

Credit
Capacity
Cash reserves
Collateral

Character and personal characteristics
Competency and experience
Compensating factors

Credit Scores and Credit Record

If your credit record shows imperfections (or worse), you can still qualify for financing. Owner will carry (OWC), lease options, lease purchase, co-signers, FHA, VA, some state housing programs, and subject-to properties all represent possibilities. But there's no getting around the fact that if (in today's market) your credit score falls below 720 or so, you will face tougher qualifying paperwork, and more than likely, pay an interest rate that exceeds the lowest rate available. To build credibility and confidence, manage your credit to enhance your credit score (at least to achieve a responsible number).

Good credit increases your possibilities. Without a strong credit score, you'll limit yourself to government programs, seller financing (most likely with above-market price or terms), subject-to loan or purchase agreements, or subprime B, C, or D loans that carry higher discount points, origination fees, and interest rates (if such loans are even available). When you show an excellent credit score and credit record, lenders will welcome you with competitive rates and terms. You become a sought-after customer for lenders, sales agents, and sellers.

Nevertheless, some mortgage lenders will accept borrowers who have experienced foreclosure, repossession, or bankruptcy. To qualify with these lenders, you typically need to (1) have paid on time, every time, for the past 18 to 24 months; (2) attribute previous adverse credit to divorce, unemployment, accident, illness, or other outside-your-control misfortune; and (3) convince the lender that your present and future financial well-being stands on a concrete foundation. (To improve your credit score, see myfico.com.)

Capacity (Monthly Income)

To judge your capacity to pay, mortgage lenders evaluate your monthly income from employment and other sources, as well as the expected rents and NOI of the financed property. For owner-occupied properties, a lender will (directly or indirectly) emphasize qualifying ratios. A qualifying ratio is the percentage of your income that you can safely allocate to mortgage payments (principal, interest, property taxes, and insurance, or PITI). If a lender sets a 28 percent housing-cost qualifying ratio and you gross $4,000 a month, the lender may limit your mortgage payments (PITI) to $1,120 a month.

If you are buying your first or second rental house, the lender may count 75 percent of the rents toward your qualifying ratios—but on this point lenders differ. Some will count more and some will count less. When financing your first few investment properties, lenders rely most on your personal credit and income. As you gain investment experience, they become more willing to look at your individual properties on a stand-alone basis. In times of strict underwriting, credit counts as much or more than capacity—even for investment-sized properties.

To judge capacity for apartment buildings and commercial properties, lenders apply a debt coverage ratio (DCR). A debt coverage ratio shows the lender whether the property brings in enough rental income to cover operating expenses and debt service (principal and interest). Here's an example of DCR for a fourplex whose units each rent for $750 a month:

Gross potential income (4 × $750 × 12)	$36,000
minus	
Vacancy and collection losses (6% of GPI).	$2,160
Operating expenses and upkeep	$7,200
Property taxes and insurance equals	$2,360
Net operating income (NOI)	$24,280

If a lender sets a 25 percent margin of net income over debt service, divide the property's annual NOI by a debt coverage ratio (DCR) of 1.25:

$$NOI/DCR = \text{Annual mortgage payment}$$
$$\$24,280/1.25 = \$19,424$$

To check, we reverse the calculations:

$$NOI/\text{Debt Service} = \text{Debt coverage ratio}$$
$$\$24,280/\$19,424 = 1.25$$

From these figures, you can see that with a required 1.25 DCR, the property will yield enough income to support a monthly mortgage payment of $1,619 ($19,424 annual mortgage payment ÷ 12). To figure how much loan a mortgage payment of $1,619 a month will pay off (amortize) over a 30-year term, refer to Table 2.1.

Table 2.1 Monthly Payment Required per $1,000 of Original Mortgage Balance

Interest (%)	Monthly Payment	Interest (%)	Monthly Payment
2.5	$3.95	7.5	$6.99
3.0	4.21	8.0	7.34
3.5	4.49	8.5	7.69
4.0	4.77	9.0	8.05
4.5	5.07	9.5	8.41
5.0	5.37	10.0	8.77
5.5	5.67	10.5	9.15
6.0	5.99	11.0	9.52
6.5	6.32	11.5	9.90
7.0	6.65	12.0	10.29

Note: Terms = 30 years.

At mortgage interest rates of, say, 6.0, 7.5, or 9.0 percent, the lender could lend you up to $270,284, $231,617, or $201,118, respectively.

> 6.0% Mortgage Interest Rate
> $1,619/$5.99 = $270,284 loan amount
> 7.5% Mortgage Interest Rate
> $1,619/$6.99 = $231,617 loan amount
> 9% Mortgage Interest Rate
> $1,619/$8.05 = $201,118 loan amount

DCRs represent guidelines, not absolutes. Given the strength (or weakness) of your other Cs, lenders will adjust their desired DCR either higher or lower. The quality of the property's income stream will also count. A property leased to a AAA-rated corporate tenant (or perhaps even one rented to long-term Section 8 tenants) will deserve a lower DCR than a property that produces less stable rent collections—such as a small strip shopping center with frequent vacancies and an extensive turnover of its small business tenants.

Cash Reserves and Source of Down Payment

Your lender sets a 70 percent LTV for its first mortgage. Your seller will carry back a second mortgage for the balance of the purchase price. Will the lender approve your loan application? Maybe, maybe not. (Today, probably not—but expect an easing up when normal underwriting returns.)

Regardless of LTV, lenders like to see their borrowers invest their own cash into their properties. The lender will also want to know where you're getting the cash. The best source is ready money from a savings account (or other liquid assets). More than likely, the lender will require a seasoned, proof-of-funds bank statement. Most lenders would not like to learn that you're taking a $10,000 cash advance against your credit card.

Likewise, lenders want you to retain cash (or liquid assets) after you close your loan. Often, they like to see enough reserves to cover two or three months of mortgage payments. However, the larger the cash balances that you maintain on hand, the better you look. Just as important, the larger your cash balances, the less likely a storm will capsize your investment plans.

Collateral

Lenders want to be repaid. If you default on your loan obligations, the lender wants an asset (or assets) to seize. They want collateral.

Until you move up to larger multifamily or commercial-size properties (at least several million dollars or more), lenders will rate your personal Cs more than they will consider the property itself (hard money lenders excepted). Nevertheless, lenders do set standards for properties (not just borrowers).

Though their standards and practices vary, some lenders won't finance properties larger than four units (or even two units). Some won't finance properties in poor condition or those located in deteriorating neighborhoods or states hit hard by foreclosures. Many lenders verify that a property is serviced by all utilities (for example, some lenders avoid properties with septic tanks instead of sewer lines). Lenders set standards that apply to property age; construction materials; type of roof; central heat and air; electrical system; paved streets; conformance with zoning and building regulations; convenience to schools, public transportation, shopping, and job centers; land/building ratio; and other criteria.

Before you look at properties and write up an offer to buy, verify whether that property meets the criteria of the lender and loan program that you intend to use. Otherwise, you may waste time and money (loan application costs, appraisal, and other miscellaneous fees). Often, lenders will not refund these prepaid expenses.

Loan-to-Value Ratios

As we talked about earlier, lenders lend up to a specified percentage of a property's market value (or contract price—whichever is less). After your property meets the lender's features and location profile, the lender will arrange for an independent estimate of market value, which, as Chapter 3 explains, may or may not prove accurate or reasonable.

In boom times, appraisers tend to overappraise—which is one reason why so many borrowers are now underwater and lenders have pleaded for government to rescue them from the effects of their ill-conceived and reckless lending practices. During the boom, rarely did any appraisal come in with a low, deal-killing valuation. Whatever amount the lender needed to support the loan, that's the amount the appraiser delivered. As the old joke goes, Member of the Appraisal Institute (MAI) stood for Made As Instructed. Perhaps unfair, but there's no doubt that appraisers felt pressured to hit the numbers (market value estimate) that would please the parties to a transaction.

In tough markets as exist now, appraisers are more likely to underappraise. They feel pressure from government regulators. New federal rules prohibit lenders from directly ordering appraisals. Loan reps must submit their appraisal requests to a supposedly impartial appraisal management company. That company then chooses the appraiser to assign to the subject property.

Complaints now arise that the assigned appraisers don't know the territory. If their value estimate comes in too low to support the requested LTV, the borrower, lender, and/or seller will claim that the comps are not really similar to the subject property. The subject property's location (or features) stand far superior to the comparables that the appraiser flagrantly ignores.

Thus, as an investor, you face two potential pitfalls: (1) in times of easy money lending, the lender may approve a loan that exceeds the safe amount you should borrow (without accepting undue risk); and (2) in tough times, the appraisal may come up short. It will either kill your deal or force you to increase the amount of your down payment. To avoid any or all of these underwriting issues, carefully evaluate the lender's appraisal (see Chapter 3).

Recourse to Other Assets or Income

In addition to the subject property, lenders might also require you to pledge other assets (property, bank accounts, stocks, and so on) to strengthen their security. At times, you might offer cross-collateralization (or pledged collateral) to a bank in exchange for an LTV that's higher than you might otherwise receive. In close calls (and sometimes not so close), a boost in the collateral you provide will tip loan approval in your direction.

Besides collateral, banks (and sellers) will probably ask property investors to sign a personal note to further guarantee repayment of the monies owed. If you default, a recourse loan gives the lender (note holder) the right to go after not just the mortgaged property or other pledged assets, but also, more generally, other assets in which you own an interest or income you earn or receive. Check your state law for the recourse rights that mortgage lenders typically place in their loan agreements—and how (whether) courts enforce these lenders' rights.

Because during the boom, lenders easily granted *nonrecourse* property loans, a New York City private equity firm recently walked away from a $5.5 billion property (now worth maybe $2.6 billion) and left the banks that had financed the deal with a loss of more than $2.4 billion. With loss experience like that, you can see why lenders have become gun-shy about offering nonrecourse mortgages.

Will times change? Will nonrecourse again become standard operating procedure on mega-million and billion-dollar deals? Probably. Monitor the credit cycle. Liberal lending will come back (if, as they say, history repeats itself).

Character

U.S. lenders cannot legally exclude borrowers because of their age, race, religion, sex, marital status, or disability. They can and do look at character and personal characteristics such as the following:

♦ Education level
♦ Career advancement potential
♦ Job stability
♦ Stability in the community
♦ Saving, spending, and borrowing habits
♦ Dependability and consistency
♦ Dress and mannerisms

A mortgage lender will not arbitrarily reject your loan application because you dropped out of high school, dyed your hair purple, tattooed every piece of flesh on your body, wear a silver nose ring, change jobs every six months, or have not registered a telephone in your own name. Nevertheless, subtle (and not so subtle) influences still count—especially for investors, and especially when tight underwriting prevails.

Property investment requires commitment. Smart lenders trust you to fulfill your responsibilities. Convince the lender that you are a solid and dependable worker, investor, and borrower. The legendary banker J. P. Morgan once testified to a U.S. congressional committee, "Money cannot buy credit. A man I do not trust could not get credit from me on all the bonds of Christendom." Character does count. Not merely with lenders, but even more so with potential partners and equity investors.

As liars' loans proliferated from 2001 to 2006, many lenders ignored (to their later regret) J. P. Morgan's wise advice. And more than likely, during some future boom period, lenders will again lose their senses and overlook loan application mistakes and exaggerations. Yet, in all of your personal and business transactions, resist temptation. Become known as someone whose words, actions, and promises evoke trust and confidence.

Competence and Experience

Borrowers default on their property investment loans more frequently than homeowners. That's why lenders apply stricter underwriting standards to investors—and charge them a higher rate of interest and apply lower LTVs. Lenders would like to feel confident that you know what you are doing—and you're not getting in over your head. Many investors today face foreclosure not only because they paid too much (relative to a property's reasonably expected cash flows), but because they did not understand that rental properties (except for NNN properties) require management know-how.

To establish experience and competency, submit a business plan (of sorts) along with your loan application. Illustrate the managerial changes that you will execute to increase the property's cash flows and boost its value. Convince the lender that you understand the market and can price and position your rentals to attract a well-defined target market of tenants who will prefer the units that you offer relative to those of your competition. Share with the lender your well-thought-out market strategy (see Chapter 11 and the example of Craig Wilson).

If you lack experience with property, relate other practical experiences that might seem similar. Or show the lender how you have succeeded in other ventures—that you have consistently performed your responsibilities diligently and competently. Show the lender that you are serious about long-term investing. You will bring the lender repeat business—and you will honor your commitments such that the lender will strive to retain you as a valued customer.

Compensating Factors

As you learn a lender's underwriting guidelines, remember, these are guidelines. Most lenders do not evaluate their mortgage loan applications by inflexible rules. Lenders weigh and consider. You can persuade a lender to approve your loan. Emphasize your positives and play down or explain away negatives.

If your debt coverage ratio falls below a lender's desired minimum, show the lender how you plan to improve the property and increase rents. If you have accumulated credit problems, compensate with a higher down payment or pledged collateral. Explain past foolishness or adverse circumstances. Show the new foundation for sound finances that you have laid. If you've frequently changed jobs, point out the raises and promotions you've received. If you lack experience in property ownership or property management, tell the lenders how you've educated yourself by reading real estate books and how you've developed a winning market strategy for your property.

Use employer letters, references, prepared budgets, a business plan, or any other written evidence that will increase the lender's confidence that you will succeed with your property. Compensating factors can make the decision swing in your favor. Lenders differ—especially when they underwrite investors. What one rejects, another accepts. To obtain the loan (and loan amount) you want, search the mortgage market. With thousands of competing lenders and loan brokers, chances are you can find a lender (or seller) who's right for you. If not, those lenders have just sent you a powerful signal: you must improve your financial fitness and borrower profile—your 7 Cs.

Automated Underwriting (AUS)

For the past 20 years, mortgage lenders have relied on automated underwriting. Using such a system, a loan rep gathers your pertinent underwriting facts and enters them into a software program.

If your borrower (and property) profile aligns with the standards written into this loan-qualifying program, great. It likely means a faster, less cumbersome path to closing, and a shorter stack of paperwork. But if your profile needs outside-the-box attention, work with a savvy loan rep who can apply the skill and knowledge necessary to get your loan approved—or at least tell you the reasons why your application falls short and how you can work to overcome deficiencies.

Automated underwriting (AUS) looks at more than your credit score. These programs incorporate calculations that evaluate your qualifying ratios, earning power, cash reserves, debts, and assets. When your credit scores exceed, say, 720 (or so), the AUS might relax on other standards. Whereas a score of, say, 640 (or so) will cause the AUS to subject your financial profile to stricter standards and more documentation of income, savings, and other pertinent financial data, though today, even 800-credit-score borrowers can expect excessive and often silly document requests and verifications.

An automated system *never* firmly approves or declines a loan. If your information registers a reject, you can still try to override the system with compensating factors and perhaps a direct appeal to the underwriting department or management higher-ups. Similarly, a looks-great feedback from AUS does not necessarily mean clear sailing. Underwriters—especially in tight credit markets—pore over every detail of your application and may ask you to further document anything from your grandmother's maiden name to your dog's birthday. Well, maybe not quite that demanding, but a green eyeshade underwriter can and will look to dot every *i* and cross every *t*. Today, rules rule over common sense. Prepare, persevere, and pray. The odds are good that your loan will eventually close.

3

APPRAISAL: INS AND OUTS
OF MARKET VALUE

Market value remains a centrally important metric (measure) to real estate investors, mortgage lenders, and homebuyers. Only the foolish would buy, sell, or loan against a property without knowledge of its market value. Nevertheless, hundreds of bank failures and millions of foreclosures has laid bare the idea that this popularly relied upon figure should serve as the only figure that matters.

Never again should anyone believe the once-entrenched view, "Buy for less than market value, you've scored a good deal. Pay more than market value, you've overpaid."

Never again should anyone rely upon appraisers (without question) to provide accurate, disinterested estimates of market value. Although always known among real estate insiders, the market value estimates of appraisers are not only subject to unintentional errors of fact, interpretation, or both, in many instances, appraisers manipulate their numbers to deliver whatever value estimate makes a deal work (at least, that is, appear to work—in the short run.)

So, this chapter will help you in two ways:

1. You will understand how to review and critique a professionally prepared market value appraisal; and, correspondingly, you will wisely decide how much confidence you should place in the appraiser's estimate of value.
2. You will see that for purposes of investment, even an accurately prepared market value appraisal fails to provide a figure that offers a fair or reasonable price to pay. For that guide, forecast future demand and supply, not rely on past sales prices.

WHAT IS MARKET VALUE?

To the naive, appraised value, sales price, and market value all refer to the same idea. But, actually, appraised value might refer to an insurance policy appraisal, a property tax appraisal, an estate tax appraisal, or a market value appraisal. Sales price itself reveals the nominal price at which a property has sold. That sales price might equal, exceed, or fall below market value. Sales price represents market value only when a property is sold according to these five assumptions:

1. Buyers and sellers are typically motivated. Neither acts under duress.
2. Buyers and sellers are well informed about the market and negotiate in their own best interest.
3. The marketing period and sales promotion bring the property to the attention of willing and able buyers.
4. No atypically favorable or unfavorable terms of financing apply. Easy money inflates demand. Tight money suppresses demand. (During the most recent property boom, lenders offered dangerously easy financing, thus pushing demand and sales prices far above the market values that would have prevailed under normal loan underwriting standards.)
5. Neither the sellers nor the buyers offer any extraordinary sales concessions or incentives. (For example, the builders in many countries offered off-plan buyers three years of rent guarantees— clearly a red flag that the builders' prices exceed market value.)

   To illustrate the assumed conditions underlying the concept of market value, say that two properties recently sold in a neighborhood where you might like to invest:

   The house at 37 Oak sold at a price of $258,000, and 164 Maple sold at a price of $255,000. Each of these three-bedroom, two-bath houses was in good condition, with around 2,100 square feet. You locate a nearby house of similar size and features at 158 Pine. It's priced at $234,750. Is that a below-market price? Maybe, maybe not. Before you accept this sales evidence, investigate the terms and conditions of the other two comparable sales.

   What if the sellers of 164 Maple had carried back a nothing-down, 4 percent, 30-year mortgage for their buyers (that is, favorable financing)?

   What if the buyers of 37 Oak had just flown into Peoria from San Francisco and bought the first house they saw because "It was such a steal. You couldn't find anything like it in San Francisco for less than $1.2 million" (that is, uninformed buyers)?

What if the sellers of 37 Oak had agreed to pay all of their buyer's closing costs and leave their authentic Chippendale buffet because it was too big to move into their new condo in Florida (that is, extraordinary sales concessions)? What if 37 Oak were a bank REO?

Sales Price Doesn't Necessarily Equal Market Value

When you value property, learn more than the past prices at which so-called similar properties have recently sold. Investigate whether the buyers or sellers in these transactions acted with full market knowledge, negotiated any favorable terms of financing, bought (or sold) in a hurry, or conceded something that pushed up the nominal selling price—or perhaps pulled it down. If you find that the sales of comparable properties do not meet the conditions of a market value sale, then that sales price (unadjusted) does not necessarily imply a market value price.

To confidently rely on comp sales prices: verify the accuracy of your information, verify the date of sale, and verify the terms and conditions of the sale. Faulty information about a comp property's features or terms of sale can make overpriced deals look good (or vice versa). Market value assumes no hidden defects or title issues. A comp (or subject) house with a termite infestation or unpaid tax liens should sell at a price less than market value (see later discussion).

Underwriting Rules Determine the Value in LTV

Banks loan against market value, not purchase price, unless your purchase price falls below market value. When you apply for a mortgage, you may tell the lender that you've agreed to a price of $200,000 and would like to borrow $160,000 (an 80 percent LTV). Yet the lender will not necessarily agree that this price matches the property's market value.

The lender will ask about special financing terms (for example, a $20,000 seller second) and sales concessions (for example, the seller's plan to buy down your interest rate for three years and pay all closing costs). If your transaction differs from market norms, the lender won't lend 80 percent of your $200,000 purchase price—even if it routinely does make 80 percent LTV loans. The lender may find that easy terms of financing or sales concessions are worth $10,000. So, the lender may calculate your 80 percent LTV ratio against $190,000, not the $200,000 nominal purchase price.

To verify that your purchase price of $200,000 equals or exceeds market value, the lender will order a market value appraisal. If that appraisal report comes back with a figure that's less than $200,000, the lender will use the lesser amount to calculate an 80 percent LTV loan. Take notice: Do not passively accept the results of any low (or high) appraisal. Review and critique the report. Ask the appraiser to correct errors. Or you can ask the lender to order a new appraisal with another firm. The lender needs a file document (appraisal) to justify its lending decision. If you provide an acceptable (revised or remade) appraisal of a satisfactory amount, you'll often get the loan you want.

Danger: Just because a lender's appraiser comes up with a market value estimate that matches your purchase price, never assume that the appraisal accurately sets market value. Accept personal responsibility for your offering price. In the past, loan reps routinely told their appraisers the value estimate they needed to make a deal work. In return, appraisers know that if they fail to hit the desired numbers, loan reps will select another, more accommodating appraiser to prepare their reports.

If you're a good customer of a bank (or if the bank would like you to become a good customer), the loan rep may encourage the appraiser to issue an MAI (made as instructed) appraisal. I know of many instances in which appraisers have acquiesced to not-so-subtle hints from a loan rep and submitted appraisals that overstated a property's value. (Indeed, as early in the property boom as 2003, government investigators found that loan reps were pressing appraisers to lift their value estimates.)

New lender and appraisal regulations supposedly will stop this abuse. I would not bet on it. People in the business know each other—and word gets around. There's no Chinese Wall in real estate. Recently, a property that I own was reappraised so that I could refinance and pull cash out (to reinvest, not spend) some of that almost free money (3.75 percent interest rate). When inspecting the house, the appraiser asked me what I thought it was worth. His market value estimate came in a mere $5,000 less than the number I suggested. In this instance, my estimate was accurate. I am not accusing the appraiser of over- or undervaluing. But it does illustrate that he did not want to nix the loan with an out-of-range opinion.

You will work with appraisers, and you will solicit their opinions, but never accept those opinions as the final word. To protect yourself against inaccurate appraisals (your own, as well as others), understand how to calculate, apply, and interpret the three basic methods used to estimate market value.

HOW TO ESTIMATE MARKET VALUE

To estimate market value, rely on multiple methods. During the property and credit boom, appraisal practice focused on the comparable sales approach and ignored (or slighted) the cost and income approaches.

In doing so, appraisers missed the danger signals that the cost and income methods were flashing.

Cost approach
♦ Calculate how much it would cost to build a subject property at today's prices.
♦ Subtract accrued depreciation.
♦ Add the depreciated cost figure to the current value of the lot.

Comparable sales approach
♦ Compare a subject property with other similar (comp) properties that have recently sold.
♦ Adjust the prices for each positive or negative feature of the comps relative to the subject property.
♦ Estimate market value of the subject property from the adjusted sales prices of the comps.

Income approach
♦ Estimate the rents you expect a property to produce.
♦ Convert net rents after expenses (net operating income) into a capital (market) value amount. Alternatively, estimate the gross amount of rents that a property could bring in and multiply that amount by an applicable market-derived GRM.

When you evaluate a property from three perspectives, you check the value estimates of each against the others. Multiple estimates and techniques enhance the probability that your estimate reflects reality. If your three value estimates don't reasonably match up, either your calculations err, the figures you're working with are inaccurate, or the market is acting crazy and property prices are about to head up (or down).

Figure 3.1 shows a sample residential appraisal form for a single-family house. Refer to this form as you read the following pages and you'll see how to apply these three techniques to appraise properties. Photocopy this form (or print a copy from the Internet). Use the forms to fill in property and market information as you value potential property investments.

PROPERTY DESCRIPTION

To accurately estimate the market value of a property, first describe the features of the property and its neighborhood in detail. List all facts that might influence value favorably or unfavorably. Investors err in their appraisals because they casually inspect rather than carefully detail and compare. Focus on each of the neighborhood and property features listed

Uniform Residential Appraisal Report

File #

The purpose of this summary appraisal report is to provide the lender/client with an accurate, and adequately supported, opinion of the market value of the subject property.

SUBJECT

Property Address	City	State Zip Code
Borrower	Owner of Public Record	County
Legal Description		
Assessor's Parcel #	Tax Year	R.E. Taxes $
Neighborhood Name	Map Reference	Census Tract

Occupant ☐ Owner ☐ Tenant ☐ Vacant Special Assessments $ ☐ PUD HOA $ ☐ per year ☐ per month

Property Rights Appraised ☐ Fee Simple ☐ Leasehold ☐ Other (describe)

Assignment Type ☐ Purchase Transaction ☐ Refinance Transaction ☐ Other (describe)

Lender/Client   Address

Is the subject property currently offered for sale or has it been offered for sale in the twelve months prior to the effective date of this appraisal? ☐ Yes ☐ No

Report data source(s) used, offering price(s), and date(s).

CONTRACT

I ☐ did ☐ did not analyze the contract for sale for the subject purchase transaction. Explain the results of the analysis of the contract for sale or why the analysis was not performed.

Contract Price $ Date of Contract   Is the property seller the owner of public record? ☐ Yes ☐ No Data Source(s)

Is there any financial assistance (loan charges, sale concessions, gift or downpayment assistance, etc.) to be paid by any party on behalf of the borrower? ☐ Yes ☐ No

If Yes, report the total dollar amount and describe the items to be paid.

NEIGHBORHOOD

Note: Race and the racial composition of the neighborhood are not appraisal factors.

Neighborhood Characteristics			One-Unit Housing Trends				One-Unit Housing		Present Land Use %	
Location ☐ Urban	☐ Suburban	☐ Rural	Property Values ☐ Increasing	☐ Stable	☐ Declining		PRICE	AGE	One-Unit	%
Built-Up ☐ Over 75%	☐ 25–75%	☐ Under 25%	Demand/Supply ☐ Shortage	☐ In Balance	☐ Over Supply		$ (000)	(yrs)	2-4 Unit	%
Growth ☐ Rapid	☐ Stable	☐ Slow	Marketing Time ☐ Under 3 mths	☐ 3–6 mths	☐ Over 6 mths		Low		Multi-Family	%
Neighborhood Boundaries							High		Commercial	%
							Pred.		Other	%

Neighborhood Description

Market Conditions (including support for the above conclusions)

SITE

Dimensions	Area	Shape	View
Specific Zoning Classification	Zoning Description		

Zoning Compliance ☐ Legal ☐ Legal Nonconforming (Grandfathered Use) ☐ No Zoning ☐ Illegal (describe)

Is the highest and best use of the subject property as improved (or as proposed per plans and specifications) the present use? ☐ Yes ☐ No If No, describe

Utilities	Public	Other (describe)		Public	Other (describe)	Off-site Improvements—Type	Public	Private
Electricity	☐	☐	Water	☐	☐	Street	☐	☐
Gas	☐	☐	Sanitary Sewer	☐	☐	Alley	☐	☐

FEMA Special Flood Hazard Area ☐ Yes ☐ No FEMA Flood Zone   FEMA Map #   FEMA Map Date

Are the utilities and off-site improvements typical for the market area? ☐ Yes ☐ No If No, describe

Are there any adverse site conditions or external factors (easements, encroachments, environmental conditions, land uses, etc.)? ☐ Yes ☐ No If Yes, describe

IMPROVEMENTS

General Description	Foundation	Exterior Description materials/condition	Interior materials/condition
Units ☐ One ☐ One with Accessory Unit	☐ Concrete Slab ☐ Crawl Space	Foundation Walls	Floors
# of Stories	☐ Full Basement ☐ Partial Basement	Exterior Walls	Walls
Type ☐ Det. ☐ Att. ☐ S-Det./End Unit	Basement Area sq. ft.	Roof Surface	Trim/Finish
☐ Existing ☐ Proposed ☐ Under Const.	Basement Finish %	Gutters & Downspouts	Bath Floor
Design (Style)	☐ Outside Entry/Exit ☐ Sump Pump	Window Type	Bath Wainscot
Year Built	Evidence of ☐ Infestation	Storm Sash/Insulated	Car Storage ☐ None
Effective Age (Yrs)	☐ Dampness ☐ Settlement	Screens	☐ Driveway # of Cars
Attic ☐ None	Heating ☐ FWA ☐ HWBB ☐ Radiant	Amenities ☐ Woodstove(s) #	Driveway Surface
☐ Drop Stair ☐ Stairs	☐ Other Fuel	☐ Fireplace(s) # ☐ Fence	☐ Garage # of Cars
☐ Floor ☐ Scuttle	Cooling ☐ Central Air Conditioning	☐ Patio/Deck ☐ Porch	☐ Carport # of Cars
☐ Finished ☐ Heated	☐ Individual ☐ Other	☐ Pool ☐ Other	☐ Att. ☐ Det. ☐ Built-in

Appliances ☐ Refrigerator ☐ Range/Oven ☐ Dishwasher ☐ Disposal ☐ Microwave ☐ Washer/Dryer ☐ Other (describe)

Finished area above grade contains: Rooms   Bedrooms   Bath(s)   Square Feet of Gross Living Area Above Grade

Additional features (special energy efficient items, etc.)

Describe the condition of the property (including needed repairs, deterioration, renovations, remodeling, etc.).

Are there any physical deficiencies or adverse conditions that affect the livability, soundness, or structural integrity of the property? ☐ Yes ☐ No If Yes, describe

Does the property generally conform to the neighborhood (functional utility, style, condition, use, construction, etc.)? ☐ Yes ☐ No If No, describe

Figure 3.1 Appraisal Report

Uniform Residential Appraisal Report

There are	comparable properties currently offered for sale in the subject neighborhood ranging in price from $			to $	.
There are	comparable sales in the subject neighborhood within the past twelve months ranging in sale price from $			to $	.

FEATURE	SUBJECT	COMPARABLE SALE # 1		COMPARABLE SALE # 2		COMPARABLE SALE # 3	
Address							
Proximity to Subject							
Sale Price	$		$		$		$
Sale Price/Gross Liv. Area	$ sq. ft.	$ sq. ft.		$ sq. ft.		$ sq. ft.	
Data Source(s)							
Verification Source(s)							
VALUE ADJUSTMENTS	DESCRIPTION	DESCRIPTION	+(-) $ Adjustment	DESCRIPTION	+(-) $ Adjustment	DESCRIPTION	+(-) $ Adjustment
Sale or Financing Concessions							
Date of Sale/Time							
Location							
Leasehold/Fee Simple							
Site							
View							
Design (Style)							
Quality of Construction							
Actual Age							
Condition							
Above Grade	Total Bdrms. Baths	Total Bdrms. Baths		Total Bdrms. Baths		Total Bdrms. Baths	
Room Count							
Gross Living Area	sq. ft.	sq. ft.		sq. ft.		sq. ft.	
Basement & Finished Rooms Below Grade							
Functional Utility							
Heating/Cooling							
Energy Efficient Items							
Garage/Carport							
Porch/Patio/Deck							
Net Adjustment (Total)		☐ + ☐ -	$	☐ + ☐ -	$	☐ + ☐ -	$
Adjusted Sale Price of Comparables		Net Adj. % Gross Adj. %	$	Net Adj. % Gross Adj. %	$	Net Adj. % Gross Adj. %	$

I ☐ did ☐ did not research the sale or transfer history of the subject property and comparable sales. If not, explain

My research ☐ did ☐ did not reveal any prior sales or transfers of the subject property for the three years prior to the effective date of this appraisal.

Data source(s)

My research ☐ did ☐ did not reveal any prior sales or transfers of the comparable sales for the year prior to the date of sale of the comparable sale.

Data source(s)

Report the results of the research and analysis of the prior sale or transfer history of the subject property and comparable sales (report additional prior sales on page 3).

ITEM	SUBJECT	COMPARABLE SALE # 1	COMPARABLE SALE # 2	COMPARABLE SALE # 3
Date of Prior Sale/Transfer				
Price of Prior Sale/Transfer				
Data Source(s)				
Effective Date of Data Source(s)				

Analysis of prior sale or transfer history of the subject property and comparable sales

Summary of Sales Comparison Approach

Indicated Value by Sales Comparison Approach $

Indicated Value by: Sales Comparison Approach $ Cost Approach (if developed) $ Income Approach (if developed) $

This appraisal is made ☐ "as is", ☐ subject to completion per plans and specifications on the basis of a hypothetical condition that the improvements have been completed, ☐ subject to the following repairs or alterations on the basis of a hypothetical condition that the repairs or alterations have been completed, or ☐ subject to the following required inspection based on the extraordinary assumption that the condition or deficiency does not require alteration or repair:

Based on a complete visual inspection of the interior and exterior areas of the subject property, defined scope of work, statement of assumptions and limiting conditions, and appraiser's certification, my (our) opinion of the market value, as defined, of the real property that is the subject of this report is
$, as of   , which is the date of inspection and the effective date of this appraisal.

Left margin vertical labels: SALES COMPARISON APPROACH, RECONCILIATION

Figure 3.1 (Continued)

ADDITIONAL COMMENTS

COST APPROACH TO VALUE (not required by Fannie Mae)

Provide adequate information for the lender/client to replicate the below cost figures and calculations.

Support for the opinion of site value (summary of comparable land sales or other methods for estimating site value)

COST APPROACH

ESTIMATED ☐ REPRODUCTION OR ☐ REPLACEMENT COST NEW	OPINION OF SITE VALUE .... = $
Source of cost data	Dwelling Sq. Ft. @ $ .... =$
Quality rating from cost service Effective date of cost data	Sq. Ft. @ $ .... =$
Comments on Cost Approach (gross living area calculations, depreciation, etc.)	
	Garage/Carport Sq. Ft. @ $ .... =$
	Total Estimate of Cost-New .... = $
	Less Physical Functional External
	Depreciation =$( )
	Depreciated Cost of Improvements........................... =$
	"As-is" Value of Site Improvements........................... =$
Estimated Remaining Economic Life (HUD and VA only) Years	Indicated Value By Cost Approach .... =$

INCOME APPROACH TO VALUE (not required by Fannie Mae)

INCOME

Estimated Monthly Market Rent $ X Gross Rent Multiplier   = $ Indicated Value by Income Approach

Summary of Income Approach (including support for market rent and GRM)

PROJECT INFORMATION FOR PUDs (if applicable)

PUD INFORMATION

Is the developer/builder in control of the Homeowners' Association (HOA)? ☐ Yes ☐ No   Unit type(s) ☐ Detached ☐ Attached

Provide the following information for PUDs ONLY if the developer/builder is in control of the HOA and the subject property is an attached dwelling unit.

Legal name of project

Total number of phases   Total number of units   Total number of units sold

Total number of units rented   Total number of units for sale   Data source(s)

Was the project created by the conversion of an existing building(s) into a PUD? ☐ Yes ☐ No   If Yes, date of conversion

Does the project contain any multi-dwelling units? ☐ Yes ☐ No   Data source(s)

Are the units, common elements, and recreation facilities complete? ☐ Yes ☐ No   If No, describe the status of completion.

Are the common elements leased to or by the Homeowners' Association? ☐ Yes ☐ No   If Yes, describe the rental terms and options.

Describe common elements and recreational facilities

Figure 3.1   (Continued)

This report form is designed to report an appraisal of a one-unit property or a one-unit property with an accessory unit; including a unit in a planned unit development (PUD). This report form is not designed to report an appraisal of a manufactured home or a unit in a condominium or cooperative project.

This appraisal report is subject to the following scope of work, intended use, intended user, definition of market value, statement of assumptions and limiting conditions, and certifications. Modifications, additions, or deletions to the intended use, intended user, definition of market value, or assumptions and limiting conditions are not permitted. The appraiser may expand the scope of work to include any additional research or analysis necessary based on the complexity of this appraisal assignment. Modifications or deletions to the certifications are also not permitted. However, additional certifications that do not constitute material alterations to this appraisal report, such as those required by law or those related to the appraiser's continuing education or membership in an appraisal organization, are permitted.

SCOPE OF WORK: The scope of work for this appraisal is defined by the complexity of this appraisal assignment and the reporting requirements of this appraisal report form, including the following definition of market value, statement of assumptions and limiting conditions, and certifications. The appraiser must, at a minimum: (1) perform a complete visual inspection of the interior and exterior areas of the subject property, (2) inspect the neighborhood, (3) inspect each of the comparable sales from at least the street, (4) research, verify, and analyze data from reliable public and/or private sources, and (5) report his or her analysis, opinions, and conclusions in this appraisal report.

INTENDED USE: The intended use of this appraisal report is for the lender/client to evaluate the property that is the subject of this appraisal for a mortgage finance transaction.

INTENDED USER: The intended user of this appraisal report is the lender/client.

DEFINITION OF MARKET VALUE: The most probable price which a property should bring in a competitive and open market under all conditions requisite to a fair sale, the buyer and seller, each acting prudently, knowledgeably and assuming the price is not affected by undue stimulus. Implicit in this definition is the consummation of a sale as of a specified date and the passing of title from seller to buyer under conditions whereby: (1) buyer and seller are typically motivated; (2) both parties are well informed or well advised, and each acting in what he or she considers his or her own best interest; (3) a reasonable time is allowed for exposure in the open market; (4) payment is made in terms of cash in U. S. dollars or in terms of financial arrangements comparable thereto; and (5) the price represents the normal consideration for the property sold unaffected by special or creative financing or sales concessions* granted by anyone associated with the sale.

*Adjustments to the comparables must be made for special or creative financing or sales concessions. No adjustments are necessary for those costs which are normally paid by sellers as a result of tradition or law in a market area; these costs are readily identifiable since the seller pays these costs in virtually all sales transactions. Special or creative financing adjustments can be made to the comparable property by comparisons to financing terms offered by a third party institutional lender that is not already involved in the property or transaction. Any adjustment should not be calculated on a mechanical dollar for dollar cost of the financing or concession but the dollar amount of any adjustment should approximate the market's reaction to the financing or concessions based on the appraiser's judgment.

STATEMENT OF ASSUMPTIONS AND LIMITING CONDITIONS: The appraiser's certification in this report is subject to the following assumptions and limiting conditions:

1. The appraiser will not be responsible for matters of a legal nature that affect either the property being appraised or the title to it, except for information that he or she became aware of during the research involved in performing this appraisal. The appraiser assumes that the title is good and marketable and will not render any opinions about the title.

2. The appraiser has provided a sketch in this appraisal report to show the approximate dimensions of the improvements. The sketch is included only to assist the reader in visualizing the property and understanding the appraiser's determination of its size.

3. The appraiser has examined the available flood maps that are provided by the Federal Emergency Management Agency (or other data sources) and has noted in this appraisal report whether any portion of the subject site is located in an identified Special Flood Hazard Area. Because the appraiser is not a surveyor, he or she makes no guarantees, express or implied, regarding this determination.

4. The appraiser will not give testimony or appear in court because he or she made an appraisal of the property in question, unless specific arrangements to do so have been made beforehand, or as otherwise required by law.

5. The appraiser has noted in this appraisal report any adverse conditions (such as needed repairs, deterioration, the presence of hazardous wastes, toxic substances, etc.) observed during the inspection of the subject property or that he or she became aware of during the research involved in performing this appraisal. Unless otherwise stated in this appraisal report, the appraiser has no knowledge of any hidden or unapparent physical deficiencies or adverse conditions of the property (such as, but not limited to, needed repairs, deterioration, the presence of hazardous wastes, toxic substances, adverse environmental conditions, etc.) that would make the property less valuable, and has assumed that there are no such conditions and makes no guarantees or warranties, express or implied. The appraiser will not be responsible for any such conditions that do exist or for any engineering or testing that might be required to discover whether such conditions exist. Because the appraiser is not an expert in the field of environmental hazards, this appraisal report must not be considered as an environmental assessment of the property.

6. The appraiser has based his or her appraisal report and valuation conclusion for an appraisal that is subject to satisfactory completion, repairs, or alterations on the assumption that the completion, repairs, or alterations of the subject property will be performed in a professional manner.

Figure 3.1   (Continued)

APPRAISER'S CERTIFICATION: The Appraiser certifies and agrees that:

1. I have, at a minimum, developed and reported this appraisal in accordance with the scope of work requirements stated in this appraisal report.

2. I performed a complete visual inspection of the interior and exterior areas of the subject property. I reported the condition of the improvements in factual, specific terms. I identified and reported the physical deficiencies that could affect the livability, soundness, or structural integrity of the property.

3. I performed this appraisal in accordance with the requirements of the Uniform Standards of Professional Appraisal Practice that were adopted and promulgated by the Appraisal Standards Board of The Appraisal Foundation and that were in place at the time this appraisal report was prepared.

4. I developed my opinion of the market value of the real property that is the subject of this report based on the sales comparison approach to value. I have adequate comparable market data to develop a reliable sales comparison approach for this appraisal assignment. I further certify that I considered the cost and income approaches to value but did not develop them, unless otherwise indicated in this report.

5. I researched, verified, analyzed, and reported on any current agreement for sale for the subject property, any offering for sale of the subject property in the twelve months prior to the effective date of this appraisal, and the prior sales of the subject property for a minimum of three years prior to the effective date of this appraisal, unless otherwise indicated in this report.

6. I researched, verified, analyzed, and reported on the prior sales of the comparable sales for a minimum of one year prior to the date of sale of the comparable sale, unless otherwise indicated in this report.

7. I selected and used comparable sales that are locationally, physically, and functionally the most similar to the subject property.

8. I have not used comparable sales that were the result of combining a land sale with the contract purchase price of a home that has been built or will be built on the land.

9. I have reported adjustments to the comparable sales that reflect the market's reaction to the differences between the subject property and the comparable sales.

10. I verified, from a disinterested source, all information in this report that was provided by parties who have a financial interest in the sale or financing of the subject property.

11. I have knowledge and experience in appraising this type of property in this market area.

12. I am aware of, and have access to, the necessary and appropriate public and private data sources, such as multiple listing services, tax assessment records, public land records and other such data sources for the area in which the property is located.

13. I obtained the information, estimates, and opinions furnished by other parties and expressed in this appraisal report from reliable sources that I believe to be true and correct.

14. I have taken into consideration the factors that have an impact on value with respect to the subject neighborhood, subject property, and the proximity of the subject property to adverse influences in the development of my opinion of market value. I have noted in this appraisal report any adverse conditions (such as, but not limited to, needed repairs, deterioration, the presence of hazardous wastes, toxic substances, adverse environmental conditions, etc.) observed during the inspection of the subject property or that I became aware of during the research involved in performing this appraisal. I have considered these adverse conditions in my analysis of the property value, and have reported on the effect of the conditions on the value and marketability of the subject property.

15. I have not knowingly withheld any significant information from this appraisal report and, to the best of my knowledge, all statements and information in this appraisal report are true and correct.

16. I stated in this appraisal report my own personal, unbiased, and professional analysis, opinions, and conclusions, which are subject only to the assumptions and limiting conditions in this appraisal report.

17. I have no present or prospective interest in the property that is the subject of this report, and I have no present or prospective personal interest or bias with respect to the participants in the transaction. I did not base, either partially or completely, my analysis and/or opinion of market value in this appraisal report on the race, color, religion, sex, age, marital status, handicap, familial status, or national origin of either the prospective owners or occupants of the subject property or of the present owners or occupants of the properties in the vicinity of the subject property or on any other basis prohibited by law.

18. My employment and/or compensation for performing this appraisal or any future or anticipated appraisals was not conditioned on any agreement or understanding, written or otherwise, that I would report (or present analysis supporting) a predetermined specific value, a predetermined minimum value, a range or direction in value, a value that favors the cause of any party, or the attainment of a specific result or occurrence of a specific subsequent event (such as approval of a pending mortgage loan application).

19. I personally prepared all conclusions and opinions about the real estate that were set forth in this appraisal report. If I relied on significant real property appraisal assistance from any individual or individuals in the performance of this appraisal or the preparation of this appraisal report, I have named such individual(s) and disclosed the specific tasks performed in this appraisal report. I certify that any individual so named is qualified to perform the tasks. I have not authorized anyone to make a change to any item in this appraisal report; therefore, any change made to this appraisal is unauthorized and I will take no responsibility for it.

20. I identified the lender/client in this appraisal report who is the individual, organization, or agent for the organization that ordered and will receive this appraisal report.

Figure 3.1   (Continued)

66

21. The lender/client may disclose or distribute this appraisal report to: the borrower; another lender at the request of the borrower; the mortgagee or its successors and assigns; mortgage insurers; government sponsored enterprises; other secondary market participants; data collection or reporting services; professional appraisal organizations; any department, agency, or instrumentality of the United States; and any state, the District of Columbia, or other jurisdictions; without having to obtain the appraiser's or supervisory appraiser's (if applicable) consent. Such consent must be obtained before this appraisal report may be disclosed or distributed to any other party (including, but not limited to, the public through advertising, public relations, news, sales, or other media).

22. I am aware that any disclosure or distribution of this appraisal report by me or the lender/client may be subject to certain laws and regulations. Further, I am also subject to the provisions of the Uniform Standards of Professional Appraisal Practice that pertain to disclosure or distribution by me.

23. The borrower, another lender at the request of the borrower, the mortgagee or its successors and assigns, mortgage insurers, government sponsored enterprises, and other secondary market participants may rely on this appraisal report as part of any mortgage finance transaction that involves any one or more of these parties.

24. If this appraisal report was transmitted as an "electronic record" containing my "electronic signature," as those terms are defined in applicable federal and/or state laws (excluding audio and video recordings), or a facsimile transmission of this appraisal report containing a copy or representation of my signature, the appraisal report shall be as effective, enforceable and valid as if a paper version of this appraisal report were delivered containing my original hand written signature.

25. Any intentional or negligent misrepresentation(s) contained in this appraisal report may result in civil liability and/or criminal penalties including, but not limited to, fine or imprisonment or both under the provisions of Title 18, United States Code, Section 1001, et seq., or similar state laws.

SUPERVISORY APPRAISER'S CERTIFICATION: The Supervisory Appraiser certifies and agrees that:

1. I directly supervised the appraiser for this appraisal assignment, have read the appraisal report, and agree with the appraiser's analysis, opinions, statements, conclusions, and the appraiser's certification.

2. I accept full responsibility for the contents of this appraisal report including, but not limited to, the appraiser's analysis, opinions, statements, conclusions, and the appraiser's certification.

3. The appraiser identified in this appraisal report is either a sub-contractor or an employee of the supervisory appraiser (or the appraisal firm), is qualified to perform this appraisal, and is acceptable to perform this appraisal under the applicable state law.

4. This appraisal report complies with the Uniform Standards of Professional Appraisal Practice that were adopted and promulgated by the Appraisal Standards Board of The Appraisal Foundation and that were in place at the time this appraisal report was prepared.

5. If this appraisal report was transmitted as an "electronic record" containing my "electronic signature," as those terms are defined in applicable federal and/or state laws (excluding audio and video recordings), or a facsimile transmission of this appraisal report containing a copy or representation of my signature, the appraisal report shall be as effective, enforceable and valid as if a paper version of this appraisal report were delivered containing my original hand written signature.

APPRAISER

Signature_____
Name _____
Company Name _____
Company Address_____
_____
Telephone Number _____
Email Address_____
Date of Signature and Report_____
Effective Date of Appraisal _____
State Certification #_____
or State License #_____
or Other (describe) _____ State # _____
State _____
Expiration Date of Certification or License _____

ADDRESS OF PROPERTY APPRAISED

_____
_____
APPRAISED VALUE OF SUBJECT PROPERTY $ _____
LENDER/CLIENT
Name _____
Company Name _____
Company Address_____
_____
Email Address_____

SUPERVISORY APPRAISER (ONLY IF REQUIRED)

Signature_____
Name _____
Company Name _____
Company Address_____
_____
Telephone Number _____
Email Address _____
Date of Signature _____
State Certification #_____
or State License #_____
State _____
Expiration Date of Certification or License _____

SUBJECT PROPERTY

☐ Did not inspect subject property
☐ Did inspect exterior of subject property from street
     Date of Inspection _____
☐ Did inspect interior and exterior of subject property
     Date of Inspection _____

COMPARABLE SALES

☐ Did not inspect exterior of comparable sales from street
☐ Did inspect exterior of comparable sales from street
     Date of Inspection _____

Freddie Mac Form 70   March 2005   Page 6 of 6   Fannie Mae Form 1004 March 2005

Figure 3.1   (Continued)

on an appraisal form. You will judge properties more profitably. (Here I focus on *market value* inspection and description. Valuing for investment and entrepreneurial improvements differs in perspective and purpose. We address those perspectives in following chapters.)

Identify the Subject Property

To identify the subject property seems straightforward. But all is not as simple as you may think. The street address for one of my previous homes was 73 Roble Road, Berkeley, California 94705. However, that property does not sit in Berkeley. It is actually located in Oakland. The house sat back from Roble Road (which is in Berkeley) about 100 feet—just far enough to place it within the city limits of Oakland. As a result, the city laws governing the property (zoning, building regulations, permits, rent controls, school district, and so forth) were those of Oakland, not Berkeley.

Similarly, Park Cities (University Park and Highland Park) are high-income, independent municipalities located within the geographic boundaries of Dallas, Texas. Among other amenities, Park Cities are noted for their high-quality schools. Yet (in the past) if you lived in Park Cities on the west side of the North Dallas Tollway, your children would attend the lesser-regarded schools of the Dallas Independent School District.

The lesson: Street and city addresses don't tell you what you need to know about a property. Strange as it may seem, a property may not be located where you think it is. The property may not receive the services you think it does. The laws of zoning and other regulations may not apply as you think they do. (See also the discussion of site identification further on.)

Neighborhood

As the appraisal form shows, a neighborhood investigation should note the types and condition of neighborhood properties, the percentage of houses and condominiums that are owner occupied, vacancy rates, property price (and rental) ranges, the types and quality of government services, and the relative convenience of the property to shopping, schools, employment centers, and parks and recreational areas—the appeal of the neighborhood to potential buyers.

Next, bring the future into view. Envision the changes that are likely to occur in the neighborhood during the coming three to five years. Is the neighborhood stable? Is it moving toward higher rates of owner occupancy? Are property owners fixing up their properties? Do neighborhood residents and local merchants take pride in their properties and the surrounding area? Is a neighborhood (or homeowners') association working to improve the area? If not, could such an association make the neighborhood a better place to live, shop, work, and play?

Have builders added large numbers of new housing units to the area? Is the neighborhood filled with foreclosures, For Sale signs or For Rent signs, or both? Has excess supply driven down property prices? How many months (or years) might be needed to clear existing and pipeline inventories?

Investment value looks to the future. Market value chiefly looks to past sales of similar properties. When you invest, you buy the future more than the present. View the neighborhood with a magnifying glass and with the use of a crystal ball. How will (or could) the neighborhood appear, look, feel, and be made to live in within the coming 5 to 10 years?

Site (Lot) Characteristics

Depending on the neighborhood, the size and features of a lot can account for 20 to 80 percent of a property's current and future value. Smart investors pay as much attention to the lot (and its potential) as they do to the building(s).

In addition to site size and features (see appraisal form), review the rules and restrictions that govern a site. Determine whether the buildings conform to zoning, occupancy, environmental, and safety regulations. Many two- to four-unit (and larger) properties have been modified (rehabbed, cut up, added to, repaired, renovated, rewired, reroofed, and so on) in ways that violate current law. Laws also change. Even if the property originally conformed to all rules and regulations, it may now violate today's legal standards.

Land use law classifies properties as (1) legal and conforming, (2) legal and nonconforming, and (3) illegal. When a property meets all of today's legal standards, it's called legal and conforming. If it met past standards that don't meet current law, but have been grandfathered, the property qualifies as legal but nonconforming.

If the property includes features or uses that violate standards not grandfathered as permissible, those features or uses remain illegal. Even work that conforms to the law might place the owners (present and future) in jeopardy if such work was performed without a valid building or renovation permit.

If you buy a property that fails to meet current law, buy with your eyes open. Lower your offering price to reflect risk. At some future time, city inspectors may require you to bring the property up to code. Or if the property suffers major fire damage, the city may not permit a rebuild (for example, a grandfathered office building in a single-family-zoned district). Health, safety, and environmental violations may present these risks:

♦ Subject your tenants to injury.
♦ Motivate a rent strike.
♦ Expose you to a lawsuit.
♦ Expose you to civil or criminal penalties (fines and, in serious cases, prison).

Before you decide upon the price to pay for a property, verify code compliance. To bring a nonconforming property up to code (or to tear out and reinstall unpermitted work) can cost thousands (or even tens of thousands) of dollars.

Improvements

After you investigate the legal restrictions relative to site size, features, and improvements (for example, parking, driveways, fencing, landscaping, utilities, sewage disposal), detail the size, condition, quality, and appeal of the house or apartment units located on the site. Building size itself ranks as one of the most important determinants of value. To determine size (room count, square footage) requires more than pulling out a tape measure.

As you inspect properties, you'll see converted basements, garages, and attics; you'll see heated and cooled and unheated and uncooled living areas; you'll see bedrooms without closets and dining areas without space for a family-size table and chairs, let alone a buffet or china cabinet; you'll see rooms with 6-foot ceilings or lower, and rooms with 12-foot ceilings or higher; you'll see some storage areas that users can access easily and others that you can reach only by crawling on your hands and knees or standing on a ladder. You'll see decks, patios, and porches constructed of all sorts of materials in all shapes and sizes.

You'll see that all space does not live equally well. You must look beyond measured size, purported space use, or room count. Judge quality, livability, traffic patterns, and functionality.

Even more challenging, not everyone measures square footage in the same way: a builder asked five appraisers to measure one of his new homes. In sales promotion literature, the builder listed the home as 3,103 square feet. One appraiser came up with a square-footage count of 3,047 square feet. The other appraisers came up with measures that ranged between 2,704 square feet and 3,312 square feet. Differences such as these occur not only by mistake but because no square-footage police prescribe or enforce measurement methods.

When you read or hear a property's room count or size, verify that information. Judge the quality, size, and desirability of the space. I once owned a lakefront house with a large master bedroom (MBR) that faced the lake through a full, wall-sized window. In valuing that house, an appraiser rated as equivalent another lakefront home—only its MBR was 40 percent smaller and faced street-side.

In his report, the appraiser made no note of that huge difference (as perceived by most would-be buyers). To compound his errors, the appraiser also rated the lakefront lots equivalent—even though the subject's lot was 40,000 square feet with 165 feet of frontage versus the comp lot at 20,000 square feet with 100 feet of lake frontage. Never accept—without verification—an appraiser's comparable data, properties, or feature adjustments. (I might note that as part of my verification process, I actually visited the owner of that comp house and he even invited me in to look around. Throughout my career, I have often been amazed at how accommodating and forthcoming people will become when you speak with them in a courteous and curious manner.)

THE COST APPROACH

The cost approach recognizes that you can either build (or buy) a new property or buy an existing one. Replacement cost typically sets the upper limit to the price you would pay for an existing property. If you can build a new property for $380,000 (including the cost of a lot), then why pay $380,000 for a like-kind existing property located just down the street? In fact, why pay $380,000 for that older property? It suffers (at least some) physical deterioration.

Calculate Cost to Build New

To follow the logic of the cost approach, refer to the appraisal form. First, calculate the cost to build the property using dollars per square foot. Use a figure that would apply in your area for the type of property you're valuing. To learn these per-square-foot costs, talk with local contractors or consult the Marshall & Swift construction cost manuals in the reference section of your local library or on the Internet (marshallswift.com).

Because replacement costs correlate directly with the size and quality of buildings, accurate measurement precedes accurate valuation. Notice, too, that you add the expense of upgrades and extras (crystal chandelier, high-grade wall-to-wall carpeting, Italian tile, granite countertops, high-end appliances or plumbing fixtures, sauna, hot tub, swimming pool, garage, carport, patios, porches, and so on) to the cost of the basic construction.

Deduct Depreciation

After you calculate today's building costs for the subject property, deduct three types of depreciation: physical, functional, and external.

As a building ages, it becomes less valuable than new construction because of physical depreciation (wear and tear): The property is exposed to time, weather, use, and abuse; it deteriorates. Frayed carpets, faded paint, cracked plaster, rusty plumbing, and leaky roofs bring down a property's value when cocontrasted to new construction. What amount of depreciation remains is your call. To fill in a physical depreciation figure for a building in good condition, estimate, say, 10 percent or 20 percent; if the property appears run-down, you might justify 50 percent depreciation or greater. Or instead of applying a percentage depreciation figure, itemize the costs of the repairs and renovations that would restore the property to like-new condition.

Itemized repairs do not work as well as percentage estimates, because you can't economically upgrade an eight-year-old roof, four-year-old carpeting, or a nine-year-old furnace to like-new condition. Still, one way or another, estimate the degree to which the subject property has depreciated relative to a newly built property of the same size, quality, and features.

Next, estimate the amount of functional depreciation. Unlike wear and tear, which occurs naturally through use and abuse, functional depreciation creates loss of value due to undesirable features such as outdated dark wood paneling, a weirdly designed floor plan, low-amperage electrical systems, fuse boxes, out-of-favor color schemes, or linoleum flooring. A property may show little physical depreciation but still lack appeal to most potential buyers or renters.

External (locational) depreciation occurs when a property fails to reflect the highest and best use for a site. You find a small, well-kept house located in an area now filling up with offices and retail stores. Zoning of the site has changed. More than likely, the house (as a house, per se) may not add much to the site's value. The investor who buys the house would likely tear it down or renovate it and create a retail store or offices.

For such duck-out-of-water properties, external (locational) factors make the buildings obsolete. External depreciation can approach 100 percent. With or without the building, the site should sell at approximately the same price. This principle also applies when neighborhoods move upscale, and well-kept three-bedroom, two-bath houses of 1,600 square feet are torn down and replaced with 5,000-square-foot McMansions. Investors and builders refer to these smaller existing houses as teardowns—even though their owners may have lovingly maintained them. The house adds nothing to the property's value. In fact, it diminishes value to the degree of teardown costs and permitting fees. (Yes, you often pay a permit fee to knock down a structure.)

Lot Value

To estimate lot value, find similarly zoned (vacant) lots that have recently sold, or lots that have sold with teardowns on them. When you compare sites, note all features such as size, frontage, views, topography, legal restrictions, subdivision rules, and other features that can affect the values of the respective sites.

In the Vancouver, Canada, neighborhood where I spend summers, 40- to 50-year-old 1,200-square-foot houses on 33-foot by 120-foot lots sell to builders for $600,000 to $700,000. A lot with a 50-foot frontage and a teardown can sell for $800,000. In Vancouver's Point Grey area, similar neighborhood teardowns on 50-foot lots will easily sell for $1.2 million (perhaps $2 million with bay or mountain views).

Although most people refer to the price increases for *houses*, more often than not, the real increase occurs in the *site*. If you seek price increase as a primary goal, choose your property's site with that goal in mind (see Chapter 4).

Estimate Market Value (Cost Approach)

As you can see on the appraisal form, after you complete these steps (calculate a property's construction cost as if newly built, deduct depreciation, and add in site value), you have computed market value. Because you can't precisely measure construction costs, depreciation, or site value, the cost approach won't give you a perfect answer (of course, neither do the comparable sale or income approaches—reason and judgment rule). But the cost approach does provide a reference point to use with the comp sales and income approaches. It also helps to reveal when a market (or property) is overvalued—priced beyond reason—or perhaps priced below investment value.

Here's an example of the cost approach:

Property description: Six-year-old, good-condition, single-family house of 2,200 square feet. The house includes a two-car, 500-square-foot garage, a deck, in-ground pool, sprinkler system, and premium carpets, appliances, and kitchen cabinets. Nearby vacant lots have recently sold for $60,000.

Dwelling (2,200 × $108 per-square-foot base construction costs)	$237,600
Upgrades	13,500
Deck, lap pool, sprinklers	21,750
Garage (500 × $33 per square foot)	16,500
Total	**$289,350**
Less	
Physical depreciation at 10 percent	(28,935)
Functional depreciation at 5 percent	(14,438)
Depreciated building value	$245,978
Site improvements (sidewalks, driveway, fencing, landscaping)	18,750
Lot value	60,000
Equals	
Indicated market value, cost approach	$324,728

Builders typically build only when they think they can construct properties that will sell (or rent) to yield enough revenue to cover their construction costs and a competitively determined profit margin. You can usually expect market prices of existing properties to increase when construction costs for newly built houses significantly exceed the market values of those houses (or apartments).

Why? Because without the expectation of profit, builders stop building. When growing demand begins to push against a scarce supply, builder profit margins eventually return. The real estate construction cycle starts anew.

When builder profits fatten, sooner or later, they overbuild. High, expected profits lead to a surplus of new construction. Too much housing inventory brings down market values for new as well as existing properties.

Did I hear someone say Las Vegas, Miami, Dublin, or Dubai? Easy financing encouraged buyers to pay prices that (temporarily) supported inflated builder profit margins. Builders overbuilt. Buyers overpaid and overleveraged. Indeed, they overpaid because they could borrow excessive amounts with few qualifying standards.

During the boom, the house valued at $324,728 by the cost approach example would likely have sold for $550,000 to $600,000. The cost to build was far less than the prices at which older properties were selling—a sure sign that home prices had reached unsustainable amounts. But many appraisers paid little attention because they were being paid so well to justify such excessive prices.

Investors rejoice. Overbuilding leads to underbuilding. During the current downturn, new housing starts have nosedived to fewer than

400,000 units—down from 1,600,000 units in 2006. Only large price gains will bring builders back into the game. Until market values significantly increase, homebuilders will not build many new houses (and even fewer condominiums—as their prices in many cities have fallen even more than single-family residences). As new construction sinks—and as inventories of foreclosures and REOs are eventually sold—the market generates the conditions to support the next cyclical upswing.

THE COMPARABLE SALES APPROACH

For houses, condominiums, co-ops, townhouses, and apartment buildings, the comparable sales approach often provides a good estimate of market value. Understand the recent sales prices, terms of sale, physical features, and locational differences of similar properties. Even income approaches require knowledge of comp sales to derive market rent levels, GRMs, and capitalization (cap) rates.

Select Comparable Properties

To apply the comp sales approach, the appraiser (or you) finds recently sold properties that closely match a subject property. Ideally, find comp sales that resemble one another in property size, age, features, condition, quality of construction, room count, floor plan, and location. As a practical matter, you seldom find perfect comp matches because each property, each location, displays unique characteristics.

But you don't need a perfect match. When you find comp sales that appear to be similar to a subject property, ballpark a market value estimate: compare price per square foot of living area.

You research three sales: (Comp 1) 1,680 square feet, (Comp 2) 1,840 square feet, and (Comp 3) 1,730 square feet. These properties sold recently for the respective prices of $225,120, $213,440, and $211,060. To figure the selling price per square foot of living area for these houses, divide the sales price of each house by its total square footage.

Comp 1
$225,120/1,680 = $134

Comp 2
$213,440/1,840 = $116

Comp 3
$211,060/1,730 = $122

If the house you're interested in has 1,796 square feet of living area, it will probably sell in the range of $120 to $130 per square foot, or $215,520 to $233,480.

Approximate Value Range–Subject Property

$120 × 1,796 = $215,520
$130 × 1,796 = $233,480

Sales price per square foot provides a first-pass estimate. To gain more insight, compare and contrast similar properties to your subject property on a feature-by-feature basis. You adjust the sales price for each of the comps—up or down—depending on whether its features look inferior or superior to the subject property.

Adjust for Differences

Here's a brief example of this adjustment process:

Adjustment Process (Selected Features Only)

	Comp 1	Comp 2	Comp 3
Sales price	$225,120	$213,440	$211,060
Features			
Sales concessions	0	−10,000	0
Financing concessions	−15,000	0	0
Date of sale	0	10,000	0
Location	0	0	−20,000
Floor plan	0	5,000	0
Garage	11,000	0	17,000
Pool, patio, deck	−9,000	−13,000	0
Indicated value of subject	$212,120	$205,440	$208,060

As you adjust the selling prices of similar houses, you move toward your best estimate of the market value range for the subject property. Whereas price-per-square-foot indicated a market value range for the subject property between $215,520 and $233,480, after adjustments, a price range between $212,120 and $205,440 seems closer.

Explain the Adjustments

To adjust for differences in size, quality, or features, equalize a subject property and each of its comparables: "At what price would the comparable have sold if it exactly matched the subject property?" Look at the $15,000 adjustment to Comp 1 for financing concessions.

In this sale, the sellers carried back a 90 percent LTV mortgage (10 percent down) on the property at an interest rate of 5.5 percent. At the time, investor financing usually required a 75 percent LTV (25 percent down) and a 6.50 percent interest rate. Without this favorable owner financing, Comp 1 would probably have sold for $15,000 less than its actual sales price of $225,120. Remember, favorable terms of financing often gain sellers a bonus in price. Because the definition of market value assumes financing on terms typically available in the market, the sales price premium generated by this OWC (owner will carry) financing is subtracted from Comp 1's actual selling price. Here are the explanations for other adjustments:

> *Comp 1 garage at (+) $11,000.* The subject property stands superior with its oversize double-car garage, whereas Comp 1 has only a single-car garage. With a larger garage like the subject's, Comp 1 would have brought an $11,000 higher sales price.
>
> *Comp 1 pool, patio, and deck at (–) $9,000.* Comp 1 is superior to the subject property on this feature because the subject lacks a deck and tile patio. Without this feature, Comp 1 would have sold for $9,000 less.
>
> *Comp 2 sales concession at (–) $10,000.* The $213,440 sales price in this transaction included the seller's custom-made drapes, a washer and dryer, and a backyard storage shed. Because these items aren't customary in this market, the sales price is adjusted downward to equalize this feature with the subject property, whose sale will not include these items.
>
> *Comp 2 floor plan at (+) $5,000.* Unlike the subject property, Comp 2 lacked convenient access from the garage to the kitchen. The garage was built under the house; residents must carry groceries up an outside stairway to enter the kitchen. With more conventional and convenient access, the selling price of Comp 2 would probably have increased by $5,000.

Comp 3 location at (–) $20,000. Comp 3 was located on a cul de sac, and its backyard bordered an environmentally protected wooded area. In contrast, the subject property sits on a typical subdivision street, and its rear yard abuts that of a neighbor. Because of its less favorable location (heavier traffic four-lane street), the subject property could be expected to sell for $20,000 less than Comp 3.

Now, you might ask: "How can I or anyone else come up with accurate amounts for each of these adjustments?" Sorry, there's no easy answer. Stock up knowledge by talking with sales agents and tracking sales transactions over a period of months and years. Or, use the PFA technique that many appraisers rely on. What's PFA? Pulled from the air. That's why appraisers offer opinions of market value—not definitive answers.

Even without professional (or PFA) knowledge, critique the opinions of appraisers and real estate agents against your own judgment. Ask questions. Explore their reasoning. Verify their facts. As you look at properties, discipline your mind to list and detail all features that make a difference. Before you attach adjustment numbers to each property's unique features, first observe those differences.

[Investor Alert: Properties with similar features make the best comps for purposes of market value. As far as an appraiser is concerned, the more closely the comps mirror the subject, the easier the market value appraisal. Your discovery process should also look elsewhere. As an investor, you seek to differentiate your property from others. Search out those differences that make a difference. What unique features provide the WOW! appeal that attracts and retains tenants? Discover what few appraisers ever look for: those differences that deliver a compelling value proposition to prospective tenants. For market value appraisals, unique differences add difficulty to the appraisal task. For entrepreneurial investors, unique differences can create value.]

THE GRM INCOME APPROACH

Near the bottom of page 3 on the appraisal form, notice a line labeled "Indicated Value by Income Approach (If Applicable)." This income approach refers to the gross rent multiplier (GRM). To calculate market value using the GRM, find the monthly rents and sales prices of similar houses (or apartment buildings).

Say you discover the following single-family rental houses: (1) 214 Jackson rents for $1,045 a month and sold for $148,200; (2) 312 Lincoln rents for $963 a month and sold for $156,000; and (3) 107 Adams rents for

$1,155 a month and sold for $168,400. With this information, you calculate a range of GRMs for rental houses in this neighborhood:

$$GRM = Sales\ price/Monthly\ rent$$

Property	Sales Price		Monthly Rent		GRM
214 Jackson	$148,200	÷	$1,045	=	142
312 Lincoln	156,000	÷	963	=	162
107 Adams	168,400	÷	1,170	=	144

If the house you value could rent for $1,000 a month, calculate a value range using the GRMs indicated by these other neighborhood rental houses:

GRM		Monthly Rent		Value
142	×	$1,000	=	$142,000
162	×	1,000	=	162,000
144	×	1,000	=	144,000

Thus, the value ranges between $142,000 and $162,000.

The GRM method does not directly adjust for sales incentives, financing concessions, features, location, property condition, or property operating expenses. This technique yields a rough estimate of market value. Nevertheless, for property investors, it works as a rule of thumb. As with the comp sales approach, the GRM derives from similar properties in the same neighborhood.

For apartment buildings, the GRM is calculated from annual rent collections rather than monthly. For example:

Multiunit Income Properties

Property	Sales Price		Total Annual Rents		GRM
2112 Pope (fourplex)	$280,000	÷	$35,897	=	7.8
1806 Laurel (sixplex)	412,000	÷	56,438	=	7.3
1409 Abbot (sixplex)	367,000	÷	53,188	=	6.9

The GRMs shown in these examples do not necessarily correspond to the GRMs that apply in your city. Even within the same city, neighborhoods differ in their GRMs. During the boom within the San Diego area, GRMs for single-family houses in La Jolla exceeded 400; in nearby Claremont, you could find GRMs in the 250-to-300 range. Within the same market area, GRMs for single-family houses typically range higher than those of condominiums. In San Francisco, small multiunit buildings sold for annual GRMs of 14 or higher.

Did such historically high GRMs in San Francisco and San Diego signal overvalued? Absolutely! With such high price and rent multiples, renting cost 50 to 65 percent less than owning. Financially, buying made sense only if you assumed that home prices would continue climbing higher and higher, that is, speculators would continue to buy—no matter how high the price. (Income investors had long before dropped out of the bidding—as per John Burr Williams, p. 30.)

Today in Detroit, Michigan, I have seen annual GRMs of less than 4. Has the market overreacted to Detroit's economic problems? In my area of Florida, I am buying well-kept and appealing properties with annual GRMs of 6 to 8—down from the 10 to 12 GRMs of six years ago.

Unlike Detroit, whose price drops relate to a 40 percent decrease in population and jobs (economic base), the Florida population and job base will continue to grow (especially as the retiring boomers relocate to warmer, higher-quality-of-life Sunbelt states). With construction of new homes in Florida at post–World War II lows, patient investors can wait for inventories of foreclosures to become absorbed. Price gains are virtually assured. Fortunately, too, positive cash flows make that wait profitable.

INCOME CAPITALIZATION

To value apartment buildings, investors also use direct capitalization:

$$V = NOI/R$$

V represents market value. NOI represents the net operating income of the property. R represents the overall rate of return on capital that buyers of similar investment properties require.

Net Operating Income

Net operating income equals the annual gross potential rental income from a property less expenses (vacancy and collection losses, operating expenses, replacement reserves, property taxes, and property and liability insurance). Look through this net income statement for an eight-unit apartment building. Each unit rents for $725 a month:

Income Statement (Annual)

1. Gross annual potential rents ($725 × 8 × 12)	$69,600
2. Income from parking and storage areas	6,750
3. Vacancy and collection losses at 7%	(5,345)
4. Effective gross income	$71,005
Less operating and fixed expenses	
5. Trash pickup	$1,440
6. Utilities	600
7. Registration fee	275
8. Advertising and promotion	1,200
9. Management fees at 6%	4,260
10. Maintenance and repairs	4,000
11. Yard care	650
12. Miscellaneous	3,000
13. Property taxes	4,270
14. Property and liability insurance	1,690
15. Reserves for replacement	2,500
Total operating and fixed expenses	$23,885
16. Net operating income (NOI)	$47,120

The following list explains each of the NOI statement entries:

1. *Gross annual potential rents.* The largest possible sum of rents that you could collect at market rent levels and 100 percent occupancy.
2. *Income from parking and storage areas.* This property has a 16-car parking lot. A shortage of on-street and off-street parking in the neighborhood makes it profitable for the owner to rent the parking spaces independently of the apartment units. Also, the owner built storage bins in the basement of the building that are available for rental to tenants.
3. *Vacancy and collection losses.* Market vacancy rates in the area range between 5 and 10 percent. All units in this building are rented. But even the best-managed apartments experience some vacancies when apartments turn over. Add in some losses for tenants who disappear owing rents that exceed the amounts of their security deposits.
4. *Effective gross income.* The amount of cash that an owner receives net of vacancy and collection, but before operating, fixed, and financing expenses.
5. *Trash pickup.* Self-explanatory.
6. *Utilities.* Tenants pay their own unit utilities. The property owner pays for lighting in the hallways, basement, and parking area.

7. *Licenses and permit fees.* Apartment building owners must sometimes pay for business licenses and other fees. For this property, the owner pays a rental property registration fee.

8. *Advertising and promotion.* These units rent by word of mouth, craigslist.org, or a For Rent sign that's posted on the property. To be safe, however, an advertising and promotion expense of $150 per year per unit is allocated to the operating budget.

9. *Management fees.* The owner of this apartment building self-manages the property. Nevertheless, he should pay himself the same amount he would otherwise have to pay a property management firm. Labor deserves pay and is distinct from return on investment. Do not reward the seller for the work that you will contribute to the property. Count self-management as an expense.

10. *Maintenance and repairs.* The current owner and her husband clean, paint, and make small repairs around the property. These labors deserve payment from the property's rent collections.

11. *Yard care.* The owner pays this amount to one of the tenants to keep the grass cut, rake leaves, and shovel snow off the walks.

12. *Miscellaneous.* This expense covers legal fees, supplies, snow removal from the parking lot, municipal assessments, auto mileage to and from the property, and other items not accounted for elsewhere in the income statement.

13. *Property taxes.* City, county, and state taxes annually assessed against the property. *Beware:* Tax assessors periodically revalue properties to reflect increases in market prices. Future tax bills could jump 30 to 40 percent over the amount of the previous tax years. Similarly, if your purchase price comes in less than the assessor's current assessed value, request that the assessor reduce your taxes (see Chapter 14).

14. *Property and liability insurance.* This insurance reimburses for property damage caused by fire, hail, windstorms, sinkholes, hurricanes, and other perils. It also pays to defend against, and compensate for, lawsuits alleging owner negligence (for example, slip-and-fall cases).

15. *Reserves for replacement.* Building components wear out. The roof, plumbing, appliances, and carpeting must be replaced periodically. Average these costs on a per-year basis.

16. *Net operating income (NOI).* Total all operating expenses and subtract this sum from the effective gross income. The resulting figure equals net operating income (NOI).

When you calculate NOI, include all expenses for the coming year. Never accept a seller's income statement as accurate. Sellers notoriously omit and underestimate expenses. (Corporate CEOs aren't the only ones who try to dress up their numbers to paint a pretty picture.)

Ask to see the seller's tax return IRS Schedule E for the subject property. The truth will probably sit somewhere between the owner-prepared income statement for sales purposes (where income is likely to be overstated and expenses understated) and a tax return (on which some owners understate income and overstate expenses). Even if the seller truthfully reports the most recent past year's income and expenses, estimate how each of those amounts might increase (or decrease) in the coming years. You buy the future, not the past.

Are property tax assessments headed up? Are vacancy rates (or rent concessions) increasing? Have utility companies scheduled any rate increases? Has the seller deferred maintenance on the property? Has the owner allocated sufficient amounts for replacement reserves? Has the seller self-managed or self-maintained the property and therefore failed to include his unpaid managerial and maintenance work as cash expenses? When calculating NOI, accept no numbers on faith. Savvy investors reconstruct seller-prepared NOIs.

Estimate Capitalization Rates (R)

You pay now for the rents the property will produce over the next 20, 30, or 40 years (more or less). The question becomes how much these future rents are worth in today's dollars (that is, the property's market value). If the appropriate capitalization (cap) rate is 8.5 percent, then the market (capital) value of this eight-unit apartment building equals $554,365:

$$\$47,121 \ (NOI) / .085 \ (R) = \$554,365 \ (V)$$

But where does that .085 percent cap rate come from? You estimate it from the cap rates that other investors have applied to buy similar properties. Say a real estate agent provides you NOI and sales price data on four similar apartment buildings that recently sold:

Market Data

Comparable Property	Sales Price	NOI	R
Hampton Apts. (8 units)	$533,469	$43,211	.081%
Woodruff Apts. (6 units)	427,381	35,900	.084
Adams Manor (12 units)	694,505	63,200	.091
Newport Apts. (9 units)	671,241	53,700	.080
Subject (8 units) (estimated)	554,365	47,121	.085

From these data, calculate a market-derived cap rate for each property (after verifying that each sale meets the criteria of a market value transaction). When investors in this area buy small income properties similar to the subject property, they figure cap rates between 8.1 and 9.1 percent. So it appears that the market of comp sales indicates a cap rate of around 8.5 percent for the subject property.

Compare Cap Rates

In your market, you may not discover sufficiently similar properties with such a narrow range of cap rates. You might find that some apartment buildings have recently sold with cap rates of 5 to 6 percent (or lower) and others have sold with cap rates of 8 to 9 percent (or higher). Why such differences?

You pay for a quantity of future rental income, and you pay for the quality of that income. Today's price also incorporates expectations about the future price or income gains for that property. The greater its *expected* rate of appreciation, the higher the price you pay now. Therefore, the higher the quality of the income stream, and the larger the expected gain in price, the lower the capitalization rate (or, conversely, the lower the quality of the property's income and price gain potential—in the eyes of the market—the higher its cap rate).

To illustrate: You compare two fourplexes. Santa Fe Villas is a relatively new property located in a well-kept neighborhood near a city's growth corridor. Several nearby office towers are under construction. Dumpster Manor is located in a deteriorating part of town. Major employers have moved out, closed, or laid off workers. Crime rates are high and moving higher. Two recent drug-related murders made front-page news.

If the annual NOIs for these two fourplexes are, respectively, $24,960 and $12,480, how much would investors pay for each property? If investors applied a 10 percent cap rate to each property's income stream, they would value the properties as follows:

> a. Santa Fe Villas
> $24,960 (NOI)/.10 (R) = $249,600 (V)
> b. Dumpster Manor
> $12,480 (NOI)/.10 (R) = $124,800 (V)

But in the real world, investors would not apply the same cap rate to these very unlike properties and neighborhoods. The *quality* of their income streams differs. Santa Fe Villas offers more stable rents, safe neighborhood, greater convenience to good jobs, and market-expected price growth. Investors might actually capitalize the respective NOIs of these two fourplexes at rates of, say, 6 percent for Santa Fe Villas and 15 percent for Dumpster Manor.

Investors would rather own a property in a prospering area. They will pay more for each dollar of income produced by such a property. But more is not really the issue. The real issue is, how much higher price is justified for the better properties? When market expectations run ahead of reasoned analysis, prices overshoot their real potential for price and income growth. Likewise, a surfeit of bad news and pessimistic expectations can drive prices below (and, correspondingly, cap rates above) the actual risk-and-reward prospects of a disdained property.

Relative Prices: The Paradox of Risk and Appreciation (Depreciation)

Odd as it sounds, higher-priced seemingly low-risk–high-appreciation properties may actually produce more risk and slower gains in price (or even more rapid declines in price) than their low-rent, highly troubled cousins who are located on the wrong side of the railroad tracks. That's why many investors now buy rental houses in Detroit.

Consider this stock market analogy. If you could buy a quality, high-growth company's stock at a price-to-earnings ratio (P/E) of 10 or a low-growth company's stock at a P/E of 10, by all means invest in the high-growth company. If you could buy a low-risk, high-appreciation-potential property with a cap rate of 10 percent or a higher-risk, lower-expected-appreciation property with a cap rate of 10 percent, buy the low-risk, high-appreciation property. However, that's not how markets price either real estate or financial investments.[1] In the real world, investors bid up prices for high-quality, growth-area properties and reduce their bids for so-called high-risk properties in less desirable neighborhoods. To figure out which type of property and location offers the most profit potential, compare their relative prices, cash flows, amortization, and 19 other potential sources of return (see p. xxvi).

When investors optimistically bid up the prices of some properties, neighborhoods, and cities relative to other properties, neighborhoods, and cities, you can profitably redirect your investment strategy (or even withdraw and wait for good sense to return to the market—after the crash). In

---

[1]If you bought Microsoft and JCPenney stock in 1998 and sold in 2004, JCPenney stock would have paid you higher returns. As a high-profile growth company, in 1998, Microsoft's stock included a too-hefty price premium for its expected growth.

other words, don't calculate market cap rates for just one type of property or neighborhood. Learn as much as you can about a variety of submarkets and areas of the country.

You *overpay* for a property when: (1) you apply a cap rate that's too low relative to the property and neighborhood you're buying; or (2) you do not detect that market cap rates themselves may sit too low relative to cash flows, other types of properties, other locations, or even other available investments. In some areas during the boom, cap rates for rental houses fell as low as 3 to 4 percent—well below their historical level of, say, 5 to 10 percent. And well below the level necessary to generate positive cash flows (after paying debt service).

VALUATION METHODS: SUMMING UP

Market value does not necessarily equal appraised value or sale price. Market value refers to the sale price of a property when a sale meets the criteria of a market value transaction. To estimate the market value of a subject property as it compares with other similar properties that have sold, first investigate the terms and conditions under which the comparative properties sold. A property down the street that sold for $600,000 after just three days on the market does not necessarily indicate that a similar property nearby will sell for $600,000. It depends on the terms of sale and the detailed features of each property.

You can apply at least three approaches to estimate the market value of a property, but those three approaches do not necessarily produce the same number. Investors and appraisers rely on imperfect and incomplete data. Decide which approaches best serves your purposes. The accuracy of your market value estimate directly relates to how well you identify and evaluate a property's features. Observe the differences (positive or negative) that make a difference. Wise investment decisions require you to identify and understand features, properties, neighborhoods, construction costs, and lot values. Technique never substitutes for knowledge, close reasoning, and well-informed (but rarely perfect) judgment.

Past price increases (or decreases) do not forecast the future. Market value itself does not warn against buying a property that's about to fall in price. And if you buy at less than market value, you have not necessarily chalked up a bargain. You can make great returns—even when you pay market value (or above)—if you have identified a property (or location) that's about to gain increased popularity or identify a property in which you envision spectacular ways to create value. (Of course, some property investments combine all of these advantages and more: lumps of coal are transformed over time into diamonds.)

Appraisal Limiting Conditions

Property appraisers hedge their estimates of value with limiting conditions. Especially relevant (Figure 3.1) are limitations 1, 2, 6, and 7.

- ♦ Appraisers do not investigate title. They assume that a property's bundle of fee simple rights is good and marketable. For a legal guarantee of property rights, consult a title insurance company.
- ♦ Appraisers do not survey the boundaries of a site, nor do they necessarily note encroachments or other potential site problems. To precisely identify site dimensions, encroachments, and easements, employ a surveyor and walk the property lines.
- ♦ Appraisers examine through casual inspection. To thoroughly assess the soundness of a property and its systems (heating, cooling, electrical, plumbing), hire a competent building inspector and skilled tradespersons.
- ♦ Appraisers gather much of their market information from second-hand sources (real estate agents, government records, mortgage lenders, and others). Appraisers seldom go inside the comp properties that they include in their appraisal reports. Because they incorporate unverified secondhand data, appraisals often err in fact and interpretation. Accept an appraisal report as for-what-it's-worth information. Never weight it more than reason warrants. (As noted, I always verify the appraiser's comp property data before I decide how much respect I should give to an appraiser's estimate of value.)

Valuation versus Investment Analysis

Before you buy, understand the property's market value. Yet market value does not inform sufficiently. Besides figuring out a best guess of market price (or, more accurately, a price range), answer these questions:

- ♦ Will the property generate adequate cash flows?
- ♦ Can you expect the property to increase in price?
- ♦ Can you add value to the property?

To address these investment issues, we turn to the following chapters.

4

MAXIMIZE CASH FLOWS AND GROW YOUR EQUITY

As one technique to estimate market value, divide a property's net operating income (NOI) by the market capitalization rate (R). That estimated value figure can help you judge the merits of a potential investment, but it will not tell you the rate of return that you can expect to earn from a property.

Most investors make mortgage payments from their rents, so all of the NOI does not go into the investor's pocket. Nor does the cap rate measure the return on the amount of cash you invest (that is, the down payment). As a result, your return on investment will differ from the property's cap rate—and if you use leverage wisely, your rate of return will exceed the market-derived cap rate.

To figure *investment* returns (ROI), calculate the cash flows that remain after paying debt service.

WILL THE PROPERTY YIELD GOOD CASH FLOWS?

Calculate before-tax cash flow (BTCF) as follows:

NOI less debt service (annual mortgage payments) equals BTCF

Return to the eight-unit apartment building example from Chapter 3. We calculated NOI for that property at $47,121. Applying an 8.5 percent market cap rate, we figured the property's market value as $544,365:

$$\$544,365(V) = \$47,121(NOI)/.085(R)$$

If you finance this property with a mortgage loan-to-value (LTV) ratio of 80 percent (20 percent down) at 7.5 percent interest, amortized over a term of 25 years, your mortgage and annual payments equal:

$544,365 (capitalized value)
.80 LTV
$443,492 loan amount

With mortgage terms of, say, 7.5 percent, fully amortized over 25 years, the monthly mortgage factor equals $7.39 per $1,000 borrowed (see Table 2.1, p. 50). Your payment equals $3,218 a month—a yearly total of $38,618:

$435,492 ÷ 1,000 = 435.492
435.492 × $7.39 (monthly payment per $1,000 borrowed) = $3,218
12 × $3,218 = $38,618 (yearly amount paid)

Given this amount of mortgage payments (debt service), this eight-unit apartment building brings in a first-year BTCF of $8,503:

$47,121 (NOI)
less $38,618 (yearly debt service)
$8,503 (BTCF)

To calculate your annual cash-on-cash return on investment (that is, your annual rate of return on the actual amount of out-of-pocket cash that you have invested), divide the down payment (original cash investment) into your annual BTCF:

Cash ROI = $8,503 (BTCF)/$108,873 (down payment) = 7.81%

Not bad in today's low interest rate world. But can you increase rents with creative improvements? Is the property strategically positioned for appreciation? If you see strong potential for the property, you might accept a relatively low return from cash flows. Still, maybe you're not happy with an annual BTCF of $8,503 and a cash-on-cash ROI of 7.81 percent. Does this mean you should cross this property off your list? Not necessarily. Before you reject a property that fails to produce satisfactory cash flows, you might look for ways to increase those returns with different terms of financing:

♦ Could you arrange alternative financing with lower annual payments?
♦ Should you decrease (increase) your down payment?
♦ Can you buy at a bargain price?

Arrange Alternative Terms of Financing

As explained in Chapter 2, smart investors think through their financing alternatives. You can restructure the cost and/or terms of financing to improve cash flows. In a first pass through the numbers for this eight-unit apartment building, we assumed a 7.5 percent interest rate amortized over 25 years with a 20 percent down payment. To improve the cash flows, try the following:

♦ Seek a lower interest rate.
♦ Lengthen the term of the mortgage.
♦ Use some type of balloon second mortgage.
♦ Combine several of these alternatives.

To obtain a lower interest rate, switch to an adjustable-rate mortgage, ask for below-market seller financing, buy down the interest rate, or perhaps assume a seller's lower-interest-rate mortgage. Here's how an interest rate of, say, 6.7 percent would boost cash flows:

> Monthly payment per $1,000 at 6.7% for 25 years = $6.88
> 435.492 × $6.88 = $2,996 monthly payment
> 12 × $2,996 = $35,954 annual payments (debt service)
> $47,121 (NOI)
> less $35,954 (yearly debt service)
> $11,167 (BTCF)
> ROI = $11,167 (BTCF)/$108,873 (down payment) = 10.26%

If this BTCF and ROI still fall short of your investment goal, extend the amortization period from 25 to 40 years (with, say, a balloon payment at year 10 or 15, if the lender requires).

> Monthly payment per $1,000 at 6.7% for 40 years = $ 6
> 435 × $6 = $2,610 per month
> 12 × $2,610 = $31,320
> $47,121 (NOI)
> less $31,320 (debt service)
> $15,801 (BTCF)
> ROI = $15,801 (BTCF)/$94,242 (down payment) = 16.77%

As another possibility, assume you obtained bank financing at 7.5 percent interest with a 25-year term. Then say the sellers offer you a $100,000 balloon second mortgage due in five years, with interest only payable at 6 percent. You borrow $335,492 from the bank on its terms, and $100,000 from the sellers on their terms. Here's what your cash flow would look like under this alternative financing arrangement.

335.492 × \$7.39 × 12 = \$29,775 (principal and interest to the bank)
.06 × \$100,000 = \$6,000 (interest only to the seller)
Total annual debt service = \$35,775 (\$29,775 + \$6,000)
\$47,121 (NOI)
less \$35,776 (debt service)
\$11,345 (BTCF)
ROI = \$11,345 (BTCF)/\$108,873 (down payment) = 10.42%

Although the cash flow here falls below the seller-financed transaction, it still beats the baseline bank financing.

My intent is not to suggest which type of financing works best. Rather, it is to encourage you to calculate possible returns through alternative financing possibilities. Then discover which (if any) financing might make an acquisition work—for you and the sellers. In just the few possibilities shown here, your first-year BTCF ranged from a low of \$8,502 to a high of \$15,765. Change the terms of financing and you materially improve (or diminish) the financial performance of a property.

Decrease (or Increase) Your Down Payment

Decrease your down payment and boost your ROI (sometimes, sometimes not). Instead of placing 20 percent down (\$108,873) on this eight-unit property, you close the deal with a 10 percent down payment of \$54,436.50. The seller finances the balance of \$489,928 at 7.5 percent interest for 25 years (with perhaps a shorter-term balloon payoff):

489.9285 × \$7.39 × 12 = \$43,446 (debt service)
\$47,121 (NOI)
less \$43,446 (debt service)
\$3,675 (BTCF)
ROI = \$3,675 (BTCF)/\$54,436 (down payment) = 6.75%

A lower down payment here only leaves a thin margin of cash flow (that is, safety) and drops your cash-on-cash ROI to 6.75 percent. By comparison, here's what happens to cash flow and ROI if you buy with 10 percent down, seller financing at 6.5 percent interest, amortized over 40 years:

459.928 × \$5.85 × 12 = \$32,287 (debt service)
\$47,121 (NOI)

less $32,287 (debt service)
$14,834 (BTCF)
ROI = $14,834 (BTCF)/$54,436.50 (down payment) = 27.25%

This outcome looks attractive. Combine the benefits of the lower interest rate with the leveraged gain from higher LTV and you beat the returns realized with the baseline bank financing (20 percent down, 7.5 percent, 25 years).

In areas of the country with generally high property prices, you may find that well-kept properties (single-family houses, duplexes, fourplexes, small apartment buildings), when financed with high LTV loans, produce negative cash flows. Say that our eight-unit building is located in a prime neighborhood that's in high demand by both owner-occupants and investors. Instead of a cap of 8.5 percent, the market prices properties in this neighborhood with a 7.0 percent cap rate. Given this lower cap rate, this building commands a higher value ($673,157 versus $544,365):

$$\$673,\!157(V) = \$47,\!121(NOI)/.07(R)$$

If you finance 80 percent LTV, you'll invest $134,631 and borrow $538,526. With a 7.5 percent interest rate and a 25-year term, your annual mortgage payment would total $47,756:

538.526 × $7.39 × 12 = $47,756 (debt service)
$47,121 (NOI)
less $47,756 (debt service)
equals
−$635 (BTCF)

In situations of negative cash flow (an alligator), search for low-cost financing. If that doesn't work, cover the negative (feed the alligator) from other income or increase the amount of your down payment. With 30 percent down ($201,947) on a price of $673,157, you would borrow $471,210 and then pay back $43,242 a year:

471.210 × $7.39 × 12 = $41,786 (debt service)
$47,121 (NOI)
less $41,786 (debt service)
$5,335 (BTCF)
ROI = $5,335 (BTCF)/$201,947.10 (down payment) = 2.645%

At least the larger (30 percent) down payment converts your negative cash flow into a positive, but your cash-on-cash return looks anemic. Buy such a property if you can profitably improve it, or when neighborhood property values are about to escalate.

But wait: Before you buy a low-, no, or negative cash flow property, think. Are you overestimating the gains from property or managerial improvements? Do you optimistically believe that strong rates of price gain will occur within your time horizon? Do you possess cash reserves to cover a fall in rents, an increase in vacancies, or both? Where is your margin of safety? Use financing to increase your returns—not to foolishly multiply your risks.

Buy at a Bargain Price

Motivated sellers, short sales, lender-owned properties (REOs, foreclosures, tax sales, uninformed sellers, and other sources of bargains now account for between 30 and 60 percent of all property sales. Distress sales—in some cities—have exceeded 75 percent of total sales.

Some appraisers argue that distress sales now define the market. Not-in-distress sellers who want to sell must compete with the pricing of short sales, foreclosures, and REOs. Sales prices have become so beaten down in some cities that most sales represent bargains—especially when compared to replacement costs, cash flows, and price-to-household-income (affordability) ratios.

Three points of caution:

1. Even if an asking price looks like a bargain relative to the preceding three metrics, hold back your excitement. Verify bargain potential with detailed and accurate feature and price information on comp sales. Even when the asking price seems low relative to cash flow, replacement cost, and affordability ratios, you might still buy for a lower price. The new dominant standard for price is whatever amount the seller will (or must) accept.
2. Keep peak price in perspective. Rarely did peak prices during the boom represent anything but speculative fever. Buying today at, perhaps, 60 percent below peak price does not necessarily imply that you have scored a bargain—much less paid a below-market value price. As I have mentioned, I recently bought a package of condominiums for $36,500 apiece. Each had sold (2005–2006) for $120,000. Before my purchase, recent sales of similar units had occurred at around $45,000. Even a price of $60,000 would have compared favorably to peak price, replacement cost, and cash flow. Yet, at $45,000, it still would not have represented a bargain relative to today's distressed market values.

3. My price of $36,500 per unit looks outstanding compared to all met-
   rics that I applied. Yet, maybe in six months, similar units will sell
   for $25,000. With indefinite economic conditions and what seems
   like a never-ending pipeline of loan defaults and foreclosures,
   prices could sink further before recovery takes hold. But will they?
   I do not think so—at least not in the markets where I am buying.
   But your market may appear more problematic. If supplies of distressed sales or employer layoffs and business closings loom large,
   maybe you should tread more cautiously—yet, remember, during
   "busts" (periods when fear and uncertainty reign) more investors
   err through procrastination than because they invest too soon.

Return to the eight-unit example that was valued with an 8.5 percent
cap rate at $554,365. With the hypothetical baseline bank financing of 20
percent down and 7.5 percent, 25-year terms, the property produced a first-
year cash flow of $8,502. But what if you could buy that property (or a similar
one) at a true bargain price (say, 10 percent under market)? You would pay
$489,928.50, place $97,935.70 down, and borrow $391,942.80 (80 percent).
Your annual debt service would fall to $34,757, and your cash flow (BTCF)
would increase to $11,539:

> 391.943 × $7.39 × 12 = 34,757 (debt service)
> $47,121 (NOI)
> less $34,757 (debt service)
> $12,364 (BTCF)

Your first-year ROI would increase to 12.62 percent:

> ROI = $12,364 (BTCF)/$97,985.70 (down payment) = 12.62

In markets where properties priced at market value fail to give you
the cash flows you want, search for a property that you can buy at a bargain
price. Look for owners plagued by their poorly executed property management, dumb financing, high vacancies, or deferred maintenance. Then offer
them quick relief from their pain.

Should You Ever Pay More than Market Value for a Property?

Recall the negotiating ploy in which you tell sellers that you will pay their
price if the owner will sell on your terms. You stroke the sellers' egos and
give them a price they can brag about. But (ostensibly) you'll earn good

cash flows and a high ROI because you receive a high LTV and low-cost financing.

Staying with the eight-unit example, say the sellers accept a "your price/my terms" offer and set a price of $600,000 ($554,365 market value). You say, "Fine, here are my terms: $25,000 down, 5.75 percent interest, and 40-year payoff period with a balloon note due in 12 years." This arrangement means that the sellers would carry back a mortgage (or contract for deed) in the amount of $575,000. Here's how the numbers work out:

> 575.000 × $5.33 × 12 = $36,777 (mortgage payment)
> $47,121 (NOI)
> less $36,777 (debt service)
> $10,344 (BTCF)
> ROI = $10,344 (BTCF)/$25,000 (down payment) = 41.38%

Wow! These numbers look terrific. Compared with a market value price and bank financing, you've achieved three important objectives: (1) you reduced the cash you need to buy the property; (2) you increased your cash flow; and (3) you lifted your ROI into superstar territory. You can readily see why some authors encourage you to trade off a higher price for low down payment, low-cost OWC financing.

Nevertheless, you created a serious problem. You owe more than the property is worth. Absent a strong increase in market price, you could not sell the property for an amount high enough to pay off the outstanding mortgage balance (a dilemma faced by millions of buyers in the country's recent downturn). Just as troubling, if a newly available refi rate of 5.0 percent becomes available, you could not refinance your outstanding mortgage balance. Your originally favorable financing locks you into a higher-than-market interest rate for what could turn out to be an extended period (especially in a less-than-robust market).

To protect against these risks, negotiate these two financing clauses:

1. *The right to assume.* If a buyer can take over your 5.75 percent seller financing, you increase your ability to sell the property without cash coming out of your own pocket.
2. *The right to prepay the loan balance at a discount.* To help you overcome the owe-more-than-you-own mortgage problem, insert a prepayment discount clause into your financing agreement. If you pay off the seller within the first five years (for example), the seller will discount the payoff balance by, say, 5 or 10 percent. Sellers who are eager to cash out their loan on a property may agree to this discount. (Even when an OWC mortgage does not include a prepayment discount clause, sellers may later accept

such an offer. But if you offer a discount, play it coy. First raise the possibility of early payoff to prompt a reaction from the seller. Generally, the more eager the seller, the greater the discount you negotiate.)

"You set the price, I'll set the terms" can work to decrease your down payment, increase your annual cash flow, and leverage up your ROI. Yet if such prices and terms leave you with negative equity, you've crossed into a minefield of risks. Calculate whether the benefits of the deal outweigh the lurking possibility of loss. Remember Ben Graham's dictum: The first rule of making money: Don't lose it.

And one more time, never assume that market appreciation rates of 6, 8, or 10 percent a year will bail you out of the excessive mortgage problem. Maybe you feel lucky, but most who have bet the ranch . . . have lost the ranch.

The Debt Coverage Ratio

You've seen how financing (mortgage amount, interest rate, amortization period) can increase or decrease your annual cash flows and ROI. Now, recall that the lender may apply a debt coverage ratio (DCR) as one of its underwriting criteria. The lender wants to see whether the property's NOI is large enough for you to pay back the loan and provide a margin of safety. For example:

$$DCR = \$47,121 \ (NOI)/\$36,618 \ (debt\ service) = 1.22$$

For moderate- to high-quality apartment buildings, a DCR range of 1.1 to 1.3 usually proves acceptable to lenders (though today more will push the higher number). If a property's NOI fails to provide enough cushion for the lender, rework the terms of the financing. Investors frequently work their deals not only to meet their own cash flow requirements but also to meet a lender's required DCR.

Numbers Change, Principles Remain

Previous discussions focused on the cash flows of an eight-unit apartment building with a variety of interest rates, loan balances, amortization periods, cap rates, and purchase prices. The numbers used in these examples illustrate techniques and principles—not the specific numbers you should apply in your market or for your investment goals.

In Tulsa, not long ago, you could buy a good eight-unit rental property for less than $300,000. In San Francisco, you can pay $2 million for a similar building. In Tulsa, I've seen cap rates over 10 percent. In San Francisco, I've seen them at less than 4 percent. Property markets differ. Even within the same city, properties, neighborhood quality, gross rent multipliers, and terms of financing vary.

When you buy condos, single-family houses, or small apartment buildings, search throughout your local area. Talk with *well-informed* and *investment-savvy* realty agents, mortgage loan officers, real estate appraisers, and property managers, as well as other experienced real estate investors.

As you discover the numbers that seem sensible in your market, work through market value, cash flow, and ROI figures. Investing profitably means *structuring* deals to yield positive cash flows and high ROIs while avoiding foolish financial and operational risks. Buy at a below-market price and you increase your odds of success. But price represents just one variable. Without positive cash flows, a seemingly bargain-priced acquisition can quickly turn against you.

WILL THE PROPERTY YIELD PROFITABLE INCREASES IN PRICE?

Over longer periods, average price increases of 3 or 4 percent per year can add hundreds of thousands of dollars to your net worth.

Buy just one rental unit at a price of $100,000 and finance it with a $90,000 mortgage at 6.5 percent interest over a 30-year term. After 15 years, at an annual price growth rate of 4 percent, that $100,000 unit would be worth $180,000. Subtract your outstanding mortgage balance of $64,803, and your $10,000 down payment has grown 11-fold to $115,197. After 30 years, your mortgage balance would drop to zero. The value of the property at an assumed long-term 4 percent (appreciation rate + inflation rate) yearly average rate of price growth) would total $324,340.

With fear and uncertainty prevalent today, perhaps any rate of price growth may seem like a stretch. That's the way most people felt during the severe Vancouver housing recession of 1981, the California housing recession of 1991, and the Hong Kong property price crash of 1998. Yet, property prices in these areas today are up 3 to 10 times from those earlier years when bleak outlooks clouded vision. During the 1973–1974 U.S. housing collapse, a home I owned at the time fell in value from $50,000 to $40,000. Three years later in 1977, that house sold for $72,000. In 2004, it sold for $218,000 (though I no longer owned it at that time).

When does price growth for properties look most promising? When prices have accelerated 10 to 20 percent per year for six years running? Or now, when prices have cratered, home affordability ranks near an all-time high, and market values sit below replacement costs? Of course, you know the answer. Now—or at least soon.

Buy just three or four $100,000 (more or less) investment properties within the next several years—before recovery moves into high gear—and within 15 to 20 years, your net equity from those units will total somewhere between $500,000 and $750,000. With modest increases in rents, your income from these properties could reach $5,000 to $8,000 a month. As Einstein supposedly observed, "Compound interest represents the most powerful force in the world."

And these amounts result from only three or four units! After 18 years, today's rent of, say, $1,000 a month would grow to $2,000 a month—assuming a long-term average annual increase of 4 percent. The GRM for this price/rent ratio equals 100. The properties that I have purchased this year yield monthly GRMs of 65 to 80. Over time, I expect rents to increase, but I also expect the GRM to climb back up to its long-term average (in my area) of 110 to 130. Higher rents plus a higher rent multiple will double the prices of these properties within 10 years—at least, that's my (possibly optimistic) forecast. If this forecast falls short, no problem. My cash-on-cash returns are outperforming any other investment alternative available today (CDs, bonds, stock dividends).

I might add that a doubling of prices in 10 years from now would still leave my current acquisitions at prices below their peak of 2006. In other words, their prices at that future time would not have returned to the prices they had attained 15 years earlier. Anything's possible, but such a result has never occurred in U.S. history—though it has in Japan and Germany.

Low-Involvement versus High-Involvement Investing

Buy and hold investment properties for income and price growth (appreciation plus inflation) for a period of 15 to 30 years (or more) and you've put in place a low-involvement investment strategy. Anyone who seriously wants to build a secure net worth can come up with the limited time and money necessary to make this modest strategy pay off.

If you want to build equity in property over a shorter period, however, then pursue high-involvement strategies to boost value. High involvement won't necessarily require more cash, but it will require more time, effort, knowledge, and market research.

To beat the market average price increases, spot communities, neighborhoods, and properties that are positioned for increased popularity and faster appreciation. Especially in perilous times (when fear and confusion drives others to the sidelines), opportunities to score large price increases multiply. Look for those areas that signal strong potential. Here's how to find these promising performers.

Compare Relative Prices of Neighborhoods (Cities)

An oft-cited cliché in real estate tells investors to "buy in the best neighborhoods you can afford; the best neighborhoods always appreciate the fastest." On closer inspection, this advice makes no sense. No neighborhood or community can persistently outperform all others. The law of compound interest proves the statement false. (Similarly, recall that the stock price of Microsoft—a great company—was higher in 1999 than it was in January of 2012.)

Here's a numeric example of this point: You can choose between a neighborhood where apartment buildings are priced at $100,000 per unit (Summerville) and a neighborhood where apartment buildings are priced at $50,000 per unit (Modest Manor). Within the recent past, properties in Summerville jumped in value by 8 percent a year. Units in Modest Manor have moved up by only 3 percent a year. Can Summerville outpace Modest Manor forever? Not likely. A look at projected price growth shows why.

Future Price Growth
Summerville versus Modest Manor

Years	$100,000 Units at 8% p.a.	$50,000 Units at 3% p.a.
3	$125,970	$54,635
6	158,690	59,700
9	199,900	65,200
12	251,820	71,250
15	317,222	77,900
20	466,100	90,300

Today, rental units in Summerville are priced *twice as much* as those located in Modest Manor. But after 20 years of (assumed) faster price growth, these superior higher-priced units would cost *more than five times as much* as their inferiors. Unless some rare market forces were at work, such an unbalanced situation would not occur.

Long before such exaggerated price differences could result, increasing numbers of potential investors, homebuyers, and tenants would become priced out of Summerville. In response, they would switch their buying (or renting) to Modest Manor. Price gains in Summerville would slow. Price gains in Modest Manor would accelerate.

The intelligent investor never assumes that past rates of price growth (or decline) will trend line into the future. Intelligent investors compare the prices and features of a variety of properties, neighborhoods, and cities. They compare local economies. They note changes up or down in the number of for-sale and for-rent properties. Then they search for properties and locations that show the best possibilities for price growth.

Undervalued Neighborhoods and Cities

At any time and in any area, no fixed relationship applies to neighborhood or community potential. Sometimes lower-priced areas represent a great buy. At other times, higher-priced areas look best. Sometimes new developments beat established neighborhoods; sometimes established beats new. Nor can anyone advise definitively about close-in versus far-out, well-kept versus run-down, or low-crime versus high-crime. Neither racial nor ethnic composition, nor household income level, nor occupational status necessarily relates to the potential price gains of a neighborhood.

The neighborhood or city that offers the best outlook for price gains is the neighborhood (city) where growth prospects, property prices, and rent levels look good relative to the growth prospects, prices, and benefits offered by other areas. Also, today, some neighborhoods, cities, and states have experienced far more foreclosures and distressed sales than others.

Accordingly, their current situation looks bleak and their prices have fallen more than prices of peer or superior areas. In many instances, property prices in such areas now sit proportionately lower than at any previous time. They present an all-time price/feature/benefit advantage (relatively speaking). I will bet that such areas—once their problems are alleviated—will rebound faster and stronger than the areas that are now experiencing less pain.

Consider one of my favorite examples of how modest can appreciate faster than classy.

Beverly Hills versus Watts (South Central Los Angeles)

Between 1985 and 1989, property prices in prestigious Beverly Hills had shot up by 50 percent or more. During the same period, property prices in the troubled neighborhood of Watts had barely budged. But by 1995, $5 million (1989) properties in Beverly Hills were selling at reduced prices of $3 million to $4 million, whereas $85,000 (1989) properties in Watts were selling at the increased price of $125,000. Between 1989 and 1995, property investors who owned units in troubled South Central Los Angeles outperformed investors or homeowners who owned properties in the movie star haven of Beverly Hills.

In response to this fact, here's what I wrote in 1995 in the second edition of this book: "Will appreciation rates in South Central continue to outpace Beverly Hills? I don't think so. Relative to other premier neighborhoods in world-class cities, houses in Beverly Hills now stand as terrific bargains. With the California economy at last climbing out of recession, house prices and rentals in Beverly Hills may now be positioned to hit new record highs."

Looking back now, you can see that this forecast proved correct. Between 1995 and 2005, upscale property prices in California did hit record highs. Although South Central prices also continued to climb, you would have made better returns from price growth had you invested in Beverly Hills. (Of course, Watts still yielded higher cash on cash returns.) Between 2008 and 2009 in Dubai, the multimillion-dollar villas located on world-famous Palm Jumeira suffered price declines of 50 percent or more. During this same period, the modest town homes of Dubai's International City held their value. Dubai had built an excess supply of top-end condominiums and villas, whereas affordable units such as those located within International City remained in short supply relative to the demographics of the population. (I am just contrasting relative drops in price between high class and declass—for other reasons, I advised against investing in International City—then and now.)

Investors can profit (or avoid loss) when they study neighborhood property prices relative to features, benefits, and buyer/renter demographics. Savvy investors never prejudge. They gather facts about supply and demand. They reason. They forecast the future. They neither extrapolate the past into the future nor do they apply clichés and slogans to anticipate price movements.

Apart from relative prices, what facts should you compare?

◆ Demographics
◆ Accessibility
◆ Job centers
◆ Taxes, services, and fiscal solvency
◆ Construction and renovation
◆ Land use laws
◆ Civic pride
◆ Sales and rental trends

Demographics

Demographics refers to income levels, occupations, education, ages, household size, household composition, and other population characteristics. You can obtain such data from the U.S. Bureau of the Census and commercial market research firms (see www.census.gov). The magazine *American Demographics* alerts its readers to emerging demographic trends. Truly news you can use.

More important than *current* neighborhood demographics, learn who is moving *into* the area. A historically lower-income area that's attracting middle- or even upper-middle-income younger residents points toward appreciation potential. Likewise, an area in which many residents are moving from welfare to jobs signals turnaround.

To learn about the people in an area, get out of your car. Talk with residents who are working in their yards or walking their dogs. Talk with Realtors, mortgage loan reps, retail shop owners, schoolteachers, postmen, taxi drivers, policemen, government planners, and others whose firsthand, everyday experience places them in the know about an area.

Ask anyone and everyone how the area is changing and whether they see these changes as positive or negative. Ask the people you talk to what they like least and what they like most about the neighborhood. Evaluate what you hear, see, and research. Then form your own conclusions. Do you think the people moving into the neighborhood are likely to push up home prices and rental rates? Or does filtering down point to deterioration?

Accessibility (Convenience)

Areas don't change their position on the face of the earth. Nevertheless, they can become more or less convenient relative to other areas and relative to their own past. Several years back, I chose to buy property in the southeast part of town rather than the more popular northwest corridor. Why? Lower prices, similar quality, and easier accessibility. Because of rapid growth and development, the freeway leading to the northwest corridor had become congested. What had been a 15- to 20-minute drive to town from those suburban neighborhoods was now taking 45 to 60 minutes. And traffic was getting worse.

As a result, increasing numbers of renters and homebuyers decided that they did not want the hassle of fighting traffic every day. They switched their preferences to the east and southeast developments. Within three years, my properties jumped in value by 40 percent. Momentum feeds upon itself for a while.

Improved (Increased) Transportation Routes

Find out whether an area might become more (or less) convenient because of changing (or lower or higher cost) commutes. Are any new or expanded freeways or toll roads planned or under construction? What about bridges, ferries, subways, trains, or bus service? Will travel to and from a neighborhood or community become easier, cheaper, or faster? After the Eurotunnel connected England to France, British demand for vacation homes doubled the (historical) appreciation rate of attractive French properties. Discount airlines such as Jet Blue have increased the demand for Florida properties—especially among New Yorkers and the Northeast.

Can you recall 15 or 20 years ago when some of those outlying developments were built in your area? Are they still outlying? Perhaps now they are situated just minutes from shopping centers, office complexes, and restaurants. Developments, cities, or even countries that yesterday seemed remote are now positioned for easy access.

Close-in can also increase the relative attractiveness of neighborhoods. High gasoline prices, traffic congestion, walk-to-shops-and-restaurants lifestyle preferences, and environmental consciousness have invigorated demand for many in-city neighborhoods throughout the United States and other countries. In fact, my investment choices run heavily toward close-in and especially revitalizing or gentrifying close-in.

Jobs and Economic Base

People prefer to live close to their jobs. When you search for price growth potential, discover neighborhoods that are situated near employers or employment centers that will add jobs to their payrolls. Look for new or expanding office districts, factories, shopping centers, and distribution facilities. As these job sites fill up with employees, they will push up the prices and rents of nearby housing. When Sarasota Regional Medical Center underwent a major expansion, home prices in nearby neighborhoods jumped 40 percent within just a few years.

Today, layoffs and employer closings seem more prevalent than growth. Yet, when an area shows longer-term potential, dark days reflect bright days for investing. Believe it or not, I am betting on a comeback (of sorts) for Detroit. No, I doubt that this city will ever regain the economic base and prosperity it enjoyed in 1950—when it was the fourth-largest city in the United States. But community effort, rock-bottom property prices, and the rebirth of a profitable auto industry might reward investors who buy now. Communities require basic employers.

Taxes, Services, and Fiscal Solvency

As you ferret out neighborhoods, communities, and even countries in which to invest, check their property taxes, government services, political stability, and fiscal fitness. Does the area offer a high level of services and social programs? Are the public finances of the area well managed? Does the tax/benefit ratio for the community compare favorably with other areas? Consider all taxes and services. Do community governments provide residents relatively good value?

Co-ops, condos, and housing developments governed by homeowners' associations present another layer of inquiry. A homeowners' association (HOA) functions as a government within a government. It issues rules and regulations, it provides services and recreational amenities, and it charges legally enforceable fees and assessments.

If you plan to buy a property that is governed by an owners' association, check out the association's bylaws, services, fees, financial reserves, and fiscal solvency in the same way that you would check out a local government. Some property owners' associations have failed to put aside enough money to fund repairs and improvements.

Especially troubling today, many condo complexes are suffering high rates of foreclosure and defaulting unit owners are not paying their HOA fees and assessments. The remaining unit owners are getting stuck with higher fees to make up the difference. Higher HOA fees incite more defaults and depress condo prices further. A vicious cycle is set in motion. Nevertheless, many state laws do provide homeowner association priority liens against units with unpaid fees and assessments. Eventually, the HOAs should be able to collect amounts owed.

When that collection occurs (if it occurs), when condo complexes stabilize their budgets and fees; and when the number of foreclosures recedes, condo prices will again see strong price gains. Massachusetts, Connecticut, and Florida, for example, have experienced these vicious condo cycles previously—and each time, after their crash, condo prices recovered stronger than ever.

If you are willing to invest patient money, accept some risk, and satisfy yourself with a reasonable current return in terms of cash flow, I suggest you look at the condo bargains that now are flooding markets in many cities.

(For more discussion of condominiums, see my book, *Make Money with Condominiums and Townhouses* [John Wiley & Sons, 2002]. At the time I wrote that book, condo prices had been down for a decade. But their rents had increased. Condos cash flowed much better than single-family houses—and they were more affordable. I believe that they offer even greater opportunities for price growth today than in 2002—though possibly with more risk now.)

New Construction, Renovation, and Remodeling

Are neighborhood property owners (especially those who have recently bought into the area) upgrading their properties? Are they painting exteriors, remodeling interiors, building additions, or installing amenities such as central heat and air, decks, patios, hot tubs, or skylights? Do you see properties brought back to life after years of neglect? Do you see front yard dumpsters loaded with remodeling debris? Check with contractors, home improvement stores, and government building inspectors. Note trends in building permits for the area. Learn whether spending for property improvements is increasing.

Look for new construction of housing, office buildings, manufacturing plants, retail stores, or parks and recreational facilities. New construction not only creates jobs, but if properly integrated into an area, it increases the area's desirability. Research the prices and rental rates of any housing that's newly built or under construction. Is the new housing more expensive than the existing homes and apartments? If so, these higher prices indicate that a neighborhood is moving upscale.

Of course, now, construction of new houses and condominiums has nearly stopped. We experienced somewhat similar—though not so dramatic— curtailment of construction of rental apartments during the 1990s—after the bust of the late 1980s.Then, as now, lenders tightened financing for new subdivisions, condominiums, and apartments. Builders today struggle to find reasonable cost financing. During the 1990s, fewer new rental units were built than in any other 10-year period since the 1960s. Eventually, pent-up demand (fueled by easy money) ignited the 2002–2007 boom.

After 2002, new construction accelerated. Builders set new records for construction of housing units—especially in such hot spots as Miami, Phoenix, and Las Vegas. Even worse, much of this excess was sold to speculators and shaky credit buyers. A severe downturn was sure to follow such excesses.

Before you invest, check whether new housing in competing areas is renting (selling) without difficulty and that vacancy rates aren't flying up toward 10 percent or higher. (Your local planning and building permits agency keeps detailed records of past, present, and planned construction.) Smart investors position themselves to profit from a down cycle. When foreclosures and REOs pile up and new housing starts collapse, they pluck out the bargains.

Land-Use Laws

Land-use laws include zoning, building codes, health and safety rules, occupancy codes, rent controls, environmental protection, historical preservation, architectural review boards, and many other laws, rules, and regulations. These laws may restrict growth and increase costs of development.

To forecast price gains for an area, learn community attitudes toward growth. Do current (or pending) land-use laws limit construction and drive up building costs? Is government restricting new supply? Is the amount of buildable land in short supply over the mid to long run? While debates rage between pro-growth and no-growth forces, experience shows that in desirable areas where no- or slow-growth attitudes prevail, rent levels and housing prices are pushed up. Compare the rate of increase in housing starts to the rate of growth in new households. A shortage of zoned, buildable land primes an area for above-average price gains—as long as the jobs, incomes, and desirability of the area increases.

Pride of Place

You're not buying the past; you're investing in the future. You and other property owners in an area can join together to improve the prospects of an area. Civic pride, community spirit, and community action can upgrade a neighborhood with a poor reputation into one that becomes the place to be. Contrary to received opinion, you can change and improve the location of a property. Do neighborhood residents display pride of place? Are they working individually and collectively to make their community a better place to call home? Are they cooperating with the people responsible for government services such as schools, libraries, police, street maintenance, parks and recreation, and public health? Are residents and public officials solving problems such as crime, graffiti, school quality, traffic congestion, or littered public areas?

Locate a neighborhood with plans for improvement, and you locate a neighborhood with strong potential for price gains. When you, other property owners, and tenants work together, civic pride and community action can transform an ugly duckling into a peacock. (For dozens of examples, see *Fixing Broken Windows*, by George Kelling and Catherine Coles [Free Press, 1996].)

Sales and Rental Trends

Among the leading indicators of rising (or falling) property prices are sales trends and rental trends. As you move forward to a profitable career in real estate investing, create a system for tracking and recording trend data such as the number of for-sale listings, new housing starts, sales prices, time on market, rent levels, and vacancy rates. Watch these trends. Detect market changes as they occur and you can earn large short-term gains.

Sales Trends. As prices begin to increase in a neighborhood, time-on-market data will show increasingly faster sales. In slow markets, properties can sit unsold for months (180, 270, or 360 days, or longer). As average time on market falls from, say, 270 days to 180 days to 120 days, prices are about to go up. A decreasing inventory of for-sale properties also points the way towards an upswing in property prices. Today, the pipeline of foreclosures is still spilling out supply. When these numbers begin to trend down (and hopefully) as the numbers of people working show meaningful gains, and when the number of For Sale and For Rent signs begin to disappear, recovery can be seen on the horizon.

At the ebb of San Diego's major recession of the early 1990s, the local MLS included 18,000 homes for sale. By 2004, that number had fallen to 6,000. No wonder prices increased as for-sale properties declined in number while jobs, population, households, income, and wealth continued to grow. In 2004, the Las Vegas MLS listed 2,700 houses for sale. By 2007, that number had exploded to more than 17,000. Should a crash in prices have surprised anyone?

Rental Market Trends. Rental market trends include: (1) vacancy rates, (2) time on market, (3) annual rent increases (or rental concessions), and (4) rates of owner occupancy.

Review the past 12 to 24 months. Are area vacancy rates falling or increasing? How long do vacant apartments or rental houses sit empty before they're rented? Visit a sampling of vacant units. Then follow up to learn their lease-up periods. What types of units rent the quickest? How do vacancy rates differ among various neighborhoods and communities? Do some types of buildings or units enjoy waiting lists? What features and locations?

Follow postings on Craigslist. Telephone or e-mail listings posted a week or two earlier. Have they rented? What similarities and differences do you note among the units that rent quickly and those that linger unrented for weeks. How do rent level, unit size or room count, neighborhood, specific complex, pet policies, and so forth, correlate with time on market? Slow movers? Fast movers?

Are rents steady or increasing? Or are property owners offering concessions like one or two months' free rent for a 12-month lease? Are homes in the area primarily owner occupied or tenant occupied? In which direction is the area trending? Look for areas where tenants are being squeezed out by homebuyers. Higher proportions of homeowners usually signal higher property prices and higher rental rates for the relatively few rental units that remain.

Every general principle gives rise to exceptions. During the latest boom, houses in family-dominated neighborhoods close to the University of Florida jumped 50 to 100 percent in value in less than five years—even though renters were increasingly displacing homeowners.

Why? Investors had discovered that they could lease these houses to groups of students and collect rents of $1,500 to $2,500 per month. They bid up prices. Out-of-town parents also entered the market. They would buy a house for a son or daughter—who would then bring in several other students as roommates and charge each one $400 to $500 per bedroom.

The lesson: Learn trends early. Track the data. Talk with those who live and work in the area. Accumulate and act upon insider information.

SUMMING UP

To discover properties that will gain from higher-than-average price growth, track market data. Monitor changes in job base, property selling prices, housing inventories, vacancy rates, accessibility, pride of place, and community action. Property prices and rent levels gallop ahead or fall behind because buyers and tenants shop neighborhoods and communities to discover the most attractive *relative values*.

5

PAY LESS THAN MARKET VALUE

When stockbrokers and financial planners compare the profit potential of property to stocks, they often err: They ignore the return-boosting power of leverage; they forget that property cash flows alone can yield 7 to 12 percent (more or less); they fail to recognize that investors can enhance value through market research and smart management. And they miss the fact that (unlike with stocks), investors often buy property at a price less than its current market value.

If the NYSE market for Wal-Mart shares sets a price of $20 each, you will pay $20 per share. No shareholder need sell for less. The stock market instantly accommodates all sellers at the market price. From Apple to Xerox, no shareholder ever needs to cut his price below the current market value. Property markets work differently. If you want to pay $200,000 to $225,000 for a $250,000 property, you can find sellers who will oblige. Every day, some properties sell at below-market prices.

Of course, the fact that sales take place at below-market prices begs the real question: Does a below-market price mean that you have negotiated a good deal or a bargain purchase? Does a below-market price guarantee that you've made a wise investment? Absolutely not. Should you try to buy at a below-market price? Absolutely. Do I contradict myself? No. Here's what I mean.

If market values are about to head south in a hurry, then your price of $225,000 for a $250,000 property might not look so good. If the property suffers undiscovered defects and never-ending maintenance and repair expenses, you may regret that you ever saw the place. If the property eats up all of your rent collections (and more), any perceived gain from that below-market price quickly disappears. If you can't clear the title you obtained by a sheriff's deed, or evict a recalcitrant foreclosed homeowner from the property, your legal costs, efforts, and delays might overwhelm your price savings. If you could have newly built a similar property for 20 percent less than the below-market price you paid, then you probably should have chosen the new construction.

Never confuse below-market price with great bargain or wise investment. Sometimes yes—when other pieces fit. Sometimes no. Those motivated sellers that we all like to find may have become motivated for reasons other than the reasons they disclose to you. Below-market value represents *one* metric by which you can evaluate a potential investment. Never rely on this measure as the only measure.

Cash flows, replacement costs, appreciation (or depreciation) potential, market timing, affordability ratios—rely on these and other metrics along with below-market price. Below-market price does not assure profits. But below-market value often points in that direction.

WHY PROPERTIES SELL FOR LESS (OR MORE) THAN MARKET VALUE

Recall from Chapter 3 that a *market value* sale assumes these five conditions:

1. Buyers and sellers are typically motivated. Neither acts under duress. *Today:* More than 50 percent of sellers suffer emotional and financial stress.
2. Buyers and sellers are well informed and knowledgeable about the property and the market. *Today:* Out-of-town distressed owners and bank REO managers may never have seen the property. (Yes, during the boom many investors bought properties they had never seen—and even in cities they had never visited.)
3. The marketing period and sales promotion efforts are sufficient to reasonably inform potential buyers of the property's availability (that is, no forced or rushed sales). *Today:* Auctions, foreclosure sales, distressed sellers, and REO managers do not market and promote their properties effectively, nor do they want to wait for a sale to occur through a normal time-on-market sales period.
4. Ordinary terms of purchase: bank financing on terms typically available apply (for example, no low- or nothing-down seller financing, all cash purchases, below-market interest rate). *Today:* Anything's negotiable—though clearly, cash and 800 credit scores are king.
5. No unusual concessions by either the seller or the buyer (for example, sellers are not permitted to stay in the house rent free for three to six months until their under-construction, new house

is completed, buyers' offer contingent upon the sale of their current residence). *Today:* Anything's negotiable with lender owners (REOs), properties mortgaged with nonperforming loans (for example, short sales), and motivated sellers.

Today, the entire meaning of a normal sale or market value transaction is open for debate. If the market is dominated by homebuyers or investors who are searching for a super deal *and* sellers who want or need to sell now—often without firsthand knowledge (for example, bank REO departments) of the market, location, and property, then such a market offers both heightened opportunities and enhanced dangers.

Opportunity because motivated sellers remain abundant. Anything may be open for negotiation. Danger because market value itself has become a moving target. Without the standard or normal terms of sale and marketing process—at least, normal according to traditional criteria—investors must verify below-market price with more diligent research than was typically necessary in the preboom, normal years.

Today, it's easier than ever to buy at a below-market price, but it remains more difficult than ever to accurately estimate market value. That's one reason wise investors double and triple check their bargain price offers with multiple value metrics and other market indicators (especially trends in new home and apartment construction, the for-sale and for-rent markets, employment numbers, and mortgage defaults and delinquencies. (In fact, investors often selectively use such information, when negative, to support a lower-price offer.)

Owners in Distress

As news stories vividly report, every day people hit hard times. They lose their jobs, file for divorce, suffer accidents or illness, experience setbacks in their business, fall behind on their car loans, credit cards, and mortgage payments, and get hit by a freight train of other problems. Any or all of these calamities can create financial distress. For many of these property owners, their only way out of a jam is to raise cash by selling their property fast.

Some investors find it distasteful to prey on the down and out. Yet owners who find themselves in financial distress long to get rid of their sleepless, toss-and-turn nights. If that means selling their property for less than it's worth, then that's what they're willing to do. These people do not just sell a property; they buy relief.

Under such circumstances, when the sellers believe they have gained more from a sale than they've lost, both parties win. If you want to help people cope with adversity—as opposed to fleecing them—seek out distressed owners who will give you the bargain price (or favorable terms) you want. In exchange, the sellers can begin to rebuild.

Today, the long-standing practice of negotiating a below-market price with troubled property owners has taken on an additional element. Because most (but not all) of these distressed owners owe more on their properties than they could ever hope to realize from a sale (market value or otherwise), the investor must negotiate a reduced loan payoff (called a short sale) with the sellers' mortgage lender. (For the short sale technique, talk with a forclosure pro. See pp. 149–150.)

The Grass-Is-Greener Sellers

In contrast to distress sellers, grass-is-greener folks see better pastures elsewhere. One day Karla Lopez is sitting in her Boston office. In walks the executive vice president of her firm. "Karla," he says, "Lucinda Jackson, head of the Denver branch, just quit. If you want her job as district manager, you can have it. We will pay you $40,000 more a year plus bonus. But you must relocate within 30 days."

"Do I want it?" Karla responds. "Of course I want it. A promotion like this is why I've been working 70-hour weeks for these past four years."

Think about it. In this situation, does Karla think, "Well, the first thing I must do is put my house up for sale and go for top dollar"? Hardly. More than likely, Karla wants to strike a deal with the first buyer who gives her any type of offer she can live with. Karla has her sights set on the greener grass of Denver. Optimistic about her career and facing a time deadline, Karla wants to get her house sold as quickly as possible.

("Well, she could rent it out," you might think. And that's what I might recommend. But, so many times I have found that people only prefer this choice in hindsight—after a period of years when they look back and say, "You know, I never should have sold that property." Indeed, I confess, I have said that myself on several occasions.)

Grass-is-greener sellers stand opposite to the financially distressed. Whereas distressed owners sell on bargain terms or price to relieve themselves of pain, grass-is-greener sellers will accept an offer of less than market value so they can quickly grab better opportunities that lie elsewhere.

On one occasion when I was a grass-is-greener seller, I not only gave my buyers a slight break on price, but more importantly from their perspective, I let them assume my below-market interest rate first mortgage and carried back an unsecured note for the amount of the difference between the price they paid and the outstanding balance on the mortgage they assumed (that is, they bought with nothing down and below-market terms). On various occasions, I've bought from sellers who were eager to pursue better opportunities elsewhere. Each time, I negotiated a good (if not great) price and favorable financing.

If looking for distressed owners doesn't appeal to you, turn your search in the opposite direction. Sellers who want to move to greener pastures (especially under a deadline of time) are frequently the easiest people to work with and the most accommodating in price and terms.

Stage-of-Life Sellers

When shopping for below-market-price deals, find bargains among stage-of-life sellers. These sellers include owners whose lifestyle now conflicts with their property. They may no longer enjoy a big house or yard, collecting rent, or dealing with tenant complaints. They eagerly anticipate their move to that condo on the fourteenth green at the Bayshore Country Club. Or perhaps they would rather not go through the trouble of renovating, updating, and repairing their current property. Whatever their reasons, stage-of-life sellers are motivated to get on with their lives.

In addition—and this fact makes these sellers good prospects for a bargain price or terms—stage-of-life sellers have typically accumulated large amounts of equity in their properties. And because they're older, they may have large savings or other investments. Stage-of-life sellers remain open to offers. They don't need to squeeze every last penny out of their sale—or pocket all cash from the deal. Because stage-of-life sellers often do not face a pressing need for cash, they make excellent candidates for OWC (owner will carry) financing.

Not only will OWC terms help them sell their property more quickly, but an installment sale reduces or defers the capital gain taxes that a cash sale might otherwise trigger (if the property does not qualify for the principal residence tax exclusion benefit; see Chapter 14). As another advantage, OWC financing—even when offered at below-market interest rates—will often net the sellers a higher cash income return than they could earn in a savings account, certificate of deposit, bonds, money market fund, or stocks—especially at today's almost insignificant CD (and bond) interest rates and the never-can-know-where-its-going stock market.

As a college student who wanted to invest in real estate, I sought stage-of-life owners of small apartment buildings. These people were tired of managing their properties. Yet, they valued a monthly income and (most) didn't want to settle for the meager interest paid by banks or the low-income yield and big risks of stocks. They also didn't want to sell their investment properties and get hit with a tax bill for capital gains.

Their choice: Sell on easy OWC terms to an ambitious young college student who was willing to accept the work of rental properties in exchange for an opportunity to start building wealth through investment real estate. This opportunity remains today. Because properly selected, well-managed rentals will pay for themselves—if you will work—you can substitute ambition and perseverance for a large down payment.

Seller Ignorance

Some sellers underprice their properties because they don't know the recent prices at which similar properties have been selling. Or they do not know of a unique advantage that favorably distinguishes their property from others. I confess that as a seller, I have made the mistake of selling too low because I was ignorant of the market.

Some years ago, I lived in Palo Alto, California. The rental house I decided to sell was located in Texas. A year earlier, this house had been appraised for $110,000, which at the time of the appraisal was about right. So I decided to ask for $125,000. I figured that price fair and still left some room to negotiate.

The first weekend the house went on the market, three offers came in at my asking price of $125,000. Immediately, I knew I had underpriced. What I had not known but soon learned was that during the year I'd been away, property prices in that neighborhood had jumped 30 percent. After learning of my ignorance, I could have rejected all the offers and raised my price. Or I could have put the buyers into a bidding war. But I didn't.

I decided to sell to the person with the cleanest offer (no contingencies). I was making a good profit; why get greedy? Also, at that time, I was teaching at Stanford University , writing a book, and consulting for Wells Fargo Bank. In other words, I did not want to give this property sale much attention. In part, my grass-is-greener-in-California attitude also contributed to my desire to go for the quick dollar rather than top dollar.

Sellers sometimes mistakenly and at other times intentionally underprice their properties. Stay on the lookout for this possibility. When you spot a good deal, jump on it. Underpriced properties often get snapped up quickly.

Although good deals go fast, I will again issue this caution: Not all (seemingly) bargain-priced properties represent good deals. Beware of booms about to go bust (which was the fate of my Texas buyers). Watch out for long-term declining markets where a low price today morphs into an even lower price tomorrow. Accurately evaluate fix-up expenses, hidden defects, and environmental problems (for example, lead paint, underground oil storage tanks, asbestos, contaminated well water). Ration your cash. Match your planned improvements to the tastes, preferences, and rent levels that your prospective tenants will find attractive.

Temper your eagerness to buy a bargain-priced property with a thorough physical, financial, market, and legal analysis. Go slowly for low- or nothing-down seller financing. Delay the temptation to jump without looking. Apply the observational powers of Sherlock Holmes. The less you know about a property and the more you assume, the greater your risk. Balance your urge to act with an itemized appraisal of potential pitfalls. *Prepare* to buy before you buy.

PREPARE SCREENING CRITERIA

Select properties. You cannot buy every property (bargain-priced or not) that grabs your attention. Before you move to the buy stage, narrow your choices:

♦ What neighborhoods and locations look promising?
♦ Do you want a single-family house, condominium, co-op, town house, or multiunit rental property? If multiunits, how large a property will you accept?
♦ Would you prefer to occupy and invest simultaneously? If owner occupancy is important, how does this desire limit your choice of neighborhoods and properties?
♦ How much repair, renovation, or remodeling work are you willing and able to take on?
♦ What types of improvements will you try? Structural? Cosmetic? Environmental? Fire damaged? Earthquake damaged? Other?
♦ Which is more important: bargain price or bargain terms? Would you buy a property that did not yield positive cash flows? If no, what is your minimum cash-on-cash return on investment?
♦ Would you accept a property occupied by problem tenants?
♦ How much risk will you tolerate? When buying fixer-uppers, your repairs and renovation costs may exceed your estimates. If you buy in a turnaround neighborhood, the turnaround may take longer than you expect.
♦ How much cash or borrowing power can you draw on to carry you through a period of impaired rent collections (vacancies, bad tenants)?
♦ What's the minimum time you would accept on a balloon mortgage or other short-term financing?
♦ How long do you plan to own the property? When all costs are considered, will the property command a selling price or rent level high enough to meet your profit objectives?
♦ What are your profit objectives? Which of the 22 sources of return seem possible with this property?

Focus on potential properties, returns, and types of sellers that match your requirements. Eliminate the wild-goose chases that steal the time of many beginning real estate investors. Clarify goals and circumstances. Resist the temptation to say yes to a deal just because it is a deal. Go after those properties and owners that suit your abilities, talent, time constraints, personal finances, and inclinations.

BARGAIN SELLERS

Now that you have developed your screening criteria, how do you discover potential sellers?

♦ Networking/Get the word out
♦ Newspapers and other publications
♦ Cold call owners
♦ Agent services
♦ Internet listings

Networking/Get the Word Out/Social Media

Some time back, I was leaving the United States for several years and decided to sell my house with minimum hassle. Coincidentally, the PhD student club at the university where I was teaching wanted a faculty member to host the upcoming faculty-student party. "Aha," I thought—what better way to expose my house to more than 100 people? So I volunteered. In the week following the party, I received two offers and accepted the better one.

The buyers received a good price and excellent financing. I never had to place the property on the market and did not pay a sales agent. Win-win for buyers and seller.

Draw on the power of networks and social media. Yet, few buyers and sellers try to discover each other through contacts among friends, family, relatives, coworkers, church groups, clubs, business associates, customers, parent-teacher groups, social media, and other acquaintances. Make your search common knowledge. Tell everyone you know. Describe what you're looking for. Notify all of your Facebook friends.

Why search alone when you can enlist dozens (hundreds?) of others to help you? Nearly all property owners prefer a quick direct sale—even at a lower-than-market price. No one likes the hassles and costs of listing and selling through a realty firm.

Network searches also awaken sleeping sellers—owners who are open to offer, but for various reasons are not yet marketing their property(ies). Indeed, right now I am a sleeping seller on a property located in North Carolina.

Newspapers and Other Publications

Some investors browse the real estate classified and display ads with a highlighter, then call owners or Realtors, obtain cursory information, and when a property sounds promising, set up an appointment to view it. This method might work, but it can fail for two reasons: (1) if a property isn't advertised (as is more and more the case today as sellers migrate to Internet sales sites), you won't learn about it; and (2) you may pass by ineffectively written ads—even though the property itself deserves attention.

One solution: Run your own advertisement in the real estate want-to-buy column. Describe the type of property and terms that you seek. You will invite serious sellers to contact you. When I began investing, I used this technique to locate about 30 percent of the properties I bought. (Websites and networking are better choices today most likely—but if you can economically buy space, you might give it a try. Many older sellers still have not migrated to web-based marketing. Also, many people will casually glance through classified ads, but not take the trouble to go web browsing.)

As another way to use the newspaper, read the "houses for rent," "condos for rent," and "apartments for rent" ads. This research helps you gauge rent levels. You will also see properties advertised as lease-option or "for rent or sale." These ads generally indicate a flexible and motivated seller.

When you search for bargain sellers, look beyond the real estate classified ads. Identify potential sellers from the public notices: births, divorces, retirements, deaths, bankruptcy, foreclosure, or marriage. Each of these events can trigger the need to sell real estate. If you contact sellers before they list with a sales agent, you stand a fair chance of buying at a bargain price. (You might, too, subscribe to your area's default or foreclosure newsletters published in print or on the Internet. Chapter 6 tells you how to profit from foreclosures.)

Cold Call Owners

To cold call productively, adopt the Realtor technique and cultivate a neighborhood farm. Many top-selling realty agents select a neighborhood (or other geographic area) and cultivate relationships to find sellers who will list their properties for sale with that agent. Agents phone property owners from names listed in a crisscross directory, walk the neighborhood, talk with residents, circulate flyers by mail or doorknob hangers, and participate in neighborhood or community-sponsored events. By cultivating a neighborhood farm, an agent becomes known in the area. She positions herself as the first person property owners think of when they decide to sell their house.

You can beat the agent at his own game. Cultivate your own neighborhood (or community) farm. Among residents and businesses, circulate a flyer that reads:

Before you list your property for sale, please call me. I plan to buy a property in this neighborhood directly from the owners. Let's see if we can craft an agreement that will please both of us.

When property owners learn how they can save time, effort, and money selling direct, they may offer you a favorable price or terms. Also, if you talk with them before they talk to an agent, they may even quote a below-market price because they lack reliable market comp data. (Of course, uninformed sellers may also quote you an above-market price—especially when current comparable prices sit well below their previous peaks.)

Vacant Houses and Out-of-the-Area Owners. Your farm area will include some properties (vacant or tenant occupied) that are owned by people who do not live in the neighborhood. These owners may not see your flyers, nor will you find them listed in a crisscross directory. To reach these potential sellers, ask neighbors and talk with the tenants who live in the property.

If this research doesn't reveal the owners' names and addresses, contact the tax assessor's office (property data are now online in many cities). You can learn where and to whom the property tax statements are mailed. It's not unusual to find out-of-the-area property owners who are sleeping sellers. They will sell but haven't as yet awoken to the idea. You can become their alarm clock.

Broker Listings. For any number of reasons, properties listed with real estate agents may not sell during their original listing period. When this failure occurs, the listing agent will try to persuade the owners to relist with her firm. And, quite likely, agents from other brokerage firms will also approach the sellers. Here's what you can do to cut them off at the pass and perhaps arrange a bargain purchase.

When you notice a listed property that looks as if it might fit your requirements, do *not* call the agent. Do *not* call or stop by to talk to the owners. Instead, write the owners a letter stating the price and terms that you would consider paying. Then ask the owners to contact you *after* their listing has expired. (If a seller goes behind his agent's back and arranges a sale while the property is listed, the owner is still legally obligated to pay the sales commission.)

You find a property listed at its market value of $200,000. The listing contract sets a 6 percent sales commission. The sellers have told themselves that they will accept nothing less than $192,500, meaning that after paying the expenses of sale they would net around $180,000. You offer $175,000. Would the sellers accept it? Or would they relist with the agent, postpone their move, and hold out for another $5,000 to $10,000?

They just might accept your offer. It depends on their finances, their reason for moving, and any pressures they may face. But you can see that even though your offer is low relative to the market value of the house, it still provides the sellers almost as much as they could expect to net if their agent found them a buyer. (Naturally, your letter would not formally commit you to purchase the property. It would state the price and terms that you have in mind.) When you make such offers, establish your credibility and emphasize the relative amounts the seller would net (your offer versus a brokered sale—not a price, per se).

Although agents provide a service, if you buy at a bargain price or buy on bargain terms (especially with low- or no-down-payment seller financing), the seller may lack the cash to pay a commission. At times, to negotiate a bargain price, skip the agent's services and do your own legwork.

Agent Services

Investor and renovator Suzanne Brangham expresses a deep need for agent services. In her book, *Housewise* (HarperCollins, 1987, p. 163), Suzanne exclaims:

> You need realty agents as much as they need you. After you have narrowed your choice to one or two neighborhoods or towns, enlist the aid of an expert. Your real estate agent will guide you so that you can sit back, take out your notebook, ask questions, and learn. Good agents know what prices properties are selling for, which areas are strong, and which neighborhoods are getting hot.
>
> If you let your agent know that you plan to buy and sell several properties over the next few years, he (or she) will do everything short of breaking and entering to show you the properties that are available. . . . I'd been lusting after a beautiful two-unit building, but it had never been up for sale. My agent called me the minute it was listed and I bought it in less than an

hour. In fact, I became notorious for signing offers on the roof of my agent's car. When there's a race to get in your bid on a particularly juicy piece of property, a faithful agent who knows exactly what you want can make all the difference.

Wow, over the top, maybe. My experience with agents does not justify the gushing praise that Suzanne lavishes upon them. But no doubt, a skilled and motivated agent can assist with at least eight tasks:

1. Suggest sources and techniques of financing and help you run through the numbers.
2. Research comp sales and rent levels so that you can better understand values.
3. Act as an intermediary in negotiations.
4. Recommend other professionals whose services you may need (lawyer, mortgage broker, contractor, designer, architect, property inspector).
5. Handle innumerable details and problems that always seem to arise on the way from contract to closing.
6. Clue you in about what type of interest and market activity has developed around various properties.
7. Give you an insider's glimpse into an area to let you know who's doing what and where.
8. Disclose negatives about a property or neighborhood that might otherwise have escaped your attention.

Agents will sort through your neighborhood and property trade-offs, suggest possibilities for value-creating improvements, and try to persuade sellers to accept your price and terms. The best agents, as Brangham points out, "[are] those who listen when you explain what you are looking for. They will take you directly to the buried treasure you want to find."

Although not all agents will oblige, I ask them whether a seller has accepted or rejected any previous offers and, if so, at what price. Agents often disclose juicy facts about why a seller is selling and their level of motivation. Although presumably confidential, I want to know the prices agreed to on pending sales of comp properties, too. As I discuss later, many types of REOs (FHA, Fannie Mae, Freddie Mac, and many banks) are available only through property brokers. Likewise, when arranging a short sale, a specialist who has gained insider know-how can prove a valuable ally.

Civil Rights Caveat. Real estate agents (like everyone else) must constantly guard what they say out of fear of lawsuits alleging discrimination. If you ask, "What's the quality of the schools in this neighborhood?" the agent may hedge an answer if, say, at one time school busing or racial strife spurred exodus to suburbia, and correspondingly, student achievement test scores fail to meet acceptable levels.

Likewise, if the ethnic, religious, or racial composition of a neighborhood affects property values (either up or down), a sales agent could not (lawfully) mention this trend. The U.S. Department of Justice (DOJ) and the U.S. Department of Housing and Urban Development (HUD) have decreed that neither ethnic, religious, nor racial demographics influence property values. Although originally intended to discourage blockbusting, fear-mongering, and panic sales, this government decree now flies in the face of fact.

Changing demographics do influence values. And in today's multi-ethnic, multiracial world, an ethnic or religious group that begins to favor a given neighborhood or community can push values up substantially—not bring them down as the HUD/DOJ decrees seem to suggest.

Even if real estate appraisers and sales agents are supposed to turn a blind eye, knowledgeable investors should not fancy such illusions. They do track changing neighborhood demographics and psychographics—and their resulting impact on future demand.

Property Condition Caveat. In addition to civil rights issues, most agents tread lightly in response to questions about the condition of a property. "How's the roof?" you ask. The agent answers, "As far as I know, it's eight years old and hasn't had any leaks." You buy the property, and three months later the roof begins to leak. On the basis of the agent's statement, you sue the brokerage firm for misrepresentation and fraud. Even though the agent told the truth as far as he or she knew it, many judges or juries would find the agent liable.

Buyers have sued agents so many times for giving "to the best of my knowledge" answers concerning property condition that smart agents avoid such questions. They prefer to refer you to appropriate property specialists and inspectors. In one precedent-setting case in California, a realty agent was held liable for not informing his buyers that a property was located in a mudslide area—even though the agent did not know that the area was risky. In response to this case, the California Association of Realtors persuaded the California legislature to enact a *seller disclosure* law (p. 124). Most other states have followed California's lead.

Many sales contracts and offering memorandums for investment properties explicitly state that buyers cannot rely on agent-provided information—and must solicit their own expert advisors for all matters of due diligence. In today's legal climate, agent-provided information arrives with many hedges, caveats, and exculpatory wrappings.

To buy at a (true) bargain price, rely on accurate information about neighborhoods and properties. A top real estate agent will provide you with some of these data, but not all that you need. Recognize the practical and legal limits that restrain even the most knowledgeable agents.

Buyer Loyalty. For every real buyer they work with, most real estate agents encounter many pretenders—wannabe investors who steal an agent's time and knowledge but feel no obligation to buy from that agent. Or if they do buy, the first thing they do to make a deal work is to try to cut the agent's commission. Such an approach does not build a relationship. To gain the benefits Suzanne Brangham celebrates, demonstrate buyer loyalty.

Show loyalty to your agents and, in turn, they will favor you as a client who gives them repeat business (and referrals). In return, they provide top service and include you among the first to learn of those juicy deals as soon as they hit the market—and sometimes even before a listing goes into the MLS (Multiple Listing Service).

Internet Listings

Property investors not only cruise neighborhoods, they cruise the Internet to look for properties. Thousands of web sites now list properties for sale. Property buyers and lookers can directly access the Realtors' Multiple Listing Service (MLS) at www.realtor.com.

A huge entrepreneurial industry of content providers publish specialized listings of everything from foreclosures to commercial properties to FSBOs. Online, you can locate investors looking for money—or money looking for properties. Nearly all real estate information that in the past had been available from Realtors, government records, newspaper ads, newsletters, and other sources is now (or will soon be) accessible online. Electronic shopping for real estate (and mortgages) has rendered the MLS book as obsolete as a slide rule. In addition to the web sites referenced in this book, search engines will guide you to a cornucopia of useful data and topical discussions.

SELLER DISCLOSURES

What you see is not all that you get. That below-market price won't seem like such a great deal once you learn the roof leaks, the foundation is cracking, and termites are munching on floor joists. If the next-door neighbors make *Animal House* look tame, quality tenants will not rent your property—or if they do move in, they will not stay.

Prepare against such unwanted surprises. Thoroughly inspect the property, talk with existing tenants, walk the neighborhood, and avail yourself of knowledgeable and trustworthy real estate agents. Get the property checked out by a property inspector, a structural engineer, a pest control expert, or other specialists who accurately assess the condition of the property. Be wary of plumbing and heating pipes that lie within or below a concrete foundation. When these pipes leak, detection and repair can present difficult and costly measures. Last, but not least, ask the sellers to complete a seller disclosure statement.

The Disclosure Revolution

More than 40 states now require (or encourage) sellers to complete a seller disclosure statement that lists and explains all *known* problems or defects that may plague a property. But even if your state doesn't yet mandate seller disclosure, obtain a disclosure form (most realty firms keep blank copies on hand) and ask the sellers to fill it out. (Or Google "seller disclosure statements." Your hits will include forms from multiple states.)

As you review a seller-completed disclosure statement, watch for these six issues:

1. Sellers cannot disclose facts or conditions of which they are unaware. Disclosures do not substitute for inspections.
2. Disclosures reveal the known past. They make no guarantees. Sellers do not warrant the present or future condition of the property. They report only what they know.
3. Disclosure questions permit subjective answers. Are playing children a neighborhood noise problem? Is a planned street widening an adverse condition?
4. Disclosure statements may not require sellers to disclose property defects that you can readily see. Inspection supersedes disclosure.
5. Beware of seller (or agent) statements that begin, "I believe," "I think," "as far as we know," and other similar hedges. Do not accept these answers as the final word. Follow up hedged statements or assertions with definitive inquiry or inspection.
6. Insist on a past written record of all maintenance calls, repairs, receipts, diagnoses, and replacements. You want a full history. A full history alerts you to so-called solved problems that may point toward future expenses. Although few sellers are likely to fully comply with such a request, it will reveal useful information and give you more evidence if it later turns out that the sellers hid defects from you.

Seller disclosures help you understand and value properties. But even so, give them only as much weight as they deserve. Some sellers forget that their boiler bangs like a tin drum; or maybe a circuit breaker pops each time the toaster and microwave operate at the same time. Sellers (disclosure statements or not) often fail to disclose. (Foreclosure sales and REOs typically sell as is with no disclosure statements.)

Independently check out the condition and risks of the property. A building that passes inspection with flying colors may still lay down a minefield of risks. Accompany your inspectors and question them thoroughly. Discount your offering price for existing, known defects *and* potentially costly future expenses.

Income Properties

Some seller disclosure laws apply only to one- to four-family owner-occupied properties. If you buy an apartment building or shopping center, the law may not require the seller to fill out a disclosure statement. If, in this situation, the seller refuses, offset this additional risk by scaling down the price you offer—and enhance the rigor of your prepurchase inspections.

Rental properties also give sellers an out. Many nonoccupant owners claim no knowledge as to defects and condition. Their disclosure forms often lack substantive answers. But they will maintain a record of service calls, maintenance, and replacements—as these records are required by the IRS. Ask the seller to produce or adjust your offer accordingly.

Verify rental income and operating expenses. Ask the sellers to sign a statement whereby they swear that the income and expense figures that they have reported to you are true and factual. Some owners place friends, relatives, and employees into their buildings at inflated rent levels. These tenants do not pay the rents shown in the lease (or if they do, they get kickbacks in cash or other benefits), but their signed leases sure look attractive to unsuspecting buyers.

SUMMARY

To find owners who will sell at a below-market price is like panning for gold. Even when you know a stream is loaded with potential, you will sift through a ton of muck and rock before you discover the nuggets that yield the profits. When searching for below-market deals, expect to work. As you gain experience and reputation, deals will come to you. But as stock speculator Gordon Gekko (Michael Douglas) tells Bud Fox (Charlie Sheen) in the movie *Wall Street*, "Kid, I look at 100 deals a day. I may choose one." Prepare yourself.

Among the properties that sellers (or agents) promote as bargains, many turn out otherwise. Through skillful negotiation and financial structuring, you can sometimes transform an apparently mediocre deal into a winner. Except in cases of luck, pocketing gold nuggets will require intelligence, knowledge, and possibility thinking. But like the industrious and fortuitous miner who pans for gold, those bargain-priced properties you do find will generously reward you for that sifting, sorting, and sacrifice.

6

PROFIT WITH FORECLOSURES

"**B**uy properties for pennies on the dollar," so say the self-proclaimed gurus of the easy money foreclosure game who want you to buy their seminars, mentoring programs, courses, books, and audio CDs. "Just learn the foreclosure secrets that will bring you the riches you deserve." Certainly, the news is filled with the sad plights of millions of people who can't (or won't) pay their mortgage loans and other debts.

But are foreclosure gurus correct? Are foreclosures really the mother lode of real estate bargains? Gold nuggets lying around for anyone to pick up with ease? Hardly. When you are propositioned with stories of easy money (foreclosures or otherwise), ponder these questions: "If a guru knows how to make so much money with so little time, effort, cash, credit, or risk, why is he telling you, me, and millions of others who will compete with him for these deals?" Does he remain ignorant of the *fallacy of composition*—that fundamental axiom learned by every student of Econ 101?

In the real world, earnings from foreclosures—like earnings from other property investments—will not just fall into your lap because you learn a few secrets and tricks of the trade. To profit with foreclosures—and at the same time alleviate risks—you must understand the foreclosure legal process, diligently research markets, intelligently value properties, prepare reliable cost-to-cure estimates, and develop your powers of persuasion.

It is true that today's market includes an oversupply of properties and an abundance of motivated sellers. This perfect storm of potential presents you with more foreclosure possibilities than any market I have experienced throughout my career. But as any sane investor knows—or as experience soon teaches—the low risk–high reward foreclosure opportunities are captured by investors who prepare.

THE FORECLOSURE PROCESS

Borrowers default because they fail to pay back their loan as agreed. Defaults also occur when owners fail to pay their property taxes; fail to pay some related obligation (homeowners' association fees, a superior mortgage claim, special assessments); transfer a mortgaged property without lender approval; or undertake renovations, remodeling, or demolition that diminish the value of the property.

Lender Tries to Resolve Problem

Compared with the late 1980s and early 1990s (the years marking the last serious downturn in the property cycle), most lenders today provide (or are supposed to provide) delinquent borrowers generous opportunity to restructure, reinstate, or refinance their mortgages. That's why even though the number of mortgages in some stage of delinquency or formal default now exceeds 8 million, the number of properties actually sold at foreclosure auctions comes in at less than 2 million.

With more loan workouts, a smaller percentage of troubled borrowers lose their properties through a foreclosure sale. Nevertheless, mortgage lenders (or loan insurers and guarantors such as FHA and VA) will receive the keys to more than 1 million properties (REOs) this year. And the number of borrowers who have fallen seriously behind in their payments (and thus would benefit from a workout) now exceeds 4 million. Given these huge numbers, the foreclosure business (preforeclosure workouts including short sales, government foreclosures, and postforeclosure REOs) provides a continuing stream of problems that investors must help solve.

Filing Legal Notice

When a lender believes that its soft approach to collecting past-due payments and penalties has failed, its lawyers file either a legal notice of default or a lawsuit to foreclose (depending on the state). This legal filing and its subsequent posting of notice on the Internet or in newspapers formally announces to (1) the property owners, (2) any other parties who may hold legal claims against the owners or their property, and (3) the public in general, that legal action is moving forward to force a courthouse sale of the property.

At least one month passes between the date of legal filing and the foreclosure sale. More typically today, this waiting period ranges from 120 days up to two years. If the property owners file a legal defense to the lender's foreclosure lawsuit (for example, lender violated due process, fraud, consumer rights, truth in lending, robosigning, false affidavits, and so on), the foreclosure sale may have to wait for a lender victory in settlement or trial. These battles in litigation can drag on for a year, two years, or longer.

The volume of defaults today also extends the period between the date of the original default and the actual day of the foreclosure sale. Lenders and mortgage servicing companies lack the personnel necessary to steer a defaulting borrower into foreclosure (or workout) in a timely manner. To halt the foreclosure sale for *at least* a month or two longer, defaulting property owners sometimes file bankruptcy. A bankruptcy filing by the property owners automatically stays a foreclosure action. To proceed further in its efforts to force a sale, the lender petitions the bankruptcy court. Only after the court grants permission will the foreclosure process start running again. (In fact, in some situations, a bankruptcy court can annul a foreclosure sale that has already occurred.)

The Foreclosure Sale

Eventually, if defaulting property owners meet defeat with their legal defenses or delaying tactics, the foreclosure sale date arrives. At this point, the property is auctioned to the highest *cash* bidder.

Sometimes a real estate investor (foreclosure specialist), speculator, or even a homebuyer submits the winning bid. More likely, the lender who has forced the foreclosure sale bids, say, one dollar more than the amount of its unpaid claims (mortgage balance, late fees, accrued interest, attorney fees, foreclosure costs) and walks away with a sheriff's deed to the property. Next, the lender eventually sells the property through a listing with a real estate brokerage firm, or in troubled times like these, through auction where dozens—or even hundreds—of REO properties are sold at the rap of the auctioneer's gavel.

REOs

Remember these words: *Lenders do not want to own foreclosed real estate.* For a lender (or institutions such as the Federal Housing Administration [FHA], Department of Veterans Affairs [VA], Fannie Mae, Freddie Mac), holding on to an REO that has been acquired through foreclosure rarely seems like a good idea. No matter how much potential the property offers, owners of REOs want to sell quickly. Lenders expect to lose money on their sales of REOs—but they lose even more by holding these properties.

Lenders will not rent out their properties and wait for better times to sell. Lenders remain ill suited to operate or supervise property management companies.

With foreclosures, you can pursue one or more of these three approaches:

1. Negotiate with the distressed property owners and, if necessary, the foreclosing lender (that is, to obtain a short sale or refinance).
2. Bid at the foreclosure auction.
3. Buy an REO from the lender or the agency (FHA, VA, Fannie Mae, Freddie Mac) that owns the property. (This topic is covered in Chapter 7.)

BUY PREFORECLOSURES FROM DISTRESSED OWNERS

Each year in every community, hundreds (sometimes thousands) of property owners hit the financial skids. Divorce, job loss, accident, illness, business failure, payment shock (ARM adjustments upward, teaser rates expire), underwater loans, and other setbacks render borrowers unable or unwilling to make their mortgage payments. (In these times, increasing numbers of property owners and other mortgagors who could pay, who suffer no financial distress, are choosing to walk away from their loans and their properties because the borrowers owe more than the current market value of their properties. In fact, several lawyers and economists have written books that encourage underwater mortgagors to breach their loan agreements.)

Rather than effectively deal with financial difficulties as soon as default is imminent, many distressed owners hang on too long, hoping for a miracle to bail them out. Since miracles occur rarely, most of these people end up waiting for the sheriff's knock at their door—or they just abandon their property. Many other borrowers who have sought lender workouts have just given up because their lender either failed to respond, or perpetually delayed authorizing a feasible plan for loan reinstatement.

In such cases where the borrowers have failed to remedy their loan delinquency, you can try to design a solution. If the owners have some equity remaining in their property, profitable workouts become possible without necessarily involving the lender—though lender participation may still prove desirable. If the distressed homeowner owes more than the value of what he owns, you will likely need a short sale agreement with the lender and the property owners (mortgagors).

Approach Owners with Empathy

No one can give you a magic system to buy property from people who face foreclosure. These owners must contend with financial troubles, personal anguish, and indecisiveness brought on by emotional depression. They have probably been attacked by foreclosure sharks, speculators, bank lawyers, and recent attendees of get-rich-quick foreclosure seminars. These owners live with the public shame of failure. For all these reasons and more, they are not easy people to deal with.

To succeed, approach them with a sensitive, empathetic, problem-solving approach. Think cooperation. Think win-win. You gain a bargain price. The sellers shed their burdens and limit their potential losses. To find and persuade sellers, you may compete against foreclosure specialists and other potential buyers. Design your negotiations to preserve what little may be left of the owner's dignity and self-esteem. Never rely on a "Here's my offer—take it or leave it" approach. It antagonizes the owners. It does not favorably distinguish you from the preforeclosure sharks that hover around the bleeding victim. Share personal information about setbacks you have lived through. Emphasize win-win outcomes. Dire straits or not, no one wants his home (property) stolen away.

The Difficulties of Dealing Profitably with Owners in Default

Some get-rich-in-foreclosures seminars, CDs, and books exaggerate the possibilities of profiting from property owners who face foreclosure. The enticing scenarios imagined by these promoters place you in the picture with high-equity sellers who hold a nonqualifying assumable mortgage. You offer the sellers a few thousand dollars in cash and agree to make up their past-due mortgage payments. The sellers deed you their property and move out. You then place a tenant in the property, collect rents, and pay the property expenses and scheduled mortgage payments. Or, alternatively, you fix up the property, put it on the market, and sell for a fat profit.

Such easy pickings are great when you can find them. Deals rarely move forward, though, with step-by-step simplicity. When you talk with property owners in foreclosure, you uncover a minefield of problems that you must crisscross with skill and creativity. Here are some of the issues you will need to deal with.

Mortgage Debt Exceeds Market Value. Property owners who contend with foreclosure often owe more than their properties are worth. To make a deal work, you must talk the lender into a short sale, that is, the lender voluntarily reduces the balance due on its loan so that you receive a fair profit for agreeing to make up past-due payments and take over (or, far more likely, pay off) the reduced loan balance.

Today, a majority (perhaps nearly all lenders) accept short sale investors. But you must thoroughly prepare your short sale package. Then you wait, suffer runarounds, and sometimes lose the deal to a higher bidder. (With some lenders, a realty agent who specializes in short sales can smooth this process.)

Nonqualifying Assumptions Rarely Exist. Long gone are the times (1970s through early 1990s) when foreclosure specialists could step right in and automatically take over the defaulting borrowers' mortgage—and pocket a large chunk of the owner's equity for doing so. Few mortgages today automatically permit assumptions. Finding a homeowner in foreclosure who actually has a nonqualifying assumable is like finding the proverbial needle in a haystack. Great if you run across a nonqual that offers potential. But not worth looking for.

Qualifying Assumptions Are Limited. Today's FHA and VA mortgages do permit assumptions, but only by credit-qualifying owner-occupants. If your credit or income is shaky, or if you plan to flip the property without taking occupancy or hold the property as a rental, neither FHA nor VA will let you assume an existing homeowner's mortgage.

(However, this rule may change. Some in Congress and the federal agencies want to open up more financing and purchase opportunities for investors as a means to more quickly clear the excess of foreclosures and REOs that plague the country's economic recovery. Without a recovery in housing, a more general recovery seems less likely. In addition, both FHA and VA do finance investors [and investment properties] in some instances).

Adjustable rate loans also permit qualifying assumptions. And another option for taking over a loan is called a *subject-to purchase*—sometimes with and sometimes without lender permission. Relatively few lenders will consent to a write-down of the loan balance with these types of loans (for an investor). To find out, ask—or better yet, submit an offer and justify why your offer makes sense from the lender's point of view.

Multiple Creditors, Multiple Title Problems. Property owners who suffer foreclosure often get hit by claims of other creditors. Check to see if one or more of these creditors has filed a *lis pendens* or a tax lien (Internal Revenue Service or other taxing authority), or has secured a judgment against the homeowners. To clear title, you may have to clean up and settle with several creditors—not just one mortgage lender.

Workout with Credit Counselors. Most lenders today (especially FHA, VA, Fannie Mae) encourage financially troubled property owners to seek credit counseling and loan workout with nonprofit agencies such as CCCA (Credit Counseling Centers of America). Neither the homeowners nor the lenders may need a profit-minded workout specialist. Various government and lender foreclosure rescue programs also compete to a degree with profit-motive investors.

Save Equity through Bankruptcy. In many states, homeowners can file bankruptcy and save all or part of their home equity. Fifteen or 20 years ago, only the most bold or financially ruined Americans pursued bankruptcy. Now, bankruptcy serves as just another tool of financial planning. Approximately 1.5 million couples and individuals elect to file for bankruptcy each year.

When someone can get rid of all those credit card balances and unpaid medical bills—and at the same time save most (or all) of their most valuable asset (their home equity)—why let a foreclosure investor come through the door?

Note: In 2005, Congress passed a revised bankruptcy law that intends to make debtors pay back more of the money they owe as well as to tighten the bankruptcy homestead exemption. Lenders lobbied that too many deadbeats were defaulting on their bills and filing bankruptcy to remedy their foolish (or intentional) financial follies.

(Unlike the banks themselves—which can carry out the most irresponsible and morally reprehensible practices and then run to the federal government pleading for taxpayers to fund bank financial follies—Joe and Peggy Lunchbox must own up to their moral and legal obligations. I wonder if the banks see the irony and hypocrisy of their 10-year lobbying campaign to make "deadbeats" pay.)

Because personal bankruptcy combines both state and federal law, talk with an attorney in your area. Learn how much equity a bankrupt homeowner can protect from creditors. (In Florida, Texas, and several other states, that amount is unlimited.)

Bankruptcy Doesn't Ruin Credit. The threat of ruined credit doesn't frighten Americans today as it did two decades ago. In fact, it's not easy to *ruin* your credit. After a bankruptcy discharge, people with steady jobs can shortly thereafter obtain credit cards (albeit secured), car loans, and home loans (e.g., lease option, seller financing). After bankruptcy, with two years of clean credit, FHA, VA, and sometimes even Fannie Mae and Freddie Mac lenders will approve reestablished borrowers for home mortgages (though bank investor loans do remain more difficult to obtain).

The somewhat easy credit-rebuilding techniques reduce the probability that you can persuade homeowners to transfer a large chunk of their home equity to you so that they can save their credit. In decades past, a bankruptcy or foreclosure would turn a debtor into a credit leper—no longer does this shunning occur.

It also seems likely that after the current credit tightness abates, seeing the vast number of credit wrecks that populate the United States, subprime lending will again become a growth industry.

Estimate Repair and Renovation Costs. Before you finalize a preforeclosure purchase with a property owner, thoroughly inspect the property and accurately estimate the costs of necessary repairs, renovations, and perhaps environmental cleanup. In their enthusiasm to do a foreclosure deal, unsuspecting buyers gloss over the inspection and make only an eyeball guesstimate of expected costs. To their dismay, they soon learn that slick foreclosure sellers can deceive unsophisticated buyers, just as slick foreclosure sharks take advantage of distressed property owners.

PREQUALIFY HOMEOWNERS AND PROPERTIES

By warning of potentially difficult preforeclosure issues, I want to prepare you. Investors who close their minds to facts rarely earn long-term (or even short-term) profits. You *can* earn generous rewards through foreclosures—but only if you prequalify the homeowners *and* the property. Before moving forward toward a workout, evaluate your possibilities and probabilities. Answer these eight questions:

1. What amount of equity have the owners built up in their property?
2. If necessary, will the lender cooperate in a short sale? Or will the lender sell you the mortgage at a discount from the loan balance owed by the borrower or property owner (see p. 328–331)?
3. Will the lender permit you to assume (or subject-to) the mortgage as an investor? As an owner-occupant? At what interest rate? If no assumption, will the lender waive the mortgage prepayment penalty (if any)?
4. Can you satisfy yourself, through a title check or title insurance, that the sellers can convey a marketable title, that is, a title free of consequential clouds (actual and potential)?
5. Will the homeowners work to avoid bankruptcy or foreclosure to alleviate their financial distress? (When sellers refuse to cooperate— as they sometimes do—your chance to succeed drops to zero.)
6. Would the property owners lose more economically in a bankruptcy than they would stand to gain? (As noted, bankrupts may emerge from bankruptcy with their unsecured debts extinguished and their most valuable assets [IRA, 401(k), home equity, life insurance cash value, furniture, clothing, car] preserved.)
7. Can you *firmly* establish how much you must spend to repair, redecorate, and renovate the property?
8. Does the potential profit margin justify your investment of time, money, effort, and opportunity cost (that is, the profits of other deals you pass up to invest in this one)?

What do your answers to these eight questions reveal about unknowns and uncertainties? Is the forecasted profit high enough to justify cost and market risk?

Complete the following revenue and cost schedule to evaluate risk and profit potential:

Sales price after improvement	$_____
Less	
Acquisition price (cash, notes, assumed mortgages)	$_____
Mortgage assumption fee	$_____
Legal fees	$_____
Back property taxes and assessments	$_____
Back payments and late fees	$_____
Closing costs	$_____
Cost of improvements	$_____
Holding costs until sold or rented	$_____
Miscellaneous	$_____
Time and effort (imputed value)	$_____
Opportunity costs (imputed value)	$_____
Equals	
Profit potential	$_____

FINDING HOMEOWNERS IN DEFAULT (PREFILING)

Ideally, learn the names of homeowners who have defaulted on their mortgages before their lender files formal legal notice. Although such discovery can prove difficult, these techniques often work.

Networking

Choose an area that offers potential. Then develop a network with people who know the neighborhood, such as mail carriers, delivery truck drivers, school personnel (teachers, principals), social service workers, busybody residents, real estate agents, local merchants, church leaders, and credit counseling personnel. Through this network of insiders, find out who's thinking about selling their home, who's been recently laid off, who spends above their means, who can't pay their bills.

Mortgage Collections Personnel

In the past, some foreclosure specialists developed relationships with attorneys, collection agencies, and personnel who pursue delinquent accounts. Today, privacy laws and policies may limit employees from revealing information about a person's financial arrears. But even now, what is forbidden and what is practiced can run opposite to each other. If you can obtain such information without breaching ethics or endangering a friend's job, that knowledge might help you locate people whose problems you can solve.

Another obstacle other than privacy detours this approach to finding about-to-default borrowers. That obstacle is distance. In the good old days, local lending personnel handled a majority of mortgage lending and collections. Now, a mortgage loan in Peoria, Illinois, may be owned by a bank headquartered in Zurich and serviced by a company operating out of Boston. When out-of-town personnel deal with the early stages of homeowner delinquency, your chances of nurturing a relationship becomes difficult.

Drive Neighborhoods

When you know your farm area, watch for properties that appear unkempt, or perhaps experience a sudden, mysterious, or extended vacancy. Such indicators may signal abandonment by a property owner who faces financial distress. Ask a neighbor or two to confirm your suspicions. Informal inquiry may turn up a prime prospect with whom you can negotiate.

FIND HOMEOWNERS (POSTFILING)

Once a lender files suit, you can learn the names and addresses of distressed property owners in at least four ways:

1. Inquire at the clerk of civil court's office and ask to see the list(s) of foreclosure filings or otherwise learn how the filing and public notice process operates.
2. Subscribe to a specialized legal newspaper or e-mail newsletter that reports court filings.
3. Read the legal notices section of your local daily (or weekly) newspaper.
4. Go online. Although some counties throughout the United States lag behind, within a few years even the most backward will post foreclosure filings on the web.

As soon as the foreclosure shows up in the publicly available records, competition for quality deals heats up. To succeed, present yourself and your offer to the distressed property owners in a way that *distinguishes* you (not merely differentiates you) from the crowd.

Cultivate a Relationship with Property Owners

During periods of stress, debt-burdened property owners hide the truth. Loss of home or property stimulates emotional anguish. You cannot rely on owner statements. Verify all details about the property and its liens.

Here are several (suggestive, not scripts) approaches to open negotiations with an owner in foreclosure:

> "Please allow me to complete a financial analysis of the property. I can be back within 24 hours with a firm offer that might solve your current dilemma."
>
> "I would like to pay you cash for your equity, which you otherwise could lose in a foreclosure sale. By working together, we can salvage your credit and you can begin to reestablish your life."
>
> "May I review the loan documents on your home? Can you locate a copy of the mortgage, the title policy, and the monthly loan statements?"

Act faster and offer better results than anyone else. Do not insult or criticize the owners or their property—even though their house may show cosmetic blemishes and deferred maintenance. (In fact, the worse it looks, the better for you.)

As you inspect the property, realistically estimate costs and evaluate its potential market value. You are now prepared to begin discussions of price and terms.

Position your critique as polite inquiry. "Do you think I might have to replace the roof?" "I wonder how I can remove those stains from the carpet?" "Do you think most buyers today prefer the dark kitchen cabinets like these—or the lighter ones like I see in many new model homes?" In this way, you lead the owners to the deficiencies of their property without sharp-edged criticism.

Two More Issues

So far, we have *assumed* that you were able to: (1) meet directly with the property owners; (2) explore the exact nature of their situation; (3) evaluate the financials of the property; and (4) work through potential win-win-win (owners-lender-you) possibilities. But you may not be able to meet directly with the owners if they are represented by a realty firm, or if they have abandoned the property and relocated.

Sales Commissions Eat Up Owner's Equity. I have found it difficult to work with property owners in foreclosure when they have listed their home for sale with a realty firm. Most run-of-the-mill real estate agents know next to nothing about bank workouts, although I see this lack of knowledge changing. Given the market today, more agents are honing their skills in foreclosure and short sale opportunities. Still, rather than help, many do hinder the creative, cooperative process that workouts require.

(In fact, agents will sometimes advertise a short sale even though the lender holding the loan on the property has never expressed a willingness to complete a short sale. It's the agent's way of attracting buyer attention for a property that an underwater owner could not afford to sell—if the lender required them to bring money to the closing table.)

Another block to agent deals: Real estate agents want to be paid in cash at closing. When a sales agent expects to pull out 6 percent of the sales price—an amount that eats up a large chunk of the owner's equity (providing the owner has accumulated any equity), it squeezes your negotiating range. The amount of that commission comes straight from monies that could otherwise go to you, the lenders, or the property owners.

I have on occasion dealt with savvy agents who understand that if they insist on a full commission, they will kill the deal. In one such transaction, the agent agreed to accept just $1,000 in lieu of $4,500. (As this agent realized, he wasn't giving up a fee of $4,500 for a fee of $1,000. He was instead earning a fee of $1,000 in lieu of earning nothing at all.)

Realty Agents Can Price Too High. Sometimes realty agents hurt the property owners' chance to sell their home when they overprice the listing. Say the distressed owners owe $280,000 on a property with a market value of $300,000. To get the listing, an agent may lead the owners to believe that they can sell the property at a price of $325,000. "Great!" the owners think, "We will net $20,000 to $25,000."

Sixty, 90, 180 days pass, and the overpriced property doesn't sell. The owners panic. The foreclosure lawyers are closing in for the kill. But the listing has become stale. To grab buyer attention (or more directly, the attention of other sales agents) requires a price cut to maybe $275,000. By this time, the unpaid mortgage balance along with missed payments and late fees could total $300,000. There's no way a sale will clear out the mortgage debt and the sales commission. More often than not, the foreclosure sale date rushes closer like a speeding freight train.

Quick FSBO Beats Realty Listing. When you talk with low-equity (no equity, underwater) distressed sellers, persuade them not to list with a realty firm in hopes of getting some pie-in-the-sky sales price. Property owners almost always stand a better chance of minimizing loss by going for a quick, discounted FSBO (for sale by owner) sale. In some cases, they should even *pay* someone (cash, note, barter) to take over their loan—or to buy the property and arrange new financing.

Property owners in foreclosure must forget attempts to maximize gain. Rather, they should minimize pain. They must eliminate the possibility of severe (credit and financial) loss. Lead distressed property owners to see that time is not their friend. Time is their enemy. The frequently heard homeowner refrain, "We're going to try this for a while and see what happens," does not make sense. What does happen? They lose the property to foreclosure—and they may incur a deficiency judgment to pay for the loan balance still remaining, plus late fees, legal costs, and lender attorney fees.

Sometimes you fish; sometimes you cut bait. Foreclosure means it's time to cut bait. It's not prudent for property owners to keep throwing the line into new waters. To work successfully with these distressed property owners, repeatedly encourage them to act now. Delay brings regret. Action brings relief.

Vacant Houses

When you discover a vacant house in foreclosure, you discover both a problem and an opportunity. It's a problem because you may have to do some detective work to locate the owners. Unless the owners have purposely tried to disappear, though, you can probably locate them in one of the following five ways:

1. Contact nearby neighbors to learn the owners' whereabouts, or the names of friends or family who would know.
2. Call the owners' telephone number and see if you get a number-changed message. Call the owner's cell phone number.
3. Ask the post office to provide the owners' forwarding address.
4. Find out where the owners were employed and ask coworkers.
5. Contact parents, friends, teachers, or students at the school the owners' children attended.

After you locate the owners comes opportunity. Because they have abandoned the property, they probably aren't entertaining any fanciful hopes for a sale at an inflated price. At this point, they may view any offer you make them as found money.

In some cases, you will learn that the owners have split up and gone their separate ways. This type of situation raises another problem: especially in hostile separations, working out an agreement with one owner in the belief that you can persuade the other(s) to go along often proves futile. To avoid this difficulty, bring all owners into the negotiations early. Never rely on, "Oh, she will go along with whatever agreement you and I work out."

SATISFY LENDERS AND LIEN HOLDERS

Before you talk numbers in your preforeclosure negotiations, identify who holds legal claims against the property and in what amounts. Ask the property owners for this information. Do not commit yourself, however. Verify the owners' figures through a preliminary title report issued by a lawyer or title insurer. Also verify claims through direct contact with claimants. Your investigation may turn up claimants in the following categories:

- ◆ Mortgage holders (first, second, third . . .)
- ◆ Taxing authorities (federal, state, local)
- ◆ County or city special assessments
- ◆ Homeowners' association fees and assessments
- ◆ Unpaid sewage or water bills
- ◆ Special assessment or bonding districts
- ◆ Judgment creditors
- ◆ Mechanics liens for labor or materials provided to the property
- ◆ Spouse (or ex-spouse) rights, including dower and curtsey
- ◆ Unfound heirs of previous owners

One way or another, figure out how to satisfy the claimants you find. Use some combination of the following four techniques:

1. Pay off immediately any or all claimants for the full amount of their claims.
2. Pay off over time any or all claimants for the full amount of their claims.
3. Pay off immediately any or all claimants at a mutually agreed discount.
4. Pay off over time any or all claims at a mutually agreed discount.

Consider a preforeclosure in Phoenix that would likely sell for $110,000. The owner agrees to deed the property to you if you pay off all outstanding liens, which total $105,000:

First mortgage	$78,000
Second mortgage	$18,000
Roofing contractor	$3,000
Credit card judgment	$6,000
Total	$105,000

Facing these numbers, no possibility of gain for an investor. The potential profit margin of $5,000 is much too low. But what if you could persuade the first mortgage lender to extinguish its old $78,000 balance and write you a new loan on the property in the amount of $88,000 (80 percent loan-to-value ratio) and waive all closing costs? You then work out discount deals with the other creditors. After negotiations, your total *payoff* looks like this:

First mortgage	$78,000
Second mortgage	$10,000
Roofing contractor	$2,000
Credit card judgment	$1,500
Total	$91,000

By combining $88,000 in proceeds from the new loan and $3,500 in out-of-pocket cash, you have just bought a $110,000 property for $91,500.

All Parties Are Better Off

If this property had completed its trip through foreclosure, only the first-mortgage lender stood a chance of emerging whole. But more than likely, after adding up continuing lost interest payments, late fees, attorney fees, foreclosure expenses, and REO risks and carrying charges, the first-mortgage lender, too, may have ended up worse off. As for the other parties, here's how they would gain from this workout proposal:

The property owners. Theoretically, they lost $5,000 in equity, but as a practical matter, that was $5,000 they were never going to see. Far more important, the workout not only kept a foreclosure entry off their credit record but also rescued them from a possible deficiency judgment.

The second-mortgage holder. Again, the property theoretically held enough value to liquidate the full $18,000. As a practical matter, this second mortgagee was better off to take a quick and sure $10,000 and cut its potential losses. Owing to the low prices bid at foreclosure sales, in all likelihood, this lender would not have recovered the full loan balance owed. Alternatively, the second mortgage lien holder could have bid at auction and bought the property for the payoff of the first lien holder. Or you could have bought the second lien at a discount and then bought at foreclosure. (See p. 330.)

Roofing contractor. Not a chance of collecting any money from a foreclosure sale. (Accepting $2,000 beats nothing.)

Credit card judgment. Not a chance of collecting any money from a foreclosure sale. (Again, $1,500 beats nothing. Besides, at this point, this debt is probably held by an asset-recovery company that paid less than 5 cents on the dollar to buy the claim. So, if that's the case, you could probably clear it for maybe $500—more or less.)

All foreclosure situations differ. The numbers could come out better or worse for the respective parties—including you. It all depends on the parties' relative negotiating power and skills, their need for cash, their need to avoid risk, and their capacity for understanding. To succeed in the face of this ambiguity, entrepreneurial workout specialists size up people and situations. You have to figure out fast whether mutual agreement looks doable.

Who is willing to settle for how much? Who stands to lose the most? Who needs cash now? Who is willing to wait? What concessions will the first-mortgage lender make, if any? Do the parties understand the likely adverse outcome of a foreclosure sale?

Win by Losing Less

In a foreclosure sale, more often than not, everyone loses except the lawyers. But think what happens when all principals agree to work with—rather than against—one another. You can create an outcome whereby everyone walks away better off. Maybe they receive less than they hoped for, certainly less than they were theoretically entitled to, but far more than they could expect from a bidder at a foreclosure auction.

PROFIT FROM THE FORECLOSURE AUCTION

Although foreclosure sales typically lose money for lenders, lien holders, and property owners, savvy bidders can turn these sales into big profits. But you must prepare. Bidding blind can buy you problems you do not see.

Why Foreclosures Sell for Less than Market Value

Foreclosure (court-ordered) properties sell at prices much lower than their market values. Why? Because court-sanctioned auctions do not satisfy the criteria of a market value transaction:

Sale Characteristics

Market Value Sale	Foreclosure Auction
No seller or buyer duress	Forced sale
Buyer and seller well informed	Scarce information
60- to 180-day marketing period	5 minutes or less selling time
Financing on typical terms	Spot cash (or within 24 hours)
Marketable title	No title guarantees
Warranty deed	Sheriff's (or trustee) deed
Seller disclosures	No seller disclosures (as is)
Close inspection of physical condition	No physical inspection
Yard sign	Rarely a yard sign
"Homes for sale" ads	Legal notice posting
Sales agent services	No sales agent services

Foreclosure auctions seem purposely designed to sell at the *lowest possible sales price*. They take place under conditions that run contrary to all principles of effective marketing.

Adverse Sales Conditions. The auction sellers (sheriff's office, clerk of court, trustee) provide potential buyers no information about a property other than its legal description. They insist on cash. They offer no contingency contracts to allow buyers time to arrange financing. The seller rarely holds an open house or sets up appointments to show the property. Buyers accept the property as is with no guarantees or assurances about title quality, physical condition, or environmental hazards. No sales agents offer advice, counseling, MLS listing, or persuasive reasons to buy.

No Guarantee of Vacancy. The foreclosure authorities don't even agree to convey the property free of occupants (owners, tenants, squatters). You may buy a property at a foreclosure auction and spend several months (or longer) to evict the people staying there. Clever occupants use delay tactics. Here are several:

File bankruptcy.
Claim that the foreclosure sale violated due process.
Organize a people's protest of some sort.

Continuously make idle promises, like "We'll be out by the end of next week."

Seek intervention from some type of child welfare office or other social service agency.

Claim a female in the household is pregnant.

Seek protection under a lease agreement (even though foreclosure sales nullify leases if made after the mortgage on the property was recorded in the public records).

Threaten you or the property with physical harm unless you permit the occupants to stay on for "just a little while."

It's rarely a question (in the United States) of *whether* you can get the people out—as a rule you can—it's more a question of *when,* and at what cost and effort—and in what condition will you receive the property?

For most would-be buyers, the risk, expense, and aggravation of foreclosure sales deter them from even showing up to bid. When you consider the lame marketing efforts, the adverse conditions and risks of sale, and the potential occupancy problem, is it any wonder that foreclosed properties deserve to sell at a fraction of their market value?

Make the Adverse Sales Efforts Work for You

You might look at the foreclosure sales process and say, "Too many potential problems. No way do I want to take those risks. Besides, how could I ever come up with so much cash on short notice?" That's the attitude of most real estate homebuyers and investors. It explains why at most sales the foreclosing lender wins the bid at a price equal to (or slightly above) its outstanding balance.

Overcome the Risks of Bidding. Risk looms large to block your path to foreclosure profits. To bid smart, know as much about the property as due diligence demands.

How can you obtain this information? First, meet with the defaulting property owners to talk over preforeclosure workout possibilities. Even when those discussions end without agreement, you still learn about the property (market value, fix-up needs, improvement opportunities), the neighborhood, and the owner's intentions. This step places you ahead of the game. Second, research the title records. Look for recorded liens and encumbrances. You can research property records in the clerk of court's office or, increasingly, on the clerk of court's website. If you find no obvious title problems, ask for a preliminary opinion of title from a lawyer or title insurer.

Time and Money. To meet with owners and check the title will cost you time, legwork, and perhaps several hundred dollars. Yet, if you buy only one property out of every five you seriousy investigate, you still gain a good payback for your efforts. Just confirm your numbers. Question whether the sales price of the fixed-up property will exceed the total amount of your bid price and fix-up costs by a healthy profit margin.

Inferior Liens Wiped Out. When you buy a property in foreclosure, all liens inferior to the one foreclosed will usually get wiped out. Assume that the first mortgagee is forcing the foreclosure. You win the auction by out-bidding this lender by $500. The first mortgagee takes what it's owed. The next claim in line takes whatever money is left.

Judgment creditors, mechanic's liens, second mortgagees, tenant leases, and any other claims disappear. Only existing tax liens, special assessments, and perhaps past-due homeowners' association fees may survive. (Lien priority and survival laws differ throughout the United States and throughout the countries of the world.)

For any specific property, discuss the priority and wipeout issues with legal counsel. But realize that many (if not all) of those preforeclosure liens that clouded the title will vanish. This fact torques up the preforeclosure negotiating leverage that you hold with lien holders. Creditors who don't settle before foreclosure will likely lose all after foreclosure—unless, of course, they attend the foreclosure auction and submit a winning bid (or perhaps force the bidding up to a price high enough to clear their lien.).

How to Arrange Financing

After you put together enough information to adequately manage the risks of buying at foreclosure, you face the problem of financing. How are you going to get the cash to close the sale? If you lack wealth or credit, you're probably out of luck. Unless you bring in a money partner, it's difficult to buy at the foreclosure sale.

If you can temporarily raise cash—for example, take out a home equity loan, get a cash advance on a credit card, sell (or borrow against) stocks, or maybe take out a signature loan—you can bid at a foreclosure auction. Then, after the foreclosure paperwork clears, you can place an interim or longer-term mortgage loan against the property (as long as your lawyer or title insurer can clear liens or clouds) and pay off your short-term creditors.

Investors who buy foreclosed properties sometimes establish a line of credit at a bank. Then they draw on the money whenever they need it. Or they maintain cash balances in amounts sufficient to cover their usual buying patterns.

THE FORECLOSURE SALE: SUMMING UP

Few real estate investors bid regularly at foreclosure sales. Most prefer to avoid the time, expense, risks, and financing difficulties that foreclosure buying entails. You, too, may agree with this view.

But when you learn the foreclosure game (as it's played in your locale), diligently prepare, and manage risks, you can earn quick rewards. You can buy properties in foreclosure for less (sometimes much less) than their market value. Your challenge is to learn which of these properties meet the test of a true bargain—and which ones carry outsized risks, expensive problems, or excessive (upside-down) financing. Good reasons explain why properties sell at less than market value.

Naturally, too, foreclosure opportunities expand and diminish as real estate markets weaken or strengthen. In up-cycle real estate markets, foreclosure bargains become more difficult to locate, whereas the 100-year-flood cyclical downturns like today serve up boom times for foreclosure buyers (and other investors who will buy while the herd remains uncertain, fearful, or incapacitated). True investors celebrate the pessimistic news reporting. They know that even perfect storms clear out. Blue skies again appear.

Perhaps you missed buying stocks when the Dow fell to 6300 in March 2009; maybe you missed buying gold before it awoke from its 20-year slumber; you did not think to buy oil futures in early 1999. You even passed up Google's IPO. No need to regret. Within a risk-reward matrix, today's profit potential with property matches or exceeds these earlier "once-in-a-lifetime" opportunities.

7

PROFIT FROM REOs AND OTHER BARGAIN SALES

Banks own more than 1 million foreclosed properties (REOs). VA, FHA, Fannie Mae, Freddie Mac, private mortgage insurers, and even OWC sellers hold for sale perhaps another million (or more) houses, condominiums, apartment buildings, retail stores, mobile home parks, and vacant lands. And this flood of REOs may continue to rise before it recedes.

Although the Resolution Trust Corporation (RTC) sales and auctions during the early 1990s created abundant REO opportunities in some areas (mostly Texas, Oklahoma, Southern California, and Arizona), today's REO bargains extend widely throughout the United States, the United Kingdom, Ireland, Spain, and other countries.

Indeed, the sale of REOs at distressed prices (as well as the sale of preforeclosure short sales and foreclosure auctions) have caused the drop in values for nearly all properties. As REOs pile up, even sellers free of financial distress must cut their prices to compete. Likewise for new homebuilders. Today, in many developments, recently constructed, unsold houses now compete directly with similar houses that builders had sold during the boom—only now competition occurs at the much lower, distressed-seller prices—as those former boom-time homebuyers default on their over mortgaged properties.

SAD FOR SELLERS AND BUILDERS, BARGAINS FOR YOU

Sad news for sellers means bargains for homebuyers and investors in two ways: (1) You not only can buy properties today at prices 25 to 75 percent below peak prices, but also at prices less than replacement cost. And (2) during the next several years, the high numbers of REOs that now crowd the market will gradually fall back to lower levels. Their depressing effect on market prices will slow and eventually disappear. Accordingly, until REOs dwindle and property prices climb substantially above replacement costs (the costs of construction), new housing starts will remain well below long-term demand (as supported by growth in population, immigration, household formations, incomes, and jobs).

As emphasized throughout this book, you are witnessing the perfect right time, right price opportunity to buy low and sell for a nice-sized gain within 5 to 10 years. Even better, REOs provide these benefits without unusual risks. Unlike a foreclosure auction where you face uncertainty about property condition and title defects, REOs provide a safer alternative. As standard operating REO procedure, lenders clean up title problems, evict unauthorized occupants, and bring all past-due property tax payments, assessments, and HOA fees up to date. REO lenders may also permit buyers to write contingency offers subject to appraisal, financing, and professional inspection. You can buy REOs with less fear of nasty surprises.[1]

HOW TO FIND REOS

In desperate times like these, REO lenders often sell REOs through highly advertised auctions. Property agents even organize foreclosure bus trips to tour distressed neighborhoods and properties. (In stable and strong markets, lenders play it low key. No lender likes to publicize the fact that it's "throwing down-on-their-luck families out of their homes.") In addition to big auctions, you can find REOs in two other ways: (1) follow up after court-ordered foreclosure sales, and (2) locate Realtors who specialize in REO listings.

Follow Up with Lenders after Foreclosure Sales

Attend the sheriff's foreclosure sale. When a lender wins the bid for a property that interests you, buttonhole the bidder and start talking business.

---

[1]Several exceptions might include (1) states where the foreclosed owners may have a right of redemption; (2) cases in which the foreclosed owners still retain some legal right to challenge the validity of the foreclosure sale; or (3) instances in which a bankruptcy trustee or the Internal Revenue Service (tax lien) is entitled to bring the property within their powers. Rarely would any of these potential claims be worth losing sleep over. But before closing an REO purchase, talk over these issues with a real estate attorney.

Also, visit the REO (loss mitigation) departments of lenders. Show a lender how your offer saves (makes?) the bank money. If you run into a bureaucratic stone wall, persevere. Today, many lenders do not know what they are doing. Your perseverance may not only reward you with a good property, but more importantly, you'll build relationships that open the bank's doors for future transactions.

Sometimes, too, lenders acquire REOs without foreclosure. Lenders occasionally open their morning mail to find the keys to a house, a deed, and a note from the distressed owners, "We're out of here. It's your problem now."

To learn about REOs that lenders now hold in their portfolio of properties, cold call mortgage lenders. Ask for a list of their REOs. Or, rather than ask for a complete list of REOs, narrow your focus. Tell lenders what you're specifically looking for in terms of location, size, price range, floor plan, condition, or other features. In that way, a lender can answer your request without disclosing the full number of REOs within its inventory. Loss mitigation might also refer you to a Realtor.

Locate Specialty Realtors

Many mortgage lenders do not sell directly to REO investors for two reasons: (1) they do not want to invite unfavorable publicity; and (2) they do want to promote good relations with Realtors.[2] Because most mortgage lenders expect Realtors to bring them new mortgage loan business, the lenders can't then turn their backs on Realtors and become FSBO (for sale by owner) dealers. In the real estate business, network relationships generate reciprocating referrals.

Cultivate relationships with Realtors who specialize in this market. (In fact, HUD, VA, Fannie Mae, and Freddie Mac almost always sell their REOs through Realtors.) In most cities, you can easily find REO specialists by looking through newspaper classified real estate ads, Realtor.com, and the foreclosure websites. Increasingly, too, some Realtors are creating foreclosure listing brochures and even office window displays.

Hire a Foreclosure Pro. Once you have identified several advertised foreclosure specialists, call them or stop by for a visit. Learn their backgrounds. Do they only dabble in the field of REOs, short sales, and foreclosures? Or do they make this field their full-time business? When I telephoned REO specialist John Huguenard in Orlando, Florida, he talked with me for an hour and a half about property availability, detailed

---

[2] Also, most lenders don't want to waste time with all of those investor wannabes who have just read a nothing-down book or graduated from a foreclosure guru's seminar.

financing and purchase procedures, hot areas of town, rehab potential, estimating repair costs, portfolio lenders, strategies for buying and managing properties as well as selecting tenants, and a dozen other related topics.

During our conversation, John asked me, "I'll bet you haven't talked to any other agents who know as much as I do about REOs and foreclosures, have you? I've been doing this for 23 years. Last year, I sold 90 houses and rehabbed 16 others for my own account."

John is the kind of REO pro you want to work with. When you build a relationship with an agent who's really in the know, you won't have to do your own legwork and door knocking. Your REO agent will screen properties as soon as—if not before—they come on the market. He will then notify you immediately.

Specialty agents stay on top of the finance plans that portfolio, government, and conventional lenders offer to homebuyers and investors. John Huguenard knew of portfolio lenders doing 100 percent LTV investor loans for investor acquisition and rehab. Tighter underwriting makes such loans more difficult—if not impossible—to find now. But a good REO specialist will know the best loan products available no matter what phase of the credit and property cycle we are going through.

HUD HOMES AND OTHER HUD PROPERTIES

Each year the FHA (Federal Housing Administration), a division of HUD, insures hundreds of thousands of new mortgage loans. (Nationwide, the total number of outstanding FHA mortgages runs into the millions.) FHA loans are originated by banks, savings institutions, mortgage bankers, mortgage brokers, and credit unions.

If borrowers fail to repay their FHA loans, the owner of the mortgage may force the property into a foreclosure sale. Rather than keep the property in its own REO portfolio, that lender turns in a claim to HUD (FHA's parent). HUD then pays the lender the amount due under its mortgage insurance coverage and acquires the foreclosed property. Next, HUD puts the property (along with all the others it has acquired in similar fashion) up for sale to the general public. To see HUD's inventory, go to hud.gov and follow the HUD homes for sale link (http://portal.hud.gov/hudportal/HUD?src=/topics/homes_for_sale).

Although HUD is best known for selling single-family houses, it also sells:

♦ Vacant lots
♦ Duplexes or two units on one lot

- Triplexes (three units)
- Fourplexes (a four-unit building)
- Condominiums
- Apartment complexes

Homeowners versus Investors

In the contest for HUD *homes*, HUD favors owner-occupants over investors in two ways: (1) owner-occupants get the first right to bid; and (2) HUD offers FHA low- or nothing-down insured mortgages only to owner-occupants of one- to four-family properties.[3] HUD does not presently finance HUD homes for those who do not intend to live in the property. (Do not lie to HUD and falsely claim that you plan to occupy a property. Do so and you commit a felony, which HUD will prosecute.)

Given HUD's owner-occupant bias, you might think that homebuyers snap up all of the great buys and investors are stuck with the dregs. On the one hand, that may be true. If, as an investor, you look for red ribbon deals at a bargain price, your HUD pickings might prove few and far between. That type of HUD home typically sells fast at a good price. When HUD homes pile up in an area, your odds look better. On the other hand, if a fixer-upper fits your fancy, you can find great HUD buys because first-time homebuyers (HUD's primary market) scare easily.

As one HUD investor told me, "I always look for properties with the highest fear factor. Most homebuyers are afraid of homes that need work. They don't want the risk of cost overruns. They think they lack the knowledge and time to handle the fix-up. And they're right. But I do know how to deal with these things—and that knowledge gives me the advantage to earn good profits through HUD home rehabs for either rental or resale."

As-Is Condition

HUD does not warrant the condition of any of the properties that it sells. Even when HUD/FHA offers insured financing, HUD inspects the property for its own benefit only, *not* for the benefit of the buyer.

HUD Recommends Professional Inspections. Because HUD sells its properties as is, HUD encourages prospective bidders to obtain professional independent inspections *before* they submit a bid. HUD does not accept

---

[3]This section discusses procedures for HUD homes. We address other types of properties later.

offers with an inspection contingency. What you see (or don't see) is what you get.

However, HUD's refusal to accept inspection contingencies does make buying somewhat risky. Because professional inspections cost $250 to $400, hopeful buyers are expected to incur this fee up front without knowing whether they will actually win the bid.

This fact explains why most first-time buyers avoid HUD fixer-uppers. Inspection fees can easily get wasted. HUD's policy of *as is–no contingencies* favors experienced investors who can estimate fix-up costs *and* accept the risks.

Disclosures and Repair Escrows. Although HUD refuses to permit offers with an inspection contingency, before closing a sale, HUD does allow the winning bidder to run a lead paint assessment on the property if it was built before 1978. HUD may disclose property defects that it knows about. In some cases, HUD will agree to insure a mortgage for a property only if a buyer agrees to make specified repairs.

None of these actions by HUD cancels HUD's as is–no warranties policy. Partial disclosure doesn't mean full disclosure. At HUD, caveat emptor (let the buyer beware) rules.

Potential Conflict of Interest

Although most foreclosure specialists will work to find you a good deal, potential conflict of interest does arise in the sale of HUD properties. First, if you do not submit a winning bid, your sales agent does not earn a commission. An unethical agent could pressure you to raise your bid even if the value of the property doesn't justify a higher price. Second, sales agents may submit bids from competing buyers who bid on the same property. If you bid $80,000, an agent could tell another, more favored buyer to bid $80,100. You (may) lose. Third, HUD typically pays brokers who submit a winning bid a 5 percent sales commission plus, on occasion, a $500 (or more) selling bonus for designated properties. Again, this reward may encourage your agent to push you to bid high on a property because she will receive an extra reward.

As another quirk in HUD offers, HUD calculates your bid price net of the sales commission that HUD will pay. If your agent tells HUD that she will accept a 2 percent sales commission, that effectively increases your net bid price. If you bid $100,000 and your agent wants 5 percent, you have submitted an effective bid price of $95,000. If the agent will accept a 2 percent commission, your $100,000 bid is viewed by HUD as if it were $98,000. To increase HUD's net, you can increase your gross bid price—or your agent could reduce her percentage fee.

Although you should not unjustly insinuate that your agent is likely to engage in underhanded sales tactics, it shows good sense to ask your agent how she handles these potential conflicts.

Buyer Incentives

When hard times hit, HUD foreclosures accumulate to unmanageable and costly numbers. To reduce this big inventory of REOs and create quicker sales, HUD may offer buyers easy financing, cash bonuses, and steep discounts. If unsold HUD properties pile up in your area, you could land a particularly good deal.

The Bid Package

As might be expected of a government agency, HUD does not make buying simple. Unlike a private purchase, where you simply write out your offer on any valid contract form, HUD requires a specific contract submission package. Bidders must use only HUD-approved forms and documentation. To bid, complete the required forms, addenda, and enclosures fully and accurately. Also, your contract package must arrive in HUD's regional office according to HUD's posted schedule.

HUD may (and does) refuse to accept bid packages that do not conform to its instructions. Given HUD's well-known inflexibility, work only with conscientious foreclosure pros who know in detail the ins and outs of HUD's requirements. Not only does HUD specify a tangle of bureaucratic bidding rules—those rules can vary by locale and are always subject to change. Your success demands a HUD-experienced sales pro.

DEPARTMENT OF VETERANS AFFAIRS (REOs)

To sell its foreclosed properties, VA follows rules similar to those of HUD. However, as noted, HUD and VA rules are subject to change—or may vary by region according to the number of REOs in their inventory. As advised earlier, change and detail stand as compelling reasons to submit bids only through a foreclosure pro with HUD/VA experience.

At present, here are 12 major ways the HUD/VA programs resemble each other:

1. The VA sells through a sealed bid process. Likewise, as either a potential homeowner or an investor, you may submit multiple bids during the same bid period.

2. You cannot *directly* negotiate with, or submit a bid to, the VA. You must submit your bid through a VA-approved broker (your foreclosure pro).

3. The VA sells its homes on an as-is basis. Even though it may partially disclose a home's defects, it offers no warranties. Caveat emptor.

4. The VA does guarantee title, and it permits buyers to obtain a title policy.

5. The VA accepts bids that yield it the highest net proceeds (not the highest price). If you agree to pay closing expenses or sales commissions, you can win the bid over others who offer higher prices, but pass these costs (a lower net) on to the VA.

6. Just as HUD/FHA charges FHA buyers an insurance fee, the VA charges buyers who choose its financing a guarantee fee of around 2 percent of the amount financed (more or less, depending on the amount of your down payment).

7. The VA accepts bids only on VA forms. If you err in completing the forms, your bid gets tossed out.

8. The VA publicizes its properties through a combination of newspaper ads, broker lists, and Internet postings. You can access VA REOs through the links at hud.gov.

9. Local VA offices report to regional directors, who may issue policies and procedures that differ from those in other regions throughout the country.

10. The VA may choose to keep your earnest money deposit if you fail to close a winning bid for any reason other than inability to obtain financing. (Preapproval for VA and HUD bids is strongly advised.)

11. As with HUD sales contracts, VA purchase offers do not include a contingency for postbid property inspections. You may, though, inspect a property before you bid.

12. When necessary, the VA evicts holdover tenants or homeowners before placing a VA property on the market. At closing, you receive the keys to a vacant property.

Big Advantages for Investors

Although the VA follows rules similar to HUD, investors gain more from the VA in two ways:

1. The VA gives equal status to investors. The VA looks for the highest net offered by any credible buyer—homeowner or investor.

2. Unlike HUD, the VA offers REO financing to investors. At present in my area, for example, investors can close financing on a VA home with total cash out of pocket of less than 6 percent of a property's purchase price. Also, the VA typically applies relaxed qualifying standards. VA buyers (who need not qualify as veterans) must show *acceptable,* not perfect, credit records. (For specifics in your area, talk with your foreclosure pro.)

With relatively attractive investor or homebuyer financing, VA homes in good (and even not-so-good) repair sometimes sell at or near market value prices. At today's depressed market values, however, even market value can look good to investors for these three reasons:

1. Leverage permits you to accelerate your wealth-building returns.
2. Even at market value prices and 80 percent LTV, many VA properties pull in rents high enough to provide a positive cash flow from day one of ownership.
3. The VA allows future buyers to assume your VA financing. For investors who want to fix and sell, an assumable loan makes a great benefit. Plus, when market interest rates go up, a lower-rate assumable VA loan gives your sales efforts a big competitive advantage over other for-sale properties.

VA REOs provide an excellent source of properties and financing for beginning and experienced investors alike. Investigate this opportunity.

FANNIE MAE AND FREDDIE MAC REOs

Fannie Mae and Freddie Mac are the two largest players in the nation's secondary mortgage market. These mortgage companies don't loan to homebuyers, but they do provide the loan funding for more than 80 percent of the one- to four family properties that are made by other mortgage lenders. (In normal times, Fannie and Freddie account for around 50 percent of one- to four-family properties. Today, these players dominate the game by themselves.)

Sometimes, when their loans go bad, Fannie (or Freddie) may force the originating lender to buy back its loan. Then this lender ends up with a foreclosed property in its REO portfolio. Typically, however, lenders who satisfied Fannie's (or Freddie's) underwriting guidelines can require Fannie (or Freddie) to take ownership of the foreclosed property. (At this time, just in the state of Florida, Fannie holds nearly 1,000 properties for sale.)

Agent Listings

Fannie and Freddie do not often use the bid sales procedure that's common to HUD and VA. Instead, both companies choose a realty firm and give that firm an exclusive right-to-sell listing. The realty firm then places that REO into MLS. The realty agent who takes on responsibility for a foreclosed property first inspects it and then recommends the best way to fix it up to maximize its sale price.

Price to Market. Fannie and Freddie might spend thousands of dollars to recondition and repair a property, and then price that property aggressively. So, you won't necessarily buy Fannie or Freddie properties at a steep discount to market value.

But these times are not typical. Fannie and Freddie hold record numbers of REOs that they must sell. Especially in markets hardest hit, Fannie and Freddie are open to offers. Talk with local foreclosure pros. You will likely find some bargains. (I recently bought a Fannie property at 20 percent below market—and market was 60 percent below the sales price of 2005. GRM equals 67—and that was for move-in ready condition, although to offer the unit to the type of tenant I wanted, I had it painted and installed new carpet.)

First-Time Homebuyers—Special Financing. Fannie and Freddie prefer credit-qualified homebuyers (especially first-time homebuyers). In addition to the bargain price appeal, these companies attract buyers with well-presented homes and special financing.

Freddie even permits homebuyers to "customize your Homesteps home." Under this option, Freddie invites buyers (for a price, of course) to upgrade their home's carpeting, padding, vinyl, appliances, and window blinds. Freddie also offers to sell owner-occupied properties for 5 percent down, no private mortgage insurance (which saves buyers $50 or $80 per month, possibly more), lower closing costs, and an attractive interest rate.

All Properties Sold As Is. Even though Fannie and Freddie often fix up their properties, neither warrants nor guarantees the condition of a property. Unlike buying from HUD or the VA, though, as a Fannie or Freddie buyer, you may submit a purchase contract offer that includes an inspection contingency. You can purchase a home warranty plan, too, just as you (or the sellers) can with most other property sales. Mortgage preapproval is either highly recommended or required.

Investors Invited

Both Fannie and Freddie have accepted investors with no priority-listing period that applies only to owner-occupants. Both companies also have offered favorable financing for credit-qualified investors. You pay just 15 percent down (in contrast to the conventional down payment of 20 to 30 percent for investor-owned properties). Closing costs may come in a little lower, too. Investor interest rates usually sit on the low side of market. You can locate Freddie and Fannie properties, and their latest loan programs, at www.homesteps.com and www.homepath.com. You can also access them through links at hud.gov.

However, investor treatment now is in flux. To protect and maintain predominantly owner-occupied neighborhoods and condo complexes from tipping to majority rental, investors are not as welcome as they once were. Yet, too, there's growing political pressure to liquidate REOs and stabilize housing supply and demand. Without investor purchases, economic recovery will continue to sag. In other words, as is usually true with political forces, they operate in opposite directions. My guess is that Congress will act to open up more Fannie and Freddie REO opportunities for investors. But no one can forecast for sure. Stay informed and ask your REO pro to alert you to any favorable changes that may occur.

FEDERAL GOVERNMENT AUCTIONS

Each year, the federal government (in addition to HUD and the VA) sells seized and surplus real estate, including houses, apartment complexes, office buildings, ranches, and vacant and developed land. Among the most active sellers are the Internal Revenue Service (IRS), General Services Administration (GSA), and the Federal Deposit Insurance Corporation (FDIC). On occasion, you can also find properties offered by the Small Business Administration (SBA).You can locate government agency properties and sales procedures through the following link at HUD.gov (http://portal .hud.gov/hudportal/HUD?src=/topics/homes_for_sale).

BUY FROM FORECLOSURE SPECULATORS

A speculator wins the bid for a foreclosed property at $135,000. The property would sell for $195,000 if it were fixed up and marketed effectively. Soon after the foreclosure sale, you offer the speculator $150,000 (or whatever). To minimize risk, you attach several contingencies to your offer that permit you to get the property thoroughly inspected, evict any holdover owners or tenants, clear up title problems, seek title insurance, and arrange financing. If the property checks out satisfactorily, the sale closes, and the speculator makes a quick $15,000 (more or less). You obtain the property at an attractive discount without costly surprises that can turn a superficially promising foreclosure into a loss.

PROBATE AND ESTATE SALES

Probate and estate sales present another potential source of bargain-priced properties. When owners of properties die, their property may be sold to satisfy the deceased's mortgagee and other creditors. Even when the deceased leaves sufficient wealth in cash to satisfy all claims against the estate, most heirs prefer to sell the property rather than retain ownership.

Probate

To buy a property through probate, submit a bid through the estate's administrator (usually a lawyer) or executor. Then all bids are reviewed by the probate judge assigned to the case. Depending on local and state laws, the judge may then select a bid for approval or reopen the bidding. Because of legal procedures and delays, bidding on probate properties can require you to persevere. Judges wield discretion about whether to accept a probate bid. You cannot know for sure where your bid stands.

For example, a probate property came up for sale in an area of $150,000 houses. The probate administrator listed the house for sale at $115,000. A flurry of bids came in that ranged from a low of $105,000 up to a high of $118,000. Several months later, the judge looked at the bids, announced the high bid at $118,000, and then solicited additional offers. Eventually, the judge approved the sale at a price of $129,850 to someone who had not even been involved in the first round of bidding. You cast your bid and take your chances.

Estate Sales

Sometimes, a decedent's assets are not dragged through the probate process. Then you can buy directly from the heirs or the executor of an estate. Some investors regularly read the obituary notices, contact heirs, and try to buy before the property is listed with a real estate agent. To succeed in this approach, develop an empathetic approach.

Estate sales frequently produce bargain prices because heirs eagerly want cash. They may also need the money to pay off a mortgage, other creditors, or estate taxes. Out-of-town heirs (especially) may not want to hold a vacant property for an extended period until a top-dollar buyer is found. Once again, pressures of time or money can lead to sales prices that fall below a property's market value.

PRIVATE AUCTIONS

In these times of REO stress, Freddie and Fannie, HUD and VA banks, and other owners of distressed properties are increasingly holding auctions. Attend one. Observe. You'll have fun. Often music is playing, and food and drinks are served. A festive mood prevails. The auction company works to make potential bidders feel good. Beyond this display of cheer, though, the auction company is really setting up its prey. The auctioneer wants to sell every property at the highest possible price. Auctioneers earn a percentage of the day's take, plus, perhaps, a bonus for exceeding a certain level of sales.

To gain a bargain price, enjoy—but remain aloof from—the festive frenzy. Attend the auction armed with market and property information. Prepare to walk out a winner—not merely a buyer. Here's how you can make that happen:

♦ *Thoroughly inspect a property.* During the weeks before most private auctions, the auction company will schedule open houses at the properties to be sold. If you can't visit an open house, contact a real estate agent and ask for a personal showing. (Many auction companies cooperate with Realtors. If an agent brings a winning bidder to the auction, that agent earns a 1 or 2 percent sales commission.) Sometimes, auction properties sell cheap because they are nothing more than teardowns waiting for a bulldozer. Or they may suffer any of a number of other defects. Even new properties aren't necessarily defect free. Inspect before you bid.

♦ *Appraise the property.* If the property is free of defects, you still can't assume value. Study recent selling prices of comparable properties. Don't count on the auctioneer's list price to guide you. Just because you buy a property 25 percent below its previous asking price doesn't mean you have bought at 25 percent below the property's market value. Asking price doesn't equal market value—past, present, or future.

♦ *Set a maximum bid price.* Remember, you seek a bargain. Market value tells you what a property might sell for if fixed up and marketed by a competent and aggressive real estate agent. Market value does not tell you the price you should bid. Before the auction, set your maximum bid price. Don't let the auctioneer's boosters (often, attractive younger women) cajole, excite, romance, bamboozle, or intimidate you into going higher.

♦ *Review the paperwork that will accompany a successful bid.* Before the auction begins, review the property tax statements, environmental reports, lot survey, legal description, and purchase contract you'll be asked to sign.

♦ *Learn what type of deed the seller will use to convey the property.* A general warranty deed assures title subject to certain named exceptions. Other types of deeds convey fewer warranties. Understand a deed's limitations (liens, easements, encroachments, exceptions, missing heirs, and so on). Title insurance is your best safeguard. If a property's title is uninsurable, consult a real estate attorney or title company to obtain an opinion of the title risks a buyer might take on.

♦ *Pay the deposit.* To become eligible to bid, register with the auction company before the auction begins, and present a cashier's check or other acceptable proof of deposit funds (amount and verifications differ by auction). You will then receive a bid card that tells the auctioneer that you are approved to bid. Without a bid card, the auctioneer won't recognize your bid.

♦ *Find out if financing is available.* Auction companies often prearrange financing on some or all of their properties. Find out terms and qualifying standards. If no financing is provided, determine how much time the auction company gives you to arrange your own financing. Unlike most forclosure auctions, private auction companies typically do not insist that bidders pay cash for their properties within, say, 24 to 48 hours.

♦ *Learn whether bid prices are absolute or subject to a reserve minimum.* Auction properties are either priced absolute or with reserve. If absolute, the property sells no matter how low the top bidder's price. With a reserve price, the top bid must exceed a prearranged minimum amount, or the property is pulled out of the auction. On occasion, the owner of a property may nod to the auctioneer and approve a bid that does not meet the reserve minimum.

How to Find Auctions

Most auction companies advertise their upcoming auctions in local and sometimes national newspapers (for example, the *Wall Street Journal*). Fannie and Freddy announce their auction times, dates, and places on their websites. Auction companies not only want to attract as many bidders as possible, they want to draw large crowds so that they can create a sense of anticipation and excitement. In addition to advertising, most auction companies will place your name on their e-mail lists.

Local auction companies are listed in the Yellow Pages. Large-scale local auctions, though, are frequently handled by auction companies that operate nationwide. These include, among many others, Fisher Auction Company, Hudson and Marshall, J. P. King, Kennedy-Wilson, Larry Latham, NRC Auctions, Ross Dove and Company, and Sheldon Good and Company. Even if you decide not to bid, large auctions are fun to attend. Try one. You'll learn the tricks of the trade as you watch the professional auctioneers and investors vie with each other.

8

PROFIT BY CREATING VALUE

During the boom years, herds of speculators stampeded property shows, model homes, hotel ballrooms, and any other venue where builders sold off-plan properties. These buyer-speculators typically placed 5 or 10 percent down to book a new house, villa, or condominium. Then, within months, they flipped their purchase contract to score a quick $25,000 to $100,000 gain. Great way to make fast, easy money (but not nearly as risk-free as buyers thought).

Alas, those giddy days have disappeared. But flipping itself continues. Your possibilities to earn short-term (but not easy) profits have actually grown. Only now, instead of buying off-plan, you buy a bargain-priced, neglected or distressed property. Then work your magic to create value.

FIX, SELL, PROFIT!

Are you willing to research properties? Do you enjoy creative work? Then rely on fix, sell, and profit to jump-start your wealth building through real estate. Of course, by employing the word *fix*, I refer not only to repairing broken windows and patching holes in the plaster. I mean cost-effective improvements that excite your target market of buyers (or renters), especially the features and design that elicit the oohs, aahs, and "Wow, look at this, honey."

To see the possibilities of fix and sell, follow the examples of Pat Williams and the Browns (Ray and Annie B.). As California was heading into its last deep recession, Pat Williams and her husband split up. Out of work and with two kids to support, Pat needed money. She chose fix-and-sell real estate. At the time, given the deteriorating economy of the Golden State, you might think that Pat was off her rocker. Not at all: Pat learned how to capitalize on adversity.

During the next five years, as California home prices fell by 20 to 30 percent or more, Pat bought and resold six homes. After each sale, she banked between $20,000 and $40,000. Her total profits exceeded $150,000. What was her secret? A keen eye for a bargain, hard work, and perseverance. "The best deals are not marked with a big red flag," Pat says. "I had to weed through a lot of properties and get up to speed on the market."

When Pat says she had to weed through a lot of properties, she means that literally as well as figuratively. Relying on seller financing, Pat ferreted out run-down, bargain-priced properties. She studied market values and competing properties, and then renovated and revitalized the houses she had bought. Next, Pat sold for a nice-sized gain. Applying her newly acquired market savvy, Pat didn't wait for the California real estate market to turn around. She created her own added value.

Would you like to earn an extra $25,000, $50,000, or more during the next two years? Would you like to create instant equity and boost your potential rental income? Locate a property that offers great promise for improvement. Don't focus on whether the property suits your tastes. Just find a house, condo, or apartment building that you can buy low, design improvements, boost rents, and then sell (or hold and refinance) to realize the extra value that you have created.

While the media moan about foreclosures, failing banks, and unemployment, self-starters are not waiting for things to get better. They know that today's property and mortgage markets offer a dynamic combo of profit-generating possibilities. (For a *strategic* fixer-upper example, see the value-creating strategy of Craig Wilson in Chapter 10.)

YOUR FIXER-UPPER SEARCH

As you drive through neighborhoods and see properties, focus. Generate ideas that you can use to improve each property. List and describe each property's features, site/yard, and neighborhood—desirable and undesirable. Notice color schemes, floor plans, storage, parking, renovations, landscaping, and out-of-date turnoffs. Inspect site, egress and ingress, basements, attics, and garages. Know the relevant zoning codes.

Most real estate books and articles tell you to buy fixer-uppers, but realize that *any property* you can decorate, design, remodel, expand, or romance qualifies as a fixer-upper. The property improvement game refers to profitable creativity. You can make nearly any property live better, look better, and feel better.

Throw away the false belief that only run-down properties make good fixer-uppers. Sure, poor maintenance offers potential for value-enhancing improvements. But for savvy investors, even well-kept properties aren't immune to profitable change. Stay alert to opportunity, and you will find ways to make a property more desirable to potential buyers or tenants. Want more evidence? Turn to the experience of Raymond and Annie Brown.

The Browns Create Value in a Down Market

When Raymond Brown and his wife, Annie B., bought a vacation retreat they called Woodpecker Haven, Raymond says, "I thought it was a done property. It was only five years old."

To Annie B., though, the house invited her talents. An interior designer with a forward-looking imagination, Annie B. modestly observed that the home "presented great potential." As Raymond tells the story, "Here are some of the improvements my enterprising wife accomplished to transform a livable property into an exquisite home":

♦ Landscaped the front and rear yards.
♦ Installed a drip irrigation system.
♦ Built a stone fence around the pool.
♦ Added decks around the rear of the house.
♦ Installed French doors in both bedrooms that led out to the decks.
♦ Remodeled the guest bedroom and bath to create a master bedroom for visitors.
♦ Built a fireplace, bookshelves, and cabinets and installed track lighting in the living room.
♦ Trimmed overgrown trees and shrubs to enhance a picture-perfect view from the front porch.

Although Raymond and Annie B. invested $75,000 in these and other improvements, they added around $175,000 in value—throughout a rapidly falling market. "We bought our Sonoma retreat," says Raymond, "just as home prices were peaking, and sold several years later, two months before market prices again turned up. . . . Yet we made a $100,000 profit. Our secret? Woodpecker Haven was a fixer-upper we renovated inside and out."

The experience of the Browns shows that even a relatively new or well-kept property can be enhanced to look better, live better, feel better, or both. (Remember, at the time of purchase, Woodpecker Haven was only five years old. Recall, too, both the Browns and cash-starved Pat Williams made their big gains in a *falling* market.) To fix up a property may require you to scrape encrusted bubble gum off floors and counters, patch holes in the roof, fight a gnarled mass of weeds and debris in the backyard, or pull out and replace rusted and obsolete kitchen and bathroom plumbing. But the fun of fixing up a property should also excite your imagination.

Visualize ways to redecorate, redesign, remodel, expand, or bring romance into the property.

To profit from fix-up work, you need not dirty your hands. Sure, sweat equity pays dividends, but market research, creativity, and imagination pay more. To create value: (1) search for a property that needs work; (2) search for a property whose creative possibilities are overlooked by most buyers; or (3) search for a property to improve its physical condition, appeal, *and* livability. Strive to perceive opportunities that other, less alert investors pass by. Unnoticed potential diminishes competitive bidding and enhances your profit potential.

Research, Research, Research

When you fix up to create value, no set rules apply. Cities, properties, tenants, and buyers differ. Features that one person loves, another may hate. What's popular in California may look out of place in Alberta. Today's fads may become tomorrow's green shag carpet. What suits you may not appeal to the tastes and lifestyles of most people. Money spent for a remodeled bathroom in Atlanta may return $3 for each $1 invested. In Ottawa, a similar fix-up might net 50 cents on the dollar.

Multiple variables enter the value equation. Learn what features your future tenants or buyers covet. Plan for profits. Refuse to let your personal tastes or preconceived notions stand unchallenged. Like smart home builders who want their homes to sell, research your market. Develop a target-market improvement strategy.

Ask Realtors and property managers to tell you the turn-ons and turn-offs for tenants and homebuyers. Identify unique niches for rare, yet desired features. Tour new-home developments and waiting-list-only apartment complexes. Watch house makeover TV shows. Notice colors, decorating themes, floor coverings, and floor plans. Discover the models, room counts, features, and amenities that sell best. Which ones stand lonely and unloved? Which features stand functionally? Which ones merely add glitz? What types and sizes of apartment units command the highest rents and display the lowest vacancies? Which properties suffer turnover and vacancies?

Visit open houses to excite your creative impulses.[1] Look for ways other property owners have remodeled, redecorated, or redesigned their properties to make them more livable or more appealing.

---

[1] On slow traffic days, you can often talk in-depth about the market with the on-duty sales agent.

Talk to your friends, relatives, and acquaintances who have remodeling experience. Buy a boxful of those supermarket and bookstore guides with titles like *1,001 Ideas to Improve Your Home or Apartment*. Google images for before-and-after photos (e.g., kitchens, baths, yards, garages, exteriors, family rooms, and so on). Stockpile creative ideas. The greater the number of ideas you can draw from, the more easily you can design a profit-generating improvement strategy.

IMPROVEMENT POSSIBILITIES

When you shop properties with an eye toward creating value, corral your enthusiasm as well as negative first impressions. Avoid reacting to whether you like or dislike a property. Instead, answer this question: Based on what you've learned from market research, can you spend $5,000 to reap a return of $15,000? Or maybe $50,000 to reap a return of $150,000? Evaluate a property for its potential profitability. Think: What combination of the following possibilities can boost the value of the property?

♦ Clean thoroughly.
♦ Add pizzazz.
♦ Create usable space.
♦ Create a view.
♦ Capitalize on owner (builder) nearsightedness.
♦ Eliminate a negative view.
♦ Bring in more natural light.
♦ Reduce noise.

Deep Clean the Property

Before you advertise a property for sale or rent, deep clean it. You may think I'm stating the obvious, but go out and inspect vacant rentals. You'll see that many owners of small rental properties offer unkempt and even nasty units. Many owners say to themselves, "Why clean this place thoroughly? The tenants will leave it like a pigsty anyway." As you can guess, owners who express such belief generate a self-fulfilling prophecy.

Uncared-for rentals turn off (and turn away) top-quality tenants. Tenants who accept units with dirt-encrusted windows and light fixtures, stained carpets, grease-layered stoves, and dust-laden window blinds are likely to treat your property as a pigsty.

Display pride-of-ownership cleanliness. You attract better-quality tenants; you show your tenants the degree of cleanliness you expect. When I first became a landlord, I did operate with the "why clean thoroughly?" attitude. After seeing how badly undesirable tenants can wreck a property, it's easy to reduce maintenance standards. But I soon learned that this attitude brings about a downward drift. When I offered units that stood clearly above the competition, I could choose the best tenants from a list of qualified applicants.

The cleanliness principle applies not just to investors who buy, fix, and rent. Fix-and-sell investors must also apply it. Whether you plan to sell the property to another investor or to a homebuyer, a spotless unit will sell (or rent) more quickly and at a higher price. Tenants and buyers alike discount heavily for dirt and debris. Cleaner units attract higher-quality tenants, and investors pay more for properties with better tenants because better tenants mean lower risk, less trouble, and surer rent collections.

Add Pizzazz with Color Schemes, Decorating Patterns, and Fixtures

Before you paint or redecorate your properties, tour new home developments and recently built, upscale apartment projects. Look through home decorator magazines. Can you enhance the appeal of your units with modern color schemes, wallpapers, or special touches like chair moldings, mirrors, faucets, light fixtures, or patterned tile floors? Avoid going wild with creativity or personal flair, but do add sufficient pizzazz (or romance) to distinguish your units from competing houses or apartments.

Create Usable Space

Have you seen the ads of the California Closet Company? This company transforms cluttered, space-starved closets into masterpieces of design and utility. Beginning with this simple mission, CCC and its imitators have grown into a $3-billion-a-year industry. These companies now apply the same design and utility principle to garages, workshops, and offices. You can mimic their success. Figure out how to create more usable space (or how to make existing space more usable), and you've increased the value of your property.

But look beyond the use of existing space. Can you convert an attic, garage, or basement to additional living area? Can you enclose a porch or patio, add a second story, or build an accessory apartment? Ask, "How can I use or create space to enhance sales appeal or generate more rent from these units?"

Think about right-sizing the living area within the units. *Right-sizing* means that you reduce the size of large rooms by adding walls, room dividers, or separate areas. Or perhaps you can combine small rooms to make larger areas. To a practical and profitable degree, every storage and living area within a house or apartment should fit proportionally to market tastes and preferences. When tenants perceive areas of space as too large or too small, they won't pay top rents or a top price. Right-sizing matches space to buyer or tenant needs.

You right-size when you enlarge (or reduce) the total size of the living area. Several years ago, research by a Manhattan investor revealed that two-bedroom apartments glutted the market and depressed rent levels. Those few buildings that did offer four-bedroom apartments enjoyed waiting lists. This savvy investor bought a building of two-bedroom apartments at a steep discount, combined apartments into four-bedroom units, and rented all of them immediately at premium rent levels. He then sold the property for twice the price that he had paid 28 months earlier.

Create a View

When I was looking for a lakefront home in Winter Park, Florida, I discovered a startling fact. Nearly all lakefront houses (having been built in the 1950s, 1960s, and earlier) failed to fully capture the view potential of their sites. I found closed-in kitchens, master bedrooms on the street side of the houses, and unbelievably (to me), even the lakefront rooms of these houses often lacked large windows.

When I was touring a new housing development in northwest Albuquerque, I came across a house situated such that it could have offered spectacular views of the Sandia Mountain Range. But it didn't. Although I entered the house full of anticipation, disappointment soon set in. None of the windows in the rooms downstairs faced the mountains. Surely, though, the upstairs would prove different. I imagined a master bedroom suite with large windows and perhaps a deck facing out to the mountains. But again, no. The master bedroom was situated to look straight at the house next door. And on the mountain side of the house was a small bedroom with no view window.

The mass production builder of this house had just plopped down a standard model with no attention to the differential advantages of the individual lots within the development.

When you find properties that fail to fully capture a potential view of a lake, ocean, mountain range, park, woods, or other pleasant surroundings, you discover a great way to add value to a property.

Capitalize on Owner Nearsightedness

Often the owners of ill-designed properties become accustomed to the property as it exists and they don't realize its possibilities. After remodeling the lakefront home (that I did buy) in Winter Park to achieve expansive views from eight of the nine rooms in the house, the previous owners stopped by and exclaimed, "Wow! If we had imagined the house could have looked this good, we might never have sold it."

Profitable improvements begin with imagination. Don't rush into fixing up a property. Before you begin your fun, inventory possibilities. Many fix-and-sell investors think property improvement means slapping on a fresh coat of paint and laying down laminate flooring or beige carpeting. These improvements help, but look beyond commonplace ideas. Close your eyes. Then, open your mind and imagine how to transform the property—not merely fix it up.

Eliminate a Negative View

Some buildings suffer diminished value because their windows look directly out into an alley, another building, or perhaps a tangle of power lines. For such properties, eliminate the negative view and convert it into something attractive. Can you change the location of a window? Can you plant shrubbery, bamboo, or leafy trees? Can you add decorative fencing?

The owners of the Black Oak Bookstore in Berkeley, California, transformed an area that had looked out directly into a plain concrete block wall. To remedy this negative, they planted ivy to run up the wall, added hanging plants, a rock garden, and a wooden lattice. These changes created a stunning improvement over the drab concrete wall.

You can even turn a backyard into a beautiful view. The owner of a house I almost bought in La Jolla, California, did just that. In her backyard, this seller had created a large, multitiered, spectacular shrub, flower, and plant arrangement designed and built up within 8-inch by 8-inch lawn timbers. To accent this view from inside the home, she had replaced the rear walls of the house with sliding glass doors. (My description fails to convey the buyer impact this improvement actually achieved.)

This owner had spent around $15,000 to create this eye-pleasing landscape, but in doing so, she added $35,000 to $50,000 to the price. Her house clearly displayed a competitive advantage over other so-called similar houses in the neighborhood.

Enhance the Unit's Natural Light

Most homebuyers and tenants prefer properties with loads of natural light. To achieve this effect, add or enlarge windows, change solid doors to those with glass, or install skylights. In addition to the positive influence of sunshine itself, brighter rooms seem more spacious. To enhance this effect, determine if you can add volume to interior rooms by tearing out a false ceiling; it might even pay to eliminate an attic area. Create a brighter, more spacious look and you elevate the experience of how a home lives and feels.

Consider the experience of home seller Joan Phelps: "The previous owners fully bricked an inside wall of the house, so it was very dark and dreary," says Joan. To solve this problem, Joan and her husband invested $2,620 to tear out much of the brick and add windows on each side of the fireplace. The result was terrific. When the couple put their home up for sale, "We had two offers and a backup buyer the first weekend. First impressions really sell," Joan advises.

Not only did the Phelpses get the price they wanted, but another nearby house with the same basic design sat on the market unsold for months. Tenants and buyers will pay a premium for a bright, cheery property. Can you add windows, skylights, and light-colored window treatments in place of those heavy, dark drapes? Can you rip out low ceilings? With more height, you bring in more light as well as vanquish that closed-in feeling that low ceilings create.

Reduce Noise

Homebuyers, investors, and tenants pay for quiet and discount for noise. Insulation, caulking, earth berms, trees, shrubs, and soundproof windows can help restore quiet. I recently attended a home improvement fair where one exhibitor had a boombox blasting hard-rock music. But this offensive noise machine sat behind the exhibitor's product: sound-insulating windows. As shoppers approached, the man at the exhibit closed the window. The noise disappeared. Quite an effective demonstration of how soundproof windows can muffle or eliminate outside noise.

Many window manufacturers now offer noise-reducing windows. For a sampling, google "soundproof windows." In fact, this year, at a cost of $10,000, I installed new triple-pane, laminated windows ("sound and security" option in manufacturer's model description) in a 2,800-square-foot house that I own. The aesthetic effects of reduced traffic noise and clear visibility achieved a truly transformative difference. Given that every room in the house had expansive windows, the cost proved quite modest relative to the value gained. (A savings of $75 a month in heat and AC also added to the value received.)

As another point about noise, before you buy a multi-unit building, test the soundproofing between units. If you can hear a television, people walking or talking, or toilets flushing, beware. Unless you can solve the noise problem, tenants will complain and you will suffer higher turnover.

REQUIRED REPAIRS AND IMPROVEMENTS

Market your properties in tip-top condition. Creative, appealing improvements add to value. But to realize those potential profits, the property should not show unsightly signs of wear or abuse; all systems must operate; and the property must remain free of hazards to health or life. When thinking about how to improve your property, assess the following areas. The more of these problems you overcome, the fewer criticisms buyers (or tenants) will voice during property showings and negotiations.

Plumbing

Check faucets for leaks and drips. Where washers are needed, replace them. Avoid tightening the handle until the seat is damaged. Buyers (and renters, too) may turn all the faucets on and off to detect damage in the internal workings. All sinks should drain quickly. Check toilets to see whether the water shuts off automatically as it is supposed to. Replace toilet seats that are discolored or cracked. Check the perimeters of all bathroom fixtures, showers, and bathtubs. Repair cracks with caulking compound, especially where leaks are present. If it is cold outside, protect pipes exposed to the weather. Remove stains that were caused by previous leaks. A stain tells buyers that your plumbing needs work.

Electrical System

Verify the condition and location of all electrical outlets. Older properties often lack a sufficient number of outlets to handle today's electrical demands. Check the adequacy of the amperage and the circuit breakers (or fuse boxes). Replace burned outlets. Residents should never need to overload outlets or circuits with adapters and extension cords.

Bring outdated electrical systems up to code and up to modern, tenant-preferred standards.

Heating and Air Conditioning

The heating and air conditioning system should heat and cool effectively and efficiently. Install new filters before you show a property to potential buyers. Some prospects will inspect the filters. If they find a dirty filter, they'll assume that the filters have not been changed regularly and that the system itself suffers damage. New filters signal that you have properly cared for the equipment. Also clean the heating and air conditioning duct outlets. If the property has gas heat (or a gas water heater), remove burnt matches from previous manual pilot lightings (if such still exists). Otherwise, the pilot light will appear defective.

Windows

Replace all cracked or broken windows. Repair broken pulleys and damaged frames and sills. Test windows to see if they lift up and down easily. Never show a property in which the windows have been painted shut. That's a turnoff to buyers. Replace broken and torn screens.

Appliances

Appliances such as a built-in oven, range, garbage disposal, dishwasher, or refrigerator that are to be included in the sale (or rental) should operate properly. Keep refrigerators defrosted and ovens clean while the property is on the market. (If tenants occupy the property, ask them to cooperate. They must maintain the appliances and their living units in neat and clean condition during the sales effort. Unkempt tenants reflect poorly on a building.)

Walls and Ceilings

Repair cracks or holes in plaster or drywall. Repaint or wallpaper faded or dark-colored walls. Aim for a bright, cheerful look to the property. To reduce your work, buy prepasted wallpaper and good-quality paint that will cover with just one coat. (I now favor high gloss—interior and exterior—for its reflective quality and ease of cleaning. I would never use flat or satin, even though they remain popular with many painters.) Wallpaper and paint, relative to their cost, normally pay back high returns. Use color schemes that accent the overall effect that you want to achieve for the property.

Doors and Locks

Inspect screen or storm doors. Replace screens, door panels, and closing springs as needed. Doors must open and close easily without being too tight or too loose. Replace cheap, flat-panel hollow-core doors with doors more substantive in strength and decor. Plane tight doors that drag. Because security ranks high with many buyers (or tenants), replace worn locks, or locks that are easily picked or broken, with a sturdier variety. Strike a balance. Excessive locks, chains, and bolts prompt buyers (or tenants) to question the safety of the neighborhood.

Landscaping

Well-kept yards magnify resale potential. Cut the grass and rake the leaves. Remove dead or unattractive shrubbery. Add privacy fences and hedges. If the season permits, plant flowers and install flower boxes. Again, I suggest, google images "before and after landscaping." You immediately recognize that landscaping creates buyer (and tenant)-pleasing curb appeal.

Storage Areas

Clean storage areas. Throw away items of little or no use. You'll have to do it before you hand over the property to a buyer anyway. Empty storage areas appear far more spacious than full ones of the same size. Buyers can't imagine the real size of a closet, attic, or basement when that area is crammed full. Buyers love space. When flipping or selling a rental, persuade your tenants to cooperate.

Clean Well

As noted earlier, most buyers (and tenants) want a property that looks like it has been well taken care of. Bathrooms and kitchens are especially important. Special efforts to remove stains on sinks, toilet bowls, and bathtubs, as well as countertops and cabinet areas, can add luster to the property. Potted flowers in bathrooms and kitchens also add appeal. Scrub floors. Vacuum and shampoo carpets. Wash windows and mirrors. (One more reminder: If tenants occupy the property, encourage them to keep it in top condition. Investors judge the quality of your tenants from how neat and clean they maintain their units. If your tenants won't practice tidy housekeeping, replace them with tenants who will honor your requests. (See lease clauses in Chapter 12.)

Safety and Health

When you clean and repair the property, notice danger. Watch out for loose carpeting, broken steps, torn linoleum, loose handrails, and scattered wires and cords. You are responsible for the safety of all the people who enter your property. Safety sells. Likewise for environmental concerns such as asbestos, lead paint, radon, or underground oil tanks. Check with state and federal EPAs to get their booklets that tell property owners how to safely and legally remedy environmental hazards.

Roofs

Inspect the roof for aesthetics and function. If the roof leaks, repair it. Don't do a quick fix to hide a serious problem for just long enough to get the property sold. Clear the roof of debris and plant growth. If the roof is discolored, see if you can use some type of roof paint to enhance its appearance. Buyers hate old roofs. Buyers love new roofs. If the roof is near the end of its life, replace it. As with repairs, don't go the cheapest route. Search out cost-effective solutions, not the cheapest. Smart buyers pay for quality.

Improvements and Alterations

If you add a room, modernize a bath or kitchen, or convert a garage to a recreation room, position your redo within range of other properties in the neighborhood. Use designs that flow naturally throughout the property. Seek harmonious improvements that you integrate (blend together into a unified form and aesthetics).

YOU CAN IMPROVE EVERYTHING ABOUT A PROPERTY–INCLUDING ITS LOCATION

"What should you look for when buying a house?" asks the *Dallas Morning News* in one of its feature articles: "Location, location, location." Why? Because, as the article reports through interviews with so-called experts, "You can change nearly anything about a property—anything except its location. That's why location is so important."

What do you think? Are these so-called experts right? Is it true that "you can't change the location of a property"? If you answer yes, you have fallen for a cliché. Conventional wisdom errs. You can improve a property's location. Location does not just refer to a fixed geographic position on the face of the earth. It includes a complex set of attributes such as neighborhood demographics, appearance, prestige (reputation), school quality, crime rates, convenience to shopping, accessibility to employment, zoning laws, deed restrictions, property tax rates, government services, and dozens of other influences. Working together, you and neighboring property owners (and tenants) can favorably affect any or all of these neighborhood features. One of my favorite examples is South (Miami) Beach, Florida.

South Beach: From Derelicts to Fashion Models

In the mid-1980s, the South Beach area (SoBe, as locals call it) of Miami Beach had deteriorated to the point where crack dealers and prostitutes openly sold drugs and sex. Derelicts and criminals filled SoBe streets and flophouse hotels. Tourists visited the area at their own peril. Most locals wrote off the neighborhood as another loss to urban decay. But visiting New York entrepreneur Tony Goldman saw things differently. "I took a ride around the area, and it was love at first sight. I was smitten," recalls Tony.

Instead of problems, Tony focused on potential. In his mind's eye, he imagined rehabbing the neighborhood buildings to highlight their art deco architecture. He envisioned sidewalk cafés and restaurants. He saw a tree-lined, beautiful Ocean Drive that would invite tourist visits. He saw streets free of criminals. He imagined new residents exhibiting pride of place.

To bring this dream to life, Tony, along with friends, investors, and Miami Beach civic leaders, formed a community action group. The group persuaded the police to rid the neighborhood of crime. They began a cleanup and rehab campaign. They persuaded the city to issue $3 million in bonds to fund public improvements. They generated enthusiasm and community spirit.

How successful were they? As one resident remarked, "Tony put the chic back into SoBe." Within just a few years, SoBe became one of the sought-after in-crowd neighborhoods in the Miami area. Condo sales, rent levels, and home prices jumped. Restaurants, cafés, and clubs filled the neighborhood. Because of these improvements, SoBe has become one of the foremost locations in the country for fashion photography shoots. Hundreds of former New York models now call South Beach home. Desirable condos in South Beach are now priced upward of $500,000 (though in today's market, lower-priced REOs and foreclosures can offer better bargains—yet such bargains will not last indefinitely).

Community Action and Community Spirit Make a Difference

The best of its genre, the classic guide, *Safe Homes, Safe Neighborhoods* illustrates how community action and community spirit can improve neighborhoods and lives. Many city and suburban neighborhoods must tackle problems of one sort or another. Besides crime, such problems can include anything from barking dogs to speeding high schoolers to a lack of parks, sidewalks, or storm sewers. But regardless of the specific problems to be solved (or prevented), as Tony Goldman proved with South Beach, people acting together can make a difference. In his book review of *Safe Homes, Safe Neighborhoods*, real estate advisor Robert Bruss wrote, "This is an action book. . . . This is a welcome and a long-overdue book for [property owners and community leaders] who want to learn how to improve a neighborhood."

"While it may seem that everywhere crime is on the rise," observed Stephanie Mann and M. C. Blakeman, authors of *Safe Homes, Safe Neighborhoods* (Nolo Press, 1993), "in many neighborhoods, residents are revitalizing and renewing their properties and the quality of their living environment. In cities and towns across the country, local crime prevention groups have reduced burglaries and car break-ins; helped catch muggers, rapists, and kidnappers; established Block Parents and other child-safety projects; driven out drug dealers; eliminated graffiti; and, in general, made their homes and streets safer. All it takes is a few people to get things started. By identifying and focusing on a neighborhood's main concerns—and working with police, schools, and city planners, and each other—neighbors can make a difference" (p. 143).

For more ideas, see another classic that has stimulated the revitalization of hundreds of neighborhoods throughout the country, George Kelling and Catherine Coles's *Fixing Broken Windows* (Free Press, 1996).

Neighborhoods Offer Potential

When you search and compare neighborhoods, see beyond the present. Imagine potential. Fixing broken windows and neighborhoods can create far more value than fixing properties.

List all of a neighborhood's good points. How can you and other property owners, tenants, police, concerned citizens, and community leaders join together to highlight and take advantage of these features? List the neighborhood's weak points. How can you and others eliminate negative influences? Who can you enlist to promote your cause? Can you mobilize mortgage lenders, private investors, Realtors, not-for-profit housing groups, church leaders, builders, contractors, preservationists, police, local employers, retail businesses, school teachers, principals, community redevelopment agencies, elected officials, civic groups, and perhaps students, professors, and administrators of a nearby college or university?

Throughout the United States and in cities throughout the world, people of all income levels, occupations, races, and religions have joined together to revitalize and reinvigorate hundreds of neighborhoods. From South of Market in San Francisco, to Madison Valley in Seattle, Lakeview in Chicago, Boston's North End, Manhattan's SoHo, Miami's SoBe, and the M Street neighborhood in Dallas, neighbors, merchants, real estate investors, homeowners, and tenants have organized campaigns to make living, working, and shopping in these areas more desirable. "We liked the community," says real estate investor Rob Rowland of Cumberland (Atlanta), "but the community association was too passive. It needed some oomph, so we incorporated and worked hard to get to know people and inspire them to upgrade their yards and properties."

In speaking of a San Diego neighborhood that's poised for turnaround and redevelopment, Lori Weisberg says, "To the outsider, there's very little here that seems inviting. . . . Yet, where most people see a shabby area . . . visionaries see an exciting new downtown neighborhood adorned with a grand, tree-lined boulevard, a central plaza, artisans' studios, loft housing, and crowned with a sports and entertainment center. . . . [Already] there are pockets of gentrification—a budding arts district, scattered loft conversions, and . . . structures well suited for preservation. . . . But [the total revitalization and redevelopment] does have to be imagined."

There's no doubt," says Pam Hamilton, an executive with San Diego's Centre City Development Corporation, "this project will happen—it's just a question of when." What's true of San Diego is true in cities throughout the United States. When you locate a neighborhood that's poised for turnaround or gentrification, your property fix-ups will multiply the dividends you receive.

WHAT TYPES OF IMPROVEMENTS PAY THE GREATEST RETURNS?

Newspapers and home improvement magazines publish articles that tell you a remodeled kitchen will pay back, say, 75 percent of its cost; a remodeled bath, 110 percent of its cost; or a swimming pool, 40 percent of its cost. Balderdash! Never rely on any of these specific payback figures. Instead, evaluate each property and its potential improvements according to the market in which it competes for buyers or tenants.

Before you estimate potential returns, research competing properties and tenant (or buyer) preferences. Learn what you need to do to design a cooperative advantage. Budgets for any project can vary enormously, depending on who does the work, what materials are selected, and the skill and creativity with which the job is undertaken.

Your profits flow directly from how much your tenants (buyers) value your units relative to what other owners offer. Relative comparisons differ in time, place, and pricing.

How Much Should You Budget for Improvements?

As you plan improvements for income properties, develop a cost and income estimate. Study market housing prices and rent levels. Figure out how much you can increase the sales price or rents for each project you undertake. As one rule of thumb, each $1,000 you invest in improvements should increase your net operating income at least $200 a year. You can see the logic of this rule by applying the value formula explained in Chapter 3:

$$V = NOI/R \text{ or } NOI/V = R$$

(Recall that V is the value to be estimated, NOI is net operating income, and R is the overall rate of return on unleveraged capital.)

If your improvements of $1,000 yield $200 more a year in net income, you earn 20 percent on your investment.[2] Choose whatever rate of return you want to aim for. Some investors use 10 percent; others may go as high as 40 percent. The profit margin you use is not the issue. What matters is that before you jump into renovation, temper your enthusiasm with a realistic look at the amount of increased rents (or selling price) your investments of time, effort, money, and entrepreneurial talents are likely to yield.

Beware of Overimprovement

When you estimate your costs of improvements, guard against spending too much relative to the property's neighborhood and relative to the prices (rent levels) your buyers (tenants) are willing and able to pay. Learn the high-end rental rates in the neighborhood relative to the size and quality of units you intend to offer. If $850 a month is tops and your inferior units

---

[2] With smart leverage (financing), of course, your returns will jump up greatly.

now rent for $700 a month, using the 20 percent rule, you should limit costs to no more than, say, $6,000 to $9,000 per unit. These amounts assume that after renovations, you could raise your rents to $800 or $850 a month and pocket another $100 to $150 a month in income:

$$\$1{,}200\ (12 \times \$100)/.20 = \$6{,}000 \text{ cost of improvement}$$
$$\$1{,}800\ (12 \times \$150)/.20 = \$9{,}000 \text{ cost of improvement}$$

These illustrative returns won't necessarily match your market, but you can apply the same methodology. Run your numbers to verify whether the market supports the selling price or rent level you ask. These calculations tell you whether your hoped-for rent level (if achieved) will yield your desired payback.

Other Benefits

When renting rather than selling, you may want to invest more in your improvements than rent increases would seem to justify. Besides higher rents, your renovated units should attract a better quality of tenant, reduce tenant turnover, and cut losses from bad debts and vacancies. More attractive units provide greater pride of ownership. Notwithstanding these points, work the numbers. Good tenants and pride of ownership will prove desirable only if you collect enough rents to pay your property expenses and mortgage payments.

No-No Improvements?

Some real estate investors have developed their no-no list of improvements. Robert Bruss writes, "Smart fixer-upper homebuyers and investors look for properties with 'the right things wrong.'" To Bruss, the "right things wrong" include cosmetic improvements such as painting, landscaping, carpets, and lighting. On his list of no-nos are roofs, foundations, wiring, and plumbing.

Although Bruss makes sense, you deal in specifics. Whether you can profitably improve a property depends on the price you pay for that property, the amounts you spend to improve it, and its sales price (or rent levels) after you complete the work. By this standard, cosmetic fixer-uppers can cost too much and serious fixer-uppers may offer that steal of a deal. No universal rule governs. Analyze the financial details of the property in front of you.

I know of a house that sat on the market for nearly a year because of serious foundation problems. No one wanted it. Eventually, an investor bought the property at a near give-away price. He jacked up the house 12 feet, repaired the foundation, built a new first story, set the old house (renovated) back on top, and resold the completed two-story house for an $82,000 profit. Not bad pay for three months' work.

BUDGETING FOR RESALE PROFITS

To budget formally for fix-and-sell profits, estimate (1) the eventual sales price of the property, and (2) the total amounts that you will invest from purchase until resale.

Estimate the Sales Price First

Buyers (or tenants) decide the price at which you can sell (or rent) your rehabbed property. Never add fix-up costs to your purchase price to estimate a future sales price. Cost-plus pricing rarely works. Many times I have heard sellers say something like, "We have to get $395,000. We've got much more than that invested in it. We just put $40,000 into remodeling the bathrooms."

No one will care how much money they spent on the house—or the bathrooms. Buyers care whether you offer the best value for the money. When you plan for profits, start with the price that a reasonably well-informed buyer is willing and able to pay for your creation.

Price your beautifully rehabbed property relative to the properties in the neighborhood where it is located. Aim for a sales price that sits at least 20 percent below the highest-priced property in the target area. As you push toward (or above) the top price limit of the neighborhood, you will find it difficult to attain your price (or rents)—even when your property towers over the others.

(Yes, exceptions test this rule. Donald Trump prides himself on "breaking through the comps." But before you mimic Donald Trump, check and recheck your market research and cost and revenue calculations. And is your target market Fortune 500 CEOs or an investment banker who's looking to spend his $10 million bonus?)

Estimate Costs

After you set a realistic future sales price for your energized creation, total your cost estimates. When you set a realistic price, you intuitively recognize that extravagant expenses will blow the budget and vanquish the possibility of profits. Second, a realistic future price helps you figure out the most you could pay for a property and still earn a profit.

Future Sales Price − (Costs + Profit) = Maximum Acquisition Price

You find a property that after improvements would sell for $280,000. You further figure that your costs and desired profit add up as follows:

Acquisition expenses and closing costs	$3,750
Cost of borrowed funds (interest)	4,000
Selling expenses	16,800
Materials for fix-up	22,000
Labor	12,000
Seller closing costs at sale	2,500
Profit	25,000
Total	$86,050

Because $280,000 equals the realistic sales price, you calculate that you can pay no more than $193,950 for the property:

Your future selling price	$280,000
Less	
Costs to fix up	61,050
Profit goal	25,000
Equals	
Maximum acquisition price	$193,950

When you deduct costs and desired profit from your expected (realistic) sales price, you set a top limit for your acquisition price. This technique guarantees you a profit—as long as you reasonably estimate each cost necessary to buy, hold, fix up, and market the property.

Reasonable and Comprehensive Cost Estimates. You might ask, "Okay, so how do I learn how much my rehab will cost?" Good question. Although experience counts heavily, so will these six guidelines:

1. *Shop, look, listen.* Visit home improvement suppliers, lumber yards, and hardware stores to learn the various costs of materials. Talk with knowledgeable store personnel. Compare price and quality trade-offs. Learn alternative solutions to common problems.

2. *Attend classes.* Community colleges and home improvement centers offer classes and seminars for beginning remodelers, renovators, and rehabbers.
3. *Read.* Property improvements now total more than $350 billion a year. An entire industry of book and magazine publishers caters to the do-it-yourself (DIY) homeowner and investor.
4. *Consult property inspectors.* Accompany your property inspector as he performs your prepurchase inspections. Ask for advice about potential costs and remedies.
5. *Obtain multiple estimates.* Contractors and tradespersons typically provide free cost estimates. Use this opportunity not only to solicit bids but also to discuss alternative ways of curing a property's deficiencies.
6. *Talk with other property owners.* You know people who have improved their properties. Ask them to tell you what they learned from experience. Then you learn from their experiences.

Estimating and executing requires due diligence. Yet, even due diligence does not and cannot provide definitive answers. Asking around, shopping, comparing, and trying to obtain firm diagnosis and remediation often produces conflicting contractor opinions, choices, and cost estimates. And that explains why fixer-uppers can prove so frustrating.

Only experience can help you sort out the charlatans, incompetents, and money-grubbers, from the reliable. But even among the reliable contractors and tradesmen, good-faith differences can arise. Budget large margins to allow for error, failed experiments, and change orders (which serve as a prime profit center for many contractors).

COMPLY WITH LAWS AND REGULATIONS

Plan your improvements to comply with all laws. Your plans may fall within a myriad of rules and regulations issued by homeowners' associations, zoning boards, health officials, fire marshals, building inspectors, environmental agencies, and other departments of government. Obtain required permits. Repairs or improvements that fail to comply with applicable codes place you at risk.

How will the authorities find out? Complaining neighbors, spiteful tenants, drive-by patrol, your buyer's prepurchase property inspector, your seller's disclosure statement, property tax assessment appraisers, and tradespeople who may at some later date visit the property to give repair estimates—to name just a few. Include the cost of regulations and permits into your cost estimates. Noncompliance can transform expected profits into losses.

SHOULD YOU BUY A FIXER-UPPER?

As I travel throughout the United States (and other countries), I talk with realty agents, investors, and homebuyers. I'm amazed at the number of people I meet who have bought properties that sat on the market for months, if not years. After buying a property that dozens of others had rejected, these alert buyers turned that unloved orphan into a Cinderella.

I'm not saying that just because a property sits unappreciated for months or years it offers undiscovered promise. Many properties remain unloved because they're overpriced money traps. And more likely, clearly underpriced bargains sell within days after the For Sale sign goes up (which is one reason why you might want a market-savvy sales agent working for you to identify these gems before they're picked up by someone else).

Nevertheless, many buyers reject properties too quickly. They walk in, do a quick-take with a pass-through tour, and then say something like, "Let's get out of here. It's way too dark, the rooms are too small, and did you not almost puke when you saw that soiled and ragged dark green carpet in the bedroom?"

"Yes," the spouse replies, "and how about those harvest gold kitchen appliances and that yellowed linoleum floor—not to mention the garbled floor plan and water marks on the ceiling? This house needs too much work. Anybody would be crazy to buy this white elephant. We could get stuck with another 'Mr. Blanding's dream house.'"

Well, yes, anybody would be crazy to buy that house—unless, of course, you could buy it at a steep discount, rehab, redecorate, and resell it for a profit of $25,000 to $100,000 (or more). Or perhaps a discounted fixer-upper might get you started in a neighborhood that otherwise was priced beyond your limit. Then no one would call you crazy—and I would call you smart.

Too Little Time?

If you are busy with kids, jobs, church, clubs, charities, social engagements, or school activities, investing in properties that need work may seem like a chore to avoid. But it's for this reason that buying a fixer-upper—remember, a fixer-upper is any property you can improve to look better, live better, or exude enhanced charm and romance—not just those that are run-down—can yield good profits. Lacking time, many investors (and homebuyers) want red-ribbon deals. Move in the tenants (or furniture) and start collecting rents. On top of that immediate benefit, buyers lack creativity, imagination, and knowledge. They see things they don't like. They can't imagine value-enhancing ways to solve. With relatively few buyers who will perceptively renovate and redesign properties, fixer-uppers can get discounted steeply.

You can't expect to easily find a $400,000 house discounted to $275,000 simply because it needs paint, carpets, and cleaning. In *normal* times, properties with readily solved problems tend to sell with small discounts. Yet today, we remain far from normal times. Any kind of discovery might present itself. Today, your dedicated search for the rejected Cinderella will almost certainly reward you.

Put Your Creativity to Work

Educate and discipline yourself to think through questions such as "How can I overcome these shortcomings?" and "What opportunities for improvements can I create?"

Now, return to the question, "Should you buy a fixer-upper?" Again listen to the wisdom of career rehab investor, Suzanne Brangham.[3] In her book *Housewise* (HarperCollins, 1987), Brangham advises beginning investors:

> Your buying power does not depend on the amount you can pay today with the funds sitting in your bank account. . . . As you learn more about real estate . . . you will understand that a little money can buy a lot—if you know how to pick the right house, bargain properly, and roll over your profits [possibly tax free, I might add] from one sale to another. . . . So get started now in property improving and property flipping so you can eventually own the properties you want, but can't afford right now. Start small and repeatedly step up from one [lower-priced] property into another [higher-priced] property. You will quickly build a magnificent net worth. (p. 185)

---

[3] Suzanne began her fix-and-sell career with a $40,000 condo in the early 1970s—just as the economy was entering the deep recession of 1973–1974. Less than 10 years later, she was magically transforming million-dollar-plus houses. Although seemingly dated, in terms of content, technique, and motivation, *Housewise* still makes for a great read.

9

MORE TECHNIQUES TO PROFIT WITH PROPERTY

Either independently or along with creative renovation, you can employ these popular techniques to profit with property:

♦ Lease options
♦ Lease purchase
♦ Conversions
♦ Master leases
♦ Assignments of contracts

LEASE OPTIONS

Many tenants would like to own their own homes. Yet for reasons of blemished credit, self-employment (especially those with off-the-books income or tax-minimized income), unstable income (commissions, tips), or lack of cash, they believe that they can't qualify for a mortgage from a lending institution. For these renters, the lease option (a lease with an option to purchase) solves their dilemma. Properly structured, the lease option permits renters to acquire ownership rights. Simultaneously, it gives them time to improve their financial profile and eventually meet the underwriting standards of a bank.

The lease option also works well for beginning (or even experienced) investors—especially in tandem with a fix-and-sell strategy. Suzanne Brangham, the author of *Housewise*, began her rehab career when she acquired a condominium through a lease option agreement. As you read the following, you might picture yourself as either the person who wants to acquire a property or an owner who wants to sell a property.

Here's How Lease Options Work

As its name implies, the lease option simultaneously creates two contracts: (1) a rental agreement and (2) an option to purchase agreement. Under the lease, the tenants sign a rental contract that covers terms and conditions of occupancy such as those shown in the following list. (See Chapter 12 for a comprehensive discussion of leases.)

♦ Monthly rental rate
♦ Term of lease
♦ Responsibilities for repair, maintenance, and upkeep
♦ Sublet and assignment
♦ Pets, smoking, cleanliness
♦ Permissible property uses
♦ House rules (noise, parking, number of occupants)

The option contract grants tenants the right to buy the property at some future date. At a minimum, the option will include (1) the up-front fee to the seller as payment for granting the option, (2) the option purchase price for the property, (3) the date on which the purchase option expires, (4) right of assignment, and (5) the amount of any rent credits that will count toward the purchase price of the optioned property.

Benefits to Tenant-Buyers (an Eager Market)

The benefits of lease options to tenant-buyers have been pointed out by the late syndicated real estate columnist and attorney, Robert Bruss, as well as most books written for first-time homebuyers. For example, written in the early days of lease options, my book *Yes! You Can Own the Home You Want* (John Wiley & Sons, 1995, p. 59), advises:

Lease options help open possibilities for property ownership in at least six ways:
1. *Easier qualifying.* Qualifying for a lease option may be no more difficult than qualifying for a lease (sometimes easier). Generally, your credit and employment record need meet only minimum standards. Many property owners will not

place your financial life under their magnifying glass, as would a mortgage lender.

2. *Low initial investment.* The initial investment to get into a lease option agreement can be as little as one month's rent and a security deposit of a similar amount. At the higher end, move-in cash rarely exceeds $5,000 to $10,000, although I did see a house lease optioned at a price of $1.5 million that asked for $50,000 up front.

3. *Forced savings.* The lease option contract typically forces you to save for the down payment required when you exercise the option to buy. Often, lease options charge above-market rental rates and then credit perhaps 50 percent of your rent toward the down payment. The exact amount is negotiable. And once you commit to buying, you will find it easier to cut other spending and place more money toward the house account.

4. *Firm selling price.* Your option should set the selling price for the property, or it should include a formula (perhaps a slight inflation-adjustment factor) to calculate a price. Shop carefully, negotiate wisely, and when you exercise your option in one to three years (or whenever), your home's market value could exceed its option price.

5. *100 percent financing possible.* Reduce the amount of cash investment you will need to close your purchase in another way: lease-option a property that you profitably improve through repairs, renovation, or cosmetics. With the property's increased value, you may be able to borrow nearly all the money you need to exercise your option to buy and pay off the seller.

   Assume your lease option purchase price equals $175,000. By the end of one year your rent credits equal $5,000. You owe the sellers $170,000. Through repairs, fix-up work, and redecorating, you increased the property's value by $25,000. The property is now worth around $200,000. If you have paid your bills on time during the previous year, a lender will finance your purchase with the full $170,000 you need to pay off the sellers.

   Or, as another possibility, sell the property, pay the sellers $170,000, and use the profit from the sale to invest in another property.

6. *Reestablish credit.* A lease option can help renters who need time to build or reestablish a credit record. Judy and Paul Davis wanted to buy a home while house prices were depressed

in their area. But the Davises needed time to clear up credit problems created by too much borrowing and Judy's lay-off. The lease option helped the Davises achieve their goal of homeownership. It locked in a low purchase price and allowed them two years to boost their credit score to meet bank underwriting standards.

When prospective tenants, homebuyers, and even investors evaluate this list of benefits, they become a ready market for lease options. As a seller, you just need to offer them the right property and terms.

Benefits to Investor-Sellers

Although you can structure lease options in many ways, they generally provide these benefits to *owner-investors:* (1) lower risk, (2) higher rents, and (3) guaranteed profits.

Lower Risk. Typically, tenants who shop for a lease option care for your property better than average renters. Because they intend one day to own the property, they will treat it as their own rather than as a mere rental. Also, they know that to qualify for the lowest available mortgage interest rate, they need to pay their rent on time every time. (If your tenant-buyers need to be reminded of that fact, stamp it on their forehead.) Lease option tenants can expect to pay first and last month's rent, a security deposit, and, more than likely, an option fee (a payment for the right of purchase) of $1,000 to $5,000 (more or less). Taken together, these up-front payments lower the risk of the property owner–lessor/optionor.

Higher Rents. Lease option tenants agree to pay higher-than-market rents because they know you will apply a part of that monthly rent to the property's purchase price. The tenants view these rent credits—actually you should name them *purchase price credits*—as forced savings that may count toward a lender's required down payment.

The higher rent payments increase your cash flow and lift your cash-on-cash return. In high-priced areas where newly bought rental properties awaken a huge alligator, the increased rent of a lease option can work to alleviate its appetite.

Guaranteed Profits. Typically, fewer than 50 percent of lease option tenants execute their right to buy the optioned property. Sometimes they change their mind. Sometimes their finances fail to improve as much as they'd hoped. Sometimes their circumstances shift (separation, divorce, job relocation, additional children).

Whatever the reason, the tenants forfeit (at least in part) their purchase price credits, option fee, and any fix-up work they have performed around the property. As a compassionate person, you may feel badly for the tenants. But as an investor, their loss provides you earnings for offering an opportunity that they were unable or unwilling to realize. You earn more than you would have earned under a straight rental agreement.

Even if the tenants do buy, you still win. In setting your option price, you built in a profit margin over the price you originally paid for the property. This technique works especially well for transactions in which you have bought at a bargain price. With a lease option, you gain more than you would have from a listed sale of the property because you didn't pay costs of promotion or Realtor commissions. You also save time and effort.

For investors, the lease option makes for a win-win agreement. You win if your tenants buy. You win when the tenants don't buy and walk away from the cash they have paid toward the option agreement.

The Lease Option Sandwich

The lease option sandwich magnifies your *potential* profit. Instead of buying a property, you find sellers who will lease-option their property to you at both a bargain rental rate and a bargain price. Typically, these sellers were not advertising their property as a lease option. In fact, they may not even have thought of the idea until you put a proposal in front of them.

Through this lease option, you control the property for two to five years. Your cash out of pocket totals less than you would probably have paid in closing costs had you immediately bought the property. .

Next, you spend some money on spruce-up expenses (if desirable) and readvertise the property specifically as a lease option. You find tenant-buyers and sign them up on a lease option with you as the lessor. Your tenant-buyers agree to pay you a higher monthly rent and a higher option price than you've negotiated for yourself in your role as lessee/optionee with the property owners. You profit from the difference.

Your rate of return skyrockets because you gain control of a property with almost no cash investment. The up-front money you've collected from your tenant-buyers exceeds the amount you paid to the property owners. Essentially, you buy wholesale and sell retail—without investing much cash in inventory.

Does the Lease Option Sandwich Really Work? Theoretically, it can work. Robert Allen and James Lumley, each one an investor and book author, claim to have used this technique successfully to generate big returns with little or no cash.

Although I have bought and sold with lease options, I hesitate to use or recommend the lease option sandwich. For my taste, giving someone an option to buy a property that I don't yet own seems fraught with dangers. *In theory*, it can yield high returns. If you're interested in biting into a lease option sandwich, read James Lumley's *5 Magic Paths to Making a Fortune in Real Estate*, 2nd ed. (John Wiley & Sons, 2004).

How to Find Lease Option Buyers and Sellers

To discover the best deal on a lease option, first talk with sellers who advertise lease options. But these sellers typically retail their properties. You might find it tougher to negotiate a bargain here. Contact motivated for-sale-by-owner (FSBO) sellers in the "Homes for Sale" ads. Or try property owners who are running "House for Rent" ads. As noted, the best lease option sellers may not realize how the idea can benefit them until you suggest it.

In your search for tenant-option-buyers, you might see three ad categories from which to choose: (1) homes for sale, (2) homes for rent, and (3) the specific category *lease option* that some newspapers and websites include. No one can say which ad category works best in your market. Experiment with each of these choices.

To learn which type ad or posting pulls the best responses, ask your callers to tell you in which category they saw the ad. Research which listings draw the largest number of qualified callers.

A Creative Beginning with
Lease Options (for Investors)

To start building equity without investing much cash up front, try the lease option approach of Suzanne Brangham. Although Brangham stumbled fortuitously into her investment career, you can follow her path more purposefully. From her book *Housewise* (p. 39), here's Suzanne's story:

> While searching for the ideal career, I was also looking for a place to live. I located a lovely but dilapidated apartment house. The building was making a painful transition from rentals to condominiums. Units were for sale or rent. But sales were practically nonexistent.
>
> With my head held high, preliminary plans, and a budget tucked under my arm, I decided to make the manager an offer he couldn't refuse.
>
> I told him that in lieu of paying the $800-a-month rent that was asked for a 2-bedroom, 2-bath unit, I would renovate the entire apartment. I would agree to spend $9,600 for labor and

materials, the equivalent of a full year of rent payments. Along with a 12-month lease, I also requested an option to buy the unit at its $40,000 asking price.

Ten months later, Brangham was on her way. She bought her reno-vated condo unit at her lease option price of $40,000. Then, simultaneously, she sold the unit to a buyer for $85,000. After accounting for renovation expenses, closing costs, and Realtor's commission, she netted $23,000. Brangham had sold her home, but she had found a career.

Twenty years, 23 homes, and 71 properties later, Brangham had become not just independently wealthy, but a nationally recognized author, speaker, and entrepreneur. In *Housewise,* she tells about her reno-vation experiences and the career she found by chance. *Housewise* includes hundreds of profit-making ideas that you can apply to buy and renovate fixer-uppers.

LEASE PURCHASE AGREEMENTS

As a practical matter, the lease purchase agreement works about the same as a lease option. However, instead of gaining the right to either accept or reject a property, the lease purchaser *commits to buying (although that com-mitment may lack true commitment).* As an investor, you might persuade reluctant sellers to accept your lease purchase offer, even though they shy away from a lease option. The lease purchase *seems* more definite because the contract obligates you to buy the property—but you would like to defer closing until some future date (six months to five years, more or less) that you and the sellers find acceptable.

Seems More Definite

I say *seems* more definite because you might escape through a loophole. You can (and should) write an "exclusive remedy for breach" clause into your purchase contract called "liquidated damages." With a liquidated damage clause, the sellers could not sue to force you to complete your purchase if you later choose to back out (that is, a lawsuit for specific per-formance). Nor could they sue you for monetary damages (more likely) that result from your failure to buy. Instead, the liquidated damage clause permits your sellers to pocket your earnest money deposit (or some other specified amount).

In effect, your liquidated damage money acts like an option payment. No matter what the purchase contract appears to say, in reality you have not firmly committed to buy. You have paid for a right to buy—if you choose to.

Amount of the Earnest Money (Option) Deposit

The strength of either a lease option or a lease purchase contract lies in the amount of the up-front money the seller receives—regardless of whether it's called an option fee, liquidated damages, or an earnest money deposit. If you want to convince a seller that you intend to complete a lease option or a lease purchase transaction, place more cash on the negotiating table. To retain walk-away flexibility, negotiate the smallest option or earnest money amount that you can, even if it means yielding more concessions in the other terms of your agreement.

Contingency Clauses

You can also escape from your obligation to buy a property through the use of contingency clauses. If the contingency (property condition, ability to obtain financing, lawyer approval, sale of another property, and so on) isn't met, you can walk away from a purchase and rightfully expect the return of your earnest money or option fee. Contingency clauses, option fees, and earnest money deposits are discussed in Chapter 10.

CONVERSIONS

Rental apartments now sold as condominiums. . . . Gas stations now operating as retail outlets (7-Elevens). . . . Old homes converted to office space. . . . Farm acreage now occupied by a shopping center. These properties are examples of adaptive use of both land and buildings brought about by a locale's growth and change.

Conversions provide opportunities for entrepreneurial investors. Converting an old house located in the downtown area can earn you good profits. Small offices sometimes rent at twice the per-square-foot rental rate of housing. The opposite can also prove true. In London and New York City, housing prices climbed so high that investors converted retail, warehouse, and offices into apartments (rental and condominium).

Badger Development in Lansing, Michigan, bought strategic corner locations in the path of the city's outward growth. The company purchased single-family homes on a good corner location with the long-term intent to convert these homes to a more profitable rental use. This method proved superior to buying similarly located vacant land. The houses generated rental income until growth made conversion profitable.

Converting land and buildings weaves straw into gold. But how can you take advantage of these changes in land use? First, obtain a zoning map from your city's planning department. Each part of the city zones areas (single-family residential, multiunit, mixed-use, agricultural, commercial, and industrial) into districts. An existing house located within a commercial zone offers good prospects. If the property you wish to convert is located in a residential zone, it requires a change in zoning to accomplish your objective. To apply for a variance or zoning change costs money, time, and effort. Somewhat easier to convert are those properties that sit near the class of zoning district that you wish to convert to. Check with your local planning department and ask about the probabilities and procedure. Also, see the book *The Complete Guide to Zoning* (McGraw-Hill, 2005).

Condominium Conversion

To convert an apartment building into individual condominium units, purchase the apartments inexpensively enough so that each unit can be easily converted to a salable condo. Because of legal procedures and incidental costs to convert, not to mention the time and effort, as much as a 1.5× to 2.0× rule of thumb is sometimes required. In other words, to earn a good profit, a $100,000 rental unit might have to sell for $150,000 as a condo. Conversions require a large price markup to cover marketing, renovation, and legal costs, plus the risk necessary to make such a conversion. Notwithstanding these financial realities, during the real estate boom of the early 2000s, investors converted more than 250,000 rental apartments into condo units.

Opportunities today have dwindled because financing for the investor-converter and the end buyer has tightened so much. But the cycle goes around. Buy a bargain-priced apartment building now. Convert to condos when recovery takes hold.

To convert rental apartments into condominiums, submit plans to the planning and zoning office. If the city planners decide that your plan complies with applicable laws, they advance your project to the public hearing stage. If not in compliance, changes, such as additional parking, bathrooms, or more handicap access may be needed before they move you to the next step. Planners may also raise the affordable housing objection. In the San Francisco Bay Area, apartment building owners could potentially convert their rental units to condos and reap large profits. But alas, the city tightly limits conversions to maintain a larger supply of rentals. Few other cities restrict conversions with such strict controls.

To calculate potential earnings from a condo conversion, consider this eight-unit apartment building example:

Acquisition price	$480,000
Rehab at $15,000 per unit	120,000
Attorney fees (condo document preparation, government permitting process, sales contract preparation, closing document review)	40,000
Marketing costs (advertising, sales commissions)	45,000
Mortgage interest (12-month renovation and sellout)	50,000
Incidentals (architect, interior design, landscaping, government permits)	35,000
Total costs	$770,000
Cost per unit	$96,250

In this example, the investor paid $480,000 ($60,000 per unit) to acquire this eight-unit rental property. After all costs of conversion, her total investment increased to $770,000 ($96,250 per unit). But these figures haven't yet considered profits. If the investor wants to net $20,000 per unit, she will need to sell the units at a price approaching $120,000 each (twice the amount of her original per-unit purchase price).

The figures in this example illustrate this conversion technique. Every cost item from acquisition to incidentals varies widely. Each depends on the local market, the specific property, the amount of renovation work, the complexity of the condo conversion laws and procedures, and the marketing strategy adopted. To estimate whether such a project is feasible in your area, research rental properties, condo prices, and conversion laws. Perform feasibility calculations. If estimates look promising, talk with a moneyed investor, contractor, and an attorney or real estate consultant experienced in the conversion process. With the knowledge gained from these talks (and follow-up research), decide whether this approach offers enough profit potential to compensate for risks such as cost overruns, slow sales, and government permitting delays.

Convert Apartments to Office Space

Office space can sometimes rent for twice the rental rate of comparable quality apartments. From this fact, it appears profitable to convert apartments to office space. But you will need to address these issues:

◆ Is the property within a commercial zone? If not, will the city change the zoning?

◆ What is the vacancy rate for office space in the area and the specific neighborhood of the subject property? If empty space remains available, what market strategy can strengthen your competitive advantage?

◆ Do you have adequate parking for office space? The city may require one parking space for every 500 to 1,000 square feet of rentable office space—depending on the specific use.

◆ How much will it cost to convert? Can you borrow money to finance the conversion? Will your costs, legal procedures, time, and effort pay off?

Study the property and the market. Figure the finances of the projected conversion. If you can convert at a reasonable cost and earn a good profit, weigh risks and rewards. Then decide.

TENANTS IN COMMON

In some parts of the country, oppressive rent control and tight condo conversion laws make it difficult to convert rental apartments into condominiums even though such conversions would prove profitable. However, innovative real estate investors and entrepreneurs created ways to work around these restrictive regulations. In Berkeley, California (commonly known as the People's Republic of Berkeley), and other left wing–dominated cities in the San Francisco Bay Area, innovative investors and homebuyers pioneered a conversion concept called TIC.

The term *TIC* (pronounced T-I-C) stands for *tenant in common* and is a popular form of joint ownership that's been given a unique twist to create a hybrid property—something between, say, a co-op and a condominium.

As the plan typically worked in the Bay Area, an investor (or group of investors) locates, say, an existing four-unit rental house that, because of rent controls, suffers a depressed market value of $600,000 ($150,000 per unit). As individual condo units, the apartments would sell for $250,000 each, for a total building value of $1 million; however, restrictive conversion laws eliminate this possibility.

But here's where creativity counts. Investors bought the property. They then advertised for four households (individuals, married couples, partners, friends, families) who would like to own one of the individual units. Once found, they sell them pro rata shares of ownership in the total building at a price of, say, $200,000 each (if the units are of unequal quality, the pro rata division would charge some owners more and others less).

Next, the respective joint owners enter into long-term leases for "their" units with all the other owners. Also, they would need to follow the law to end the tenancy of the building's current residents.

Although all of the TIC members jointly own the entire building, in a practical sense, each becomes the proprietor of a specific unit. Later, if one of the co-owners wishes to sell his share of the building, he can do so. The buyer pays the seller an agreed price for his ownership interest in the total property and obtains long-term leasehold rights to the unit.

Besides sidestepping condo conversion restrictions, you can legally form and market a TIC with much less cost and documentation than a condo conversion. In fact, with a TIC you merely sell a building to a group of co-owners; no special laws may apply.

Although the TIC concept in rental properties was implemented primarily as a response to excessive government, you need not be limited to that use. Even if you don't live in a "People's Republic," explore this investment technique in your area. Because you can more easily structure a TIC than a condo conversion, it can provide you experience in buying wholesale and selling retail. As drawbacks, though, you might find it tough to locate a lawyer who can provide competent legal counsel—and explaining the concept to potential buyers and building co-owners can require patience and close instruction.

To discover more about the TIC concept, take a (tax-deductible?) trip to the San Francisco Bay Area and talk to investors, unit owners, and attorneys who have firsthand experience with these types of properties. Maybe you can pioneer the concept in your area. [Eventually, Berkeley eased up on its condo conversion laws, but the politics of conversions, TICs, and affordable housing could likely continue for many years (decades?)].

In addition to this use of TICs, some firms also create TICs with multimillion dollar apartment complexes, shopping centers, and other types of commercial properties. They then sell shares to investors—often at a minimum stake of $100,000 to $250,000.

MASTER LEASES

To control a property, own it. But you can control a property through the use of a master lease, as well.

Say you locate a 12-unit apartment building that is poorly managed— as most are. You consider buying the property. But you don't have the financial power to arrange new financing, and the owner doesn't want to sell the property using a land contract or purchase money mortgage. At present, the property brings in barely enough rents to pay expenses, property taxes, and mortgage payments. The owner wants to turn this money pit into a moneymaker but lacks the will to invest time, effort, money, and talent.

The solution: sign a master lease for the entire building and guarantee the owner a steady, no-hassle monthly income. In return, you obtain the right to upgrade the building and property management to increase its net operating income (NOI).

A master lease provides possession of the property for a period of 3 to 15 years and an option to buy at a prearranged price. During the period of your lease, you pocket the difference between what you pay to operate the property, including lease payments to the owner, and the amounts you collect from the individual tenants who live in each of the apartments. Here's how the before-and-after numbers might look:

Before (Owner Management)

Gross potential income at $500 per unit	$72,000
Vacancy losses at 15%	10,800
Effective gross income	$61,200
Expenses	
Utilities	14,400
Maintenance	8,360
Advertising	2,770
Insurance	3,110
Property taxes	6,888
Miscellaneous (evictions, attorney fees, bad debts, vandalism, pest control, bookkeeping, and so on)	5,000
Total expenses	40,528
Net operating income	20,672
Mortgage payments	19,791
Before-tax cash flow (cash throw-off)	$881

After (New Management)

Gross potential income at $575 per unit	$82,800
Vacancy losses at 4%	3,312
Effective gross income	$79,488
Expenses	
Utilities	2,230
Maintenance and upkeep	13,200
Advertising	670
Insurance	2,630
Property taxes	7,300
Miscellaneous (evictions, attorney fees, bad debts, vandalism, pest control, bookkeeping, and so on)	2,500
Total expenses	28,530
Net operating income	50,958
Leasehold payments to owner (master lessor)	25,000
Before-tax cash flow (master lessee)	$25,958

How can you achieve such a profitable turnaround? (1) upgrade the property and implement a systematic maintenance program; (2) attract and retain better tenants through improved aesthetics and attentive management; (3) individually meter the apartment units to reduce utility expenses; (4) raise rents to reflect the appealing condition of the property and the pleasant ambience created by higher-quality, neighbor-considerate, rule-abiding tenants; (5) shop for lower-cost property and liability insurance coverage; and (6) reduce turnover and encourage word-of-mouth tenant referrals to eliminate advertising expenses.

Not only did this property turnaround increase the NOI, but correspondingly, the higher-NOI, lower-risk, and more attractive apartments added value to the property. When you execute your option to buy, you can borrow 100 percent financing to pay off the owner, yet still give the lender a 70 to 80 percent loan-to-value ratio as measured against the property's now higher market value.

In lieu of buying the master-leased property, you could sell your leasehold and option rights to another investor. Given the higher NOI that you've created, these rights will command a premium over the amounts you pay. In effect, an investor would invest to acquire the right to earn $25,958 per year (plus future increases) for the remaining term of the master lease, as well as the right to buy the property at the below-market, option-stipulated price.

The master lease follows the same principle that Four Seasons and other hotel operating companies use. Investors build and own the hotel building and then contract with a name brand hotel to manage the room rental operations. In turn, the management company may sublet the bar and restaurant businesses to specialized operators. Some retailers operate similarly.

A master lease (that is, essentially a management contract) with an option to buy can create significant profit opportunities for investor-entrepreneurs who will work to turn a poorly managed, run-down property into an attractive, effectively operated apartment building. You can also apply this strategy to offices, retail, self-storage, and mobile home parks. Harry Helmsley, the late New York property mogul, operated the Empire State Building under a 116-year (1961–2076) master lease.

ASSIGNMENTS: FLIPPING PURCHASE CONTRACTS

Some contracts to buy or option a property permit you to assign that contract to another investor. This technique, which is called contract flipping, offers profit opportunities with relatively little up-front cash investment.

A developer announces plans to build a high-rise condominium project with units priced from $225,000 to as much as $775,000. The builder promises delivery of the completed units within 18 months. With an earnest money deposit of $20,000, you contract ("off plan") to buy an apartment. You pick a choice-view unit priced at $500,000. During the construction period, this project receives rave reviews and wonderful publicity. Buyers sign up on waiting lists. The value of your reserved unit jumps to $600,000. Yet your purchase contract gives you the right to buy that unit at a mere $500,000. What do you do? If you want a quick $100,000 profit, flip your contract. Assign your right to buy this unit for a payment of $100,000. You've just made a quick five-fold return on your original investment.

If this new project receives bad reviews, if mortgage interest rates skyrocket, or if the local economy goes into the tank, if the builder does not deliver as promised (quality, timing), the market prices of these units could fall, and you may have to forfeit your $20,000 deposit. Though often called investors, contract flippers speculate; they do not invest.

You need not limit use of this technique to projects under construction. Some savvy investors scout the market for bargain-priced existing properties, place the seller under contract with a small deposit, and then locate another buyer who will pay them a fee (premium) for the right to step in and buy the property on the favorable terms previously negotiated. Although any type of contract flipping creates risks, for those who are skilled in spotting underpriced properties, this technique can yield high returns in short time periods.

(Unfortunately, many REO sellers restrict or prohibit their buyers from assigning their purchase contracts—and sometimes even restrict the property resale after closing. Carefully read the REO seller's purchase contract addendum.)

During the hot housing markets of the recent past, flipping off plan properties became almost as popular as the Super Bowl. In Dubai, UAE, where I have worked off and on for seven years, investors (speculators) flipped more than 50,000 new units at premiums of 30 to 200 percent. In Las Vegas, house-flipping bets were thought risk free—a sure bet with casino-like jackpots. Everyone who plays wins.

With fortuitous timing, flipping can make you some big piles of fast money. But when you rush for the exit too late—as many did—you can lose much more than your deposit when prices fall and your contract obliges you to pay $500,000 for a property now worth $300,000. That's why off-plan property flippers in Las Vegas, Miami, and Dubai have been scrambling to hire lawyers who can find a purchase contract loophole that will permit the flippers (now stuckees) to escape from their deals. (In Dubai, their success rate to date has not been high.)

SUMMARY

Buy, manage, and hold for increased rents and property price growth remains the best time-tested, effective way to build wealth in real estate. As an alternative strategy, buy, fix up, and resell your properties using a lease option purchase contract. Under the right market conditions, this technique can increase your returns two ways: (1) the option price you offer your tenants should exceed the price you paid for the property plus the amounts you paid for improvements; and (2) during the rental period, your rent collections and option fee monies will exceed the monthly income you would receive from a straight rental. Once you develop a system that will work in your market, the lease option investment technique can yield good returns.

Other investment tactics include the fix and sell, property conversions, TICs, master leases, and contract assignment. Although each of these techniques involves risk, specialized expertise, and market knowledge, in the right circumstances, any one of them can pay off with strong returns.

If high property prices and negative cash flows appear to block your efforts to invest in real estate, keep trying. Put one of these alternative strategies to work. Yet even these ideas don't complete your possibilities. Chapters 11, 13, and 15 illustrate other attractive—yet, relatively unrealized and unpursued—real estate opportunities.

10

NEGOTIATE A WIN-WIN PURCHASE AGREEMENT

For ease of discussion, I will classify negotiating styles as (1) adversarial, (2) accommodating, or (3) win-win. Many lawyers (especially litigators) rely on the adversarial style. They make outrageous demands. Then to land you closer to their position, they push, pull, or threaten. Adversarial negotiators don't care whether their *opponents* (which is how they see the other party) end up satisfied. All they care about is winning for themselves.

Whereas the adversarial style relies on threats and power, accommodating negotiators cave in to requests and threats. They think, "What else could I do?" Or sometimes, "It wasn't worth the fight." Accommodators feel powerless to create the negotiated result they desire. They feel a lack of money, credit, time, information, knowledge, or experience. They overestimate the strength and position of the other party. So, they substitute excuses for performance.

Accommodators detest and avoid conflict. They would rather lose face than stand their ground. When negotiating through a real estate agent (or other third party), accommodators shed responsibility. "Oh, just do whatever you think is best" or "Let's just agree and get the whole thing over" are typical responses that accommodators rely on to prematurely give up on realizing their hoped-for goal.

In contrast to the adversarial and accommodating approaches, think of "win-win" negotiation as imaginative, caring (and careful) assertiveness. Win-win negotiators recognize that every negotiation brings forth multiple issues, priorities, and possibilities. To negotiate assertively with care and caring, identify and respect the other party's (not *opponent's*) concerns, feelings, and needs. Win-win negotiators do not push and pull along a single line of contention—especially the singular goal of price.

A win-win negotiator *plans* for a secure, firm, mutually beneficial agreement that holds up over time. He leads the other party to believe that the deal was near the limit of his willingness and ability to proceed.

The adversarial negotiator wants to triumph over others and then boast of victory. The win-win negotiator prefers to lament how much he gave up—even when (as is often the case) he prevailed in reaching all (or most) of his goals. Win-win negotiators want the other parties to feel triumphant—or at least feel that they scored a lot of points and chalked up substantial gains from the transaction.

To obtain the results that you want from negotiation, inventory your strengths, weaknesses, and the benefits that others will accrue from what you are offering. Why should the other party accept your proposition? Inventory the weaknesses, soft spots, and urgencies of the other party.

Win-win agreements are thought out and developed—not simply multiple rounds of give and take. Stand against the win-lose mind-set of the adversarial hardballers. Accept responsibility for the outcomes that arise from your trade-offs, compromises, conciliations, and refusals. Stand strong with walk-away willpower. Few deals are must deals. Beware of becoming a passive accommodator whose eagerness for a deal leads to unwise, unnecessary, and perhaps regrettable concessions.

WIN-WIN PRINCIPLES

To win what you want, know what you want—not simply from this transaction, but from your higher-level investment and life goals. Beware of jumping for a deal (no matter how apparently attractive) unless it fits within the context of your life.

With this first-order perspective settled, you can negotiate effectively. Then, after you have progressed to this point, advance your negotiation skills and rewards by incorporating the following 15 principles into your discussions with sellers, buyers, lenders, prospective equity partners, government officials, and the many other parties with whom you will transact as you grow your portfolio of investment properties.

1. *Find* interests or current events to explore (and agree upon) with the other party. Defer talk about price, terms, and issues. Chitchat to warm the relationship before you get down to business. Engage in a cooperative spirit. Become likable as best you can without resort to fawning flattery or feigned sincerity (which will diminish, if not destroy, your credibility). Although often made fun of by the intelligentsia, I still recommend Dale Carnegie's *How to Win Friends and Influence People* (the original edition, first published in 1937).

2. *Cooperate.* Negotiations emotionally involve and excite. Each party feels his own needs, wants, biases, beliefs, standard operating procedures, and ego. Learn the other parties' perspectives. Empathize.

3. *When* viewpoints on negotiating issues differ, sense when to slow down. Feel tension building. Push for that next dollar in price or that one more concession and you can kill agreement and the working relationship. Push too hard, you destroy trust. When parties lose trust in each other, they tend to knock win-win off the table.

4. *Listen* to the seller reject, object, and propose. Determine what the seller really wants. People often seek results indirectly. Bring forth real wants and needs and the negotiations will yield a more rewarding outcome. Disagreements can arise because two parties do not communicate what they think they are communicating. Listen more than you talk.

5. *Use questions* to identify needs. Know that the way you phrase questions can rank as important as knowing what questions to ask. A priest asked his bishop, "May I smoke while praying?" Permission was denied. Another priest asked, "May I pray while I am smoking?" You know the answer. Phrase questions to identify a seller's needs without causing offense. ("Why did you paint the walls with such tasteless colors? I will have to repaint everything. You've got to knock another five grand off your price.")

6. *Provide credible* reasons to support your viewpoints and requests. Why do you need seller financing? Why should the seller grant seller financing? How does a below-market interest rate serve the seller's interests? Likewise, learn the seller's factual foundation, sources, and interpretations. Ask for reasons, seek understanding, and appreciate his perspectives and concerns.

7. *Never* quickly say no to a proposition suggested by a seller, even when you think it ridiculous. Take time to reflect so that the seller's views seem important. Return the negotiations to the overarching goals you hold in common with the seller.

8. *Remind* the seller of the property's negative features, but do so in a way that doesn't provoke retaliation—especially when you negotiate with a homeowner. Reference the market, the property features, or the decorating schemes that tenants prefer. Say nothing to insult the seller's tastes or handiwork. Say, "Tenants usually prefer tile or laminate flooring." Don't say, "How do you think I could get this place rented with that marbled purple and cream-colored carpeting and that pink foil wallpaper?"

9. *Sellers* expect to negotiate (as opposed to agreeing flat out with your requests). Remain flexible. Even though price and terms

may rank most critical to the negotiations, possession date, closing costs, closing date, personal property, repair escrow, and other issues provide trade-off points.

10. *Stay realistic.* You may face a seller's market or a buyer's market. You may face a timid seller or an assertive one. You may meet sellers where the wife is eager to sell, but the husband couldn't care less. Each negotiation differs. Focus on the context of the transaction. With financial distress rampant today, mixed motives and feelings can create unrealistic prices or demands from sellers. Patience and perseverance rule.

11. *Concede* slowly with reservation. Say yes too quickly and a sophisticated seller will press on for more easy victories. Hesitate. Suggest tit for tat. When you give, ask for something in return. If I can do _____ for you, would you be willing to do _____ for me?

12. *Beware* of oral concessions. Oral concessions tip your hand to a higher price or other unfavorable terms that you might accept. Or sellers may encourage you to commit orally to a price. Then, once the seller feels you are committed that far, he will write his offer for an even higher amount. Each time you offer or counteroffer, write out your price and terms. Use a contract-of-sale form and adjust the relevant terms that are subject to the negotiation. Each party then initials those changes.

13. *Negotiate* with risks in sight. When you reject a seller's counteroffer, that counteroffer dies unless the seller chooses to revive it. Likewise, when you counter a seller's offer, your counter kills the seller's proposal. A seller or buyer may withdraw an offer or counteroffer without obligation—even if the withdrawing party has promised to keep the offer open for a stated period. (If someone pays to keep an offer open for a specified time, then that person has purchased an option to buy [or sell].)

14. *Stockpile* information early. The more you learn about a seller's financial capabilities, family situation, likes and dislikes, priorities, time constraints, available alternatives, previous offers (accepted or rejected), past real estate experiences, perceptions about the property's condition and value, and any other factors that might bear on the transaction, the better you can design your offer. Match your negotiating strategy to the seller's situation and personality.

You not only need to collect this information; you need to collect it as early as possible while you are in the relationship-building stage of your negotiations. When you incite a contentious debate over price and terms before you stockpile the information you want, sellers clam up. They guard their disclosures closely. Most sellers can play coy. They put forth their own information agenda

in regard to what they would like you to believe. Don't accept seller admissions or explanations as fact. Look for nuggets of truth, but finely tune your bunkum detector.
15. *Set reference points* and benchmarks for the negotiation. Sellers derive their asking price and terms from reference points. What value measures and techniques did the seller rely on? What comps? What data? The seller may believe that comparable properties have sold with a monthly gross rent multiplier of 175, or maybe a cap rate of 6.5 percent, and will therefore apply those norms to figure a fair price for her property. Your task: Provide better norms or data that support the results that you are aiming for. Tell why; cite evidence.

When you negotiate with a seller who holds convictions that oppose your interests, ask him to identify his benchmarks and explain why they should govern. After you gain this information, discuss why those norms aren't as applicable as the seller believes and why the reference points you've selected are appropriate. Point out that the comp properties with cap rates of 6.5 percent are newer (better location, more stable tenants, better condition, and so on) than the seller's property. In fact, the comps most similar to the seller's property have typically sold with cap rates in the range of 7.5 to 8.0 percent.

Will the seller readily accept yours over his? Of course not. But it will soften his position as he sees that he is holding a less-than-tenable reference point. Competing evidence persuades more easily than flat rejection or unsubstantiated disagreement.

The seller may know the house down the street just sold for $380,000, but doesn't realize that its owners carried back financing at 5.0 percent and included $35,000 worth of personal property. You can try, "I'll give you $355,000. That's my top offer. Take it or leave it." But you set the stage for win-win only if you first persuade the seller to accept a reference point that's favorable to your offer. Then edge the seller toward the purchase agreement that achieves your primary goals. You can negotiate anything, but not everything.

THE PURCHASE CONTRACT

Perhaps the most commonly used negotiation tactic is the standard contract ploy. But no standard purchase contract exists—even though many purchase contract forms include the word *standard* in their title. Read each clause of any purchase contract you use to write your offer. As you search for win-win, any of these clauses, terms, or conditions can serve as a bargaining chip.

The following discussion identifies some—but not all—issues to look for in a sales agreement. As lawyers continue to expand their reach, all real estate contracts are getting longer. But do not let such length and unreadable prose intimidate you. Understand each clause. Then revise or omit as desired.

Names of the Parties

Name all parties to the agreement. Ideally, all of the named property owners should sign your offer as soon as you've reached agreement. Do not negotiate with a seller whose co-owner spouse or partners do not join the negotiations. Later on, if they don't sign, you lose the deal and you've wasted time and effort.

Some sellers claim that their co-owners will go along with whatever agreement they set. Yet after you commit, the seller will come back and say, "Gee, I'm terribly sorry. My partner refuses to sign. He thinks I'm giving the property away. He wants another $250,000, but I've told him I can't renege and change the terms. But he insists. So I'll tell you what—if you can just move your offer up by a mere $100,000, I'll go back to my partner and do my best to persuade him to go along. I'm really sorry, but sometimes this guy's a jerk, and there's little I can do to reason with him."

This good-guy-bad-guy gambit stands as one of the oldest tricks in the book. But it often works. Sellers (and buyers) continue to use it. Just don't be surprised when sellers try it on you—if you negotiate with someone who lacks the legal authority (or feigns to lack authority) to sign off on the agreement.

Site Description

Identify the subject property by street address *and* legal description. Walk the boundaries of the property as you refer to a survey or a plat. When walking the boundaries, note any encroachments. Verify that the size of the lot you're buying actually matches the size you think you're getting. Especially where a subject site borders a vacant lot, field, creek, or other unclear property line, assume nothing. The lot lines may not run where they appear to run. Physically verify where surveyed boundaries actually lie.

Building Description

As a matter of law (except for condominiums), a real estate agreement need only specify site description—not the building itself. The legal definition of real estate (a legally described site by definition) includes all structures permanently attached to that site.

If the seller represents that the buildings are of a specific size or are built of certain materials, or of a certain historical date or design, then write those features (whatever they are) into the property description. In Berkeley, California, buyers sued the sellers of a gracious old home because the sellers had (mistakenly) told the buyers that the home had been designed by Julia Morgan, a famous Bay Area architect of the early 1900s. The buyers claimed that they had not just agreed to buy a house on a specific site. Rather, they had contracted to buy a Julia Morgan house. Because the house lacked the Julia Morgan prestige, the buyers believed they were entitled to damages. (The court agreed and awarded damages to the buyers.)

If you buy a prewar brownstone, or maybe the house where Dwight Eisenhower was raised, write it into your agreement. Detail what you expect to receive. Should your expectations (the seller's material representations) prove false, you can rescind the contract, claim damages, or perhaps both. (Caveat: see no representations clause, p. 218.)

Personal Property

Although real estate includes land and buildings, it does not necessarily include the personal property that may form part of your agreement with the sellers. (Generally, the term *personal property* refers to items that are not permanently attached to a building or the land.) Say the sellers of a four-plex provide their tenants window air conditioners, miniblinds, ranges, refrigerators, and ceiling fans. If you offer to buy that property, expressly list these items in your written purchase contract.

While it's true that many courts have broadened the concept of real estate to include personal property that is adapted for use with a specific property, do not depend on litigation to force the sellers to convey the personal property that you believed to be included in the sale. Leave no doubt—write it out. Walk through every room of the property and iden-tify and list every item that the sellers might plausibly maintain was not a part of your purchase agreement because it was their personal property and therefore not included with the sale of the real estate.

You list personal property for another purpose, too. You want the sellers to identify what personal property belongs to them and what belongs to their tenants. Property investors who do not obtain an accu-rate list of the seller's personal property (that is, personal property to be transferred to the buyer) may later find themselves in dispute with tenants when the tenants claim, "That refrigerator is ours. That junk icebox the landlord provided was carted off to the dump two years ago. We bought this refrigerator from Amanda's parents." To deter such claims, ask the tenants to sign off on any list of personal property that the sellers prepare.

Price and Financing

When you write your offer, spell out precisely the purchase price of the property and the terms of the financing. List the amounts payable, how payable, when payable, and the interest rate(s). Make it easy for a disinterested third party to interpret your meaning. Leave nothing to decide at some later date. "Seller agrees to carry back $20,000 on mutually agreeable terms" does not meet the contractual requirements of specificity.

If you plan to arrange new financing, or even if you assume the seller's mortgage, the same advice holds: clearly state the amount and terms of financing. Several years ago, I agreed to purchase a property and assume the seller's below-market-rate mortgage. Just before closing, however, the lender pointed out that it intended to increase the interest rate to the market level. Fortunately, my contract with the sellers specified that the mortgage assumption would come to me at the same below-market interest rate that the sellers were then paying. Rather than lose the sale and risk a lawsuit, the sellers had to buy down the mortgage interest rate from the rate the lender would otherwise have charged me.

If you agree to arrange new financing, spell out the maximum terms (for example, 5.75 percent, 25 years, 20 percent down). Then, if it turns out that (in good faith) the best loan you can find is at 6.25 percent, 20 years, 25 percent down, you need not complete the purchase. You can walk away and obtain a return of your earnest money deposit. (But make your financing contingency seem reasonable to the sellers. As noted elsewhere, savvy sellers won't accept unrealistic contingencies. And the fewer the contingencies, the more certain your offer will close, the lower the price.)

Earnest Money Deposit

The validity of your purchase offer *does not* depend on the amount of your earnest money deposit or, for that matter, whether you pay a deposit. Earnest money represents a good-faith showing that you intend to complete your purchase. Choose your deposit amount as part of your negotiating strategy.

Large deposits position you as a serious buyer. Some investors use large deposits to offset their lowball offers. A large earnest money deposit affirms that "You can count on me to buy your property. This large deposit proves that I mean what I say. Wouldn't you rather go for a sure thing now rather than wait for a better offer that may never come along?"

I recently bought a below-market-priced property for cash and deposited the entire amount in escrow within three days after the seller had signed. Closing occurred nine days later. The force of my offer and the quick close persuaded the seller to take the money and run—even though the price came in well below the amount the seller wanted. Was this agreement a win-win? Yes. Quick cash in lieu holding a vacant property was the most pressing goal of the seller (a Wells Fargo REO).

Whereas a large deposit signals strength, a small deposit conveys an image of weakness, or that you're trying to tie up the property on the cheap while you review other possibilities. But here's the rub: Smart sellers tend not to accept contracts that don't commit.

Whether sellers judge your deposit as large or small, serious or trifling, depends on local custom. Judge the size of your deposit by the amounts local sellers and realty agents think reasonable for the type of transaction you're entering.

Just keep in mind that a seemingly low deposit diminishes your credibility. A relatively high deposit bolsters credibility. For the best of both worlds, employ a low deposit strategy and rely on other factors to support your credibility as a buyer, such as current ownership of multiple properties, strong FICO credit score (see www.myfico.com), high net worth, and personal integrity. But this tactic is not so easy to pull off. Ready cash persuades best.

Quality of Title

For assurance of title, retain a title insurer. Your purchase agreement will specify the title guarantees and exceptions that govern your transaction. Before you close the deal, review the title report. Especially when you buy properties through foreclosure, tax sales, auctions, probate, or other sales in which the seller (title holder) of the property does not sign a general warranty deed, your risks of title issues increase.

Probate judges, clerks of court, sheriffs, and bank officials do not warrant a title in the same way that the previous owners could. You partially overcome these risks by purchasing title insurance.[1] But like all insurance

---

[1] If available. Title insurers will not issue policies on some properties when too many uncertainties cloud the quality of the title. In such cases, you would buy the property only at a steeply discounted price. Once purchased, you would then try to resolve the title issues. If successful, you win big. A property offered with a clear title will bring a higher price than one that is burdened by major clouds or defects.

contracts, title policies list a variety of limits, exceptions, and conditions. They do not cover everything. Although a title policy offers protection, you (or your attorney) must still identify title risks that remain.

Property Condition

Address the issue of property condition in two ways: Ask the owners to complete a seller disclosure statement that lists every conceivable problem or defect that has *now* or *ever* affected the property or the neighborhood. Also ask what efforts the sellers, previous property owners, or neighbors have implemented to solve the problem. ("Oh yes, we kept blowing fuses, so we just rewired around the fuse box. Now we never have problems." Or maybe, "Well, there was a crack cocaine house down the street, but the Neighborhood Watch group got the police to close it down.") The more you can get the sellers to tell you about the property and the neighborhood, the more accurately you can judge the property's potential risks, rewards, and value. (Sellers of REOs do not typically provide seller disclosure statements. "As is" reigns.)

Although you can learn much from the sellers, you can't learn everything. Sellers can't disclose what they don't know. As added protection, include a property inspection contingency in your offer. Check out the property with one or more specialists who can assess the condition of the plumbing, heating and air conditioning, electrical system, roofing, and foundation. (Risks remain, as no inspector warrants condition.)

Your contingency clause can state that repair costs should not exceed some designated amount (say $1,000). Ideally, the sellers should pay these costs. But if you've negotiated a bargain price, you might expect to pay them. If repair costs exceed your specified amount, your contingency clause should give you the right to cancel the purchase agreement and obtain a refund of your earnest money deposit. (Remember, when you present a firm, no-contingency offer to the sellers, along with a large earnest money deposit, your power to extract price and other concessions goes up.)

Preclosing Property Damage (Casualty Clause)

Most purchase agreements require the sellers to deliver a property to the buyer on the date of closing (or the date of possession) in essentially the same condition as it stood on the date the purchase agreement was signed. If the property suffers damage (fire, earthquake, vandalism, hurricane, flood) after the purchase contract has been signed, but before the closing, the sellers must repair the property at their expense. Alternatively, in the event of damage, the sellers may be allowed to terminate your purchase agreement and return the earnest money deposit to you.

I have seen some purchase contracts used by HUD, VA, and Fannie Mae REOs, for example, shift this risk of preclosing damage to buyers. Read the precise language of your contract. If you accept the risk of preclosing property damage, check with your insurance agent. Secure coverage to protect against property losses during this interim period.

Also, you may not want contract language that gives sellers the right to return your earnest money and terminate the purchase agreement should they find themselves unwilling or unable to repair any property damage. Say you bargain hard and get the sellers down to a price of $335,000. After accepting your offer, they begin to harbor second thoughts. Then along comes another offer at $355,000. Mysteriously, the property suffers a $5,000 fire. Now what will the sellers do?

They may drag their feet on repairs and claim problems settling with their insurer. Because they supposedly can't restore the property to its previous condition in time to meet the scheduled closing date, they cancel your contract and return your deposit. The sellers effectively used the casualty clause to shut you out of your bargain price.

To eliminate unwanted seller withdrawals, set the right to cancel the contract as your option, not the option of the sellers. The contract could also impose financial penalties on the sellers for failure to repair—or set up an escrow repair credit to compensate for the amount of the damage.

If you plan to use bank financing, the bank may refuse to close your loan until the damage has been satisfactorily repaired. That puts you in a catch-22. You can't repair the property until after you close your loan, but the lender won't close your loan until after you've made the repairs. This type of problem doesn't occur often, but if you prepare for this risk ahead of time, you and your attorney can draft a casualty clause that adequately protects your interests. (To resolve this issue with a lender, you might set up a $5,000—or some other appropriate amount—repair escrow account.)

Closing (Settlement) Costs

Property transactions can eat up thousands of dollars in closing costs. Title insurance, appraisal, mortgage points, buy-down fees, application fees, lender-mandated repairs, lawyers' fees, assumption fees, recording fees, transfer taxes, document stamps, survey, property inspections, escrow fees, real estate brokerage fees, and other expenses can quickly add up to a fair-sized amount of money. Who pays each of these transaction costs—the buyers or the sellers? Local custom suggests an answer, but negotiation can override custom. If the sellers won't drop their price as low as you'd like, ask them to pay settlement costs that are typically allocated to a buyer.

Sellers who won't cut $5,000 off their asking price will sometimes agree to pay that much or more in settlement costs that custom otherwise assigns to the purchaser. (Indeed, a 3-2-1 interest rate buy-down that costs the sellers $5,500 might prove more advantageous to you than a $5,500 reduction in price. A reduced interest rate improves your cash flow or qualifies you for a larger mortgage, or both.) When it can work to your benefit, give the sellers their price, but as a trade-off, request that they pay all (or most) of the closing costs. (Caution: Recall the pitfalls of "You name the price, I'll set the terms.")

Closing and Possession Dates

Purchase agreements set dates for settlement and possession. When sellers (or buyers) strongly prefer a quick (or maybe delayed) closing date, that date can play a role in the negotiations. Because of a need for ready cash, the sellers might trade a lower price for a fast settlement. Or for tax reasons, the sellers may prefer to delay settlement for six months or more.

The same goes for the date of possession. The sellers may prefer to close quickly, but they might want to hold on to the property (especially if it's their home) for some period that extends beyond the settlement date. Maybe the construction of their new house isn't complete. Maybe they would like to postpone moving until their children finish the school term. Reasons vary, but as a smart negotiator, feel out the sellers on their preferred closing and possession dates. Then use this information to shape your offer. If you're willing to meet the sellers' needs on this issue, they will more likely move closer to the price or terms, or both, that make the deal acceptable to you.

Leases

When you buy rental properties, read each of the tenant's leases before you write your offer. Leases remain in effect after a new owner takes possession. Especially weigh these issues:

♦ *Rent levels.* How much do the tenants pay in rents? Are any tenants in arrears? Have any tenants prepaid? How long have the current

rent levels been in effect? Are today's market rents above or below the rental amounts tenants currently pay?

♦ *Concessions.* Did the tenants receive any concession for signing their leases such as one month's free rent, a new 18-speed Trek bicycle, or other incentives that lower the effective amount of rents the tenants pay? Do any tenants pay high rents only because of an under-the-table agreement with the sellers to help improve the income statement that the sellers show prospective buyers? Sometimes sellers pad their rent rolls.

♦ *Utilities.* Do the leases require the tenants to pay all of their own utilities? If not, which utilities do the owners provide?

♦ *Yard care, snow removal, and other services.* Who provides yard care, snow removal, or other services such as small repairs within the rental units? Who pays for garbage and trash pickup? Do the leases obligate the sellers to provide tenants laundry facilities, off-street parking, a clubhouse, exercise room, child-care center, or transportation?

♦ *Furniture and appliances.* Is the owner obligated to provide tenants with window coverings, furniture, or appliances? If so, precisely which ones? What quality? Who retains responsibility for maintenance, repairs, and replacements?

♦ *Duration.* What term remains on each lease? Do tenants enjoy the right to renew? If renewed, does the lease (or do rent control laws) limit the amount of rent increase that you can impose? Will the market, tenant relations, or both, support a rent increase?

♦ *Security deposits.* What amount of security deposits has the owner collected from the tenants? Have tenants prepaid their last month's rent? Do the sellers retain an inspection sheet that shows the condition of each of the units at the time the tenants moved in? Have the tenants signed those inspection sheets?

♦ *Tenant confirmation.* Ask the tenants to confirm the terms of their leases as the sellers have represented them. Determine whether the sellers (or their property manager) have entered into side agreements with tenants that would modify or override the terms of the written lease. Learn whether the sellers have orally promised any of the tenants special services, rent relief, or other dispensations.

When you buy a rental property, you must honor valid leases. Such obligations not only affect the amounts of your future rental income and operating expenses, but they also restrict your plans to retenant, renovate, or convert (for example, converting rentals into condominiums). Although you own the property, the tenants were there first. Their valid leasehold rights trump your rights of ownership.[2] Even worse, some government landlord-tenant laws grant tenants the almost-automatic right to renew—at a rent-controlled rental rate.

Contingency Clauses

Most investors hedge their purchase offers with contingencies that relate to financing and property inspections. If an investor can't get financing, or if the condition of the property doesn't meet the investor's standards (as written into the purchase contract), the investor can walk away from the contract and receive a return of his earnest money.

Other Contingencies. In addition to financing and inspection contingencies, you can condition your purchase offer on any number of issues. If you plan to renovate, include a contingency for government permits. If government doesn't approve your plans, you can pull out of the purchase without penalty. You might include contingencies when your plans are subject to regulatory review (for example, converting apartments to condominiums, rehab with rent increases, increasing or decreasing the number of rental units, eliminating on-site parking, asbestos removal, and so on).

Other contingencies might include attorney review, the sale of another property, raising funds from co-investors, professional market value appraisal, or even a market study (feasibility analysis). You can condition your purchase offer on anything ranging from the approval of Uncle Harry to an eclipse of the sun.

Contingencies and Negotiation Strategy. Even though you *can* condition your offer on anything (or everything), that doesn't mean the sellers will accept it. They may tell you, "No way are we going to take our property off the market for several months while you try to put together a syndication deal. Come back and talk to us after you've raised the money." The more you hedge your offer with deal-threatening contingencies, the less likely the sellers will sign it, whereas a clean, no-strings-attached offer might gain the sellers' approval even when price or terms you offer falls below the amount expected.

---

[2]Some owners place a "cancellation upon sale" clause into their leases. Except under unusual circumstances, most tenants should reject a lease with such a clause—if they noticed it. (As with all lease clauses, if found unconscionable, deceptive, or unfair or contrary to government-issued landlord-tenant laws, courts can refuse to enforce such clauses.)

Sellers prefer firm offers. Selectively choose your contingencies. Weigh them into your negotiating strategy. Write an offer that looks certain to close. You may find that your sellers will relax demands on other important contract issues.

Assignment and Inspection

Sales agreements may (or may not) permit buyers to freely assign their purchase contracts to another buyer. Talk this issue over with qualified counsel. As a buyer who (at least on some occasions) would like to flip a contract, verify whether the sellers can contractually object. To avoid conflict, insert an assignment clause similar to the following: "Buyers may assign this Contract and all rights and obligations hereunder to any other person, corporation, or trustee."

The sellers should oppose such broad language and try to negotiate language such as: "Buyer may assign this Contract only with the written approval of the sellers. Consent by the sellers shall not be arbitrarily withheld."

The sellers should normally want the right to approve your assignees just to satisfy themselves that the assignees possess the credit and financial capacity to complete the purchase. The sellers may want you to remain liable for damages (or specific performance) should your assignees default. You would like to avoid (or limit) that liability.

When you obtain the right of assignment, insert a clause that permits you reasonable access and entry to the property so that your potential assignees can inspect and evaluate it. Without the right to show the property, the right to assign loses its effectiveness. (When flipping *off-plan* properties—as was so popular during the boom years—the "right of entry" clause becomes a moot point.)

Public Records

If you contract for a lease option, lease purchase, contract for deed, or some other type of purchase offer that postpones closing of title for, say, more than six months, consider a clause that permits you to record a notation of your contract in the public records. Recording serves notice to the world of your rights in the property.

Without this notice, the sellers could place mortgages or other liens against the property that could jeopardize your interests. Also, without a recording, the sellers' judgment creditors, or perhaps the Internal Revenue Service, might gain a priority claim to the property. Discuss these issues with competent local legal counsel. Do not make payments to the sellers over a period of years and then learn that the sellers cannot deliver clear title.

Systems and Appliances

Whether your closing occurs within 30 days or three years, your contract should lay out who is responsible for interim maintenance, repair, and replacement of malfunctioning systems (heating, air conditioning, electrical, waste disposal, well water) or appliances. If the air conditioning (AC) stops working, the sellers may want to repair it at a cost of $450 in lieu of a new replacement unit that costs $4,200. Yet if a repair only keeps the old AC clanking and clunking for, at best, 6 to 12 months, you should insist on replacement—or discount the contract price.

Environmental Hazards

Heightened costs for environmental cleanups and extensive regulatory controls mean that your contract must address environmental hazards that could affect the property. Lead paint, asbestos, urethane formaldehyde, underground heating oil tanks, radon—and who knows what other dangers the Environmental Protection Agency may discover—can cost property owners thousands in remedial or replacement expenses.

Include a contract clause as follows: "Sellers warrant that the property complies with all current federal, state, or local environmental laws, rules, or regulations. Sellers agree to indemnify buyers for all required cleanup costs that shall be necessary to remedy environmental hazards that existed during the sellers' period of ownership."

This language only suggests, but it covers two main questions that you want answered: (1) Is the property free of hazards? (2) If hazards are discovered, who pays for the cleanup? Under federal (and many state) laws, any owner of a property may be personally required to pay for environmental cleanup—even when that owner stands innocent of creating the hazard.

No Representations

Up to this point, we've looked at contract clauses from the buyer's perspective. When you sell a property, include a clause something like the following: "All oral or written representations or promises of the sellers pertaining to this agreement, or material to inducing this agreement, are listed herein."

Why is this clause necessary? To protect you from property buyers who falsely claim that you made promises such as "We'll leave all of the appliances for you" or "The roof's in perfect condition." In their attempt to void a contract or force you (the seller) to pay for repairs or replacements, buyers (and especially their lawyers) know that claims of "fraud in the inducement" can justify damages or contract rescission in court.

Will the buyers win their lawsuit against you? Are you prepared to spend $10,000 or $20,000 in legal fees and court costs to find out? Don't believe for a minute that old saw, "It's just their word against mine." Yes, it is. But that's no guarantee a judge or jury will believe you over them. Remove from your buyers the chance to falsely claim you lured them into a contract through deception.

Default Clause

Your contract default clause should spell out what happens if you or the sellers fail to carry through the terms of your purchase agreement. These clauses address at least four areas:

1. Method of resolution
2. Damages
3. Specific performance
4. Who bears the expenses

Method of Resolution. Many people are quick to file a lawsuit when another party breaches an agreement. Other options for resolution include mediation and arbitration.

If you pursue a lawsuit, you will probably lose even if a court's decision goes in your favor: You will spend tens of thousands of dollars in legal fees; you will see truth and justice perverted beyond recognition; you will encounter lawyers whose dishonesty and incompetence are exceeded only by their arrogance; you will expose yourself and your private life to public view through intrusive discovery procedures that permit lawyers to question you (admissions, interrogatories, depositions) about anything that could *in any way* be related to your character or the issues being litigated.

The litigation process itself can require you to live through years of anxious uncertainty, and even winning verdicts can be overturned on appeal for purely technical reasons, thus starting the trial process over again.

Lawsuits enrich lawyers, judges, and a myriad of expert witnesses, jury consultants, court reporters, legal secretaries, and photocopying services. They do little to settle disputes in a fair, timely, and cost-effective manner.

Admittedly, mediation and arbitration also fail in many ways. But to their advantage, they are less costly, less adversarial, more timely, and more likely to emphasize substance over procedure. Talk with people who have sought redress through litigation. Then decide for yourself whether to specify mediation and arbitration to resolve contract disputes.

Damages. A party who breaches a real estate contract may be held liable for either compensatory damages or liquidated damages. In theory, compensatory damages are supposed to make the innocent party financially whole. Such damages measure the economic loss you've suffered because the other party didn't live up to her part of the bargain. Translating the theory of compensatory damages into an actual dollar amount is subject to legal argument. Because of indefinite calculation, no one can predict how much money a jury might award, or whether an appellate court will uphold that amount.

To avoid this legal wrangling over how much you (or the sellers) lost because of the other party's breach, some contracts specify an amount called *liquidated damages.* In case of buyer default, some real estate contracts permit sellers to keep the earnest money deposit as liquidated damages.

I won't go into all the specific pros and cons of compensatory versus liquidated damages. But, to me, liquidated damage clauses seem superior because (properly written) they reduce ambiguity and, in the case of buyer default, limit liability to a knowable amount (e.g., typically, the earnest money deposit). Nevertheless, if you can locate an experienced real estate attorney who is competent and trustworthy, and bills reasonably, discuss this issue with him or her. Understand the type of damage clause included in your purchase offer. Use this clause to limit your liability.

Note: In some states, and in some types of contract cases, winning litigants may also recover damages for emotional distress, but this is rarely the rule. In cases of fraud or other egregious behavior, some states permit awards for punitive damages. In contrast to compensatory damages, punitive damages punish the losing party for reprehensible conduct. These issues involve technical interpretations of statutes and case law in light of the facts of a particular transaction.

Specific Performance. In addition to a claim for damages, some contracts (or contract laws) give buyers (and less frequently, sellers) the right to seek specific performance. This right means that through legal proceedings (arbitration or lawsuit), a court could order defaulting property owners to sell their property on the terms specified in your purchase contract. You would pursue this remedy when a subject property uniquely fits your special need (e.g., to compel the sale of a vacant lot next door to your apartment building so that you can satisfy the city's off-street parking requirements).

Who Bears the Expenses? Whether you pursue mediation, arbitration, or litigation, the dispute resolution process can easily run up thousands (or tens of thousands) of dollars in costs and expenses. Therefore, look to your purchase contract to see what it says about who pays. Even though today we hear about "loser pays" types of laws and contract terms, accept such a clause only after you think through its potential adverse results.

First, lawyers lose many cases in which their clients are in the right. Lawyers fail to prepare; they err in tactics or strategy. Judges may rely on their biases rather than on the weight of the evidence. Or perhaps key witnesses come across poorly on the witness stand. The other side may lie in a convincing and unshakable manner. Even in the most righteous cases, victory seldom triumphs without risk.

Second, if the other side can easily spend more money than you, they can hire the best and most expensive counsel to overwhelm and intimidate you and your counsel. With such firepower against you, even if you are willing to risk losing your case, you may not be willing or able to face the opponents' legal expenses of, say, $50,000 or $100,000 (yes, even lawyers in small-time litigation can run up fees of this size if someone has the money to pay them). Regardless of the merits of your case, the potential outcome of bearing the other side's legal expenses may force you to accept an unfavorable settlement.

My purpose here is to inform, not advise. Your purchase contract will include important clauses that govern the relationship between you and the sellers. Read these contract clauses before you sign your offer. Only then can you (or your counsel) rewrite, amend, or strike out unacceptable language. Once you and the sellers commit, you're both bound to the extent of the law. Protect yourself. Fashion your offer so that you know and understand the full import of your agreement—including what recourses and costs apply if the deal falls apart.

SUMMARY

You don't just find great deals—more often, you create them. Regardless of the sellers' asking price and terms, investors should elicit and sort through the sellers' real needs and emotions. Then, negotiate an agreement that gives both parties a win-win agreement. Your contract negotiations will involve multiple deal points. Especially hold in the front of your mind these 15 primary issues:

1. Does the contract include the names and signatures of all buyers and sellers?
2. Are the site boundaries accurately delineated? Have you walked the site boundary lines?
3. Are the building and other site improvements adequately identified and described?
4. Does the contract or contract addendum list all personal property and fixtures included in the sales price? Should you ask the sellers to prepare a separate bill of sale for these items? Does the seller hold clear title to all the personal property that is to be conveyed?
5. Have the sales price, term, and financing contingency been spelled out so precisely that a disinterested third party could unambiguously interpret the agreement?
6. What is the amount of the earnest money deposit? Under what conditions will it be returned to the buyers?
7. What types of deed must the sellers use to convey title to the property? Is the title free of encumbrances? If not, what liens, easements, encroachments, or other encumbrances cloud the title? Is the title insurable? What exceptions apply?
8. What is the condition of the property? Have you obtained adequate seller disclosures and professional inspections? Have you negotiated an escrow credit for repairs?
9. Who bears liability for preclosing casualty losses? Under what conditions can the buyer (or seller) terminate the sales contract as the result of preclosing casualty losses? Who has responsibility for preclosing repair or replacement of systems and appliances?
10. What settlement costs are to be paid by the sellers? The buyers?
11. What are the dates of closing and possession?
12. Have you examined all leases that apply to the units occupied by tenants? Has the present owner of the property entered into side agreements with any of the tenants? Have you confirmed with the tenants the rental information provided by the sellers? Have you identified the tenants' personal property? Although leases provide legal recourse, tenant quality ranks just as important (if not more so). What qualifications, character, and cooperativeness do the tenants display?
13. How many contingency clauses have you included in your offer? Are your contingencies consistent with the negotiation strategy you have adopted?

14. Have you protected yourself against environmental hazards that may require expensive cleanup costs? What methods of dispute resolution are provided by your offer? What types of default remedies are available to you and the sellers? Who pays the costs?
15. Do you support your requests and positions with credible reasons, benchmarks, and evidence? If you ask for a lower price or seller terms, tell why. How will the seller benefit?

Your agreement includes multiple issues. Negotiate a full complement of trade-offs and conciliations. When you hit an impasse, shift to another issue. Rethink and recast the contract terms. Keep searching cooperatively. You will achieve win-win.

11

STRATEGIC MANAGEMENT
BUILDS EQUITY

When you own property, you control—for better or worse—the cash flows that you receive and the amount of equity that you build. Market timing and market conditions matter, but you matter more. You need not wait for market vacancy rates to fall. You need not wait for improved market rent levels. You need not wait and hope for market appreciation. Through strategic property management, you can boost the rents, occupancy, and value of your properties (leases permitting, of course) within just 3 to 12 months after your purchase—even with no favorable change in the market.

THE 10:1 RULE (MORE OR LESS)

Recall the value (V) formula:

Value = NOI (net operating income)/R (capitalization rate)

Assume that the property you buy yields an annual net operating income of $25,000 and the market cap rate equals 10 percent. The property value equals $250,000 (as estimated by this income approach). You next apply the creating value ideas from Chapters 8 and 9 to boost the property's rental income and cut its operating expenses, and thereby increase its NOI by $5,000 a year. You've just added $50,000 to the market value of your property:

Added value = $5,000/.10 = $50,000

Or, alternatively,

$$V = 25{,}000 + 5{,}000\ (\text{NOI})/.10\ (\text{R})$$
$$= \$300{,}000\ (\text{versus the old value of } \$250{,}000)$$

Can you achieve such gains in NOI? Yes! Here's why: Most small investment properties suffer from subpar management. Ill-informed, poorly motivated, and inattentive property owners dominate the field. [In fact, to build equity fast, seek out undermanaged and ill-managed properties. Strategic management + smart leverage means that within a few years you can multiply original equity (your down payment) 3 to 10 times (higher LTVs yield higher multiples).]

Think First

Undermanaged properties remain abundant because many property owners fail to clarify their personal and financial objectives. These investors know that they want to make money in real estate, but they don't think through the types of tenants, properties, and neighborhoods that best fit their temperament, lifestyle, and budget.

Instead, they buy their properties according to whether they can get a bargain price or easy financing. Or, worse, they buy a property because some professed guru has urged them to "get started now." (Notice those testimonials on the TV infomercials where people enthusiastically remark, "We were able to buy our first property just three weeks after studying your course. Thank you, guru." Do begin now, but "begin now" means to research properties and areas—it does not encourage you to rush out and buy within a matter of days or weeks.)

Through some combination of work and luck, a few of these guru protégés do achieve long-term success. Many more aren't prepared for the potential problems, difficulties, and downside of unwise acquisitions. They lack money to cover repairs, replacements, and maintenance. They find that they dislike managing their tenants and their properties. Disappointment sets in. Neglect sets their standard operating procedure. Their properties deteriorate, and their tenant relations sour. Eventually these disillusioned owners sell out and then lament to anyone who will listen, "Owning rental properties takes too much time and creates too many headaches. It's a never-ending stream of things going wrong."

To avoid this whine, know yourself, know your finances, and know your capabilities. To succeed in real estate (as well as in any other endeavor), pick through your likes and dislikes, strengths and weaknesses. Affirm that your properties, tenants, and neighborhoods match up well with who you are and how you want to live your life. Otherwise, you, too, can end up frustrated, careless, and burned out.

Know Yourself

Do you seek pride of ownership? Would you like to point out the properties you own to friends and relatives? Would you deal effectively with tenants who sit below (or above) your socioeconomic status? (Some owners detest their low-income Section 8 tenants, while other blue-collar owners despise their well-to-do, arrogant, college student tenants.) Do some neighborhoods or types of tenants threaten your sense of safety? Are you the kind of person who easily gets suckered by a hard-luck story?

Before you invest, think about the types of properties that you would enjoy (or at least tolerate) owning. No matter how good the price or how easy the financing, avoid properties that clash with your MMPI.

I know from experience. When I began to buy properties, I looked at the financials of a deal—not my personal psyche. Accordingly, my portfolio grew to include an eclectic mix of single-family houses, duplexes, and small apartment buildings with differing price ranges, types of tenants, and neighborhoods.

This odd collection of properties taught me a great deal. I learned that I liked some of the tenants and that some of the properties were great to own. Other types of tenants and properties seemed to evoke a long list of hassles. I also fell for hard-luck stories.

However, once settled on an acquisition and management strategy (including tenant selection) that matched my personality, my property operations and my life became easier. At that time, middle- to upper-middle-income single-family houses proved most desirable to me. In terms of cash flow, these more stable and higher-priced properties (less rent collected per dollar of investment, that is, lower cap rates) reduced my cash-on-cash return, but the trade-off was worth it.

Nevertheless, some prosperous investors seek out low-end tenants (see Roger Neal's *Streetwise Investing in Rental Housing* [Panoply Press, 2000]). In most cities, low- to moderate-priced properties offer the highest rental yields. And these types of properties serve up potential for management turnarounds on a silver platter. Choose the type of property that will work for you. You will make good money—as long as the property fits your personal (and financial) profile. Properties that disappoint and frustrate seldom yield satisfactory returns.

Know Your Finances

Property ownership requires a safe level of cash reserves. Without cash (or wise credit), you'll fail to invest in upkeep, maintenance, and improvements. Properties grow in value only when you give them the TLC they need. Shortchange upkeep only if you primarily hold a property for its land value (i.e., a potential teardown or a major rehab). To manage properties profitably, you can't just pull money out—you must also put money back in. Many no-down-payment gurus neglect to emphasize the need to reinvest. (Not all of your rents should go to make the lease payments on your new BMW.)

Know Your Capabilities

During my early years in property ownership, I attempted some property repairs, remodeling, and renovations. For me, bad idea! I lacked the required talent and skills. I lacked the temperament. Rather than save money (my goal), many of these do-it-yourself projects ended up over budget and low quality.

Projects that I figured would last a week often dragged on for a month or more. Sometimes my rent losses exceeded the amount I would have paid for a competent contractor. In fact, if I had hired a contractor in the first place, I would have saved myself exasperation. (Admittedly, working with contractors can exasperate, too.)

The moral: Assess your capabilities before you buy a property. Many investors fudge a property's expense numbers to persuade themselves that a proposed deal looks better than it really does. They omit expenses for this and that because of their "I can do it myself" self-talk. But even if you can do it yourself, record a bookkeeping expense for the value of your own labor.

If you focus on strategic management and supervise repairs, maintenance, and improvements, you'll typically make more money and avoid the burnout that plagues so many owners who try to do everything themselves (and then sell at a distress price to rid themselves of their headaches and money traps).

When you delegate manual labor, you free up time to think, research, and plan your investment strategy. I am convinced that most owners of small income properties could improve their bottom line if they would manage their strategy more than they fret over the small stuff. Think more, work less. That approach leads to effective, value-creating property management. (Of course, if you enjoy and hold competency in such work, DIY builds equity faster. For some investors, sweat equity pays big dividends.)

(Note: Do-it-myself did provide valuable knowledge and experience in everything from air conditioning to zoning. It improved my practical ability to manage, supervise, and negotiate the work now performed by others.)

SMART STRATEGIC DECISIONS

Owners of modern, large-scale apartment complexes research their market strategy. These owners know that market strategy returns higher cash flows and higher gains in property value. Yet real estate books aimed at small investors rarely mention the term *strategy* or *market strategy*.

Authors of such books seem to believe they have discovered the one true way to buy and manage properties. They believe that what has worked for them will work for you. Maybe it will. But more than likely, you can do better if you formulate your own strategy to match your capabilities, your finances, and current market conditions.

By strategy, I mean collect market data and design a value proposition (rent level, property benefits, location, promotion, lease clauses, etc.) to profitably distinguish your properties and management services from those of competing owners. With a well-thought-out strategy, you collect more rents, experience less turnover, achieve quicker rent-ups, and better satisfy tenants.

Tailor Strategy to Local Markets

Real estate markets differ in time and place: types of properties, price ranges, price movements, inventories, rent levels, expenses, laws, tenants, tenant preferences, employment trends, vacancy rates, and dozens of other variables. You can't mimic an investment plan created by someone who gained experience in a different city at a different time at different property prices and rent levels. To enhance your NOI and property values, monitor the ever-changing characteristics of a specific market(s). Then adapt.

Craig Wilson's Profit-Boosting Market Strategy

To see strategy in action, follow the experience of Craig Wilson. Craig bought an undermanaged 16-unit apartment building located within one mile of a small college. Craig felt that he should direct his marketing efforts toward college students.

Yet Craig also knew that college students did not define a true market segment. You cannot accurately stereotype college students any more than you can stereotype any other group of people who happen to share one characteristic. Accordingly, Craig set out to learn about those diverse college students who rent off-campus.

Discovering Student Beliefs and Attitudes. Like all smart small business owners, Craig knew that to begin his market research, he needed to understand his potential customers. To achieve this end, Craig:

♦ Thumbed through back issues of the campus newspaper to read articles and letters to the editor that addressed student-housing issues.
♦ Met with the director of the off-campus student housing office.
♦ Talked with students who stopped by the off-campus housing office to look at property listings.
♦ Talked candidly with each of the current tenants of his newly acquired building.
♦ Hired a marketing student to solicit responses to a student-housing survey (questionnaire).
♦ Reviewed "For Rent" ads in the newspapers and on the web.

Although none of Craig's survey techniques followed the sampling techniques of a Gallup Poll, they did provide insights about student attitudes and the property choices available to them. Students levied these complaints about their residences and living conditions.

Too much noise
No laundry facilities
Too little closet space
Rents too high
Inadequate parking
Authoritarian or obnoxious landlords
Unkempt appearance
Inadequate security
Lack of privacy
Plumbing and hot water problems
Too little storage space
Outdated kitchens and baths
Inadequate heating and cooling
No pets
Slow repairs
Cockroaches, ants
Too few electrical outlets
Lack of cleanliness

With this customer feedback in hand, Craig collected more data on competing properties.

Collect Details about Competing Properties. Most rental property investors never personally evaluate their competitors' offerings. Avoid this error. Without firsthand knowledge of competitors, you're shotgunning in the dark. You may hit your target, but miss the bull's eye—except by luck.

Can you create a competitive edge if you fail to inspect and evaluate the features, benefits, and rent levels of competing rental units? You cannot. Lacking such knowledge, you will set your rents too low or too high. Or you miss easy ways to improve your property's features to achieve comparative advantage.

To manage proactively, Craig researched competitors: (1) he phoned in response to two dozen ads and recorded basic property and rental information; (2) he made appointments and visited a dozen properties; and (3) he performed follow-up research after one-, two-, and four-week intervals.

Telephone Advertisers. After a search of listings from newspaper ads, property signs, Internet listings, and the off-campus housing office, Craig telephoned 24 property owners or managers. From these calls, Craig learned:

♦ The ease or difficulty of reaching these owners and managers
♦ Their degree of competency with telephone selling skills (courteous, informative, pleasant, persuasive)
♦ The addresses of their units and the specific types of property (single-family, duplex, fourplex, and so on)
♦ Property amenities
♦ House rules
♦ Important lease terms, clauses, and rental rates
♦ Amount of deposit
♦ Repair, lawn care, and utility expenses (who pays, how much?)

As expected, some owners and managers were more forthcoming than others. But, overall, this research gave Craig a knowledgeable feel for the rental housing market. To make sure he didn't forget (or ignore) pertinent facts, Craig recorded competitive data on a survey form that he had prepared for this task.

Inspecting Properties. To follow up this research, Craig scheduled viewing appointments or attended open houses for 12 of these competing rental units. During these property visits, Craig sized up both the specific property and its owner or manager. He gathered information about floor plans, bathrooms, kitchens, total square footage, room sizes, decorating patterns, cleanliness, appearance, soundproofing, views, ceiling heights, electrical capacity, laundry facilities, appliances, parking, storage, and security.

When possible, he picked up copies of leases and application forms. He also judged the personality and demeanor of the owner or manager. Would this person's attitudes, words, and behavior attract or repel good tenants? Did he seem eager to please and show sincere interest toward providing tenants a pleasant place to live? Or did he seem to issue do's and don'ts like a boot camp drill sergeant?

The Callbacks. After property inspections, Craig ranked each of the properties according to its appeal. Then he affirmed his impressions with market feedback. To learn how quickly (or slowly) each unit rented, he checked back during the month to see which units remained on the market. This information added to his knowledge of tenant turn-offs and turn-ons. He also figured out which units the prospects rejected because of cost or, perhaps, undesirable features.

When you develop your market strategy for a property, exploit the weaknesses of competitors and strengthen your offer in the eyes of the customers (residents) you plan to attract. Market data gives you clues and insights.

Without attention to detail, your strategic decisions (if the term *strategic* even applies) evolve from guesstimates or intuition. Or all too often, they arise from default—"Well, that's the way we've always done it," or "That's the way everyone else does it." Maybe so. But you can figure out a more profitable approach when you derive your decisions from thorough information about prospects and properties.

How Craig Wilson Used Market Information to Enhance Profitability

The methods you use to position your property will differ from the strategy that Craig Wilson (or anyone else) has adopted for his properties. Nevertheless, follow through the ways Craig chose tenants and designed his property features and operations to gain competitive advantage. When you execute similar methods of research, inquiry, and thought, you can plan your own strategy.

Tenant Segment. After Craig stacked up the housing complaints and comments of students against the typical rental property and owner or manager, he decided to design his property operations to appeal to students who placed high value on quiet, aesthetics, cleanliness, security, and a pleasant, easy-to-get-along-with owner. He sought students who responsibly managed their finances, class studies, college activities, and employment. From among the many students who were searching for apartments, Craig wanted to select the top tier. To attract this tenant segment, Craig knew that he had to offer the features and benefits that these students would value highly.

Privacy, Quiet, and Storage. To provide his tenants with privacy, quiet, and storage, Craig modified his property three ways:

1. *Study room.* On a portion of the roof, he built a soundproofed 20-foot-by-20-foot study room. Many students in his target market had complained that they found it difficult to read or study in their apartments while their roommates watched television, played CDs, or visited with friends. This study room also eliminated another problem: Students who wanted to get in just a couple of hours (or less) of study time no longer had to bear the inconvenience of returning to campus in the evenings.
2. *Party room.* As another benefit, residents could reserve the study room on weekend nights for social events or group gatherings. This use met the needs of not only the tenants who wanted to entertain, but also those who did not want to hear their noise.
3. *Storage.* To overcome tenant complaints of inadequate storage space, Craig bought eight-foot-by-six-foot-high gabled storage sheds and placed them behind a wooden fence on each side of his building. These facilities could store skis, infrequently used sports equipment, bicycles, boxes of books, and other assorted items.

Security. To enhance the safety and security of his building, Craig replaced the hollow-core entrance doors to each unit with solid doors equipped with double dead-bolt locks and peep scopes. He also equipped all windows with burglar pins and made certain that all window locks were strong and secure. To bolster fire safety, Craig placed a fire extinguisher in each unit and a hard-wired smoke alarm in every room.

Landscaping, Grounds, and External Appearance. Although from a street and walk-up view, this property looked okay, Craig decided he wanted its attractiveness to stand out. He painted its wood trim; added decorative flowers, shrubs, rocks, mulch, and fencing; and replaced the building entrance doors with heavier carved-wood doors. While from a narrow economic perspective such changes might seem unnecessary, Craig believed they would achieve four goals.

First, these improvements accented his pride of ownership as well as his goal to provide residents a desirable place to live. Second, since most prospective tenants judge a building from the outside before they look inside, these improvements would entice students to come in and view the vacant units when they became available. Third, by keeping the outside especially attractive, Craig felt he could appeal to students who would take better care of the property. (You cannot expect tenants to care for your property more than you do.) And fourth, by noticeably improving the exterior appearance of the property, Craig encouraged other nearby owners to do likewise and thus begin a spruce-up campaign that would benefit all of the neighborhood's tenants and property owners.

Laundry Facilities. The basement area of College Oaks provided space to install three sets of washers and dryers. Craig leased these units from a commercial vendor. Under this lease, the vendor supplied and maintained the machines, and Craig earned a percentage of all revenues. While this operation was not expected to earn much profit for Craig, it did provide convenience for tenants. (In today's market, I would hesitate to buy a property that lacked in-unit washer and dryer connections.)

Heating. College Oaks lacked individual furnaces in each unit. This deficiency created tenant discomfort. In winter months, some apartments remained cold. Others felt hot. Nearly all apartments experienced a chill from 6:30 A.M. to around 9:00 A.M. To solve this problem, Craig removed the wall air conditioning units and replaced them with units that included heating and cooling elements. Although these heating units could not produce heat as efficiently as the central gas boiler, tenant control did provide a cost-effective, much-appreciated improvement.

Kitchens and Baths. Craig knew that aesthetics and functional utility of kitchens and baths lead to tenant satisfaction (or dissatisfaction). To improve appearance, Craig painted the kitchens and added a splash of color with tile borders. To enhance function, he added four electrical outlets and six linear feet of counter and cabinet space, and by changing the location of the refrigerator, he improved the efficiency of the kitchen work triangle (see Figures 11.1 and 11.2). To sharpen the bathrooms, Craig added new fixtures, artful decorating patterns, and spacious storage cabinets and shelving.

Upkeep and Cleanliness. Following the advice of George Kelling and Catherine Coles's book *Fixing Broken Windows,* Craig implemented a cleanliness and upkeep program for his building that never tolerated trash, dirt, cobwebs, or deferred maintenance. Lack of care invites tenants to drop their respect for the property. (*Fixing Broken Windows* shows that when neighborhood and property condition "little things" are left unattended, they drift ever lower, or as my mother would say, "Leave one dirty dish in the kitchen sink, and before you know it, you've got a full sink of dirty dishes.")

Tenant Selection. Craig knew from his research that many students preferred his management style vis-à-vis those of competing owners. He also knew that to execute profitably, he must choose tenants carefully. To achieve his goal, Craig adopted four practices:

1. *Appropriate conduct.* In talking with prospective residents, Craig emphasized the advantages of his property operations and the

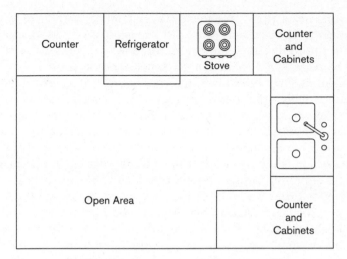

Figure 11.1 Old Kitchen Design

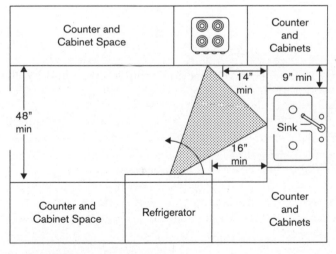

Figure 11.2 New Kitchen Design

strict types of resident conduct that he expected and required. In stressing these strict policies, Craig explained the benefits that would flow through to all tenants who lived in the building.

2. *Screening*. Craig emphasized that he wanted residents to exhibit personal responsibility. He requested credit reports and scores,

references from present and past landlords and employers. He also sought tenants who did not smoke or use drugs. He did not permit ear-splitting motorcycles or other loud vehicles. Applicants also needed a 3.0 or better grade point average.

3. *Rent level.* To offer his residents a strong value proposition, Craig priced his units equal to competing (yet inferior) properties. In this way, Craig received more tenant applications than he could accommodate; he pushed down the costly burden of vacancies and tenant turnover.

4. *Deposit.* Although Craig did not fully exploit the superiority of his property through higher rent levels, he did request a security deposit that was double the going rate. He explained to tenants that the large deposit discouraged applicants who would not live by house rules. One or two inconsiderate people can spoil the peace, quiet, and cleanliness of a property. Steering these people to other buildings enhances the quality of life for all of Craig's residents.

Results

When combined with expense reductions, Craig's market strategy succeeded. Every indicator (NOI, property value, tenant retention, occupancy rates, word-of-mouth referrals, maintenance costs, pride of ownership, management time and effort) changed for the better.

Can you achieve similarly improved results for your property or properties? Definitely! Your opportunities remain wide open because so few owners or managers of small rentals think market strategy. Yet in every housing market, some types of tenants remain underserved. In every housing market, some property features, benefits, and management services remain in relatively short supply. Discover these market (opportunity) shortcomings. Strategize your property operations to exploit them. You will profit personally and financially.

CUT OPERATING EXPENSES

Every dollar you slice from your property's operating expenses adds $10 (more or less) to your *equity*. With figures like that, meticulously keep track of expenses. Then reduce, shift, or eliminate them. The following discussion provides some ideas.

Energy Audits

Nearly all utility companies will show you how to reduce your gas or electric bills. Some will perform an energy audit and inspection of your property. Others provide booklets or brochures and perhaps a customer service department to answer questions. Find articles and books at your local library that discuss energy conservation. Google "energy audit" or "energy savings" and you'll get more than enough ideas.

Each type of building construction and area of the country presents different problems and opportunities. Seek how-to advice that fits your situation. Site placement and window positions can increase or reduce energy costs. Conduct an energy audit on a building before you buy it. Judge beforehand the extent to which you can feasibly lower these costs. Avoid energy-hog buildings for which no solution exists.

Property Insurance

When you buy property insurance: (1) Obtain enough coverage to protect your property, your rental income, and your other assets; (2) within your basic protection, reduce premiums by increasing deductibles or eliminating uneconomical coverage; and (3) shop among agents and companies for the best combination of service and low premiums.

Basic Protection. If you own a home, you obtained a homeowner's insurance policy. If you're like most homeowners, you haven't given that policy much thought. I know of this common oversight from a frightful experience. In the early 1990s, I was living in the Berkeley-Oakland, California, hills when a wildfire swept through and destroyed 3,300 houses and apartment units. Nearly one-half of the property owners who suffered losses discovered that they lacked sufficient insurance coverages and policy limits.

Property and liability insurance for income properties requires even more attention than policies written for owner-occupied residences. Rental property policies are subject to less standardization of coverage and greater variance in premiums. Before you buy a fire insurance policy and think you're covered, talk with several insurance agents and ask these questions:

1. *Who is covered?* Typically, your insurance coverage protects only the named insureds within the policy. Therefore, take care to name all persons or companies (co-owners, mortgage lenders) whose financial interest in the property deserves protection.
2. *What property is covered?* On this point, insurance policies distinguish between the property you own and the property your

tenants own. Policies seldom (if ever) cover tenants' property (advise or require them to buy their own tenant policy). Also, policies distinguish between personal property (appliances, lawn care equipment, assorted tools, and other items stored in the garage) and real property (the building itself, plants, shrubs, fencing).

Generally, the real and personal property distinction most affects rental property owners who rent their units furnished. But if you keep personal property around or within a rental property, verify coverage.

3. *What time period applies?* Insurance policies don't just begin and end on specified dates. They begin and end at specified *times* on specified dates. Assume you close a property purchase at 9:00 A.M. on June 3. A fire breaks out at 10:30 A.M. You've ordered insurance coverage to begin on June 3. You're covered, right? Not necessarily. That June 3 policy may not begin coverage until 12:00 noon. So don't assume; verify the exact dates and times of your protection.

4. *What perils are covered?* People think that fire represents the most critical peril to protect against. But what about flood, earthquake, vandalism, tenant abuse, windstorm, hail, mudslides, sinkholes, riot, theft, accumulation of snow and ice (on roofs that collapse), termite infestation, lawsuits, trip-and-fall accidents, and other potential losses too numerous to mention? Your policy will list covered perils. Read them. If not adequate, your insurer may add coverage through a rider or endorsement.

5. *What losses are covered?* Insurers usually classify losses as direct or indirect. A fire that damages your building creates a direct loss. The fact that you can no longer collect rents until the damage is repaired represents an indirect loss. Your basic policy will not cover many types of indirect losses. For these losses (if coverage is available), you need to buy a rider or endorsement.

6. *What locations are covered?* This question normally applies to personal property that you may move from location to location. But also consider the following possibility: You've just loaded your F-150 with $4,000 worth of appliances, plumbing fixtures, and carpeting from Lowe's. You plan to install these items at a fourplex you own. But while you're in the restroom at a gas station, someone steals your truck and its $4,000 worth of contents. Does your policy cover these supplies? Maybe, maybe not.

7. *How much will the insurer pay?* Every insurance contract restricts how much it will pay for losses. Most policies include some combination of deductibles, limits, and co-insurance. Also, for real or personal property, your policy might pay to replace, repair, or

rebuild the damaged items with new materials (100 percent of replacement cost). Or the policy might only reimburse actual cash value (replacement cost new, less depreciation).

Within the same policy, different types and amounts of restrictions apply to the various types of coverage. For example, fire damage might subject you to a $500 deductible, whereas earthquake damage subjects you to a $10,000 deductible. Don't assume that your policy provides the amounts of coverage you want or need. Ask your insurance agent to explain *all* of the ways the company may restrict or limit its payment for your covered losses.

Even when you buy replacement coverage for your building, your insurer may not pay for repair or construction costs mandated by stricter building codes. Without a code compliance endorsement, your policy will pay only to replace your current building as it existed before it suffered damage. If, to rebuild, current code requires additional fire sprinklers or an upgraded 200-amp electrical system, you'll pay these costs out of pocket. (A large oak tree recently fell onto one of my houses. Code compliance coverage added around $25,000 to my insurance recovery—an amount that otherwise would have come out of my pocket.)

Improve Coverage and Reduce Premiums. After choosing your basic coverages and endorsements, search through various policy deductibles and limits. Fine tune to identify the most cost-effective combinations. Avoid paying a lot for a little: save money; increase deductibles and eliminate trivial coverages that disproportionately push up your premiums. Also avoid risking a lot for a little. Purchase coverages that protect you against large-scale, budget-busting losses such as huge liability claims.

Avoid coverage for small, frequent losses and extend coverage and limits for those rare but catastrophic exposures. To further save money wisely, ask your insurance agent to suggest loss prevention and loss reduction measures that you can undertake. Some insurers reduce premiums for properties equipped with hurricane shutters, fire sprinkler systems, burglar bars, and dead-bolt locks. In earthquake-endangered areas, special foundation support systems merit a premium discount. What discounts for loss prevention (reduction) are available in your area?

Shop and Contrast. Do not rotely place your rental property insurance with your current homeowner's insurance agent. Discuss your needs with whomever you're already doing business. Then, secure competitive quotes from at least three or four other sources. You might also solicit bids through several insurance web sites that are operating, such as www .insurance.com.

Of course, don't jump for the company with the lowest premium. Through *Best's Guide* or other consumer rating reports, verify the company's financial strength and its willingness to pay claims. Because property and liability insurers are licensed by state governments, check the company's record of performance with your state department of insurance. (Insurance company financial data and performance records can be obtained at your local library or through your state department of insurance website.)

Insurance bores most people. But buying the right insurance at the right price not only affects your NOI, it just may save your net worth. Although property insurance premiums might cost thousands of dollars, failure to obtain needed coverage can cost you tens, or possibly hundreds, of thousands of dollars. Invest a few hours to review the costs and scope of your protection. For your efforts, you will receive piece of mind and smart cost savings.

Maintenance and Repair Costs

Smart investors reduce and eliminate money-wasting property maintenance and repair expenses in at least five ways:

1. *Low-maintenance properties.* Your life will prove easier when you own properties that are built to require low maintenance. The same advice applies to yards, shrubs, and landscaping. Some require frequent pruning, cutting, watering, and fertilizing. Others fend for themselves quite well.
2. *Low-maintenance tenants.* Just as with properties, you'll find low-maintenance and high-maintenance tenants. You will enjoy life more when you watch out for and avoid chronic complainers as well as people who show no house sense. In my experience, you can slice at least one-half of your maintenance, repair, cleaning, and wear-and-tear costs when you select only those tenants who consistently accept personal responsibility. Contrary to the pleadings of tenants, things seldom break by themselves—nor do toilets stop up and overflow as an act of God.
3. *Repair clauses.* To promote house sense and tenant responsibility, a growing number of property owners shift the first $50 or $100 of every repair cost onto their tenants' shoulders. High security deposits also encourage care.
4. *Handyman on call.* Ease the drain on your time and checkbook. Employ a trustworthy and competent all-around handyman (or persons) to take care of your property maintenance and repairs. Establish a relationship. My caretaker/handyman charges $25 an hour and can perform nearly any task (plumbing, carpentry, painting, minor electrical, HVAC, flooring; you name it, he can probably do it).

5. *Preventive maintenance.* You take your car in for regular servicing. Apply the same principle to your income properties. Anticipate and alleviate problems when the cost is relatively small. Ask property maintenance experts how you might replace high-maintenance materials and components with low-maintenance substitutes.

Property Taxes and Income Taxes

Taxes, especially property taxes, can severely eat into your net rental income. Although I know of no way to escape paying taxes, you can control and reduce them. We cover these tips and tactics in Chapter 14.

ADD VALUE: CLOSING WORDS

For at least the past 25 years, corporate managers have downsized, right-sized, outsourced, restructured, and slashed expenses, all the while searching for new markets, new customers, new products, and new ways to increase sales revenue. In some companies, such strategizing proved to be nothing more than cheap cosmetics to excite cheers from Wall Street and mislead investors. Yet, when executed in good faith, corporate refocus does illustrate how strategic thinking and the never-ending search to wisely cut expenses can boost net income and add value to businesses.

The same principle applies to investment property. Approach your investment properties with the attitude "I can design and develop more profitable (less costly, higher-yielding) ways to manage these properties." Your results will improve. Owners of shopping malls, office buildings, and apartment complexes strategically manage their properties through market research, property improvement, tenant selection, and cost reduction.

It's now time for owners and managers of smaller investment properties to think like an entrepreneur. For investors who adopt the entrepreneurial approach, increased cash flow and equity remain readily available.

12

DEVELOP THE BEST LEASE

In the not-so-distant past, many owners of rental houses and smaller apartment buildings relied on oral rental agreements. Today that practice has mostly disappeared. Lawyers and their legalisms have pervaded ever-greater areas of society—including the relations between property owners and tenants. To protect themselves (against litigious tenants and their lawyers), property owners now need to *draft* written rental agreements.

THE MYTHICAL STANDARD LEASE

By *draft*, I mean read and adapt any lease form that you use. Do not fall for the myth of a standard lease. Blank form leases vary widely in content and applicability. They omit clauses that you should include. They include clauses that you will want to omit or rewrite. Before you sign any lease, think through the following issues.

Your Market Strategy

As part of your value proposition to tenants (your market strategy), I advise you to become known as a friendly, caring property owner and avoid using multipage fine-print lease forms written in legal jargon. Yes, these lengthy leases seem to thoroughly lay out your contracted rights and remedies. But their long lists of authoritarian do's and don'ts intimidate tenants and tear down trust and cooperative spirit.

To justify such leases, lawyers claim, "Place everything in writing so that there's no room for dispute or faulty memory." Sounds good, but reality differs.

Legalisms Bite Both Ways. If you push your tenants to accept an oppressively legalistic approach, at some point, expect them to push back in kind. The more pages your lease entails and the more arcane its language, the more likely your tenants (or *their* lawyers) will find some word or clause to argue about. If lawyer and former president Bill Clinton could legally argue the meaning of *is,* you can bet that, when confronted, your tenants and their lawyers (or some tenant activist group or housing agency) will creatively interpret your incomprehensible lease clauses in ways to favor their own arguments.

The Myth of a Strong Lease. According to lawyers, a strong lease is one in which every clause binds the tenants into doing exactly what you want them to do. (If it were only that easy.) All too often, tenants do what they want to do—lease or no lease. Don't believe in the myth of a strong or air-tight lease. In most cases, it's not the strength of the lease that determines whether your tenants conduct themselves in a manner consistent with your wishes. Rather, it's the quality of the tenants themselves.

A strong lease never substitutes for tenant selection. When push comes to shove, a strong lease *may* help you mitigate the losses caused by troublesome tenants. But regardless of the language in your lease, only good tenants will make your days as a property owner profitable and painless. As with all contracts, the parties—not the written words—bear primary responsibility for making the relationship work.

Joint Responsibilities? Because most leases are drafted to advance the contractual advantage of property owners, they routinely slight tenant rights and owner responsibilities. As part of your market strategy to attract quality tenants, your lease might display a more balanced treatment.

Many tenants view landlords critically. When you adopt a just approach, you display your good faith. Such an approach also features you as a cut above other property owners. And, since you do intend to fulfill your responsibilities, listing these responsibilities helps to educate tenants. More than a few tenants believe that owners of rental properties do little more than collect rents and get rich. Disabuse them of this notion. List your responsibilities and the expenses you agree to pay within the lease (e.g., property insurance, property taxes, maintenance, appliances, replacement of capital items).

Joint Drafting? People feel more committed to agreements when they help shape them. Put this fact to your advantage. Discuss and draft your lease agreement with tenant participation. Naturally, you'll have a good idea of which clauses, conditions, and responsibilities you want to address (see "Crafting Your Rental Agreement" later in this chapter). But some give-and-take encourages the tenants to feel like customers rather than serfs.

Win-Win Negotiating. Joint drafting provides another benefit. Your proposed tenant may suggest issues and trade-offs whereby you both win.

When I first moved to Florida, I tried to rent a place to live for a period of three to six months. Prior to buying a home, I wanted to learn the market. But because I preferred a short-term tenancy and I owned a pet (a Yorkshire terrier), I faced slim pickings. As a result, I bought without as much search and research as I would have liked—and stayed in a Holiday Inn for 8 or 10 weeks.

Had I been able to secure a satisfactory rental house or apartment, some landlord would have gained a perfect tenant. I would have paid a premium rent and security deposit. Instead of this win-win approach, the property owners and rental managers I talked with stated their no-pets policy. None even hinted at trade-offs that could have benefited both of us.

Think before you write a lease. Even if you prefer not to draft a rental agreement jointly, keep the negotiating door open. Let the prospective tenants know that you can draft mutually advantageous changes. "Does this seem fair . . . ?" "Are you agreeable to . . . ?" "What if we . . . ?" "How does this sound . . . ?"

Notwithstanding what I have advised thus far, when talking with potential tenants, I look for hints of contentiousness and complaint. I rent only to people whom I believe will prove easy to get along with. I do not want tenants calling me or my maintenance man for every little thing that might go wrong—or to bear upon me for any whim that may pop into their mind.

If a potential tenant asks if rent is negotiable—meaning will I rent to them for less than I am asking—and they offer no proposition as to what they will do for me in exchange, I reject them with no further thought. Experience has taught me that such a request signals (1) they cannot afford the amount of rent that I have advertised, or (2) they will routinely ask for other concessions, favors, or services later.

Shun high-maintenance tenants just as much as you would shun high-maintenance buildings. When you choose to negotiate, negotiate win-win. But with many people, choose *not* to negotiate at all. Send them on their way (courteously, of course).

Search for Competitive Advantage

Most property owners view their lease strictly as a document that compels tenant performance. Although imperfect in that respect, written leases protect better than an oral agreement. But your leases should serve another important purpose: they should help you achieve competitive advantage over other owners of rental properties.

Your Lease Clauses. Before you decide on the specific clauses within your lease, review the leases of other property owners. Look for ways to differentiate your rental agreement that would encourage tenants (your target market) to choose your property over competing properties. To gain cooperative advantage, lower your up-front cash requirements, offer a repair guarantee, shorten (or lengthen) your lease term, guarantee a lease renewal without an increase in rent, or place tenant security deposits and last month's rent in the investment of the tenant's choice to earn interest for the tenant's benefit.

Alternatively, develop tight or restrictive lease clauses that position your property as rentals that cater to discriminating and responsible tenants. Severely restrict noise and other nuisances. Promote your property as "the quiet place to live."

You create cooperative advantage when you adapt the features of your property to the wants of your tenant market; but also tailor the clauses, language, and length of your lease to match tenant preferences.

Explain Your Advantages. When you adapt leases to match the needs of your target market, you increase your rental revenues, achieve a higher rate of occupancy, lower your operating expenses, or some combination thereof. To realize these benefits, inform prospective tenants of the advantages you offer. Adopt the tactics of a successful salesman. Rather than show your property, point out (from the tenants' standpoint) the desirable features of both the unit and your lease.

CRAFT YOUR RENTAL AGREEMENT

To craft a lease to fit your market strategy, you can draw from dozens of terms, issues, and contingencies. Although the following discussion presents typical practices, stay alert for ways to adapt (or omit) items to attract more profitable tenants. Ignore any of my advisories if you see a better way to structure the risk-reward balance of any specific clause. Indeed, I vary my own leases to match the tenants or the situation.

Properly drafted, your lease attracts premium tenants. Legalese and an authoritarian demeanor drive good tenants into the rentals offered by your more market-savvy, tenant-responsive competitors. Also, of course, think renewal. Tenant turnover increases operating costs and generates revenue losses. Satisfied tenants remain in their units longer and and make fewer demands.

Names and Signatures

Name (and obtain identification from) all residents who are permitted to live in the unit—including children, if any. All adult residents should sign the lease. Do not permit tenants to bring in additional tenants or to substitute new cotenants for those moving out. Require new tenants to pass your application and qualification process. (In some instances, the law might hold you liable for the negligent or illegal acts of your tenants.)

Joint and Several Liability

When you rent to cotenants (even if they are husband and wife—divorces do happen), include a "joint and several liability" clause. This clause makes all tenants individually responsible for all rents and tenant damages.

Without joint and several liability, individual cotenants might claim that they're liable only for their part of the rent. Or alternatively, "I didn't burn that hole in the carpet. Jones did. Collect from him." In such cases, Jones may have already moved out and disappeared. Joint and several liability at least provides you the contractual right to force payment from any other tenants who are financially able.

Guests

When they take in additional roommates, some tenants fail to notify and gain your written approval. When you show up at the property and ask who these new people are, you'll be told, "They're *guests*." "Joe's just staying for a couple of weeks until he's called back to work at Ford." Two months later, Joe's still there, and now his girlfriend, Jill, has also taken up "guest" status.

Whether you might have to contend with these kinds of tenants depends on the type of people your property attracts as well as your qualifying standards. As a precaution, place a "guest clause" in your lease that limits occupancy for the unit and the time period that guests can stay.

Length of Tenancy

Many rental owners reflexively set their tenancies at one year. In some markets, the preponderance of properties requiring one-year leases creates a shortage (relative to demand) of properties available for shorter terms. Because short-term (especially seasonal) tenancies command higher rents, you might boost your rental revenues by appealing to such a potentially underserved market.

As another possibility, to reduce turnover and vacancy expenses, give tenants a slight discount on their rents. In exchange, the tenants would sign up for a lease term of, say, two or three years. Either way, leases for terms shorter or longer than one year might yield higher net income.

Holdover Tenants (Mutual Agreement)

A holdover tenant remains in his rental unit after the rental period expires. In some cases, leases for holdover tenants automatically renew for the same period as the original lease. In other instances, the lease converts to a month-to-month tenancy.

Unless your properties are located in an area with strong peak and valley rental seasons—as are college towns and vacation areas—consider leases that convert to month-to-month tenancies. In my experience, month-to-month holdover tenants often end up staying for years.

Even if they stay for only two to six additional months, you still gain because you've postponed unit turnover. If, however, you require your tenants to commit for another year—or move out—you may force a move that the tenants otherwise would have postponed. Of course, you might raise the issue of renewal for a year and if they accept, great. If they hesitate (and you would like to retain them), suggest the idea of a shorter term. Then negotiate a trade-off that's win-win.

Holdover Tenants (without Permission)

Sometimes tenants notify you (or you notify them) that their tenancy is ending. If they move on schedule, all is well. On occasion, tenants decide to stay contrary to your permission or desire. To reduce this possibility, and compensate for any problems this delay causes, consider placing a penalty in your lease for unauthorized holdovers of, say, $50 or $100 per day.

Property Description

Misunderstandings sometimes arise over the exact physical property your tenants are leasing. To avoid this issue, describe precisely the space they are entitled to. Do they obtain the right to use the garage, attic, basement, or outdoor storage shed? Or do you plan to reserve areas for your own use or for others? Could you rent any of these areas to other people or businesses?

Your lease (usually through a signed addendum) should list existing damages or imperfections that the property currently suffers. Your prospective tenants should accompany you (or your rental agent) while making this inspection. Without this written and signed inventory of prior damages, your tenants may deny responsibility for damages they have caused, "Those holes in the wall were already there when we moved in. We're not paying. We didn't do it." I also use a dated photographic record and provide the tenants digital copies of the photos thus taken. The tenants are also invited to take their own photos—if they so choose.

Sometimes, too, I shift the responsibility to the tenants for finding imperfections. The lease might include a clause that requests the tenant to notify the owner in writing of any repair, maintenance, or cleaning issues that exist at the time of move-in. If no notice of deficiency is submitted within, say, 48 to 72 hours, then the tenant cannot later disclaim responsibility for deficiencies that exist at the time of move-out. (Timely notice or not, though, fairness in settlement should control.)

Inventory and Describe Personal Property

If you provide personal property for your tenants (washer, dryer, refrigerator, stove, microwave, blinds, drapes, curtains, furniture), inventory and describe (with photographs or serial numbers where possible) each separate item and include the list as a lease addendum. Unbelievable as it may sound, I know of vacating tenants who have taken their landlord's almost-new appliances and left in their place appliances that would soon find their way to a landfill.

Without a signed inventory and description of personal property (or photos), the tenants may get away with such theft. If the lease merely says, "owner provides washer and dryer," you may find it difficult to prove the exact washer and dryer that you originally placed in the rental unit. (Purchase receipts provide evidence that you bought the items. They do not prove what you did with them.)

Rental Amounts

Some owners set low rent levels to reduce their turnover, vacancy losses, and tenant complaints. (Complaints fall in number because tenants realize they are receiving a good deal and prefer not to give reason to raise their rent.) Also, slightly below-market rents permit you to select tenants from a larger pool of qualified applicants. Naturally, you need not merely use below-market rents to attract quality tenants. You can offer desirable features that are otherwise scarce. Features can lure in quality tenants even though your rents sit near the top of the market.

Late Fees and Discounts

Ideally, your well-selected tenants will pay their full rent on or before its due date. To further encourage timely payment, some owners offer their tenants an early payment discount. Others penalize tenants with late fees if the tenant's check is received, say, three to five days past its due date. Many owners say that the carrot approach creates better tenant relations, works more effectively, and is easier to enforce.

Regardless of which method (or combination) you choose, do not permit tenants to take the discount, or avoid the late fee, unless they satisfy the respective due date requirements. And never, never, *never* allow tenants to get behind in their rent. Evict as soon as your lease and local ordinances allow it. It is a fact of human nature that tenants who can't pay today won't pay tomorrow. The more money that accumulates unpaid, the greater their incentive to take a midnight exit. (Experience has taught me this lesson.)

For peace of mind and financial prosperity, rent only to people who pay their rent on time, every time. Reject excuses. Terminate swiftly in instances when your selection process erred.

Multiple Late Payments

What about the tenant who regularly pays on the eighth or ninth of every month—even though the rent falls due on the first? As long as the late fee is included, some owners tolerate this behavior. I would not. I want rents paid on time, every time.

Therefore, to enforce the "on time, every time" requirement, either I work out a new payment date with the tenants that better matches their cash flow needs, or I enforce the "multiple late payment" clause. This clause sets forth a "three strikes and you're out" rule. I realize that anyone can suffer a lapse of memory or cash shortfall once or twice, but chronic lateness warrants termination of the lease, forfeiture of deposit, and any other damages the tenant's breach of contract entails (and the law enforces).

To avoid lates, some rentals now set up their tenants with electronic fund transfers or automatic credit card billings. Although this process does not necessarily foil the financially irresponsible who goes over limit or draws down his account balance, it does accommodate the forgetful and lazy. EFT or credit card payments places you in a priority position to collect on time.

Bounced Check Fees and Termination

Do not tolerate bounced checks. Once or twice, maybe. Three times warrants termination. In my experience, tenants who won't pay their rent on time with good checks don't just create problems in this one area. As often as not, you can expect them to give you other kinds of trouble. In fact, tolerate this behavior and you ask for headaches. Don't do it. Get rid of these tenants quickly.

Tenant "Improvements"

"If we buy the paint, is it okay for us to paint the living room?" As an owner of rental properties, you will receive requests like this from tenants. Or you may end up with tenants who don't ask. They redecorate first and wait for you to ask questions later—like, "How could you paint the living room deep purple?" or "What happened to the oak tree that was in the back yard?" (True story: Tenants of a friend of mine cut down a lovely large oak tree because they didn't like it.)

To prohibit tenants from diminishing the value of your property with their so-called improvements, include a lease clause that requires them to obtain your written permission before they paint, wallpaper, redecorate, renovate, repanel, remove, or in any other way modify your property. If left to their own accord, some tenants will treat your property as if it were their own. (This may sound all right until you see how little they care for their own property.)

Owner Access

Under many laws of tenancy, you cannot enter your tenants' premises without their permission—unless their lease grants you that right. If you do want access to conduct periodic inspections, make repairs, take care of emergencies (for example, an overflowing toilet), show the unit to future prospective tenants (or buyers), or for any other reason, include an "owner access" clause.

This clause will not typically give you unlimited access at any time, night or day. Few tenants would like such an intrusive demand. But an access clause can give you an automatic right of entry within certain specified hours, say, 8:00 A.M. to 8:00 P.M. daily with 24-hour notice (emergencies excepted). Without an owner access clause, a difficult tenant may give you the runaround for days or even weeks. Or, worse, they may answer your requests for entry with a "No!"

Quiet Enjoyment

Do you want to guarantee your tenants that they will not suffer from noise and disturbances created by other tenants? Then heavily restrict their neighbor-disturbing partying, fighting, arguing, loud lovemaking, and playing of television, radio, stereo, computer, or other electronic devices. Or simply place a general clause within your lease such as:

> Residents agree not to create, generate, broadcast, or otherwise cause sounds or disturbances to emanate from themselves, their vehicles, their guests, or their residences into the residences of others. All residents agree to respect and promote the quiet enjoyment of the premises by all other residents.

Avoid buildings with those notorious paper-thin walls. While performing your prepurchase inspection, turn on a portable radio and carry it from room to room and unit to unit. Do sound volumes at reasonable levels penetrate into other rooms or other units? If so, that property presents a large source of aggravation to you and your future tenants. Unless you can economically silence the problem, don't buy the property.

Noxious Odors

As with noise and disturbances, noxious odors wafting throughout a building can stir up tenant complaints. Noxious odors include smoking, cooking (especially some types of ethnic foods), and heavy use of perfumes. If any of these (or other types of noxious odors) could present a problem, draft a lease clause that excludes the causes of these odors.

Disturbing External Influences

In some instances, your tenants may be disturbed by noises or odors whose source lies outside your property. If you know of such problems (trains, heavy traffic, school band practice, factory emissions), place a rider in your lease whereby tenants acknowledge and accept notice. If you know but do not disclose, your tenants may be able to lawfully terminate their lease and sue you for the damages they incur because of their necessary relocation— sometimes called constructive eviction.

Even if you've had no prior knowledge of neighborhood noise or odors, such disturbances may give rise to a tenant claim of constructive eviction. If successful in pursuit of this claim, your tenants might also terminate their lease and collect relocation expenses from you. Therefore, with or without knowledge of adverse external influences, you may want to include a lease clause that limits both your responsibility for damages and the tenants' right to terminate their lease.

Tenant Insurance

Because a property owner's insurance does not cover the personal property of tenants, some landlords require their tenants to buy a tenants' insurance policy. These owners have learned through experience that when uninsured tenants suffer damage to their property through fire or theft (or other peril), they may accuse the owner of negligence. Even if the building burns after being hit by lightning, these tenants (or their lawyers) will claim that you should have installed a better lightning rod.

Sublet and Assignment

When tenants leave their residence for an extended period (summer in Europe), they may want to *sublet* their unit. When tenants plan to relocate permanently (job change, bought a house), they may want to *assign* their lease to someone else. To deal with these contingencies, your lease might adopt one of four positions:

1. No right to sublet or assign.
2. Right to sublet or assign with owner's written permission. Original tenants and new tenants both assume liability for rent payments and damages.
3. Right to sublet or assign with owner's written permission. Original tenants are released from any liability for future rent payments or damages. Owner must look exclusively to new tenants for financial performance.
4. Unlimited right to sublet or assign. Original tenants remain liable.

Absent a specific lease clause, many courts rule that option 4 is the controlling default option. Because owners dislike this default option, they typically write in a sublet or assignment clause based on choice 2 or 3.

Naturally, most owners prefer number 2. When the original tenants remain liable for rents and damages, they choose their sublessees and assignees with care. As a negotiating tactic, use lease language that reflects the position of number 1 or 2. But in response to tenant objection, ease up and adopt number 3. Or, as is perhaps most common, stick with the approach of number 2 for sublessees and permit number 3 for assignees.

Pets

Many property owners prohibit pets. In my experience, responsible tenants maintain pets in a responsible manner. Irresponsible people treat pets in an irresponsible manner. If you filter out irresponsible people, you can eliminate pet problems without excluding all pets.

When you accept responsible people who keep well-behaved pets, you can boost profits. Because of widespread no-pet restrictions, owners who do permit pets can often charge a pet premium in both the amount of monthly rents and the amount of the security deposit.

If you do accept pets, draft a pet rules addendum and attach it to your lease. When drafting your pet rules, please consider the needs of the pet. I have seen pet rules that require dogs to be kept tethered in a backyard on a six- or eight-foot chain, or perhaps kept only within the confines of a basement or on a back porch.

If you feel so little for the lives of animals, exclude them from your rental properties. Any pet owner who accepts such cruel restrictions does not qualify (in my view) as a responsible person or a responsible pet owner.

Security Deposits

Security deposits present at least five issues that you may want to address in your lease:

1. Amount of the deposit.
2. When payable.
3. Rate of interest, if any.
4. Under what conditions tenants will forfeit all or part of their deposit.
5. When you will refund the deposit if tenants satisfy all terms of the lease.

To eliminate dispute, your lease (or lease addendum) should answer each of these issues. (Remember, too, that as you learn the practices of other rental property owners, craft a security deposit policy that gives your property a cooperative advantage.)

Amount and When Payable. As to amount, I typically favor high security deposits plus first and last month's rent—*always* payable in advance. (This lesson I learned the hard way.) You will undoubtedly get prospects who want to pay their deposit piecemeal over one to three months. When you agree to this request, you invite trouble. (Ditto for postdated checks.)

By urging you to require your money up front, I mean that whatever amount you set, collect it before your tenants move into the unit. I favor a large amount because I'm leasing desirable properties to people with financial capacity. However, you may find that your tenant segment doesn't (or can't) meet this requirement.

Interest. Some local and state laws require owners to pay interest to their tenants. If this law applies in your area, tell your tenants. In fact, I recommend paying interest to tenants even if the law doesn't require it. Some tenants feel upset if you insist on a deposit (especially a large one) but refuse to pass along its earnings to its "rightful owner." (When short-term interest rates are low, this issue does not stir up much conflict.)

Forfeiture. To minimize controversy, some owners develop a schedule of costs that they levy against tenants who fail to satisfy their lease obligations. This schedule might list broken windows at $75, wall holes at $100, dirty appliances at $75, and general cleaning at $250. Other owners levy actual costs after the remedial work has been performed. And some severe owners try to keep the full security deposit as liquidated damages—even when the actual damages fall substantially below the amount of the security deposit.

No matter which approach you favor, (1) inform your tenants of your deposit forfeiture policy *before* they take possession of your property, and (2) as soon as they vacate the property, perform a thorough property walk-through inspection with the tenants. In this final walk-through, compare the property item by item with the inspection sheet (photos) you prepared at the time they moved in.

Perform a final inspection with the tenants present. Never let several days pass between the date tenants move out and the date you inspect. If you ignore this advice, expect tenant dispute. When tenants sign their lease, let them know that their security deposit does not limit their liability for rent or damages. If their actual damages exceed their deposit, they pay you for the higher amount.

Deposit Return. As a courtesy to your tenants, return their deposits with interest as soon as you know the correct amount. The best time is at the end of the final walk-through. You pay. The tenants accept. You shake hands with them and wish them well in their new home.

Some owners needlessly delay returning deposits. That practice sours tenant relations and may subject you to legal penalties. In some jurisdictions, if you miss the law-imposed deadline to return a deposit of, say, $1,000, the tenants can go to court and force you to pay them $3,000. Many cities legislate security deposit procedures. Read and follow these laws. As the treble damage penalty shows, violations can cost you plenty.

Yard Care

When you rent out a house or duplex, you will probably require the tenants to care for the yard. But don't just say, "Tenants are responsible for yard care." I made this mistake with otherwise excellent tenants. To these tenants, "yard care" meant cutting the grass. To me it meant watering the lawn when needed, tending the flowers and shrubs, and trimming the hedges to maintain them at their existing height of four feet.

Because the house was located in Florida and I was living in the San Francisco Bay Area, my visits to the property were not frequent. When after two years I did return, the hedges had grown wildly, many flowers and shrubs were dead, and the lawn suffered scattered brown spots.

If your tenants care for the yard, tell them exactly what care they must provide.

Parking, Number, and Type of Vehicles

Some tenants believe that if they can't find parking in a driveway or street, it's okay to park in the front yard. Or they may routinely block other people's driveways. Or they leave unsightly junk (inoperable) cars to accumulate around the property. RVs, boats, and trailers also can create aesthetic and parking problems.

To head off such trouble, place a parking clause in your leases. Specify exactly the number and types of permitted vehicles. Then designate the *only* places where tenants are permitted to park. You may also want to deter the backyard (or front yard) mechanic who disassembles his car and leaves parts scattered around for days, weeks, or months.

Repairs

Increasingly, owners of rental properties shift costs of repair onto their tenants. Stopped-up toilets, slow drains, and broken garbage disposals seldom occur without tenant abuse. As a minimum, owners may charge their tenants, say, a $50 repair fee for each time a repair becomes necessary. In other instances, owners declare tenants fully responsible for certain types of repairs—unless the service provider establishes that the tenants were not to blame.

Appliances. Some owners tell their tenants that they may use the appliances currently in the property, but the owner will not pay for repairs or replacement. If the tenants don't agree to accept the appliances on those terms, the owner then removes them, and the tenants provide and maintain their own appliances.

Which Approach Is Best? As stands true for every lease clause, no single approach to repairs works best in all situations. It depends on the types of tenants and properties that you're dealing with. Some people will mistreat your property. At the same time, they expect you to jump into action whenever their abuse or neglect creates a problem. These are the people at whom you want to aim your tenant repair clauses. (Ideally, avoid these kinds of tenants.)

Roaches, Fleas, Ants

On occasion, roaches, fleas, ants, and other similar pests will invade a house on their own without apparent reason. More often, tenants invite them in through careless handling of food, unwashed dishes, trash, garbage, or pets. Especially in single-family houses, you may want your lease to shift the cost of extermination to the tenants.

In apartment buildings, the source of such pests may prove more difficult to determine. All it takes is one unsanitary tenant, and their roaches or ants can quickly spread to everyone else's units. As a precaution, spray periodically to reduce this potential problem.

Neat and Clean

Regardless of whether you rent out apartments or houses, your lease should recite standards of cleanliness. Proper disposal of trash and garbage are bare minimums. Other do's and don'ts may address unwashed dishes, disposal of used motor oil and broken furniture and appliances, materials awaiting pickup for recycling, bicycle storage, and vehicles that drip motor oil or transmission fluid.

Rules and Regulations

Especially for apartment buildings—or for rental units in co-ops or condominium projects—prepare a list of rules and regulations that you direct tenants to follow. Incorporate these rules into your rental agreement (usually by addendum). Note within your lease that you (or the homeowners' association) reserve the right to reasonably amend or modify the listed rules.

Wear and Tear

Leases often state that tenants retain responsibility for all damages *except* normal wear and tear. I omit this clause. It invites tenant neglect and abuse. Many tenants believe that soiled and stained carpets, cracked plaster, broken windows, and other various damages reflect nothing more than normal wear and tear.

I disagree. If a tenant cares for a property, that property will not suffer noticeable wear and tear during a tenancy of one year or less. For such short-term periods of residence, tenants should leave the property in the same condition in which they accepted it—and my leases state this rule explicitly. Eliminate the "wear and tear" clause. It will save you money and argument.

Lawful Use of Premises

As good business, and as a good-neighbor policy, require tenants to abide by all applicable laws, ordinances, and regulations. Enforce a zero-tolerance rule against illegal drugs. Ordinances may apply to property use, parking, noise, pet control, occupancy limits, yard care, and a multitude of other issues.

In some instances, the law not only punishes tenants but also property owners who tolerate those tenants who violate government rules. In addition, this clause will give you authority to stop behavior that causes offense—even though the police or other government authorities choose to let it slide from their enforcement.

Notice

To reduce rent loss during periods of turnover, require tenants to give advance notice of the date they plan to vacate the property. You can then begin to publicize the unit's upcoming availability. Ideally, you'll find a new tenant who will move in within a day or two after the previous tenants have moved out.

Most owners require 30 days' *written* notice. If you're operating in a weak or seasonal rental market, you might ask for 45 or 60 days' notice. If you expect strong and immediate demand for your rental property, you could reduce your advance notice to, say, 15 days. Tie your written notice requirement to the length of time it will take to locate a new, highly desirable tenant (or to avoid missing a peak rent-up period as exists in college and resort towns).

Failure to Deliver

Sometimes tenants will tell you that they're vacating on the 28th. Yet as of the 31st, they're still packing boxes. This holdover could create turmoil if you've already signed a lease with new tenants and promised them possession on the 30th. Although your holdover penalty clause should help avoid this dilemma, it sometimes occurs.

What do you do? Given this possibility, some property owners include a "failure to deliver" lease clause. This clause typically accomplishes two objectives: (1) it voids the liability of the property owner to the new tenants for any expenses they might suffer (motel room, furniture storage, double moving costs) as a result of the owner's failure to deliver, and (2) it does not permit the new tenants to immediately cancel their lease. Rather, it pushes back their move-in date (and accrued rentals) until the previous tenants do vacate and the owner completes her "make ready" efforts.

If your current tenants continue to remain in the property, you can't hang up your new tenants indefinitely. In that case, your lease might release the new tenants after your failure to deliver extends beyond, say, 10 days. Fortunately, you won't often experience the holdover problem. But anticipate the possibility and draft a lease clause to deal with it.

Utilities, Property Taxes, Association Fees

Tenants often pay their own utilities and waste disposal charges. Owners pay all property taxes and homeowners' association fees. However, this custom is not written in stone. Sometimes in longer-term residential leases, tenants pay all of these expenses. And frequently in short-term rentals, owners pay all expenses. Some multiunit properties don't meter individual tenants. This situation can shift utility costs to owners.

Regardless of which practice you adopt, spell out who pays what with respect to these or other similar types of expenses (e.g., heating oil, pest spraying, window washing). Clarity helps two types of tenants: (1) people who are new to renting and may not fully understand their responsibilities, and (2) people who relocate and form their beliefs from their experience elsewhere.

Liquid-Filled Furniture

Although waterbeds and other types of liquid-filled furniture aren't as common as they once were, they still remain popular within a niche market. The water damage created when one of these beds bursts is typically excluded from coverage under most rental-property insurance policies.

You can forbid this risk. Or, alternatively, require your tenants' liquid furniture to meet industry safety standards *and* require your tenants to pay a "waterbed premium" for the insurance endorsement you buy to obtain coverage.

Abandonment of Property

Sometimes tenants move out and leave some of their personal property. They promise, "We'll come back next Tuesday and pick up those boxes in the garage." Next Tuesday comes and goes, and the boxes remain.

What can you do? That depends on your lease. If it's silent on the issue, the law may require you to safeguard the items for some specified period. Then you will have to dispose of the items according to the applicable legal procedure. With a lease clause, you can contractually agree with the tenants that any items not removed by the end of the lease will go straight to the dump or to the Salvation Army. (Note: I emphasize again, verify applicable laws. In many instances a law that regulates a specific issue can trump a lease clause that runs to the contrary (for example, security deposits, fair housing, rent increases, eviction, late fees, abandoned property, and so forth).

Nonwaivers

For reasons of courtesy or practicality, you may, on occasion, permit tenants to temporarily breach a lease clause or house rule. To prevent tenants from stretching this courtesy beyond your intent, include a nonwaiver clause. In this clause, you make clear that your obliging actions today in no way waive your right to enforce the letter of the lease tomorrow.

Likewise, this clause can deal with rent collections in a similar way. Say you accept a rent check even though you know your tenant is sharing his apartment with an unauthorized cotenant. The nonwaiver clause dissuades your tenant from later claiming, "Well, you took our rent check. You can't tell me now that Joe has to move out." Yes, you can. Your nonwaiver clause voids that tenant defense.

Breach of Lease (or House Rules)

In a breach-of-lease clause, you reinforce your right to terminate the lease of tenants who breach *any* lease requirement or house rule. Absent this clause, tenants sometimes believe that if you accept the rent, you waive your enforcement of other tenant violations. Together, the nonwaiver and breach-of-agreement clauses impress on tenants their obligation to comply 100 percent—or suffer the consequences of eviction, loss of their security deposit, and your claim for damages.

No Representations (Full Agreement)

Occasionally, tenants try to extricate themselves from their lease obligations by claiming that you misled them with false promises. They could claim that when you induced them to sign their lease you promised to completely paint and recarpet their unit. You know that the tenants are lying, but a judge may not. To the judge, it's your word against the claims of the tenants.

To prevent such a charade, include a lease clause that states the lease and its addenda set the full extent of the rental agreement. Furthermore, this clause should state that the tenants did not rely on any oral or written representations or promises not explicitly included within the lease (for example, "Tenant acknowledges that owner has made no promises or representations other than those included within this agreement. All issues material to this agreement are included herein").

Arbitration

In many cities, the legal process is too slow, expensive, and complex to effect timely and affordable justice. As a result, some property owners include an arbitration clause in their leases. This clause steers unresolved owner-tenant disputes away from the courthouse and into a more informal arbitration hearing. (Alternatively, many cities have set up housing courts or panels who decide landlord-tenant disputes in a more timely and less costly procedure than the regular court system.)

An arbitration hearing typically differs from trial litigation in that it (1) requires less time; (2) costs less; (3) avoids formal rules of legal procedure; (4) reduces or eliminates pretrial discovery such as depositions, interrogatories, and requests for production of documents; and (5) severely limits the right to appeal.

All of these features may sound like a pretty good trade-off against litigation. But "the proof of the pudding is in the taste." Before you adopt this clause for your leases, investigate how well arbitration works in your area. Learn whether your local courts show any noticeable bias for or against property owners. Arbitration tends to work best for landlords faced with courts that generally side with tenants. (Unfortunately, some pro-tenant judges—at the urging of lawyers who fear a loss of business—refuse to enforce contract arbitration clauses.)

Attorney Fees (Who Pays?)

Many standard form leases include an "attorney's fees" clause that strongly favors property owners. In cases in which you prevail in court, this clause requires losing tenants to pay your "reasonable" attorney fees and court costs. When your tenants prevail, the clause (through its silence) leaves attorney fees and costs on the shoulders of each party who incurred them.

Will the Court Enforce It? Courts that honor the principle "judges shall not rewrite lawful contracts" will generally enforce this one-sided attorney fees clause. Such courts reason that a tenant who wanted to modify or eliminate this clause was free to negotiate the point before signing the lease.

On the other hand, so-called activist judges may use this clause to hold you liable for a winning tenant's attorney fees and costs. These judges declare "what's good for the goose is good for the gander." They often see their cases as "'powerful greedy landlords' versus "powerless victimized tenants." They like to upset this supposed imbalance of power by placing their thumb on the scales of justice in favor of tenants.

Include or Not? Whether you should include such a clause remains an open question. Do courts in your area enforce it as written? Also, consider how your prospective tenants might view this clause. Will it cause them to mark you down as just another landlord rather than see you as "a fair provider of housing services"?

What about the solvency of your tenants? Even if you prevail in court, is it likely you could collect a judgment? Does your area permit wage garnishments? Beware of activist tenants. These types of tenants love going to court and often get their legal fees advanced by some government agency or nonprofit tenants' rights group. Should you eventually fail to win your claim (or defense), these activists know how to work the system to stick you with thousands (or even tens of thousands) in legal bills.

Explore Your Options. Don't insert (or omit) any type of attorney fees clause until you explore its practical and legal implications. Learn from the experiences of other property owners. Investigate the legal procedure that's typically used for settling owner-tenant disputes in your area. Also, some courts follow a "loser pays" rule regardless of what your lease says—even when it's silent on the issue of attorney fees. Florida statute specifies that costs and fees are awarded to the "prevailing party"—but case law does not seem to clarify if a lease clause of "win or lose, each party bears his own costs" can override the statute.

Offer of Settlement Rule. In other areas, courts may follow some type of offer-of-settlement rule. In these cases, a party who turns down a pretrial settlement offer may end up having to pay the other party's fees and costs—regardless of who wins. Say your tenants offer to settle your $8,000 claim for $5,000. You reject the offer and go to trial. The court awards you $6,000.

Guess what? In some areas, you would pay the tenants' legal costs and fees because your court victory didn't award you at least 25 percent more than the amount the tenants offered to settle. (So much for justice!) Of course, this rule does cut both ways. In some cases, it can benefit you. Just realize that in many jurisdictions, the question of who pays costs and fees is far more complex than a simple clause in a lease may seem to indicate.

Written Notice to Remedy

A written notice to remedy requires an owner (or tenant) to notify the other party before taking legal action to legally enforce a lease provision that the tenant (or owner) is currently breaching. From your perspective, written notice helps in two ways: (1) when you wish to evict a tenant for cause, previous written notices give you a paper trail to strengthen your case, and (2) if in defense of an eviction (or suit for rent) a tenant falsely claims, "We didn't have any heat for most of January," you can force the tenants to prove that they sent you written notice of this problem. Because their claim is false, no such evidence exists. Their defense fails.

TENANTS' RIGHTS LAWS

Historically, many laws governing landlord-tenant relationships originated in feudal England (a time of serfs and royal-grant landlords). Consumerism and expansive tenant rights lacked legal standing. In modern times, reformist lawmakers, courts, and government agencies have frequently stepped in to update this legal relationship. Tenant-friendly statutes, ordinances, court decisions, and regulations can supersede written clauses in your lease. Such contemporary laws broaden tenant rights and landlord responsibilities in the following areas: (1) tenant selection, (2) property operations, and (3) evictions.

Tenant Selection

Market strategy tells you to target your rental units to defined market segments. However, laws in many countries do not permit owners (or managers) to exclude rental applicants because of their race, religion, sex, ethnicity, national origin, disability, or family status (households with children). In addition, *some* laws have lengthened this list to include categories such as homosexuals, welfare recipients, and lawyers. (Yes, some property owners do not rent to lawyers because, as a class, lawyers rank among the most troublesome tenants.) Note, too, that federal civil rights law and nearly all state and local fair-housing ordinances exempt owner-occupied properties of one to four units. If they choose, exempt property owners may discriminate without legal penalty.[1]

Conduct and Creditworthiness. Laws against excluding people because of their race, religion, or occupation do not mean that you must accept individuals who do not meet your legitimate standards of conduct and creditworthiness. You may turn down any person—regardless of protected status—whose credit, employment, income, or rental record falls below your minimums. Nor must you accept any individual who satisfies minimum standards but nevertheless ranks below the superior qualifications of other applicants.

Unlike employers who are sometimes coerced into quota hiring, small landlords are not subject to such laws or regulations. You are free to select those tenants (among all applicants) who *best* match or exceed your standards. (If you own a rental complex of 200 three-bedroom apartments that includes only two units with children—now that's a different story. Prima facie, you are discriminating against households with children.)

Inconsistency Can Cost You. You are not free to arbitrarily change your standards or to arbitrarily apply them. Discrimination laws restrict a property owner's flexibility. Assume you meet with a nice young couple from your church whose credit score has plunged about as low as it can go. You believe they're good people and make an exception to your credit standards.

Subsequently, a nice young couple of a different religion applies to rent a unit in the same building. You turn them down because of their prior credit problems. You've just opened yourself up to a lawsuit. Under the law, you must apply your standards consistently. Exceptions and flexibility can land you in trouble.

Beware of Testers. To trap property owners who set and apply their tenant selection standards in an arbitrary or illegally discriminatory manner, various government agencies and activist nonprofits employ testers. These tenant testers might differ from one another by race, religion, or family status, but their income, credit, and other lawful tenant selection criteria remain similar.

When applying to rent from you, various testers record your words and actions. If you treat any tester differently from the others ("I don't think this would be a good building for your children; mostly singles live here"), you invite a charge of discrimination. To avoid trouble with testers

---

[1]Some lawyers argue that an 1866 civil rights law voids some of these exceptions. So, beware and be wary of unlawful discrimination. On this issue, adhere to the law precisely. Legal costs and monetary damages for unlawful discrimination can ruin your net worth.

and their vigilant search for racist, sexist, and homophobic landlords, apply your tenant-selection standards consistently. Do not encourage or discourage rental applicants because of any protected status.

"I think you'd be happy here, we have many Jewish tenants," and "I don't think you'd be happy here, we have very few Jewish tenants," are equally discriminatory under the law. For your own peace of mind and financial well-being, never say or do anything that takes notice of a person's difference if that difference is covered under some type of discrimination law or regulation. (Of course, this advice applies equally to all leasing agents or property managers whom you employ. As a principal, you can face legal responsibility for the discriminatory acts of your agents and employees.)

Property Operations

Various laws govern the operation of your properties. You must abide by zoning, environmental, occupancy, health, and safety codes. Local laws may apply to rent control, lease renewal, snow removal, trash receptacles, waste disposal, tenant parking, smoke alarms, heat, security locks, and burglar bars. Some cities enforce "repair and deduct" statutes. These laws give tenants the right to pay for necessary property repairs and then deduct these costs from their rent check.

Laws governing property owners typically operate as a normal part of doing business. Occasionally, however, compliance can cost big money (lead paint or asbestos abatement, underground oil tank cleanup, earthquake retrofit). Before buying a property, investigate whether such laws might increase the amount of money that you must spend on your property to satisfy compliance issues.

Evictions

Governments set the legal steps property owners must follow to terminate a lease and evict a tenant. This procedure typically applies to (1) lawful reasons, (2) written notice, (3) time to cure breach, (4) time elapsing before a hearing, (5) allowable tenant defenses, and (6) time to vacate after an adverse ruling.

Learn this legal procedure for your area. Then follow it. Failure to dot your *i*'s and cross your *t*'s can get your case thrown out. You must then go back and start again. Never resort to self-help. Never threaten or assault a tenant; change door locks; turn off the tenant's water, heat, or electricity; or confiscate tenant property. Follow lawful procedure. Self-help exposes you to personal injury lawsuits and possibly criminal charges. (Watch the movie *Pacific Heights* (available on DVD or Netflix).

LANDLORDING: PROS AND CONS

From the preceding collection of possible lease clauses and tenant rights laws, you might say, "Forget it! Landlording involves hazards, headaches, and heartburn."

But read about the laws, regulations, accidents, breakdowns, repairs, lawsuits, hassles, and expenses that go along with driving a car. If you focus only on the negatives, you might park your car in a garage and leave it there.

Possibilities, Not Probabilities

By discussing various rental issues, I do not mean to scare you away from landlording; I want to present possibilities for your concern. It is the naïve and unknowing property owners who most often experience landlording difficulties.

In more than 30 years of dealing with rentals, I have rarely initiated an eviction. Nor have I ever used a lease that included all of the previously mentioned clauses. Nor have I been sued by a tenant, experienced a charge of discrimination, or run into any break-the-budget environmental or building safety and health code problems.

The chances are that you won't, either—if you develop leases, systems for tenant selection, and property operations that anticipate, alleviate, and mitigate potential problems. Think of the concerns discussed as possibilities to prepare for and guard against, not as certainties sure to make landlording a constant source of anxiety and expense.

Professional Property Managers

If you choose, you can employ a property manager or caretaker to deal with routine tenant relations and property maintenance. For relatively low cost, you can delegate everyday concerns. As long as you design and retain approval of leasing standards and property operations, delegating tasks to others will save you time, money, and effort. I advise you, however, not to employ a property management firm that manages hundreds or even thousands of units for dozens of property owners. How can such a firm closely watch your best interests and develop a marketing strategy that outperforms your competitors? It can't and it won't. At its best, a large property management company will deliver mediocre performance. Expect nothing more and anticipate something less.

To operate profitably and proactively, set high standards. Show your hired help how to achieve the performance results you want. Pay them well. Tell them how much you value their work and appreciate the job they're doing. With this respectful, long-run approach, you can count on your properties to bring you peace of mind, security, wealth, and financial freedom.

13

CREATE PROMOTIONS THAT SELL

You invested wisely. You worked smart. You created value. You have gained from inflation and appreciation. You have paid down the balance on your mortgage (amortization). Now it's time to harvest the wealth that you have gained through property equity.

Just one more task: Design and execute a sales promotion that attracts buyers who will pay the price you want. How do you attract these buyers? Craft a winning value proposition—and then effectively promote it. (Also, of course, you can rely on these same techniques of promotion to attract tenants.)

DESIGN A WINNING VALUE PROPOSITION

More than 50 years ago, the marketing maven Rosser Reeves coined the phrase "unique selling proposition (USP)." In that era of mass marketing, Reeves tried to pull out from traffic. He encouraged firms to differentiate— "Make your products and services stand out in a unique way," he advised.

Over the years, Reeves's ideas have become so well known that marketing pros around the world now recognize the USP concept. In fact, just ask a pro, "What's your firm's USP?" and he will know what you are referring to. Reeves and his concept of USP have achieved universal acclaim.

Yet Generic Prevails

Although Rosser Reeves holds an esteemed position among marketing hall-of-famers, and even though every textbook of marketing advocates USP, the majority of all businesses still fail to reach the standard that

Reeves set. Generic prevails. "Me-tooism" dominates. Think of banks, for example. How many offer a uniquely desirable level of services? Think of real estate sales agents. Most meander in mediocrity.

And more to our point in this chapter: What about the investors who own small rental properties? Most fail to stand out from that crowd of property owners against whom they compete for tenants—and eventually buyers. This generic mind-set that prevails—either consciously or unconsciously—explains why Craig Wilson (Chapter 11) operated his property more profitably and with less effort than other property owners who also offered student-oriented rentals.

Craig Wilson's principle of success should also guide your sales promotions. To achieve the price (and terms) you seek, you cannot shuffle down the same path that others crowd on to. To compete successfully, design a winning value proposition (WVP)—a value proposition that attracts, persuades, and closes the perfect buyer (or tenant).

USP versus WVP

Reeves's advocacy of USP moved marketing thought forward. But we can improve on his idea. A unique selling proposition might not win customers (renters, buyers). Different may not translate into desirable (much less most desired). In my years of looking at properties, I have found many owners who promote *unique* or *different* without offering a desirable difference—a difference that I or anyone else was willing to pay for.

And that brings us to my second point: even if you create a desirable uniqueness, you must offer that benefit at a price your target market will pay, and at a price that provides you a profit. In Dubai, dozens of planned residential and office towers remain unbuilt, unsold, or unrented. Yet in advertisements, builders and architects celebrated their iconic designs, their Ritz-Carlton level of services, and their "close to everything" locations.

Unfortunately, these so-called iconic projects (a most popular promotional tagline) failed because no sufficient market of buyers or tenants—now referred to as end users vis-à-vis the speculators who were actually driving the boom—would pay a price high enough to cover the costs of construction. You've seen similarly ill-conceived marketing when homeowners try to fully recover the costs of their (unique) $65,000 kitchen makeover when selling a $250,000 house.

In contrast to USP, a winning value proposition (WVP) integrates four elements: (1) the buyer, (2) your competitors, (3) the benefits you will offer, and (4) your pricing (and terms, if any). To create a WVP, think interactively.

Think Interactively. In my grade school, some kids would tease and torment their classmates who wore glasses by calling them "four eyes." In fact, to sell your property at the best price, four eyes would provide great advantage. Why? So that you could focus on four sets of details simultaneously.

1. *Which buyers (tenants)* should you appeal to? Like tenants, buyers come in all varieties. Toward which types of buyers should you design your value proposition? No-cash, no-credit buyers? First-time homebuyers? Move-up homebuyers? Old or young or disabled homebuyers? Lease option buyers? First-time investors? Professional investors? Group housing operators? Conversion specialists?

2. *Who will compete with you (substitutes)* (houses, condominiums, apartments, new home builders, foreclosures, distressed sellers)? What locations? What features and benefits do each of your potential competitors offer? What price and terms do each of the potential competitors offer?

3. *What features and benefits* should you emphasize and offer? Room counts, floor plans, amenities, landscaping, special touches? Seller financing? Fast (or delayed) closing? Strong appreciation potential? Inflation hedge? Positive cash flows? Low amount of cash to close?

4. *How should you compare* and contrast, mix and match the types of potential benefits, potential buyers, and potential competitors to arrive at your price (or terms or both)—a price that provides the target buyer (tenant) great competitive value? And provides you the profit you seek?

Think interactively. Think to find (or create) a niche in which you can outperform your competitors such that your buyers (tenants) will reward you with a deal that meets or exceeds your profit expectations. What features or benefits remain relatively scarce among competitors—yet highly prized by some segment(s) of potential customers?

How do you answer these questions? In the same way that Craig Wilson answered similar questions when he designed a winning value proposition for his College Oaks tenants: Ask market players. Inspect, compare, and contrast properties. Discover the properties that sell fastest and at the best prices. Read articles on property decor (now called home staging) and renovation. Talk with or employ a home stager. Google images for home staging. Think! What features or benefits or contract clauses will provide a competitive edge against other properties and a cooperative edge with your customer segment(s)?

Work Does Reward. Will these research efforts pay back enough to justify the time and effort required? In my experience, yes, but decide for yourself. Give systematic and organized research a try. In a property market dominated by inept sales agents, ill-informed sellers, unimaginative buyers, and woefully deficient promotions and advertising, you can create unique selling points that also create a winning value proposition.

CRAFT YOUR SELLING MESSAGE

"Build a better mousetrap and the world will beat a path to your door." Maybe Emerson correctly describes the mousetrap market, but as to property, his advice falls short. To effectively sell (or rent) properties requires thought and effort. To sell at the best price, to craft a winning value proposition—you must tell the world about it. You cannot wait for the world to find you.

When I say, "Tell the world about it," I mean craft a selling message that grabs attention, stirs interest, excites desire, and motivates action. How do you accomplish this goal? Apply these 10 criteria:

1. Use a grabber lead or headline.
2. Reinforce and elaborate.
3. Add more hot-button benefits.
4. Establish credibility.
5. Compare to substitutes.
6. Arouse emotions.
7. Reduce perceived risks.
8. Make it easy to respond.
9. Provide reasons to act now.
10. Follow up.

"Wait a minute," you might object. "How can I write a sales message that packs in all of that information? I just want to run a four-line newspaper ad." Or you might say, "I don't plan to sell 'by owner.' I'll let my real estate agent deal with advertising and sales."

True, in their print and website ads, many sellers recite a few facts about their property and expect their prospects to call and learn more. But in a sea of ads, web pages, and Craigslist postings, you must first get your prospects to notice your property; you must draw enough interest from the prospect to entice a response, and then know what to say when you answer the telephone, text message, or e-mail. A "just the basic facts—I will tell you more if you e-mail me" approach rarely sells effectively. Nor will it generate an offer that matches what you could otherwise obtain if your inception sales message proved more persuasive.

As to sales agents (discussed later in this chapter) or property managers, never walk from your responsibility to supervise, direct, and critique their sales efforts. Even high-production sales agents often fail to craft effective sales presentations.

Experience proves what common sense supports. You will close more frequently on better terms when you craft your marketing messages (ads, flyers, brochures, web postings, social media, personal selling, networks, word of mouth) to incorporate all 10 principles of effective selling.

Use a Grabber Headline or Lead

What do your prospects value highly? What do most competitors slight? When you design your WVP, discover the most salient benefits or features that would excite a targeted buyer. Choose the critically important.

The most famous book title in real estate, Robert Allen's *Nothing Down* (Simon & Schuster, 2004), illustrates this point perfectly. In just two words, he hit the burning, intense need of millions of people who wanted to buy real estate—but lacked the cash to make a down payment. The book shot to the top of the bestseller charts within a matter of weeks.

Does your property proposition offer seller financing, low price per square foot, strong potential for appreciation, easy qualifying, mountain views, a great yard for kids . . . ? Match the feature or benefit to the intensely perceived need and desire of your target market. Rely on your headline to grab your prospects' attention and pull them in to learn more about your property and your offer.

Reinforce and Elaborate

After you hook the potential buyer, reel him in. Serve more details—details that flow from and support your original promise. Provide enticing information about the financing, features, views, and so on, information that reinforces the buyer's understanding of what you offer and why your offer provides just what he has longed to find.

Add Hot Buttons

What other features or benefits of your proposition would excite potential buyers? List and describe more key benefits. If you are selling an investment property, for example, emphasize the quality of the tenants, the low maintenance expenses, or the possibility of rezoning to commercial. Is it the lowest-priced property in the area? Will it reveal strong cash flows, price growth, tax shelter, or value-add possibilities? Are condo conversion documents all set for government approval? What other sources of return?

Establish Credibility

Back up your claims with facts. If you cite numbers, show where they came from. If you say the rents sit below market, identify other rental units of equal or lesser quality that bring in higher rents. When you talk price, reveal your benchmarks of value. Know the sales prices, terms, and features of all comp properties that sold recently. Steer clear of puffing, exaggerations, rumors, and opinions unsupported or unverified.

Compare to Substitutes

Know the facts, features, and prices of currently for sale (or rent) listings. Point out the attributes and features of your property as compared to these others. Explain why your price or terms provide superior value relative to the competition. If selling to a first-time buyer, show how over time (because rents will increase) owning costs them less than renting. Plus, owning builds equity while renting yields piles of worthless paper receipts.

Evoke Emotional Appeal

Does the neighborhood offer a friendly, social environment? Will parents feel their children are safe? Can you help that first-time investor feel the joy of financial freedom? Will owning bolster feelings of prestige, security, or independence? Does the recreation room offer a great place for parties or family gatherings?

Reduce Perceived Risks

What fears block your prospect's commitment? Do you offer a homeowner's warranty? Do you credibly support your assurances that the buyer is gaining a great deal? Do all of your words and actions build a sense of trust between you and the prospect? Have you arranged for an escrow account in which you will place the buyer's earnest money deposit?

All prospects—investors, tenants, and homebuyers alike—hesitate when they fear risk and uncertainties. Identify those fears. Then bring forth facts, benchmarks, historical trends, warranties, guarantees, and explanations to alleviate them.

Make It Easy for Prospects to Respond

Prospects manage dozens of potentially promising property listings. They forget. They scribble notes and then lose them. They confuse the descriptions and details of ads. They intend to call back, but procrastinate or otherwise fall off track. More than likely, this description (at least to a degree) matches your own behavior when you are searching from the buyer's side.

What does this less-than-rigorously organized search mean? It compels you as seller to make the buyer's response as easy as possible and then to offer a persuasive narrative that will move the buyer to visit the property (if deemed qualified as to interest and finances.) Many sellers and agents fail to meet these criteria.

I recently telephoned four times about an ad for a property. No answer. No voice mail. Eventually on another try, I reached voice mail. One week later, I received the call back. I finally scheduled an appointment and showed up at the property on time. The person showing the property called 20 minutes later. "I'm running late. Sorry. I'll be there within 10 minutes."

My response: "I'm leaving. I'm going to see another property."

You might think that these FSBO sellers weren't motivated to sell. But that was not the case. They were overleveraged; they were badly managing the property; and they were running negative cash flows that they could not afford. They wanted to sell. They were just incompetent.

Prepare for the Phone Calls. Make it easy for your prospects to contact you: landline, mobile, e-mail—and prepare all of your backup information ahead of time. Open multiple channels of contact. Avoid such put-offs such as "Call 6 to 9 P.M. Tuesday through Thursday evening." When you answer the call, know every fact that a buyer might want to learn and every fact you want the buyer to learn.

During your first voice contact, you either build trust and credibility—or you lose it. In my experience, many sellers lose it. Make it easy for buyers to respond to your promotion. Then meticulously prepare for that response.

Arrive for the Appointment Prepared and Ahead of Time. When you meet the buyers personally, continue to build trust, reinforce your credibility, and don't just show the property—market it. Bring documents, facts, newspaper articles, government data, exhibits, whatever helps support the value of your value proposition.

Think, "I am not here to show this property. I am here to sell (or rent) this property." Many agents and owners confuse showing with closing. Lead the prospect through your value proposition; bring a blank purchase offer contract; set up an escrow account before you begin to market the property. Encourage the offer.

Provide Reasons to Act Now. More often than not, your prospect will demur. Every salesperson has heard buyers utter those words of delay with, "Let me think it over." Do not acquiesce. Use the buyer's delay tactics to question the prospect further.

"Mr. Prospect, perhaps I can help you weigh the pros and cons of your decision." Reiterate facts that support your value proposition. Use competitive benchmarks to illustrate relative merits of your WVP. Explore other possibilities the buyer favors. Ask for objections or critique. Isolate and address buyer fears. Then provide reasons to act now.

Are interest rates poised for increase? Are you scheduled to present the property to other prospects within the next few days? Can you sweeten the deal? Can you entice an offer to open negotiations? Before you let the prospect walk out the door and drive away, go for the close.

Banish this dialogue:

Buyer: "Well, let me think it over."
You: "Sure, just let me know if you have any other questions."

No! Never!

Learn the objections. Learn how the proposition excites. Go for the close. If the buyer still leaves without an offer—or without making an offer you want to accept, follow up.

Follow Up with Your Prospects

Sight prospects on your radar screen. Maintain contact for as long as the prospect willingly permits you to do so. Restate (or improve) your value proposition. Continue to solicit an offer.

Use this contact time with prospects to enhance your knowledge of competitive offerings. If the prospect is viewing other properties and talking with agents, sellers, and perhaps lenders, discover what he's learning. Invite comments in a nonchallenging, curious manner. Vary your prospecting and value proposition accordingly. Also invite the prospect to bird dog for you: "Mr. Prospect, based on all you've told me, maybe this property and the price or terms offered do not really fit your preferences. Perhaps, though, we can still work together. I will pay a $5,000 [or whatever] finder's fee if you refer a buyer to me."

REACH POTENTIAL BUYERS

You crafted a winning value proposition (WVP). You prepared a selling message that attracts attention, stirs interest, stimulates desire, and motivates action. How can you effectively place that sales message in front of your target market(s)?

♦ For Sale sign(s)
♦ Flyers and brochures
♦ Networking
♦ Websites and links
♦ Sales agents

For Sale Signs

Place the largest For Sale (or For Rent) sign on your property that zoning or HOA rules permit. Reduce the size of space devoted to the words "For Sale." (Passers-by know a sign in a front yard most often indicates that the property is for sale.) Instead of emphasizing "For Sale," emphasize your lead benefit. Then bullet some hot buttons. Include e-mail, website, and telephone number(s). Attach a packet container, then fill (and refill) it with *color* flyers or brochures that persuasively convey your selling message.

Flyers and Brochures

Accent the sales message on your flyers with multiple color photographs that show the property in an appealing manner. (If selling in the dead of winter, use a summer photo with vibrant landscaping and flowers blooming. If selling in summer, still use a summer photo.) Print the address of the property on the flyer—some sellers omit this vital information.

Organize Your Sales Points. Sales agents and FSBO sellers randomly slop assorted features across the page. Or worse, some lazy agents photocopy the barely readable MLS sheet with its cryptic abbreviations.

Design your flyer: more readable, more informative, more effective. Organize features and benefits into categories. Not just features, but the benefits such features will deliver to the buyer. Such categories might include exterior, yard or lot, interior, garage and outbuildings, basement and attic, neighborhood amenities, financing, warranties and guarantees, and so forth.

Provide your prospect a sales message that conveys unity, clarity, and coherence. Fit all photos and narratives together such that your flyer convincingly communicates a winning value proposition.

Distribute Flyers and Brochures. Place your flyers wherever your target market(s) might see them.

- Neighborhood bulletin boards (such as those in grocery stores, libraries, and coffee shops)
- Neighborhood residents
- People you know at work, church, and clubs
- Neighborhood churches
- Mortgage companies and real estate firms
- Technical schools and colleges
- Homebuyer counseling agencies
- Apartment complexes (if you don't get thrown off the property)
- Investor clubs
- Employers
- Hospitals

Don't wait for buyers to find you. Become proactive. Bring your opportunity to them. At any moment, many prospects for your property aren't actively searching. They procrastinate. They misalign priorities. They are waiting for your sales message to motivate them.

Multiple Targets, Multiple Sales Messages, Multiple Flyers. You can craft multiple flyers for a variety of target markets. Prepare one sales message that targets investors, another one directed toward parents of students who are attending the nearby university. Another aimed at prospects who need seller financing, or maybe those who crave the extra space your property offers.

Each of these markets will respond best to their own unique hot buttons. A one-size sales message rarely fits all. Investors might get excited over positive cash flow and low vacancy rates. A first-time homebuyer might favor properties for their affordability, school district, or spacious yard. Your market research will tell you.

Networking (Word of Mouth)

Recall from Chapter 5 how I sold my house by hosting a student-faculty party. Get the word out. Tell most anyone you meet or know. Carry flyers in your car, briefcase, or backpack. Emphasize your bird-dog fee.[1] Never speak per se about selling a property. Speak of features, benefits, profit potential, and your winning value proposition.

---

[1]Check the law in your area. Sometimes real estate licensing laws restrict referral payments to unlicensed persons.

Websites and Links

At today's low cost for IT services, set up a website for your property. Fill it with complimentary photos, your sales message, and links to articles, reports, and government records that add power and credibility to your value proposition. Weigh the cost and availability of other property-for-sale sites. Post on craigslist.org. In fact, create a variety of postings with alternative leads and sales messages. Tailor sales messages for multiple types of buyers.

Sales Agents

What about sales agents to help you sell? Agents charge high fees. The majority are mired in mediocrity. Nevertheless, a majority of property sellers (homeowners, investors) do employ a real estate agent to list and sell their properties. But should they? Should you?

SHOULD YOU EMPLOY A REALTY AGENT?

Most owners who try to sell their own properties fail. They put out their cardboard front-yard sign, run a newspaper ad for a month or two, and then give up. Do these failures mean that you should forget FSBO and list your property with a realty agent? Not at all; but it does mean that to succeed where others fail, you must avoid mistakes.

Most FSBOs do not realize that to sell properties, *top* sales agents go beyond yard signs and newspaper ads. To get properties sold, top agents provide services to sellers and buyers.

Services to Sellers

1. *24/7.* Sales agents tend to work whenever they get called, and they remain on call morning, noon, and night, every day of the week.

    Advice for FSBO sellers: Arrange to show the property ASAP at the convenience of the prospect. Consider yourself on call.
2. *Multiple media.* Agents use yard signs and newspaper ads, but they rely on referrals, networking, websites, cold calls, floor time, and personal and business relationships.

    Advice for FSBO sellers: Get the word out about your property to everyone you know or come in contact with. Circulate those flyers.

3. *Pricing.* Agents inspect and show dozens of properties every week. They know properties. They know the details of purchase contracts. They know prospect hot buttons.

   Advice for FSBO sellers: Look at properties in the neighborhood and nearby areas. Monitor sales prices, terms, and time on market. Price your property realistically in the context of other transactions. Your goal: a winning value proposition. Distinguish the *value* of your offer.

4. *Prepare the property.* Agents obtain feedback about properties from dozens of buyers each month. They learn the likes and dislikes of the market. They can use this knowledge to help sellers dress their property for success.

   Advice for FSBO sellers: Monitor buyer feedback. Talk with realty agents, contractors, home remodelers, and sales consultants at home improvement centers. Provide buyers what they want most.

5. *Sales presentations.* Top agents don't show properties; they sell them. They know how to encourage buy signals. They know how to alleviate buyer objections. They diplomatically buffer hard-edged negotiations and persistently create trade-offs, options, and alternatives. They maintain a supply of purchase agreements. They know how to get buyers to commit and sign.

   Advice for FSBO sellers: Encourage your prospects. Ask them to buy. Shy and passive won't make it. Remain flexible and open to offers. Give and take with tact and good nature. Persuasively lead your prospects into a buying decision. Don't wait for them to ask you.

6. *Troubleshoot problems.* Agents know that signed contracts do not walk to settlement by themselves. Someone must shepherd the flow of paperwork and solve problems that arise.

   Advice for FSBO sellers: Don't assume that you can travel down the road from contract to closing without hitting a few potholes. Monitor progress. Rely on a sharp escrow agent to diligently control the document shuffle.

Services to Buyers

1. *Market knowledge.* Agents know listings and can prescreen properties to save the buyers effort.

   Advice for FSBO sellers: Compare and contrast your property with others on the market. Especially highlight its competitive advantages. Know and show why your value proposition stands superior to other sellers.

2. *Agents help buyers with neighborhood selection.* People don't just buy properties, they buy locations. Agents know demographics, schools, trends, commuting distances, shopping, and culture. Buyers depend on agents to compare and contrast the pros and cons of neighborhoods.

   Advice for FSBO sellers: Understand the neighborhood. Know how it compares to others. What are its advantages? Prepare a neighborhood flyer to complement the flyer you've prepared for the property itself. Buyers who are new to a city especially need this information.

3. *Price.* Buyers depend on agents to advise about price. In turn, agents provide buyers comp sales data. Agents help buyers choose their offering price.

   Advice for FSBO sellers: Provide prospects with comp sales data. Emphasize how your price, terms, and property features and benefits beat those offered by the competition. Do not expect prospects to learn these facts on their own. Other owners (and their agents) will spin facts to their own advantage—not yours.

4. *Financing.* Agents either qualify buyers or refer them to a loan rep who provides this service. Buyers often need someone to figure out how much property they can afford, the quality of their credit profile, and how well they and the property match other loan underwriting criteria.

   Advice for FSBO sellers: Establish a relationship with several loan reps. Discuss the features and costs of loan programs with prospects. Refer prospects to www.myfico.com, where for around $39.95 they can look at three credit reports, learn their FICO (Fair Isaacs Company) credit score, and gain tips on how to improve their credit profile. Even better, help buyers with owner-assisted financing or a mortgage assumption.

5. *Negotiating assistance.* Many buyers, and especially first-time buyers, do not feel comfortable or competent when negotiating. In their role as facilitator and mediator, agents ease their buyers through the offer-counteroffer emotional roller coaster.

   Advice for FSBO sellers: Play softball, not hardball. Contemplate and conciliate. Help prospects feel comfortable in talking with you. Nurture trust. "Let's see if we can work out an agreement that will make us all happy," not, "Look, take it or leave it. If you don't want the property, I'm sure someone else will."

   (Naturally, the actual words that work best do not stand independently of the prospect whom you are talking with. That's why sales scripts represent one of the most offensive formats for selling. The sales agent delivers the same slick spiel regardless of actual buyer concerns and objections.)

6. *Follow through.* Agents help buyers follow through to submit their mortgage application and obtain a professional inspection of the property. They may hand-hold or troubleshoot for the buyers. The agent remains on call to provide assurances and intervene when an obstacle arises (low appraisal, mortgage turndown, lot encroachments, and so forth).

Advice for FSBO sellers: A sharp escrow agent can assist with some of these details. But invite the buyers to call at any time, because you want to assist with problems or answer questions about the property, the neighborhood, the mortgage loan process, or anything else that concerns them. Provide the buyers with the names of competent property inspectors, pest control companies (for termite clearance), and surveyors (if necessary).

I have reiterated here some points made earlier because to succeed as a FSBO seller, you should practice the 10 steps to an effective sales message. When you get the word out, you will outperform most professional sales agents. You can earn a higher profit margin, provide buyers a better deal, sell quicker, or achieve some combination of all of these benefits.

Co-Op Sales

If going it alone as a FSBO seller doesn't appeal to you, offer sales agents a 3 percent (more or less) commission to bring you a buyer. Act as your own listing agent and pay the co-op percentage to the buyer's agent. With this approach, you increase the chance of a sale, but if you find a buyer yourself, you owe the agents nothing. Indeed, as soon as your FSBO sign goes up on your property, agents will solicit your listing through telephone calls. Invite them in to take a look. Thoroughly present your value proposition. Ask for critique and improvements. Inform the agent of your co-op policy. As one shortcoming of this approach, though, in most cities (check yours), MLS will not list FSBO co-op sale properties.

Listing Contracts

When you agree to list your property for sale with a real estate brokerage firm, the sales agent will require you to sign a listing contract. Read that contract. Especially review the following clauses:

♦ Type of listing
♦ Commission payable

♦ Listing period
♦ Description of property
♦ Automatic renewal and cancellation rights
♦ Obligations of the agent

Types of Listings. Listing contracts include: (1) open listing, (2) exclusive agency, and (3) exclusive right to sell. Under the first two listing agreements, owners retain the right to sell their property themselves without paying a brokerage fee. Under an exclusive-right-to-sell listing, owners agree to pay a sales fee no matter who sells the property—as long as the sale takes place within the listing period.

Which contract is best? It depends on whether you want to reserve the right to sell your property yourself. Many agents hesitate to accept an open or exclusive listing. These agents prefer an exclusive-right-to-sell listing to protect the time, effort, and money that they will invest to promote, show, and sell your property.

Assume you sell FSBO—but agree to co-op with an agent; when that agent arranges a showing, sign a "named buyer" listing. A named buyer listing assures the agent that you won't go behind her back to deal with her buyer and cut her out of a commission. Such an agreement also protects you against agent claims that *your* buyer was actually someone she had brought to you first.

Commission Payable. Any listing you sign should state the amount payable to the agent—probably a percentage of the selling price of the property, or maybe a flat fee. Either way, the percentage or amount represents a negotiated agreement. Forget the notion of a standard fee. You can offer less—or more. To create an incentive, you might agree to pay a bonus for quick success.

Your agreement should set payment at closing—and only if closing occurs. Some listings in the past have specified that the agent earns his commission whenever he brings an able and willing buyer to you—even if you decide not to sell to that buyer (for example, in the meantime, before signing with the agent's buyer, you receive a better offer. Or perhaps, you choose to pull your property off the market).

Listing Period. Like commissions, listing periods are negotiable. I've seen listing periods as short as 24 hours and as long as two years. On a co-op, named-buyer showing, I advise a time limit of 30 to 90 days. If the agent can't get his buyer to commit within that period, then he loses the right to that buyer. You are then free to deal direct—without the obligation to pay a commission—if you succeed where the agent has failed.

With an exclusive-right-to-sell listing, a period of 30 to 90 days seems reasonable. Some agents want 180 days. That's too long for a condo, house, or two-to-four-unit rental property—except, perhaps, when the market is slower. Still, if you've crafted a winning value proposition, your property will sell within 90 days—if the agent does her job. In these times, most properties that remain on the market for months and months (and longer) do so because the sellers prefer to live in the past rather than the present. They believe no sale reflects a slow market—when in most instances, no sale actually announces a noncompetitive (that is, a losing) value proposition.

Describe the Realty and Personal Property. At the price you ask, what do you offer? Describe the house, lot, and personal property that you plan to include with the sale. If you plan to remove any items that buyers might expect (drapes, blinds, refrigerator, ceiling fans, chandelier, and so forth), specifically exclude them in writing.

Automatic Renewal and Right of Cancellation. If a clause in the listing agreement automatically renews the listing at the end of the listing period, omit it. Some contracts require you to notify the agent, say, 10 days before the listing expires to cancel. If you fail to provide this written notice, the listing renews for the same period set earlier. If with the first listing period the agent has not sold the property, the listing should die—unless you positively affirm its renewal.

What if during the listing period the agent does not work effectively? The agreement should give you the right to cancel, list with another agency, or sell the property yourself with no obligation to pay that realty firm. Cancellation rights should include the right to terminate the listing and take your property off the market.

Agent Obligations. Most listing agreements slight agent obligations. No surprise there. Agents (or their lawyers) drafted the contract. Remedy this self-serving omission.

You now know how to carry out an effective sales effort. You know what services a top agent should perform. You know how to design a sales message that sells. Now write these obligations into the listing contract.

For the past 20 years, real estate sales agents have tried to strike the word *sales* from their job title. They prefer to call themselves real estate professionals. But to deserve such status, they must accept responsibility to think and act like the professionals they claim to emulate. Your "obligations and responsibilities" clause will spell out the professional performance you expect, and the performance for which you are paying.

14

PAY LESS TAX

As a real estate investor, you will benefit from a variety of tax deductions, tax credits, and tax deferrals that can reduce (and sometimes eliminate) your taxable rental income. Especially in the early years of ownership, you will probably pocket your positive cash flows completely free of income taxes. Upon sale of a property, the taxes that you pay on capital gains will (more than likely) range between zero and 20 percent.

No other popular investment (stocks, bonds, gold, mutual funds, hedge funds) will let you keep as much of your investment earnings as does income property. Of course, the IRS does not alert you to all of the ways that owning property can cut your tax payments. To protect your earnings and future net worth, you must develop tax-saving tactics and strategy. And looking at the depleted finances of the United States (and many other countries), tax-saving tactics will become ever more important to anyone who wants to build financial security.

THE RISKS OF CHANGE AND COMPLEXITY

At the Constitutional founding of the United States, Publius (John Jay, Alexander Hamilton, and James Madison) wrote in *The Federalist:*

> It will be of little avail to the people that the laws are made by men of their own choice if the laws be so voluminous that they cannot be read, or so incoherent that they cannot be understood; if they be repeated or revised before they are promulgated, or undergo such incessant changes that no man who knows what the law is today can guess what it will be tomorrow.

Can anything contradict these founding principles more than the current federal income tax laws? At present, the Internal Revenue Code (IRC) court cases, regulations, interpretive rulings, and journal commentary stack up more than 1 million pages of text. Moreover, Congress, the Internal Revenue Service (IRS), and the U.S. Department of the Treasury change or threaten to change the tax laws on an almost daily basis.

Confronting complexity and instability, you may want to admit defeat and relinquish your financials to a tax pro. Apart from high fees, experience shows that such planned ignorance of the tax laws can cost you thousands (or even hundreds of thousands) of dollars in additional taxes. As a smart, tax-savvy investor, at least learn the basics. As you develop savvy and insight, you will discover what tax questions to ask your advisor, and more importantly, you will learn to plan your tax strategy to legally reduce or avoid paying more than the law requires. (If, like Warren Buffett, you feel that your legal tax liability falls below your fair share, write a check to the U.S. Department of the Treasury. It gladly accepts contributions.)

Investors who lack tax savvy act first, and then ask their tax pro to calculate their taxes. The tax-planning investor anticipates the tax effects of alternatives and then chooses with knowledge of the tax consequences. Although tax outcomes per se should never drive your investment decision, those outcomes should weigh in with all other benefits and costs that you might expect from an investment choice.

HOMEOWNER TAX SAVINGS

Because government policy favors home ownership over renting, Congress provides homeowners several tax breaks. When deciding investment alternatives, weigh heavily the tax benefits that home ownership provides.

Capital Gains without Taxes

When you sell your principal residence, you can pocket up to a $500,000 gain tax free (married filing jointly). If you're single, your maximum untaxed profit is capped at $250,000.

Although the law generally requires you to have lived in the home (house, condo, co-op) for at least two of the past five years, it does not limit the total number of times that you may use this exclusion. It just limits you to one capital gains exclusion every two years. In other words, over the next 24 years, you could buy and sell a personal residence up to 12 times—and escape capital gains taxes every time (subject, of course, to the $250,000/$500,000 limits).

Serial-Seller Paradise. For investors who buy properties, improve them, sell, and move up to bigger and better, this law offers a serial-seller paradise. Granted, you may not want to change homes every several years. But for those willing to tolerate this inconvenience, even an 8- or 10-year plan could help you earn $200,000 to $1 million in tax-free profits.

That's how Suzanne Brangham, author of *Housewise* (HarperCollins, 1987), earned her fortune: buy, renovate, sell, and repeat. She first bought a $40,000 condominium, and then over a period of 16 years, rehabbed herself up to a $1.8 million mansion (1987 prices). In contrast to Brangham's day, the benefit of the law now is that when you sell these flippers, you avoid paying taxes on the gain. (Under previous tax law, homeowner capital gains were primarily deferred, not excluded.)

Tax-Free Capital. In addition to buying and selling personal residences, you can benefit from this capital gains exclusion another way. You own a future home with large equity. The kids are gone; you want to downsize. You can now sell that large, expensive house and unlock your equity tax free (up to $500,000). Then, split your cash proceeds into several piles. Use your sales proceeds as down payments on a lower-priced replacement home as well as several income properties. Finance the newly acquired properties with 15-year mortgages. With price gains and a relatively short-term mortgage payoff you'll soon become financially set.

Admittedly, in today's market, to speak of gains—much less gains in the hundreds of thousands—sounds quite fantastical. First, remember that I speak mostly toward creating value (especially with bargain-price purchases). Second, *because* the outlook now seems fearful and uncertain, the potential for future price growth looks better than at any time since the Great Depression. Not since the 1930s has such a large percentage of properties been priced below replacement costs.

Rules for Vacation Homes

Although tight credit has temporarily slowed sales of second homes (so now's a great time to buy), demographics point to rapid growth in this market. Income tax laws define vacation homes broadly. A second home can refer to a condominium, apartment, single-family house, house trailer, motor home, or houseboat. Unlike a personal residence, the IRS will tax your profits from the sale of a vacation home as a capital gain. No exclusion allowance applies. If you earn rental income from this vacation property, however, you may deduct some of your expenses according to the following three rules:

1. If the vacation home is rented for fewer than 15 days, you cannot deduct expenses allocated to the rental (except for mortgage

interest and real estate taxes), but the rental income doesn't have to be reported to the IRS.

2. If the vacation home is rented for 15 days or more, then determine if your personal use of the home exceeds a 14-day or 10 percent time test (10 percent of the number of days the home is rented). If it does, then the IRS assumes you used the home as a residence during the year. You may deduct rental expenses only to the extent of gross rental income. The amount of rent collected in excess of expenses becomes taxable.

3. If you rent the vacation home for 15 days or more, but your personal usage is less than the 14-day/10 percent test, then tax law ignores this minor usage of the property during the year. In this case, the amount of expenses that exceed your gross rental income may be deductible against your other salary or business income. Court cases have allowed deductions for losses when the owner made little personal use of the vacation home and primarily bought the property to earn a profit on resale.

This brief description shows that the income tax laws specify how many days you can use the vacation property relative to how many days it is available for rental—and that your principal reason for buying the property will affect the amount of your tax liability (if any).

Mortgage Interest Deductions

When you buy and finance a property, you'll pay acquisition costs (purchase price, settlement fees, loan points) and, perhaps, property improvement expenses. Accordingly, you may deduct the interest you pay on these borrowed funds. However, if in the future you arrange a cash-out refinance, tax law does not permit you to deduct interest on the cash-out portion of that loan—unless you use the money for property improvements, reinvestment, or for medical or education expenses.

Credit Card Interest

Normally, you may not deduct credit card interest (as you can mortgage interest). But you might benefit from a special exception. If you use credit card borrowings or cash advances to help fund your rental property acquisitions, improvements, or operations, then you can deduct the interest you pay on those funds.

If you commingle personal and business credit card charges, fully document the business portion. For ease of record keeping, use one of your credit cards exclusively for business charges. In times of cash flow short-falls, you may have to violate this practice and dip into the credit available on your personal cards. If (or when) you resort to your personal cards, accurately segregate business from personal. Otherwise, the IRS may reject your deduction and apply the general rule against deducting credit card interest.

Rules for Your Home Office

As an owner of rental properties (and possibly other investment and business interests), you may be able to set up a tax-deductible home office. To legally claim a deduction for a home office, the area must be used *exclusively* and on a regular basis for work (a room where your spouse watches television or works puzzles while you telephone real estate agents and complete your Excel spreadsheets does not qualify).

When you operate a bona fide home office, you're entitled to deduct pro rata amounts for property depreciation, insurance, telephone, computer, office furniture, and any other items that relate to your work. If your rental properties don't show a taxable income (because of other allowable deductions), you can't deduct office expenses for that year. You can, however, carry these expenses forward and use them as deductions in later tax years.

Depreciation Expense

Real estate investors deduct the noncash expense called depreciation. Income tax law assumes that your rental buildings, their contents (appliances, carpeting, HVAC), and various onsite improvements (parking lot, fencing, sidewalks) wear out over time. Accordingly, various IRS depreciation schedules permit you to reduce your taxable income to allow for this (assumed or actual) deterioration.

Note that this deduction stands on top of already deductible expenses for repairs, upkeep, maintenance, and property improvements. That's why investors call depreciation a tax benefit. You don't have to write a check to pay for it, but it knocks down your taxable income as if you did. If you own multiple properties, the tax losses that depreciation provides on some newer acquisitions can offset taxable income that your other investment properties might yield.

Land Value Is Not Depreciable

Tax law does not permit you to depreciate the land on which your rental buildings sit. To calculate a property's depreciable basis, first subtract the value of the land from your purchase price. If you buy a property for $200,000 and its lot value equals $50,000, your original depreciable basis equals $150,000. Tax law permits an assumed life for residential rental units of 27.5 years. Divide $150,000 by 27.5 and you get $5,455. That's the amount of (noncash) depreciation that you can deduct each year to reduce your otherwise taxable rental income. (If you held this or any other residential property for 28 years, your annual depreciation deduction would then cease.)

Land Values Vary Widely

To maximize the deduction for depreciation, look for properties in neighborhoods with relatively low land values. Or, holding land value constant, look for lots with the largest quantity (or quality) of improvements. At the other extreme, several years ago, I looked at a small (900 square feet) 100-year-old rental house in Berkeley, California. That house was priced at $525,000. At that time, the land value alone probably totaled $500,000. The actual building was a potential teardown. As a result, even though the property (that is, land) was worth a half million, a buyer who placed a tenant in that house could legally deduct less than $1,000 per year depreciation expense ($25,000 ÷ 27.5).

No set percentages apply to land/building value ratios. For estimates of land value, you talk with the tax assessor's office, real estate appraisers, and sales agents familiar with the neighborhood. Other things being equal, the larger your deduction for depreciation, the larger your annual after-tax cash flow. Yet "other things being equal" seldom applies. When you compare properties and estimate returns, the potential depreciation deduction becomes just one factor among many for you to weigh.

After-Tax Cash Flows

Here's an example to illustrate how depreciation serves to reduce your taxable income. You own a property that produces a net operating income (rent minus operating expenses) of $10,000 a year. Your mortgage payments total $9,500 a year, of which interest equals $9,000 ($500 equals principal). With building and site improvement value of $135,000, you're entitled to deduct $4,909. If you're in a 30 percent marginal tax bracket, and without your rental property, your taxable wages (and other income) equal $75,000. Here's how these numbers work out to shelter your income from taxes:

NOI		$10,000
Less		
Mortgage interest		9,000
Depreciation		4,909
Tax loss		(3,909)

You use this tax loss from your rental property to offset your taxable income from a job (or other properties).

Taxable income	$75,000
Tax rate	.30
Taxes owed (excluding loss)	$22,500
Now with the tax loss from the property:	
Taxable income	$75,000
Tax loss from rental property	(3,909)
New taxable income	71,100
Tax rate	.30
	$21,330
Taxes saved because of rental property:	
Taxes owed without property	$22,500
Taxes owed with property loss	21,330
Tax savings	$1,170
Total yearly benefit (without appreciation):	
NOI	$10,000
Mortgage payment (principal and interest)	$9,500
Before tax cash flow	$500
Principal reduction	$500
Tax savings	$1,170
Total benefit (not including appreciation)	$2,170

For any specific property and investor, the tax savings could end up higher or lower than those shown here. This example serves to illustrate how investors can benefit from a property—even when, for tax purposes, that property records a tax loss. Had you generated taxable income from other investment properties, this tax loss would cancel out taxes (up to the amount of the applicable losses) otherwise owed on that rental income.

Passive Loss Rules

The tax law described in the previous section applies to many real estate investors, but not all. If you fall into a technical tax swamp called the passive loss rules, a different set of laws applies to you. Although too complex to detail here, the passive loss rules generally ensnare investors who report adjusted gross incomes in excess of $100,000 a year. Investors who take no role in the operational or managerial decisions that affect their properties may also fall under the passive loss rules.

The passive loss rules were enacted to keep high-wage earners from sheltering their earnings through depreciation—a widely adopted practice before the 1986 Tax Reform Act (TRA). (Unfortunately, the amounts that investors, as well as other taxpayers, now must pay to CPAs and tax attorneys to figure their taxes far exceeds any revenue gains to the U.S. Treasury.)

Taxpayers in the Real Property Business
(No Passive Loss Rules)

More complexity: Congress has created another investor tax category called "taxpayers in the real property business." This category includes (but is not limited to) real estate agents, contractors, property managers, leasing agents, converters, and owners of rental properties. If you can fit yourself into this category, you are exempt from the passive loss rules and may use your rental property tax losses to offset the taxable income you receive from any other source including wages, commissions, dividends, interest, and royalties.

However, here's the catch: You must work in a real estate–related trade or business at least 750 hours per year (around 14 hours per week for 52 weeks). More than one-half the personal services you perform each year must fall within the definition of a real property trade or business. In other words, you can't simply go out and get a license to sell real estate and automatically qualify for this preferred tax treatment. Nevertheless, for people who actually do (or can) work in real estate, the hours-worked test won't prove difficult to meet.

Even if you work as, say, a schoolteacher or an auto mechanic, once you begin to build a portfolio of properties, you may be able to meet the hours-worked test if you can somehow spend at least one-half the hours you work each year on your real estate activities. To do so, you could cut back on the hours you work in your regular job, and work a second job with your properties. If you put a lot of time into fixing up and renovating your properties, you might qualify. The time you spend searching, buying, renting, and selling also counts.

ALTERNATIVE MINIMUM TAX

The alternative minimum tax (AMT) defies human reasoning. You must turn to a tax pro (or tax software) for guidance. Both passive losses and capital gains may throw you into the AMT. Originally, only the wealthiest and most heavily tax-sheltered taxpayers would run into serious AMT tax liabilities. Today, the reach of the AMT has pulled in millions of other unsuspecting taxpayers. (For basic information on the AMT for individuals, see IRS Publication 909, Alternative Minimum Tax.)

CAPITAL GAINS

Lower tax rates for capital gains benefit real estate investors. Under current rules, gains realized in the sale of a property will be taxed at a maximum rate of 15 percent.

A Simplified Example

As repeated throughout this chapter, the tax law incorporates far more complexity and technical nuances than I can explain here. Still, the following example illustrates the basics of the capital gains tax:

Sales price	$600,000
Tax calculation	
Acquisition price	$300,000
Less: Accrued depreciation	100,000
Adjusted basis	200,000
Total gain	400,000
Less: Depreciation recapture	100,000 at 25% = $25,000
Capital gain	300,000 at 15% = 45,000
Total taxes	$70,000

Current law recaptures accrued depreciation at a tax rate of 25 percent, and your capital gain is taxed at a rate of 15 percent (or less). If you fit into the 15 percent ordinary income tax bracket (as opposed to the higher brackets), your capital gains are taxed at 10 percent rather than 15 percent. The depreciation recapture remains at the 25 percent rate.

To qualify for capital gains tax rates, you must own the subject property for at least one year. Also, your property buying and selling activities must not occur so frequently that they throw you into the IRS dealer category.

How often and how many deals? No one knows for sure. Occasional sales by rental property investors clearly don't cross into dealer tax territory. However, investors who fix and flip numerous properties (other than their successive personal residences) may get tagged as dealers. Don't unknowingly get caught in the dealer trap. Anticipate this potential problem. Seek the advice of a tax pro. To isolate dealer properties from your investment properties, set up segregated corporations (or other differential ownership entities).

The Installment Sale

If you carry back financing (owner-will-carry, or OWC) when you sell an investment property, you need not pay all of your capital gains taxes at that time. Instead, you spread them out on a pro rata basis as you actually receive principal payments from your buyer.

Assume that at closing you accept 20 percent down and finance the balance of the buyer's purchase price over 15 years. Your total taxable capital gain equals $300,000, which accounts for 50 percent of your selling price. You would immediately incur a tax liability on $30,000 (15 percent × 50 percent × $300,000). You would thereafter owe taxes on the pro rata amount of gain you would receive in each of the following years. (For simplicity, I have ignored recapture of depreciation.) The exact formula for calculations is shown on IRS Form 6252.

Pros and Cons. In his book *Aggressive Tax Avoidance for Real Estate Investors* (Reed Publishing, 2005), John Reed argues that investors should not sell their properties on the installment plan. Reed maintains that with the now-lower tax rates on capital gains, postponing the day of reckoning doesn't really save a great deal of money. Moreover, because of technical complexities, use of installment sales may expose you to the murky swamps of the AMT.

Reed's points are misguided and simplistic. Although he tells investors to calculate whether an installment sale will produce the large tax savings that are popularly expected, tax strategy alone should not drive your investment decisions. (That's why so many pre-1986 TRA investors ended up with real cash losses. Their deals were driven exclusively by tax-shelter benefits. After the tax shelters were reduced or eliminated by the passive loss rules, the tax shelter value of their investments collapsed.) Reed alludes to this point in bringing up the issue of opportunity costs. He says, "Why leave your money tied up in OWC financing just to save taxes when you could instead use those sales proceeds to buy more properties and earn much higher returns?"

Here's Why. As the late Robert Bruss pointed out in his real estate articles, owners should consider OWC financing because it can help them sell their properties faster and at a higher price. This is especially the case when (as today) mortgage lenders are going through one of their tight money phases and insist that investor loans carry lower LTVs and tougher qualifying standards. So, don't measure your profit from the installment sale just by the tax savings and mortgage interest your buyer pays you. Maybe OWC will bring about a quicker sale at a higher price. It probably will. (Of course, as a buyer, avoid paying an excessive price just because a seller offers you OWC terms.)

As another advantage to OWC sellers, those buyer interest payments can prove lucrative to you, especially when you use wraparound financing (p. 40–41). Plus, interest earnings on a seller-held mortgage (depending on creditworthiness, amount of down payment, and the quality of the collateral) typically deserve a lower risk premium than does property ownership.[1] And you devote less effort to pull a mortgage payment from your mailbox each month than you would to manage apartments and collect rents.

What's the Bottom Line for Sellers?

That equivocating answer, "It all depends," applies to installment sales. The tax savings from an installment sale may not loom as large as many sellers anticipate. More importantly, though, the benefits of an installment sale extend beyond tax savings. When you reach the stage in life when you want to enjoy a stable monthly income without the risks and efforts of property ownership, then when compared with so-called safe long-term bonds paying 3 to 6 percent interest, a seller mortgage that earns, say, 7 to 10 percent interest might look pretty good. And if OWC financing helps you get a faster sale and better price for your property, all the better. (Although bonds may return your principal, that principal will probably have lost much of its purchasing power.)

Implications for Buyers

Nothing in this discussion of installment sales should discourage you from *seeking* OWC financing. As a buyer, whether you borrow from a bank or

---

[1] In terms of risk and reward, to a degree, mortgages tend to pay lower returns than equity investments in property because investments in debt (when issued according to sensible rules of loan underwriting) present less risk than equity.

a seller will not change your federal income tax liabilities. If you agree to pay the seller a higher price in exchange for favorable terms, however, make sure you include a prepayment discount. If you refinance or sell the property early, you won't want to pay the seller for favorable OWC terms that you end up not using. Also, when you arrange seller terms, negotiate assumable financing that you can pass along to your buyers when you sell (or exchange) the property.

TAX-FREE EXCHANGES

When you own a corporate stock that has run up in price, you may think that now is the time to sell before the market stalls or turns down. But selling stocks creates a tax liability. Federal income taxes can pull out a large amount from your gain. As a result, many stock market investors hold their stocks long after they should have sold them because they can't bear the thought of throwing away part of their profits in taxes.

Real estate investors need not face this dilemma. As noted, the installment sale can help you defer, and perhaps reduce, the amount of the profits you lose to taxes. Just as important, but not nearly as well known, real estate investors can eliminate or defer their federal income tax liabilities by trading up. These two techniques—installment sales and exchanging—give owners of investment properties a tax advantage over investors who choose stocks and bonds.

Exchanges Don't Necessarily Involve Two-Way Trades

Many real estate investors who have heard of tax-free exchanges mistakenly believe that to use this tax benefit, they must find a seller who will accept one or more of their currently owned properties in trade. Although a direct trade represents one way to carry out a tax-free exchange, it does not represent the most commonly used exchange technique. In fact, most exchanges involve at least three investors.

The Three-Party Exchange

Three-party transactions outnumber two-party trade-in exchanges because it's difficult to find an owner of a property you want who will accept the property you plan to trade up. True, you might negotiate a two-way exchange by persuading an unwilling seller to accept your property in trade and then turn around and sell it. But to do so may cause you to spend too much negotiating power that you could otherwise apply to issues such as a lower price or OWC financing.

Instead, most real estate investors arrange a three-party exchange through the following steps: (1) locate a buyer for the property you want to trade; (2) locate a property you want to buy; and (3) set up an escrow whereby you deed your property to your buyer, the buyer pays cash to your seller, and your seller conveys his or her property to you. In effect, no property has really been exchanged for another property. Because of this anomaly, some observers suggest renaming this technique the "interdependent sale and reinvestment" strategy. Not surprisingly, that terminology has not caught on.

Beware: The law enforces strict timing dates for a 1031 exchange. Do nothing—absolutely nothing!—to sell your property or buy another one—until after you have discussed your situation and goals with a 1031 pro. I once contracted with a seller and gave him a $25,000 earnest money deposit. The seller then went to his tax advisor who sadly informed him that by accepting my deposit he had disqualified himself from the possibility of a tax-deferred exchange (in the sale of that property to me, that is).

Exchanges Are Complex but Easy

As you might suspect, anything that involves federal tax laws will entangle you in a spider web of rules and regulations, and Section 1031 exchanges (as they are called in the Internal Revenue Code) prove no exception. Yet even though exchanges must adhere to complex rules, when you work with a pro who is experienced in successfully setting up and carrying out tax-free exchanges, they need not create difficulty.

Due to intense competition among Section 1031 accommodators, the total extra costs (including fees and escrow charges) of conducting an exchange are often less than $1,000. Standard forms may be used to complete the required paperwork. Even with standard forms, use a tax or realty exchange pro. Be aware, too, that the great majority of CPAs and real estate attorneys know little about Section 1031 exchanges. Unless your accountant or lawyer has definitively mastered this area of law, find someone else who has this expertise. (If you live in at least a midsize city, there's probably an exchange club whose members include investors and commercial realty brokers who can recommend competent and experienced exchange professionals.)

Note: Some accountants and lawyers have told me things like "Oh, you don't want to get involved in something like that," or "That's more trouble than it's worth," or "Sure, I can handle it, no problem." In my naïve and inexperienced days, I simply accepted such comments without question.

"Surely, I can count on the wisdom and good faith of my accountant or lawyer." (Okay, those of you who have worked with lawyers and accountants can now stop laughing.) Note these words of wisdom: (1) To hide their own ignorance, lawyers and accountants who do not understand an issue will often advise against "getting involved with that," whatever "that" may be, so as not to disclose that they really don't know what they are talking about; or (2) depending on how much they need the business (or perhaps they don't want to lose you as a client), accountants and lawyers may claim competency, even though they lack expertise in that specific area.

Either or both of these tendencies can cost you. (Yes, you can sue for malpractice. But that's not an easy remedy.) To reduce the chance of professional error, misinformation, or just plain bad advice, don't let your accountant or attorney bluff you. Pepper them with detailed and specific questions about the issue at hand and their actual experience. Whatever you do, never *naïvely* accept the counsel of any professional (lawyer, accountant, real estate agent, medical doctor, and so on). These are not demigods but people with limited and biased knowledge and abilities. Require them to *earn* your trust and respect through performance. Do not grant trust merely because your advisors list a string of initials after their names.

Are Tax-Free Exchanges Really Tax Free?

Some people quibble with the term *tax-free exchange*. They say that an exchange doesn't eliminate taxes but only defers payment to a later date. This view is wrong on four counts:

1. The exchange itself is tax free if you follow the rules.
2. Whether you must pay taxes at a later date depends on how you divest yourself of the property. If you hold it until death, the property passes into your estate free of any capital gains taxes.
3. As another alternative, you could arrange a sale in a later year in which you have tax losses that you can use to offset the amount of your capital gain.
4. If Americans are sensible enough to elect legislators who understand the importance of productive investment, we may see the income tax, or at least the capital gains tax, abolished. (I would not bet on this outcome—especially with the multitrillion-dollar deficits and debts the U.S. government is accumulating.)

Exchanges do eliminate taxes for both capital gains and depreciation recapture in the year you exchange the property. Whether you pay in future years depends on how savvy you are in developing your tax-avoidance strategies, and on the tax law that exists in some future year. By exchanging, you eliminate a certain tax liability in the year of sale and accept an uncertain and contingent future tax liability. That's a tax trade-off you should accept.

Section 1031 Exchange Rules

Section 1031 tax-free exchanges must comply with five principal rules:

1. *Like-kind exchange.* Tax law states that only exchanges of like-kind properties qualify for the preferred tax treatment. However, like-kind doesn't mean fourplex to fourplex, or even apartment building to apartment building. Like kind actually includes "all property [types] held for productive use in a trade or business or for investment." As a matter of law, you are permitted to exchange nearly any type of real estate for any other type of real estate and still arrange your transaction to fall within Section 1031 guidelines.
2. *45-day rule.* If all parties to an exchange are known and in agreement, you can close all properties simultaneously. You can otherwise use a delayed exchange procedure that specifies two separate time deadlines. One of these is the 45-day rule, which says you must identify the property you want to acquire within 45 days after the date of closing with the buyer of your present property (that is, before midnight of the 44th day).
3. *180-day closing.* The second time-period requirement requires you to close on your purchase property within 180 days of closing the disposition of the property that you are trading up. Or if sooner, from the date your income tax filing is due for that tax year.
4. *Escrow restrictions.* Tax-free exchanges generally require exchange proceeds to be paid into and distributed out of an escrow arrangement. The escrow agent must stand independent of you (for example, not your attorney, real estate agent, bank officer, spouse, company's employees, or anyone else who is subject to your exclusive control or direction). Most importantly, you must not touch any money held by the escrow or otherwise pull out of the exchange agreement before the date the escrow agent has scheduled disbursements and property transfers.

    Beware of with whom you place your escrow monies. Choose a well-established escrow holder. During the recent boom, many exchange-investors lost their money when their 1031 escrow agents misappropriated, malinvested, or stole the funds that had been deposited with that escrow agent.

5. *Trading up.* To gain the benefit of a tax-free exchange, you must trade for a property of equal or greater price. Trading down or accepting a cash boot exposes you to a liability for capital gains taxes. If because of this tax liability, your seller doesn't want to trade down or accept a cash sale, then you can create a daisy chain of exchange participants until a property owner is found who wants to cash out or trade down real estate holdings and is willing to pay the capital gains tax. (A seller who has planned a total tax strategy may not have to pay any taxes despite realizing taxable income from a specific transaction. Also, because heirs receive properties on a stepped-up basis, they will incur little or no capital gains tax liability unless they sell their inherited property for substantially more than its estimated market value at the time it entered the deceased's estate.)

To keep lawyers and accountants fully employed, the tax law embellishes the preceding rules with various details, definitions, regulations, and requirements. So, let an experienced exchange pro guide you *before* you enter into a purchase or sale agreement, and to keep the exchange process in compliance throughout each step until all closings are completed.

REPORTING RENTAL INCOME AND DEDUCTIONS

You report rental income and expenses on Schedule E of your federal tax return. You report the gross rents received and then deduct operating and financing expenses such as mortgage interest, property taxes, maintenance costs, and depreciation. Add any net income to your other taxable income. If you book a loss, you may reduce the amount of your other taxable income within certain limitations (see passive loss limitation rules, discussed earlier).

To pay less tax, keep detailed records for all allowable deductions. Don't cheat yourself with sloppy bookkeeping. Deduct every expense that you believe reasonable and necessary to operate and maintain your properties. Among the most common deductions are the following:

♦ *Real estate taxes.* Property taxes are deductible, but special assessments for paving roads, sewers, or other public improvements may have to be depreciated or added to the cost of the land.
♦ *Depreciation.* Be sure to deduct depreciation; it is the tax-shelter benefit of real estate ownership.

♦ *Maintenance expenses.* These expenses include repairs, pool service, heating, lighting, water, gas, electricity, telephone, and other service costs.

♦ *Management expenses.* You may deduct all fees paid to a professional management firm. However, you can't pay yourself a deductible fee unless the property is owned by a separate corporation or partnership. You could, though, pay your spouse or kids for helping out and then deduct these amounts.

♦ *Traveling expenses.* These include travel back and forth from properties for repairs or showing vacancies.

♦ *Legal and accounting expenses.* These could include the costs of evicting a tenant, negotiating leases, or keeping financial records and filing tax returns.

♦ *Interest expense.* This category includes interest on mortgages and other indebtedness related to the property or property operations.

♦ *Advertising expense.* This includes the cost of signs, newspaper advertising, websites, and referral (bird dog) fees.

♦ *Insurance expense.* This includes the cost of premiums for property and liability coverage.

♦ *Educational investment.* To consistently improve your motivation and performance, read books, attend seminars and conferences, join investor organizations, and subscribe to magazines and newsletters. These educational costs are legitimate tax deductions.

♦ *Capital improvements.* Income tax law does not permit you to expense a new roof; new flooring; a new heating, ventilating, and air conditioning (HVAC) system; a major kitchen remodeling; or other long-life expenditures in the year you make the improvement. Instead, the law requires you to depreciate the cost over, say, 5 to 20 years, depending on useful life of the improvement. (For specifics, talk with a tax pro.)

TAX CREDITS

On occasion, tax law may offer property investors (or homebuyers) tax credits. A tax deduction reduces taxable income; tax credits reduce your tax liability dollar for dollar. They're much more valuable than tax deductions.

Assume you deduct all tax-deductible expenses from your gross income and calculate your taxable income at $40,000. If you are in the 28 percent tax bracket, you would owe $11,200 (.28 × 40,000) in income taxes. But let's assume that you are entitled to a tax credit of $4,000. After accounting for this credit, your tax liability falls from $11,200 to $7,200 (11,200 − 4,000).

How do you get these tax credits? As tax law stands today, tax credits aren't as easy to come by as they once were. However, Congress and state governments periodically add (or delete) tax credits. So stay alert for updates. Among the tax credits available recently are these six possibilities:

♦ *Mortgage credit certificates (MCCs).* These tax credits are available only to first-time homebuyers whose state or local governments participate in a program Congress created in 1984 (and has continued to reauthorize since then). To calculate the amount of tax credit permitted, you multiply 0.2 times the amount of your annual mortgage interest. If you paid $9,000 in mortgage interest this year, in addition you would receive a $1,800 tax credit (0.2 × 9,000). If your area offers an MCC and you haven't yet invested in your first home, get the details on this program as they apply to homebuyers where you live (or plan to live). MCCs provide free money.

♦ *Low-income housing tax credits.* These tax credits are available to real estate investors who build new or substantially rehabilitate rental housing that is rented to households with low incomes.

♦ *Nonresidential rehabs.* Nonresidential rehabilitation tax credits are available to investors who substantially renovate commercial buildings that were originally constructed before 1936.

♦ *Certified historic rehabs.* Historical societies in various states have the authority to certify residential and nonresidential buildings as "historically significant." Investors who rehabilitate and restore these structures to meet historical preservation standards are entitled to tax credits.

♦ *ADA building modifications.* The Americans with Disabilities Act (ADA) requires owners (or lessees) of some existing public or commercial buildings (not including rental housing) to adapt their properties to meet the accessibility and use needs of people who are physically disabled. Meeting the financial burden of these ADA requirements may entitle the owner (lessee) to tax credits to partially offset these expenses.

♦ *Energy Saving Improvements.* You *may* be able to obtain tax credits for new energy-efficient windows, doors, HVAC system, insulation, solar heat, and wind turbines. *May* because the rules seem to change every year. Check with manufacturers and a tax pro before you begin to shop. I recently bought a new five-ton HVAC. Even though the credit existed, for some technical reason, my system did not qualify. Both state and federal governments have been offering various types of energy-efficient tax credits. Check with each one.

Complexity, Tax Returns, and Audits

Tax complexity creates some risk of noncompliance. Income tax laws have grown "so voluminous that they can't be read, and (in many ways) so incoherent that they can't be understood."

Several years ago, *Money* magazine devised an income and expense profile for a hypothetical investor and sent the same figures to 50 certified public accountants (CPAs), tax lawyers, and the IRS. *Money* asked these tax pros to calculate this hypothetical household's federal income tax liability. Guess what? Among these 50 separately prepared tax returns, no two produced the same answer. In fact, the difference between the high and low tax bill was a whopping $66,000.

What does this mean to you? The complexity of tax law renders the rules uncertain and incomprehensible, not just to average citizens, but also to tax preparers. This doesn't mean that some parts of the law aren't relatively certain (for example, the deductibility of mortgage interest paid to finance rental properties). It does mean that in many instances, figuring your tax liability will require judgment calls (for example, the allocation of property value between land and improvements for purposes of calculating depreciation).

Therefore, you choose whether to take an aggressive stance on matters of judgment to reduce your taxes to the lowest possible level, or to play it safe, pay more, take less than the law *might* allow, and reduce your chance of an audit.

You and your tax pro can answer this question only after you weigh your total personal situation in light of current IRS audit standards and the contemporary hot issues that may flag your return for audit. Nevertheless, before you choose to play it safe and pay more than you owe, review the following points.

Audits Intend to Intimidate. The IRS prefers that you play it safe. The IRS operates through intimidation. It wants taxpayers to fear an audit. The fewer the number of people who push the envelope, the more money the IRS collects for the government. However, under the law, Congress did not authorize the IRS to maximize government revenues. Rather, statutorily, Congress authorized the IRS to enforce the tax code. As long as you support an aggressive position that reduces your taxes, you have little to fear from the audit result itself. (Of course, the time, effort, and expense an audit requires remain a valid concern—especially for investors who lack organized and documented records.)

Renegotiate Your Assessment. Even if an audit goes against your position, that doesn't mean you completely lose. When the IRS assesses more taxes, you can renegotiate the amount (based on the facts of your case and applicable tax law, not simply, "I'll give you 50 cents on the dollar") with the examiner, another examiner, or the manager of the IRS office responsible for your audit. In many cases, you (or your tax pro) can persuade the IRS to reduce its additional assessments.

Appeal Your Assessment. Absent a satisfactory resolution at the local level, you can ask the district appeals office to reduce or eliminate the additional assessment. Although under the law the appeals office can reopen your file and bring new challenges and even higher assessments, it rarely does so. The appeals office works to settle cases quickly. Appeals officers acquiesce (on the merits) to lower assessments in more than 50 percent of the cases that come before them.

Litigate Your Assessment. Some cases aren't settled on appeal. But again, you aren't compelled to accept the decision of an appeals officer. You have further appeal rights through several different court procedures. Furthermore, because of the large cost of litigating tax cases and the limited number of government lawyers to handle them, few tax cases actually go to trial.

Represent Yourself without Worry or Large Costs. You may think that audits, appeals, and court litigation will cost you far more than you could possibly save in taxes. While that may be true, it's not *necessarily* true. Up through the appeals office, you can represent yourself as long as you are willing and able to prepare your case (facts, records, laws) in a way that meets IRS standards. This task is not difficult (see the excellent book by tax attorney Fred Daly, *Stand Up to the IRS* [Nolo Press, 2008]).

Furthermore, if you move your case from the appeals office to the small-claims tax court (tax assessments of less than $10,000 for each year in question), you still can represent yourself. If you choose to litigate in regular tax court or a U.S. district court, however, retain a tax pro to carry on your battle. At that point, your legal expenses will shoot up. But do not measure the time, effort, and expenses you incur to win your position against the tax savings of just one year. If the issue affects your future tax returns (or past returns that are still open to audit), then you have more at stake than just the initial assessment. Argue for the position you believe is correct or you could pay additional taxes over a number of years.

Relatively Few Returns Are Audited. Your (law-derived) aggressive position to minimize income taxes won't be challenged automatically. Even if IRS computers flag your return, they will not necessarily call you in for an audit. In recent years, the IRS has scheduled office or field exams for less than 1 percent of all tax returns filed. Even then, most returns are not comprehensively examined. More often, a sampling of deductions are questioned as a matter of law or documentation. (Unreported income presents another, more serious, issue.)

This brings us back to where we started this IRS discussion. Because it has the personnel to investigate (not to mention litigate) less than 1 percent of all tax returns filed, the IRS realizes that it must appear more formidable than it actually is. Don't let the intimidating image of the IRS deter you from lawfully minimizing your tax payments. Even when the IRS does examine your return, as long as you (or your tax pro) can plausibly support your positions by citing case law, statutes, or revenue rulings and provide some legally acceptable (not perfect) records, you need not fear the audit.

At the worst, you will have played the game with odds in your favor. And even when you roll the dice, over the long run, an aggressive (but arguably lawful) tax position will yield more wins than losses.

Plausible Position. By taking an aggressive tax position, you should *avoid* paying taxes that you do not owe—not *evade* paying the taxes that you do owe. Do not spend $20,000 to renovate your personal residence and then claim this money was invested to upgrade your rental properties. Do not collect rents in cash so that they will leave no paper trail for the IRS to follow. Do not sell your properties privately on contract so that you can try to hide your capital gains and interest income from the IRS.

Before you act to reduce your taxable income (or, correspondingly, increase your deductible expenses), verify your position with a tax pro. A plausible position is supported by one or more recognized tax authorities (cases, statutes, regulations, or revenue rulings) and some personal records (contemporaneous or ex post). When you fail to report rental income or run personal expenses through your rental property accounts, you do not meet this test. Interpret facts and law to favor your position, and at most you'll owe more in taxes (plus interest and maybe some penalties). Purposely misrepresent the facts, and you expose yourself to steep penalties, fines, and criminal prosecution.

Use a Tax Pro

Although you can represent yourself at an audit or appeal, consult a tax pro to help you plan your tax strategy, prepare your returns, and, if necessary, prepare for an audit. Tax law complexity makes it nearly impossible for the great majority of Americans to fully understand the tax laws.

This chapter goes through some basics of income tax law as they apply to property owners. But this discussion remains a starting point—not the last word.

Consult a tax pro *before* you buy or sell a property, and *before* you develop your operating budget or plans for capital improvement or exchange.

Tax plan your transactions and document your spending to whittle down your federal (and state) income tax liabilities.[2]

PROPERTY TAXES

"If you think that your property taxes are too high," writes tax consultant Harry Koenig, "you're probably right! Research shows that nearly half of all properties may be assessed illegally or excessively" (*How to Lower Your Property Taxes* [Simon & Schuster Fireside Books, 1997]). While Koenig may overstate his point, no doubt millions of property owners do pay more in property taxes than they need to. With planning, you can avoid falling into this trap by taking several precautions:

♦ *Check the accuracy of your assessed valuation.* Tax assessors usually base their tax calculations on a property's market value. Look closely at the assessor's value estimate on your tax bill. Can you find comp sales of similar properties that would support a *lower* value for your property? Given the downturn of property prices, determine whether your properties might appraise for less today than in the past. If so, you may have grounds to request a tax reduction. (See Chapter 3 to review appraisal techniques.)

♦ *Compare your purchase price to the assessor's estimate of market value.* Apart from providing comp sales, if you can show the assessor that you recently paid $190,000 for a property that was assessed at $280,000, you have a prima facie case for a lower tax assessment.

♦ *Look for unequal treatment.* Under the law, assessors must tax properties in a neighborhood in an equal (fair) and uniform manner. This means that you might argue successfully for lower taxes even though the assessor has accurately estimated the market value of your property. How? Show that the assessor has assigned lower values to similar nearby properties. (All property tax data are

---

[2] A former secretary of mine was billed $12,500 by the IRS to recover tax benefits she had previously claimed from the sale of a property. She had timed a second sale two months too soon. Although she had been represented in both transactions by the same lawyer, he claimed that tax issues were not his specialty. So, if taxes were her concern, she should have asked specifically about them. Lesson: Don't assume! Inform yourself. Then ask. Lawyers, and to a lesser degree, accountants, rarely admit that they failed to advise you competently—even when their error is obvious to common sense.

publicly available.) If faced with this issue, the assessor will have to cut your taxes because after everyone's tax notices have been sent out, it's not politically feasible (even if lawful) for the assessor to start telling people that he has made a mistake and property owners owe more than their tax bill shows.

♦ *Recognize that assessed value and market value may differ.* Property taxes are typically based on assessed value, which may be calculated as a percentage of market value. If your tax notice shows an assessed value of $380,000 and you know your property is worth $680,000, don't necessarily conclude that you've been underassessed. If property tax law sets assessed values at 50 percent of market value, then your assessed value should come in at $340,000 (.50 × $680,000), not $380,000.

♦ *Does your property suffer any negative features that the assessor has not considered?* Even though comp properties may appear similar, might they actually differ? Does your property abut railroad tracks or a noisy highway? Does it lack a basement, built-in appliances, a desirable floor plan, or off-street parking? Does it have a flat roof? (In some areas, flat roofs reduce value because they tend to leak and are costly to replace.)

♦ *Do you or your property qualify for any property tax exemptions?* Many property tax laws offer lower taxes to various persons or properties. For example, homeowners, military veterans, age 65-plus, blind people, and hardship cases may benefit from reduced assessments. Historic properties, properties located within areas designated for revitalization, energy-efficient properties, or properties rented to low-income households may qualify for reduced assessments. Check with your assessor's office to see what exemptions apply in your area.

♦ *Verify that your property assessment meets all technical requirements specified in the law.* Tax assessors and the legislative bodies that levy property taxes must operate within a set of rules, regulations, laws, and even constitutional requirements. For example, some technical or procedural requirements may pertain to assessed value ratios, property classification, land improvements ratio, procedures for public hearings, notice of public hearings, permissible valuation techniques, and allocation of assessed value between real and personal property.

♦ *Learn tax assessment laws before you improve or rehabilitate a property.* The property tax laws of every state list the types of property improvements that are taxed and the applicable rates. Once you discover the detailed nature of these laws, you can plan improvements that add value without adding taxes. For an excellent discussion of this topic and numerous case examples, see the dated, but useful book by Steve Carlson, *The Best Home for Less: How to Drastically Reduce Your Taxes, Utility Bills, and Construction Costs When You Build, Remodel, or Redecorate* (Avon Books, 1992).

Some investors (and homeowners) who remodel or renovate do not obtain the appropriate permits. These owners think that the government won't tax what it doesn't see. But the city may not sit in the dark for long. Nonpermitted work runs the risk that someday a building inspector may discover the illegal work. In some cities, that means the inspector can require a property owner (even if the unpermitted work predates his ownership) to tear out the work and do it over. This risk arises especially when unpermitted work doesn't meet code requirements. In the past, governments often overlooked unpermitted work and failed to keep their property tax records up to date. But now, with computer data banks, buyer prepurchase inspections, and mandated seller disclosure statements, such illegal work is more likely to become known.

Furthermore, in their quest for more taxes, local governments realize that unreported remodeling and renovations are costing them millions of dollars each year in lost tax revenues. The trend throughout the country is drifting toward more thorough property investigations and harsher penalties. While many city and county governments still lack the personnel or political will to change their practices, don't foolishly bet that assessment inefficiencies will continue forever.

SUMMARY

Income taxes and property taxes take large bites out of your earnings. To reduce this drain on your livelihood and wealth building, you can practice tax evasion or tax avoidance. Tax evasion results when you maintain two sets of books, fail to report rent collections, overstate or invent expense deductions, or run personal expenses through your tax-deductible property accounts. Tax avoidance refers to legal strategies and tactics that you can use such as depreciation, tax credits, installment sales, tax-free exchanges, and income shifting (e.g., timing of receipts and converting ordinary income into capital gains).

If you evade taxes, line up trusted and competent property managers who will look after your properties while you go to prison. To avoid taxes, know the law; structure your income, expenses, and transactions to minimize, if not eliminate, income tax liabilities. Before you act, ask your accountant three questions: (1) How can I arrange and document this spending to make sure it's tax deductible? (2) How can I structure my income or capital gains to keep from losing it to the IRS? (3) Can I arrange this spending or investment to qualify for any allowable tax deferments or tax credits?

Although income taxes remain a fact of life, the amount of income tax you pay does not. Through careful planning at the *start* of each year, you will find that you can slice your income tax bill at tax time by thousands of dollars or more.

Likewise, property owners must pay property taxes. But the amount of taxes you pay need not equal the amount indicated on your property tax bill. Through negotiations with the tax assessor's office or through formal appeal procedures, you may be able to pay less than the sum the assessor originally said you owed. Learn the details of property tax laws and assessment practices *before* you remodel or renovate a property. You can then make your improvements with an eye toward keeping your assessments down while enhancing the desirability of the property for your tenants.

Although tax avoidance should not drive your investment strategy, develop an investment strategy that explores opportunities to keep more money for yourself. The stakes have climbed too high. With governments' insatiable appetites for more taxes, your best defense stands as a strong offense. And a strong offense requires wisely informed tax planning.

15

MORE IDEAS FOR PROFITABLE INVESTING

You can choose from multiple ways to invest in real estate and can pursue multiple sources of return. You might go for buy and hold, lease options, master leases, fix and sell, create value and hold, foreclosures, REOs, contract assignments, condo conversions, wraparounds, or some combination of any or all. And within each of these possibilities you might profit from more than 20 sources of financial returns such as inflation, appreciation, leverage, cash flows, amortization, subdivision of rights, subdivision of the physical property, conversion, smarter management, and savvy marketing. Property investing offers a cornucopia of diverse opportunities.

But these aforementioned possibilities do not exhaust your potential. Although less popularly recognized, each of the following types of investing can yield extraordinary returns—when pursued with research, wise calculation of risks and rewards, and large doses of due diligence.

- ◆ Out-of-area investing
- ◆ Commercial properties (office, retail)
- ◆ Triple net leased properties
- ◆ Self-storage
- ◆ Mobile home parks
- ◆ Zoning changes
- ◆ Property tax liens or tax deeds
- ◆ Discounted paper

Before you move forward with any of these investments, educate yourself about the local market, the specific opportunity, and the realistic numbers that are necessary to make a proposition attractive. Read more specialized how-to advice. Talk with unbiased and disinterested players who have succeeded—never rely exclusively on the sales messages of any promoters, gurus, or sales agents who are encouraging you to jump into a deal too good to last.

OUT-OF-AREA INVESTING

Russell Conwell's famous little book, *Acres of Diamonds* (CreateSpace, August 2011), teaches us that we might search the world for treasure, yet as often as not, that treasure we seek lies within our own backyard. Conwell's message—which he delivered as a speech more than 25,000 times—expresses more than a kernel of wisdom. Read his book. It will open your eyes and your mind to potential that sits within your immediate reach.

Still, in some instances, perhaps opportunities more to your liking will seem readily available elsewhere. And with the Internet now bringing properties into your home from throughout the nation and throughout the world, an increasing number of promoters are operating to tap into out-of-area sales. Indeed, for some investors, out-of-area investing can make sense. As I so frequently tell people who seek my advice, "It all depends."

Reasons to Invest Elsewhere

Why invest in an area away from where you live? Larger cash flows, more growth potential, greater affordability, lower taxes, less regulation, retirement planning, vacation planning, favorable currency exchange rate, favorable terms of finance, and "right time, right place, right price" represent several good reasons.

For example, if you live in the San Francisco Bay Area, you might search diligently yet never find a positive cash flow income property that's located in a desirable neighborhood. And that's assuming you could afford the price. Look further east to Las Vegas or Phoenix and you achieve affordability and cash flow. Or maybe you believe as I do that Detroit offers substantial turnaround potential with incredibly low prices and incredibly low GRMs (gross rent multipliers). No need for a 30-year mortgage in Detroit; many decent properties will pay off with positive cash flows and 10-year amortization schedules.

If you live in San Diego or Boston, you've seen small residential properties priced with cap rates as low as 4 or 5 percent. Redirect your search to the Midwest, Southwest, and South and you will find similar properties (except for location, of course) valued with cap rates of 7, 8, 10, or sometimes 12 percent.

Go to loopnet.com. Click on Texas, Florida, North Carolina (for examples). Troll through for-sale listings. You'll find hundreds of properties (multifamily as well as offices, retail, mobile home parks, self-storage, industrial, and so on) reporting attractive financials. Look at the price-per-unit and price-per-square-foot figures. Many properties are priced well below replacement costs.

Recall from Chapter 3 (Appraisal) that purchase prices that fall well below replacement cost will generally protect you against direct competition from new construction. Any builder who would try to match the price or rent levels of these lower-priced properties would soon go broke—as many builders have and many more are expected to follow. Foreclosures and REOs and other distressed sales pull down the current market values of single-family residences (SFRs), condos, and the price per unit (PPU) for multifamily properties.

Some existing properties do sell at prices far below the costs of new construction because they've fallen into disrepair, or their locations are trending toward decline, deterioration, or both. Often, though, low prices result from the *down cycle* (not deterioration)—and until market prices increase substantially, builders will hold back on constructing new SFRs, condos, or apartment buildings. At today's market prices, builders cannot compete effectively with existing properties. If over a longer term, you can reasonably expect an area to grow its jobs, economic base, and population, you are primed for extraordinary returns from multiple sources.

What about Property Management?

Can you manage properties from afar? A French colleague who is working with me in Dubai owns four rental properties that are located in France. She does not employ a local property manager. Another Dubai colleague owns rentals in Alabama. And another owns a few rental houses located in Perth. No one employs a property management firm. I currently rent out my Florida home to a medical doctor and his tax attorney wife. I do not employ (for that house) a property manager (although I do employ a caretaker/jack-of-all-trades handyman).

You can self-manage rental properties from anywhere in the world. Here's the secret: Offer good value, select great tenants. Do not fear long-distance property management. Set up a system to manage repairs, vacancies, and emergencies. Secure longer-term leases. Delegate some maintenance responsibilities to your tenants. (This type of investing does work best if you have reason to periodically visit the area where you buy your properties.)

Tenant-Assisted Management

Notwithstanding the fact that you can self-manage, you may need local assistance if you expect intermittent vacancies—as would be the case with multiunit buildings. (If you're located within several hours of your property, you could fill vacancies yourself.) Typically, for that task—as well as general property oversight—enlist the help of one of your longer-term tenants. In exchange, give that tenant discounted (or free) rent and a variety of upgrades for living quarters.

Property Management Companies

I seldom recommend large residential property management companies—although other investors I know do seem to find them satisfactory. I don't think this type of firm will strive to give my properties the competitive advantage that seek while they simultaneously work for dozens of my competitors. Nevertheless, if self-management issues deter you from out-of-your-area investing, by all means, employ a property management company. Just make sure you develop your own market strategy (see Chapter 11) and guide your management company accordingly.

EMERGING GROWTH AREAS

In San Francisco, a few years back I shared the speaker's platform with Richard Florida (author of *The Rise of the Creative Class* [Basic Books, 2003]) and Rich Karlgaard (publisher of *Forbes* magazine and author of *Life 2.0*). Neither of these authors claims expertise in real estate investing per se, but both share insights that can benefit real estate investors.

The Creative Class

In different ways, Florida and Karlgaard have both sought to identify the areas of the country (as well as specific cities) that will experience the most long-term profitable growth. Although I do not necessarily agree with some of their picks, that's not the value of their work. Their value lies in pointing out that today, people do not so much move to where the jobs are; rather, jobs (at least the best-paying jobs) move to where people (especially members of the population that Richard Florida dubs the creative class) want to live. (See, too, Florida's book, *Who's Your City?* [Basic Books, 2008])

Implications for Investing in Real Estate

As you evaluate areas for their growth (that is, appreciation) potential, do not rely exclusively on traditional statistics such as jobs, incomes, and household size. Look more closely at the types of people moving into the area; the types of employment; the restaurants, cafes, galleries, and bookstores (I hope) that are opening. Discover what festivals, tournaments, outdoor activities, and sports events are gaining in size and recognition.

Is the area—whether neighborhood, city, or rural outpost—attracting people who in turn will serve as magnets for others (as Silicon Valley attracts tech-savvy people from around the world)? In other words, look for areas that are developing a certain cachet. Look for areas where increasing numbers of people say they would like to live—even if their possibility of actually moving seems remote.

Why? Because such dreams encourage conversations and positive word of mouth. Such talk reinforces the decisions of those who do decide to make the move. Many of us do like to provoke at least a mild amount of envy from our friends, relatives, and acquaintances. As we all know, where we live and where we move to say a lot about us to those we know.

Right Place, Right Time

When I read Richard Florida's book, I could see myself writ large. Throughout my career, I never accepted a job anywhere that I did not want to live. And those places where I have chosen to live (Vancouver, Palo Alto, Berkeley, Charlottesville, Williamsburg, and now Dubai) all fit the profile as creative-class growth centers.

Yet, oddly enough, before reading Richard Florida, I thought of "where to locate" decisions more as personal choices, not a class choice—nor that millions of other members of the boomer generation would like to choose the same (or similar) locations—and thus push up their property prices at an accelerated rate.

Learn from my experience, as well as Florida's and Karlgaard's research and observations. Don't just personalize. Generalize. What places do you like that have yet to hit their full stride? What places do you hear others talking about? What locations have you read about in favorable articles? During the city's ascent, a front-page article in the *Wall Street Journal* extolled the appeal of Dubai. The *New York Times* and *Chicago Tribune* published similar articles.

Although Dubai remains—as does Abu Dhabi—a creative-class favorite, massive overbuilding has deflated its property boom. Identify these creative-class areas before they become high profile, front-page stories and you've probably identified a promising area in which to invest. (As Dubai, Miami, Las Vegas, and Dublin illustrate, beware when high growth in demand propels even higher growth in supply.)

EMERGING RETIREMENT AND SECOND-HOME AREAS

During the next 15 to 20 years, the number of persons age 60+ will double. It's the largest age-wave retirement shift in U.S. history. Just as important, millions of these emerging age-wavers rank among our country's wealthiest households. Many others of the 45-plus age still seek to build their wealth and incomes through property investment. Thus, demand for retirement and second home property will remain strong from both retirees and older investors.

Combine these numbers with increasing longevity and you can see a longer-term appreciation in prices—especially when measured against today's down-cycle market values—for properties located in areas that become favored vacation or retirement spots. If you wish to invest for high appreciation, search out the towns, cities, and rural retreats that will be favored by this coming age wave. (As a case in point, for investors looking at a 5- to 10-year horizon, I believe Sarasota, Florida (and much of the Florida Southwest coast) now represents a screaming buy opportunity. Indeed, many Canadians and Europeans agree. A weak dollar adds to the attraction for international buyers.

Which Cities and Areas?

Identify soon-to-be vacation or retirement havens similarly to how you identify emerging creative class locations. Talk with future retirees. What newfound areas are achieving attention and increasing popularity? Personalize, and then generalize. What locations seem attractive to you, your family, your friends, and your coworkers?

Pick up a pile of those books and magazine with titles such as *Where to Retire*. View entries as suggestive, not definitive. Anytime someone data crunches hundreds (or thousands) of locations to find winners and losers, or the top ranked and bottom ranked, errors and silly results often pop out. In one widely reported survey of cities, Sarasota, Florida—a top 20 pick on any sensible list—ranked number 156.

Look for ideas, not definitive answers. Whether you rely on information from publications or people you know, invest only in areas where your reliable market research reveals promise.

Income Investing

Many people who buy vacation retirement properties plan to rent them out part of the year and personally enjoy the property at other times. Although this strategy can work well, watch out for exaggerated estimates of rental revenues.

Demand for seasonal rentals can fall because of weather (too much rain, not enough snow), traffic and transportation issues (road construction, cost and availability of flights, and so on), and publicity (the SARS scare slashed travel to Toronto and Hong Kong). Also, firms typically charge high fees to manage vacation and seasonal rentals. It's not unusual for vacation management companies to charge 20 to 40 percent of gross rental receipts. (For a full discussion of issues relevant to this investing strategy, see my book, *The Complete Guide to Second Homes for Vacations, Retirement, and Investment* [John Wiley & Sons, 2000].)

OUT-OF-AREA CAVEATS

If you choose to buy away from an area where you enjoy everyday familiarity, double or triple your due diligence. Real out-of-area opportunities do exist, but the diamonds sit among far more zircons.

During the boom, investors were lured by the siren song of quick, easy profits to invest (speculate) in properties throughout the United States and throughout the world. Californians were easy prey for the property promoters of Texas and North Carolina. U.K. buyers snapped up entire floors of off-plan Dubai office buildings. South Americans flipped Miami condos. Busloads of Australians toured Phoenix developments. Hot money flew anywhere and everywhere that seemed to offer promise. Early in, early out often made money. Latecomers frequently suffered severe burns.

Today, the promoters now organize tours of distressed cities and properties. Vulture tours attract planeloads and busloads of investors wanting to buy. Or with the Internet, why travel? You can pick up your property bargains without leaving home. In the field of real estate (as well as with stocks, gold, foreign exchange, commodities), there's always those promoters and salespersons who promise low-risk, high-reward investments—especially to the ill informed and uninformed.

Whether investing out-of-area within the United States or out-of-country; whether searching on your own or following the bait of a good story, before you part with your cash: question, compare, critique, challenge, and investigate.

Laws differ: Landlord-tenant, freehold, leasehold, taxation, inheritance, conveyance, financing, escrow, property rights, land use, environmental, court procedures, contracts, and dozens of related laws, rules, and regulations *will not* mirror those with which you are familiar. Consult local competent counsel. Question thoroughly.

Compare prices locally: Even though that $600,000 Chicago apartment building looks cheap compared to Boston, it may look expensive compared to other similar properties in Chicago. Bargains exist relative to local comparables, not relative to the comps that you know of from back home.

Easy financing can cost you: Some sellers and builders will tempt you with easy terms. Buy the property, not the financing. Easy financing dulls the critical faculties. (Of course, this error occurs locally, too—but somehow easy financing seems even more irresistible when the charms and excitement of a new area intervene.

What price turnkey deals? Fearful of long-distance management, and worried about possible vacancies? "No problem," says the promotion, "we offer a turnkey operation. We even guarantee returns for three years." Sounds pretty good. But read the fine print. What costs will you pay? How do they calculate returns. How much price premium are you paying over similar properties that do not offer such enticements? Does the financial strength of the builder stand to support those golden promises.

To make their sales, many sellers, builders, and agents who cater to out-of-area buyers depend on the ill informed and uninformed. And when scouting on your own, beware of the error of overconfidence. Unless you have researched local laws, properties, neighborhoods, and markets, you almost certainly know much less than you think you do.

COMMERCIAL PROPERTIES

When most people think of investing in real estate, they think residential. Everyone's familiar with houses, condos, and apartments. In contrast, most people lack knowledge of commercial properties. Or they think such properties cost too much.

But a growing number of investors now realize that commercial properties can offer lower prices and higher yields (that is, higher cap rates, higher cash on cash returns) than houses, condominiums, and small apartment buildings. You can purchase single-unit retail or office condominiums for as little as $100,000. Similar to the boom euphoria that drove residential prices beyond the level that rents would support, so, too, the experience in small commercial properties.

As a result, many distressed and bank-owned properties are available. On a recent loopnet.com search for office buildings priced at less than $500,000, REOs were plentiful. A nearly new North Carolina dentist office that had sold several years ago for $250,000 was listed at $125,000. A search of California office buildings turned up hundreds of choices priced less than $300,000; cap rates of 6 to 11 percent set the norm; price per square foot as low as $35 with a typical range of $135 to $200.

You can find similar prices and yields among retail properties. How about a bank-owned retail center in Flagler Beach, Florida—13,000 square feet for $495,000. Or maybe you see possibilities with this 28,000-square-foot former supermarket located on a 10-acre site in Winchester, Indiana. How much? $299,000. Yes, you read that right, $299,000. A leased retail store or restaurant will yield 7 to 12 percent. If you want a value-add opportunity, buy a vacant building at a much-reduced price. Then research your market (actually better to perform the research before you buy) and sign up a tenant. Your building will immediately jump in value.

Low Effort Management

Depending on the type of property and the terms of your leases (see the discussion further on) you may not need a property management company for your commercial rentals. Likewise, you may or may not need a leasing agent.

For example, say you own a medical office condominium that is leased to a doctor for a remaining term of five years. This doctor has three five-year renewal options. If she chooses not to relocate, you enjoy a long-term, virtually carefree investment. The condo association maintains the building common areas. The doctor accepts maintenance responsibility for the interior of her offices.

You can find similar opportunities with offices for professionals such as lawyers, accountants, and insurance agents. Open your Yellow Pages. Scroll through the listings. Nearly every one of these businesses needs a place to operate. Potential tenants for your commercial properties number in the thousands. Just make them a winning value proposition (WVP.)

The Upside and Downside

One strong upside of commercial properties is that (in most but not all situations) your tenants operate businesses or professional practices. They establish themselves in a set location. This desired stability means that commercial properties experience lower tenant turnover than houses and apartments.

When a vacancy does occur, though, that vacancy could last for months. Or if you own a specialized property (or a property in an inferior location)—a vacancy could last for years—if you do nothing but place a sign in the window and list the property with a mediocre agent. On the other hand, if you think about the Yellow Pages and all of those potential tenants, if you design a WVP, you will re-lease your building promptly.

In fact, some commercial property investors seek out buildings with leases set to expire within a year or two. Expiring leases increase risk for the unskilled owner. But for the entrepreneurial minded, vacating tenants spell profit potential. The expiring leases discount the sales price. The retenanted property is valued substantially higher—especially if the new tenants pay a higher lease rate than the departing tenants.

Opportunity for High Reward

Vacant (or high vacancy rate) commercial properties sell at steep discounts. When you value a zero (or depressed) NOI by using a high (risk-adjusted upward) cap rate, you obviously compute a relatively low price. (Of course, you would also use the comparable sales and replacement cost appraisal techniques to value such a property.) Nevertheless, after balancing the three appraisal methods, you can still negotiate a low purchase price. Next, turn this lemon into lemonade. Through research of the market, develop a profitable profile of a tenant (or use) for the property. Bring that idea to life and you've created value two ways:

1. You've raised rent collections and NOI.
2. You've reduced the riskiness of the property (which justifies a lower cap rate).

Envision realistic leasing possibilities that others miss and you will be richly compensated for your insights.

Commercial Leases Create (or Destroy) Value

Generally, tenants who rent *residential* units sign leases of one year or less. If you don't like the lease (or the tenants) of the previous property owner, no problem. You can get your own lease and rental policies up and running within a short time.

With commercial properties you may confront a more tenuous situation. Many commercial leases run for 3, 5, or 10 years or longer. Plus, commercial tenants often obtain the right to renew for multiple periods (for example, an original five-year lease with three five-year renewal options).

Just as important, commercial leases differ greatly in their terms. Even tenants who rent units within the same office building or shopping center might operate under disparate terms and lease rates. That's because the terms of commercial leases depend on the market conditions when the lease is signed and the negotiating powers of the tenant vis-à-vis the property owner. You can bet that tenants who sign office leases in Dublin or Dubai today negotiate sweeter deals than those tenants who signed near the peak of the boom in 2006.

How Leases Differ. Lease terms determine your NOI. Great leases keep your NOI high. Leases with adverse terms drive your NOI down. Here are several examples:

- ♦ *Who pays what?* In commercial leases, property owners often shift some (or all) of the property's operating expenses to the tenant. In some leases—especially long-term, single-tenant properties—the tenant pays for operating expenses, building repairs, and major replacements (for example, roof, parking lot, HVAC).
- ♦ *On what space does the tenant pay rents?* Commercial tenants frequently pay rent per square foot (psf). But the rentable square footage may exceed the tenant's private usable space. Some leases require tenants to pay rent for hallways, common areas, HVAC rooms, storage areas, public restrooms, and so on. The lease may even specify the precise way the space is to be measured. The method of measurement can add or subtract 5 percent (or more) to the quantity of rentable space.
- ♦ *Are the rents inflation protected?* If the property is leased to a tenant for 5, 10, or 15 years (or longer) will your rent collections increase with inflation? When, and by how much?
- ♦ *Are the property owners entitled to percentage rents?* In retail, leases may require tenants to pay a base amount of rent plus a percentage of the tenant's business revenues (which also should be precisely defined—for example, must the tenant pay a percentage of their off-premises sales?)

Read Each Lease Clause. I don't want to make leases sound too complex. Some owners of small commercial properties write relatively simple, three- or four-page leases that involve month-to-month tenancies. However, unless you read each tenant's lease, you won't know what pitfalls lurk within the fine print.

Beware of buying a property only to learn later that an undesirable tenant can stay in place for another eight years at a rent level $6 psf under market. Beware of buying a small retail strip center with the idea of bringing in a Dollar General store only to learn that an existing tenant had previously negotiated an "exclusive right to sell general merchandise" clause in its lease.

To learn more about leases for small commercial properties, I recommend Thomas Mitchell, *The Commercial Lease Guide Book* [Macore International, 1992], and Janet Portman and Fred Steingold, *How to Negotiate Leases for Your Small Business* [Nolo, 2005]. Your lease determines your income stream. The quantity, quality, and duration of your income stream determine your building's value. Great leases and great tenants create great value.

TRIPLE NET (NNN)

If you would like to invest in real estate with virtually no managerial responsibilities, acquire properties that are leased to retail, office, or industrial tenants under a triple net (NNN) lease. Triple net means that the tenant pays all operating, maintenance, and fixed costs (property taxes, insurance) that are associated with a property. You pay only the mortgage payment, if any, which is typically covered by the tenant's rental payment to you.

To see the types of NNN deals available, google "triple net leases." One company active in this field of investment, Westwood Net Lease Advisors, for example, has listed for sale hundreds of properties with tenants such as Applebee's, Pizza Hut, Dollar General, Union 76, Taco Bell, Rite Aid, West Plains Corporate Park, Rite-Aid, McDonald's, Walgreens, Starbucks, KinderCare Learning Centers, Pep Boys, and Rivertown Commons Shopping Center. As with other types of income properties, NNN deals are priced by dividing a cap rate into the NOI the property produces.

In today's market, the respective cap rates for individual NNN properties typically range between a low of 5 and a high of 12 percent—though both higher and lower cap rates are possible. Strong credit, national tenants with established businesses (Walgreens, McDonald's) tend to command low cap rates (say, 5.0 percent to 6.25 percent because these tenants present little risk to the investor or the mortgage lender who finances the property for the investor. Higher cap rates (due to increased risk of default) apply to deals involving local companies or businesses that show high rates of failure (that is, locally owned and operated restaurants). The remaining term of the lease, option-to-renew clauses, above- or below-market lease rates, the quality of the property's location, property appreciation potential, and the cost and availability of property financing also influence the cap rate investors apply to a stream of NNN income.

Favorable deal issues tend to drive cap rates lower, and unfavorable issues tend to drive cap rates higher. No single rule applies as to the right cap rate or the best deal. For example, a Walgreens property priced with a 5.5 percent cap rate might prove to offer more long-term profit potential than a mom and pop–operated, locally owned sushi restaurant priced with a 12 percent cap rate. Before deciding, go through your due diligence checklist for each property that you consider. Then relative to the pros and cons, choose the one that seems to fit your risk-and-reward goals best. To assist in deriving the appropriate cap rate (and corresponding pricing) for any given deal, experienced and beginning investors solicit advice from an experienced, active NNN real estate sales agent.

Most triple net deals offer little or no possibility for entrepreneurial property improvement during the period of the lease (though exceptions exist), but they do offer the ultimate in carefree property investing—yet still provide returns from cash flows, appreciation, amortization, leverage, tax shelter, and inflation. As more boomers near their retirement years, I expect increasing demand for NNN properties. In a point-by-point comparison to stocks, CDs, annuities, or bonds, NNN properties—on a risk-adjusted basis—often prove superior.

Which sounds better to you: a 10-year U.S. government Treasury note that yields 1.92 percent, a 5-year bank CD that yields 1.67 percent, a portfolio of S&P 500 stocks that yield 1.9 percent, gold that yields 0.0 percent, a Walgreen's 20-year, NNN property yielding 6.3 percent with modest rent bumps every 5 years—or maybe a Dollar General (corporate guarantee) currently yielding 8.1 percent on 15-year NNN lease? (All actual yields at the time this chapter was written in January, 2012.)

SELF-STORAGE

Americans have become a population of pack rats. Their want of storage space grows larger every year. As a result, the self-storage industry has continued to grow. Although the big national players who operate 200- to 400-unit facilities attract most of the self-storage business, smaller investors, too, can profit with smaller (and sometimes more specialized) properties. Self-storage can offer cap rates of 8 to 12 percent. Earn even more if the site will accommodate expansion. Alternatively, self-storage can provide a profitable way to hold land while you wait, say 5 to 10 years, until the site becomes suitable for redevelopment into a more valuable use (for example, retail, offices).

In today's market, self-storage is difficult to bank finance unless you place 30 percent (or more) down and show evidence that your prior business experience equips you to competently manage the premises. This tight financing presents opportunity and danger.

Opportunity because motivated sellers recognize that they will need to offer OWC with favorable terms if they want to maximize the sales potential of their property. (The same situation applies to small mobile home parks; see the next section.) Danger because OWC can entice the unwary into both overpaying—as well as underestimating the business skill necessary to turn self-storage into a cash cow.

With rental rates per square foot that can almost match the rental rates of mid-range apartments, self-storage certainly looks like a no-brainer. No midnight calls about stopped-up toilets, no loud parties that command the attention of the police, little or no worries about tenants soiling the carpets or stuffing steak bones down the garbage disposal.

Although self-storage avoids problems that inept owners of residential rentals suffer, it does present some potential difficulties that only the inexperienced ignore. Here are a few:

- ♦ *Customer turnover.* By its very nature, self-storage appeals to transient customers. Effective retention and replacement reign supreme. To retain good-paying customers requires selection and service. When vacancies occur, you must quickly fill the space. Each of these tasks calls for something more than a night watchman attitude. You need marketing savvy.
- ♦ *Poor location.* To succeed typically requires a highly visible location with a traffic count of 25,000 vehicles a day. You also need effective signage and easy and convenient egress and ingress. If your property lacks any of these essentials, you had better develop a very good Plan B.
- ♦ *Rent collection procedures.* The self-storage industry persistently looks for policies and procedures that will get rents paid on time, every time. Otherwise, that cash cow you were hoping to find soon runs dry. Auctioning off contents does not substitute for rent collection.
- ♦ *Lien laws.* If you must auction contents, follow your state's lien laws precisely. Failure to abide by governing rules will subject owners to fines and lawsuits.
- ♦ *Demographics matter.* Your customers will consist primarily of middle class and perhaps some businesses (depending on your market strategy). Typically, industry experience shows that the lower-income households lack both the excess possessions that end up in self-storage and the discretionary income necessary to pay the rent. Since customers tend to select storage units by convenience, verify whether the neighborhood demographics and population density can satisfy your need for profitability.
- ♦ *Verify owner financials.* As with mobile home parks, smaller owner-operators of self-storage properties rarely provide potential buyers an accurate and comprehensive statement of current and past years' income and expenses. To protect yourself, check and crosscheck

all figures: tax records, utility companies, talks with customers (if possible), a review of leases and rental applications (if used). Seek explicit representations and warranties when negotiations give you the leverage to do so. Accept nothing on faith.

Ineptly managed, self-storage can drain your cash faster than it produces it. That's why banks have wised up from their anyone-qualifies underwriting and now want to see a business plan backed up by managerial know-how. Banks also understand—as do experienced operators—that self-storage can provide some of the highest returns available to property investors. But to earn those generous cash flows—and contrary to popular perception—the self-storage business does not run well on automatic pilot. As with most types of actively managed real estate, you—as much as, or even more than, the property itself—will bring in those good cash flows.

MOBILE HOME PARKS

Mobile home parks (MHPs) yield high cash flows—if you buy right. As with self-storage, many property investors are lured into the potential high returns of MHPs without performing the requisite competitive market analysis and property due diligence. And to an even greater degree than self-storage, sellers of MHPs entice the naïve with OWC financing and cooked books to whet the appetite.

What should your due diligence include? Here are some essentials, but prior to buying, dig much deeper into the many how-to MHP guides.

♦ *Owner financials.* Verify all income and expense figures through multiple checking and cross-checking. Compare to industry norms. Calculate annual gross income and annual gross expenses on a monthly per-space basis. Now do the figures look reasonable? Obtain park bank statements, tax returns, and operating income history for the past three years. The more reluctant the owner is to provide good financial records, the more risk you confront.

♦ *Zoning.* Zoning boards have become hostile to mobile home parks in many areas of the country. In one sense, this trend works for you because it limits new competition. But it can work against you if your park now fails to meet current zoning (or other land use) rules and regulations. Perhaps the number of park spaces exceeds the number permitted. Some zoning laws grandfather existing nonconforming uses, but only for a limited number of years.

♦ *Rent rolls.* Review the lease and personal record for all tenants who currently reside in the park as well as rent roll records for the past two or three years. Current and past tenants can provide insight about park operations. Plus, learn their source of income, rent-paying history, and length of tenure in the park—and if you can, why previous tenants moved.

♦ *Sewer/Water lines.* Many mobile home parks lack public sewer and water connections. This deficiency opens up multiple health and environmental issues. Capacity, pressure, pipe quality, size, age, and condition raise other related concerns. A professional inspection and perhaps a Phase 1 environmental report can alert you to existing and potential problems. Even if park lines are connected to city facilities, inspect them. City responsibility often ends at the property border. Repairing or replacing the park's underground piping can cost many thousands of dollars.

♦ *Police reports.* What do the police or sheriff's department think of the park and its surrounding area? Are officers called frequently to investigate crimes or disturbances?

♦ *Walk the grounds.* Walk, talk, inspect, discover. What ambience pervades the park? What demographic dominates? Do residents abide by park rules? Do park rules sufficiently control barking dogs, trash disposal, loud or offensive behavior, parking, discarded appliances and other junk and debris, inoperable vehicles, improperly muffled vehicles? Would the park appeal to the type of resident that you would like to attract?

♦ *Substitute housing.* If the residents did not live here, where else could they live? Are competing parks nearby? What are lot rental rates? What amounts do rental apartments and rental houses charge? How well can this park compete with the substitutes: surroundings, accessibility, attractiveness, price?

"Any idiot can buy a mobile home park, and many do," writes an old pro who has been in the business for more than 25 years. He continues, "Many, many people have made themselves millionaires through owning mobile home parks. In Stanley and Danko's book, *The Millionaire Next Door,* owning mobile home parks ranked as one of the top routes to build such wealth. However, these folks knew what they were doing. They learned the business, performed proper due diligence, and operated professionally."

To become a millionaire next door, you can invest in mobile home parks in two ways:

1. Own the pads, provide utilities, and maintain the site.
2. Own the pads and the mobile homes (much more labor intensive for maintenance and tenant turnover).

As with self-storage, you can hold mobile home parks for cash flow until a higher and better use for the land becomes profitable. It's also customary to delegate some day-to-day management to a park tenant who would like to earn extra money.

If you buy a park that includes mobile home rentals (rather than just the pads), value the land separately from the trailers. First, capitalize the lot rental NOI. Add to that figure the depreciated market value of the trailers. Rental mobile homes generate strong cash flows. But they lose value quickly. If you capitalize their rental income to figure a market price, you will overpay.

You can easily buy repossessed mobile homes for a fraction of their cost new and at a fraction of their capitalized value. That's why mobile homes generate so much cash flow per dollar invested. In most markets, a mobile home costing $10,000 (or less) will rent for $450 (more or less). A brick-and-mortar apartment building bringing in about the same amount of rental revenue could command a price of $30,000 to $40,000 per unit.

PROFITABLE POSSIBILITIES WITH ZONING

Research whether you can upgrade a property's use and profitability within current zoning and regulatory rules. Sometimes zoning laws change and the affected property owners don't notice—or they just don't investigate the more profitable uses that the rules now permit. Alternatively, persuade the planners and elected officials to grant your property (or area) a higher and better use. (This tactic is discussed in Chapter 9, but I wish to remind you here.)

As property investors struggle to boost their yields, zoning and land use opportunities are becoming more important. If you can add another floor to a rental house, sell off extra land as a buildable lot, or convert a house to an adult congregate living facility (ACLF), you can pocket thousands of dollars of found money. (For more details on the types of changes you might seek, see pages 54 to 88 in my book *Make Money with Flippers, Fixer-Uppers, and Renovations* 2nd ed. [John Wiley & Sons, 2008]. To help you navigate the approval process, see *The Complete Guide to Zoning* by Dwight Merriam [McGraw-Hill, 2005].)

TAX LIENS AND TAX DEEDS

Throughout the United States, nearly every state and county levies taxes against properties. If an owner fails to pay this tax assessment, the county authorities (sooner or later) begin to enforce their claim. Generally, this enforcement involves a tax lien, a tax deed, or some combination of both.

Localities Differ

Each jurisdiction proceeds according to local and state law. In my county in Florida, the assessor's office sells tax liens to investors in a reverse-bid auction. The bid winner pays the tax of the defaulting property owner. That investor then earns interest on his tax lien of 18 percent a year or less—in recent years much less.

The county starts the bid at 18 percent. Then investors bid down the rate. The lowest-rate bidder wins. In an auction that I recently attended, most tax liens were sold at an interest rate of less than 7 percent.

If the property owner does not repay the investor, including interest accrued, within four years, the investor can petition the court to order a tax sale auction. The investor who bids the highest purchase price at the tax deed sale (who may or may not be the tax lien investor) is then issued a tax deed to the property. The tax lien investor is paid from the tax sale proceeds. If the auction's sales proceeds do not cover the full amount of the tax lien (with interest), tough luck for the tax lien investor.

Upon being awarded a tax deed, the tax *deed* investor then employs a lawyer at a cost of $2,000 (more or less) to try to clear the legal issues that will cloud the title. (Tax deeds rarely qualify for title insurance.) If successful, the tax deed investor then moves to the next stage of his strategy (sell, renovate, rent out, whatever).

Are Tax Liens and Tax Deeds an Easy Way to Make Big Profits?

If you believe that you can easily earn big profits through tax liens or tax deeds, you've been watching too many infomercials. You can earn profits in this arena only if you work hard to research markets, research properties, and research legal procedures. Then bid selectively when your research indicates a satisfactory trade-off between risk and reward. For a realistic view of tax liens and tax deeds and a state-by-state listing of legal procedures, see *Profit by Investing in Real Estate Tax Liens* by Larry Loftis (Dearborn, 2005).

DISCOUNTED PAPER

Discounted paper represents another investment technique famously promoted by the moguls of mentoring, boot camp gurus, and infomercial pitchmen. In fact, one such trainer was put out of business by the U.S. Department of Justice and is serving time in federal prison. Does this clampdown mean that discounted paper itself offers no opportunities to individual investors? No. But it does indicate that some of the gurus of discounted paper—like their compatriots who infest other fields of real estate gurudom—overpromise, underdeliver, and overcharge.

What Is Discounted Paper?

To entice a buyer, property sellers sometimes carry back financing, which investors refer to as *paper* (for example, "I got a good deal on that property. The seller agreed carry back paper for me.") If at some later date, that OWC seller wants to convert his buyer's paper (a mortgage or contract-for-deed) to ready cash, he assigns the buyer's promise to pay and property lien to a note investor. How do note sellers and buyers find each other? Postings on the Internet, hundreds of note brokers, and newspaper classified ads represent the primary avenues of contact.

How much does the note investor pay for the right to receive the loan payments of the buyer or debtor? That amount is negotiated between the seller and the investor. The current outstanding balance on the loan usually sets the top price, but the note investor typically pays the seller something less (that is, a loan balance of $145,000 might sell for a price of $122,000.) On occasion, though, in low-interest-rate times like the present, some note investors might be willing to pay a premium over the outstanding loan balance—just as bond investors will pay a price premium over a bond's face value, if the bond yield exceeds the current market interest rate (for bonds of the same credit quality).

Here's How the Loan Sale Works

A seller carries back a 7 percent, $100,000 second mortgage, 25-year amortization. Based on those terms, the buyer pays the seller $707 a month. After three years, the seller needs cash. At that time, the remaining balance on the buyer's note equals $95,100. If a note investor wants to earn 12 percent on his money, he would pay the seller $65,588—which equals the present value of $707 per month for 22 years (the remaining term of the loan) discounted at 12 percent. The buyer then makes his monthly payments to the note buyer. At the reduced purchase price, the loan now yields an effective interest rate of 12 percent.

Sell the Note at a Premium

Assume that you purchased this loan two years ago, but you are not keen to hold this debtor's note for 20 years. You want fast money, and fortunately for you, market interest rates have fallen. In such a situation, you could search for a note investor who will accept a 10 percent return. For the right to receive $707 per month for 20 years, this investor would pay $73,353. Flip the note to this investor and pocket $7,765 more than the $65,588 you originally paid. The new note investor enjoys an income stream of $8,484 each year for 20 years, which includes a return *of* his $73,353 original investment plus an annual return *on* his investment of 10 percent.

Not many people know of this private paper market—even though it operates in principle just as the banks and mortgage companies buy and sell mortgages among themselves, and among mortgage investors such as pension funds and life insurance companies. Given the need for income among the 3 to 4 million people who retire every year, and given the small-to-miniscule yields offered by bonds, stocks, and CDs, I expect the demand for private paper to grow. And given the fact that most outstanding paper has been written at interest rates of 6 to 12 percent, buying at a discount and selling at a premium might become another important way to earn good returns.

Delinquent and Nonperforming Loans

Want to buy a loan at a 40 percent, 50 percent, or maybe even a 75 percent discount? Step up your risk tolerance and enter the field of buying paper that has gone bad. Although you may never collect from the debtor, that paper provides you a lien against the collateral property. If loan workout efforts with the debtor fail, you could ask him for a deed-in-lieu of foreclosure or proceed to a foreclosure sale.

Some investors accept a deed-in-lieu and then permit the homeowners to remain in the house under a lease or lease option. If you choose to take the property to a foreclosure sale you can bid up to whatever amount sets the minimum price you want. If another bidder goes higher, you're out with a nice profit. If no one outbids you, you now own the property for whatever price you paid for the discounted loan plus foreclosure costs.

If state law permits a deficiency judgment, you could go after the property owner for additional monies that he is legally obligated to pay under the original loan agreement. You pay $50,000 for a loan that shows a $100,000 balance. You let the property sell at foreclosure to another bidder for $60,000. You have earned a profit, but because the note balance is

$100,000, the debtor still owes you the difference between the outstanding loan balance (plus legal costs, late fees, and accrued interest) and the $60,000 you obtained from the foreclosure sale.

Can you collect? Probably not, if the debtor files bankruptcy—and the court permits a complete discharge. But if the debtor appears able to pay at least part of your claim (and the claims of other creditors), the law does not authorize a complete wipeout of all debts. The court will order partial payment. If the debtor does not file bankruptcy, your judgment will remain in the records (depending on the statute of limitations) for 10 to 20 years (or longer.)

When I mentioned short sales (p. 131), I said you need the cooperation of the property owner or the deal would go nowhere. Technically, that's right. But you can try another approach. Offer to buy the seller's delinquent loan from the bank. With loan in hand, you can proceed to recovery of your investment in any of the ways that we've just discussed.

With a short sale, the lender will permit you to arrange a loan with another bank to pay off the defaulted loan. If you purchase the debt, you will probably need to raise the cash to do so. Still, for investors who have or can raise the cash, buying nonperforming loans has become big business. In fact, numerous vulture funds have raised hundreds of millions of dollars to buy packages of defaulted mortgage debt. (Similarly, companies buy nonperforming car loans and credit card accounts.)

Due Diligence Issues

The discount loan market requires homework. What's the true market value of the mortgaged property? (The seller and original mortgagee/note holder may have jacked up the selling price of his property and sucked in a naïve buyer with an offer of easy financing.) What credit risk does the borrower present? What's the debtor's payment record to date? What's the quality of the property's title? Is the debtor current on all senior liens (that is, the first mortgage, property taxes, HOA assessments, federal income taxes)?

Do the mortgage agreement and note comply with applicable state and federal laws? Did the seller originate the loan with any and all required disclosures and a truth-in-lending statement? If the buyer defaults, what procedures must the note holder follow to foreclose? How long will it take? How much will it cost? Can the note holder collect a deficiency judgment? If so, under what circumstances?

No doubt about it. You can *earn* good money buying or brokering discounted paper. Just verify that the paper you buy is worth substantially more than the paper itself—which is not always the case.

SHOULD YOU FORM AN LLC?

Here's another concern that the gurus have popularized during the past several years: "Don't build your wealth only to lose it to a lawsuit or judgment creditor. Protect your assets through limited liability companies (LLCs)." In response to such publicity and promotion, many of my readers have asked me, "Should we hold our property (or properties) in LLC(s)?"

Different Strokes for Different Folks

Neither I nor anyone else can answer that question for you until we study your legal, financial, and tax situation in light of your goals and what you want your LLC(s) to accomplish. Many mortgage lenders will not permit you to borrow against a property that's held by an LLC, nor will they permit you to transfer a property to an LLC after you have closed your loan. Holding a property in an LLC might also bear upon income tax and estate-planning issues.

Court Rulings

To what degree will an LLC protect your assets against lawsuits or creditors? Those remain open questions. They have not yet been litigated enough to establish a clear body of case law. Moreover, LLC statutes are enacted by states, not Congress. What proves true for Texas may not protect in the same way for New York or Indiana.

Even within the same state, the different district courts of appeals may rule inconsistently with one another. Until (if ever) the high court of the state clarifies or overrules the LLC law in, say, Tampa (2nd DCA), the law could differ from the LLC law in Orlando (5th DCA) even though both courts presumably apply the same Florida statute.

One Size Doesn't Fit All

You need asset protection. LLCs represent one potential means to achieve it. Whether it's the best means for your situation, no one knows until they review your financial, tax, and legal situation; each of the asset protection alternatives that are available to you; and the applicable law. In contrast to the hype surrounding LLCs, one size doesn't fit all.

Please do not misunderstand. You need asset protection. But look further than off-the-shelf LLC solutions. Your circumstances and state laws will control what works best for you. This is one area for which you need tailored, expert legal advice. Remember, too, liability insurance plays a necessary part of any comprehensive asset protection program. Do not merely buy insurance. Read your policy perils, coverages, limits, and exclusions.

To guard against lawsuits and other calamities, insurance stands as your first and most important risk management technique. Even within LLCs, property and liability insurance provides the critical component of your wealth protection plan. (Of course, your property operating policies and practices actually represent your first line of preparation for loss prevention. Obey all laws, nurture good tenant relations, and maintain the premises in good repair.)

16

OPPORTUNITY *FOR* A LIFETIME

Promoters of investment schemes often talk about "the opportunity *of* a lifetime. In fact, you've probably heard someone say, "If you do not buy now, if you pass up what I'm offering, you'll miss the opportunity *of* a lifetime."

Property investing differs. Property investing provides you an opportunity *for* a lifetime. Market timing matters, but building a storehouse of knowledge, abilities, and entrepreneurial talents matters more. As you gain experience, as you find your bearings, as you develop your market wisdom, you will consistently find—and, even better—create new opportunities. You will see that the deal of a lifetime actually comes along at least once a month—if you remain alert and educated enough to recognize it.

Throughout this book, I have illustrated multiple types of investment possibilities and explained how and why these multiple possibilities can yield multiple sources of wealth-building potential. The economists, financial planners, and assorted media commentators who think that to accurately compare property to stocks, one simply compares the relative gains in price between these two asset classes err egregiously. Fortunately for you and me, their error reduces our competition. And that error especially helps now.

USA: RIGHT TIME, RIGHT PRICE, RIGHT PLACE

Although property investing does not require market timing, market timing heightens the potential for scoring great deals. By *great deal*, I not only refer to good price and good property as related to *today's* market prices. More importantly, today's investors will look back from 5, 10, or 20 years into the future and congratulate themselves for acting while the majority waited in idle worry and procrastination. Looking back from the future, today's opportunities will really stand out as great deals.

"Foreign capital has piled into apartment blocks and residential homes in the United States this past year. International investors seek a safe haven in America's rental property." This recent *Financial Times* article continues, "[Foreign] investors are seeking less risky assets whose values won't be as volatile as other investments. . . . There are strong, long-term demand drivers and limited new supply coming into the market. Apartment rent growth will outpace the economic recovery."

It seems that foreign investors have once again realized the potential for U.S. real estate. Record amounts of cash are pouring in from Canada, the United Kingdom, the Netherlands, and other nations of Europe, Asia, and the Middle East. Should not more Americans join with this thumbs-up endorsement of property investing? Low interest rates, high affordability, higher cap rates, lower GRMs, stable-to-decreasing vacancies, stable-to-increasing rents, prices below replacement costs, and a paucity of new construction—a combination of positive market indicators that remain unmatched by any other time in our living history.

No one knows or can know the future for Social Security, stock prices, bond returns, or inflation. Social Security must raise taxes and cut payouts or it will go broke. Stock prices, bond prices, interest rates, and inflation all show big, unexpected ups and downs. Examine the record for any of these and you see that uncertainty reigns.

We do know, however, that neither stocks nor bonds, and not even certificates of deposit provide an inflation-adjusted income stream that 80 million current and future retirees think sufficient or reliable. And who will act so foolishly as to count on Social Security to fund an adequate living standard and quality of life? Upon evaluating the alternatives, property investing wins by default. No other choice provides a reasonably sufficient income.

Yet, does property win only by default? I think not, but you can judge for yourself.

PERSONAL OPPORTUNITY

When you rely on stocks, bonds, or Social Security, your fate wanders outside of your control. Other than buying, selling, or perhaps voting (for Social Security increases), you can do nothing to influence the returns you would like to receive from these assets. Your financial goals mean nothing to stock markets, bond markets, or Congress. Not so with properties.

When you choose property as your opportunity *for* a lifetime, you can achieve good returns, even in a recession. (Or, as I would advise, *especially* in a recession. Because that's when you can most easily pick up bargain-priced properties.) More importantly, investing in property provides profit sources that stock, bank certificates of deposit, or bond investors can never achieve. Recall the discussion of Chapter 1:

♦ Buy properties at prices substantially less than their current market value.

♦ Through creative finance, acquire properties with little of your own cash (but heed the caveats).

♦ Accumulate large amounts of equity through amortization. Tenants pay off your loan and buy your properties for you.

♦ Improve properties to enhance their market value.

♦ Improve your market strategy to boost rents and lower vacancies.

♦ Cut operating costs to increase net operating income.

♦ Sell your existing properties and trade up without paying tax on your capital gains. Pocket your positive cash flows free of income taxes (up to the limit of your deduction for depreciation).

♦ Change the use of a property from one that's less profitable to one more profitable (apartments to condo, residential to office).

♦ Refinance your properties and pull out tax-free cash. (You can borrow short-term against a stock portfolio. But margin requirements, price volatility, and little or no cash flow overload that choice with costs and risks.)

To profit from real estate requires due diligence, knowledge, effort, time, and market savvy (though NNN properties do offer a *passive* income stream with cash flows and capital growth that exceed alternatives). Unlike those who buy stocks, real property *investors* don't whimsically follow hot tips from Internet chat rooms, barbers, hair stylists, auto mechanics, neighbors, or the chatter of talking heads on cable TV. You can't buy, own, or sell real estate with the click of a mouse. (Of course, the last boom did attract many who assumed they could profitably speculate risk-free in property while guided by a stock gambling mentality.)

But the so-called disadvantages of work, research, and reason explain why, over a period of years, real estate provides a safer, surer route to lifetime income and a comfortably secure net worth. Today, fanciful dreamers still believe that they *and* tens of millions of other Americans can achieve wealth without work. Just buy stocks, and voilà—their portfolio will grow. Supposedly, easy fortune awaits all who faithfully pay into their 403(b)s, 401(k)s, Keoghs, 529s, and IRAs. But it won't happen. It can't happen.

At some time in the future, Americans will realize that the income they receive from their stock portfolios can never exceed the amount of corporate dividends. And these dividends will never grow large enough to support the more than 50 million hopefuls who continue to send their monthly retirement savings to Wall Street. (Talk about risky behavior!)

At present, income property provides true *investment* opportunities. You can *speculate* in stocks. You can *speculate* in real estate. You can buy lottery tickets. You can buy gold or trade in foreign exchange. You can shoot craps in Las Vegas. Maybe any or all of these wealth-without-work techniques will pay off, but the odds are stacked against you. In lieu of these popular choices, selectively accumulate 6 to 12 properties (residential or commercial), and you will receive income and build assets *for* life—a monthly cash flow that will finance the quality of life you would like to enjoy. You consume the fruits: the tree continues to grow.

I wish you success. And let me know how you're progressing. I like to hear from readers and investors (gweldred@gmail.com).

INDEX

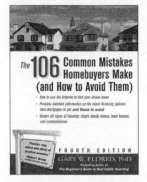
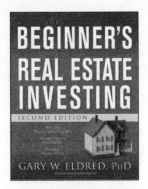

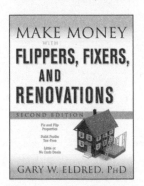
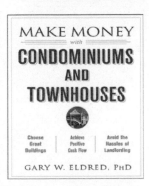
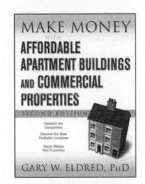